365 Amazing Pork Recipes

(365 Amazing Pork Recipes - Volume 1)

Carla Moore

Content

365 Awesome Pork Recipes

***

---

1. "PAPARA? KVIETKA" Or Flower Fern Salad With Some Twists

Serving: Serves 2 | Prep: | Cook: | Ready in:

Ingredients

- vinegar and water in a 1:3 ratio
- 1 small sweet onion, cut thinly into rings and halved
- 4 ounces excellent quality fatty ham, julienned
- 2 ounces proscuitto, julienned
- 4 small heirloom tomatoes, peeled and cut into long pieces (I added the excess juice in with the dressing)
- 1 ounce pickled fiddlehead ferns or asparagus, optional
- 1 ounce pickled green tomatoes, julienned, optional
- 6 ounces Brimskaya Brinza cheese, julienned
- 6 ounces fresh or freshly pickled refrigerator cucumbers, julienned
- 8 small dill gherkins, julienned
- 1 tablespoon capote capers
- 1 tablespoon chopped black olives, optional
- 2 tablespoons finely chopped dill, chives, and flat leaf parsley
- 1 hard boiled egg, chopped
- 2 seckel pears, julienned and spritzed with fresh lemon juice
- 2 tablespoons champagne or pear vinegar
- 4 tablespoons EVOO
- 1 teaspoon dijon mustard
- 1 teaspoon acacia or other similar honey
- 1 small bit of white anchovy, finely minced and mashed, optional, but recommended
- kosher or pink Himalayan salt to taste
- fresh milled pepper to taste
- 2-4 hearty artisan bread slices, buttered on the side
- serve on a bed of mixed seasonal greens, if desired

Direction

- Marinate the onion rings in the water and vinegar mix for 2-3 hours. Then drain and mince finely.
- Assemble all the salad ingredients together, add a dash of salt, and keep any greens you may want to use as a bed separate. Pack to travel. Keep salad chilled until serving.
- Combine the vinegar and EVOO, mustard, and honey with optional anchovy. Season with salt and pepper. Feel free to include any excess tomato juice in the dressing. Pack the dressing to travel, so it can be shaken well and poured later.
- When ready to eat, plate your salad, dress, and toss. Serve with hearty lightly buttered artisan bread.

---

2. Mama's Ham Noodles

Serving: Serves 4-6 depending on refills | Prep: | Cook: | Ready in:

Ingredients

- Egg Noodles
- 1 large packets Egg Noodles
- 1 pinch Sea Salt
- 1 gallon Water- Per Package Instructions
- Preparing Smoked Pork Butt
- 1 to 2 pounds Smoked Pork Butt
- 1/2 to 3/4 gallons Milk
- to taste or pinches Sea Salt

- to taste or pinches Black Pepper...I prefer Fresh Grounded

Direction

- Egg Noodles
- Cook egg noodles per instruction on package
- Drain...DO NOT RINSE
- Place noodles back into the pot you cooked them in
- Preparing Smoked Pork Butt
- Chop Pork Butt into small cubes approximately 1/2 inch. Fry in a Cast Iron frying pan as you would cook Bacon until tender and lightly crisp. Pour entire contents of into the pot of noodles. Add 2 cups milk to frying pan, bring to a low boil while scraping the drippings up to gather the favor. Be careful not to Scald the milk and be sure to get all of the drippings from the pan. Add this to the ham and noodles. Pour the remaining milk into the ham and noodle mixture until milk is even with the top of the noodles. Simmer on low temperature, stirring occasionally until milk begins to thicken. Season to taste with Sea Salt and Pepper. Your choice of Bread or Biscuits to soak up the juices.
- You can also fry the Pork Butt cubes in the same pot as the noodles were cooked in but I prefer a Cast Iron frying pan as it works the best for getting good scapings for the milk gravy. You may make this recipe with 1%, 2% or Whole Milk. You may also use table salt instead of sea salt. Milk Gravy will NOT be thick...just a wee bit thicker than milk. Remember DO NOT rinse the noodles as this helps to thicken the milk gravy.

3. Spicy Pork, Pepper And Zucchini Stew

Serving: Makes about 6 servings | Prep: | Cook: | Ready in:

Ingredients

- 2 pounds pork tenderloin, trimmed of any sinew and then cut into 1 to 1 1/2 inch cubes.
- Salt and pepper to season the pork
- 3 to 4 tablespoons olive oil
- 2 medium onions cut into a large dice
- 1 pound sweet mini peppers, stemmed, seeded and then cut crosswise into halves or thirds depending on their size
- 4 large garlic cloves, chopped
- 1 tablespoon ancho chili pepper
- 1 tablespoon ground cumin
- 1 teaspoon salt
- 1/2 teaspoon black pepper
- 1/2 teaspoon cayenne pepper
- 1/2 cup dry white wine
- one 14 to 15 ounce can of Italian plum tomatoes, crushed
- 12 ounces tomato or vegetable juice
- 1 cup chicken broth
- 2 small to medium zucchini cut into 3/4 to 1 inch cubes

Direction

- Season the pork cubes with salt and pepper. Heat 3 tablespoons of the oil in a Dutch oven or stew pot. Brown the pork in batches and remove to a plate or bowl.
- Add the 4th tablespoon of oil to the pot if needed and then add the onions and peppers. Sauté until they soften and then add the garlic, chili powder, cumin, salt, black pepper and cayenne and continue to sauté for another minute.
- Add the wine, and with a wooden spoon, stir and scrape up any brown bits on the bottom of the pot. Let the mixture simmer for a minute and then add the crushed tomatoes, tomato juice and chicken broth.
- Add the pork cubes along with any accumulated juices. Bring the pot up to a simmer and then simmer with the pot partially covered for about one hour. (Check and stir every so often)
- After the hour, stir in the zucchini cubes and continue to simmer for another 10 to 15 minutes. I like to make the stew early in the

day and then add the zucchini when re-heating. Serve up nice and hot in bowls.

---

4. The Hot Burrito Trilogy, # 2; "The Gilded Palace Of Sin"

Serving: Serves 4 | Prep: | Cook: | Ready in:

Ingredients

- 1/2 pound pork belly (or if you must, substitute pork shoulder or country style ribs)
- 4 10" wide soft flour tortillas
- 6 ounces rice noodles
- 1 tablespoon gochugaru (Korean pepper flakes)
- 1 tablespoon gochujang (Korean red pepper paste)*
- 1 ounce ginger, sliced into sticks
- 1 sweet onion, roughly chopped
- 5-7 whole cloves of garlic, peeled
- 2 cups (approximate) pork or chicken stock
- 1 bunch cilantro (optional)
- 8 ounces your very favorite, best kimchi
- Korean hot sauce (I like KIM) or substitute your own favorite, maybe "Rooster sauce"
- Crumbled cotija cheese or be bold with a Spanish valdeon (cheese here, VERY optional)
- salt (if needed)

Direction

- Mix the gochugaru and gochujang in a bowl. This is going to be sticky. Rub this all over the pork belly.
- Braise the pork belly in either pork stock or chicken broth along with the ginger, onion and garlic for about two hours until it's fork tender. You can hold this overnight, and probably you should. But you are not finished yet.
- Grill the pork belly and bring it back inside. This is bo ssam ma'am. Chop it into small pieces.

- Boil your rice noodles and then plunge them into very cold water. Turn them out into a colander and pat dry with paper towels. Let that rest awhile.
- The burrito station comes next. Smear some hoisen over a 10" tortilla. Sprinkle some peanuts (or sesame) over that. Follow with cheese if you are using any. Give this a squirt of hot sauce.
- Next, add a handful of noodles. Don't overstuff because we hate burrito blowouts. Finish with the pork and kimchi and chopped cilantro if using. Follow our standard burrito roll up rules.
- Set your rolls on a sheet pan and place in a 350F oven. Bake for about 8 minutes.
- *Some of the Korean condiments can be hard to find, such as the gochujang. You can substitute a Chinese bean paste and amp it up with sambal or sriracha to taste. For gochugaru you can use another flaked red pepper.

---

5. "Bonne Année" Lentil Soup For New Year's

Serving: Serves 8 | Prep: | Cook: | Ready in:

Ingredients

- 1 pound Du Puy lentils
- 2 tablespoons olive oil
- 1 packet (8-10 slices) Canadian bacon, diced
- 1 small yellow onion, diced
- 3 garlic cloves, minced
- 8 cups chicken broth (I use organic low-sodium)
- 2 bay leaves
- 1/2 teaspoon dried thyme
- salt and pepper, to taste

Direction

- Rinse lentils in a colander. (There is no need to soak them.) Sift through them carefully and extract any debris you may find. Set aside.
- In a large pot, heat the oil over medium heat until it shimmers. Add Canadian bacon, onion, and garlic. Cook, stirring, until the garlic releases its aroma and the onion appears translucent.
- Add the lentils, chicken broth, bay leaves, and thyme. Stir once and increase the heat to high. When soup comes to a boil, reduce heat to low, partially cover the pot, and simmer the lentils for 1 hour, removing the cover periodically to stir.
- Taste and, if desired, adjust seasoning with salt and pepper.
- Continue to simmer until the soup reaches your desired consistency. To serve the lentils as a soup, watch the pot closely to make sure all the broth does not cook out; it can go quickly at the end. You can also deliberately simmer until very thick and suitable for plating as a side dish. Just make sure that the lentils do not scorch on the bottom of the pot.

6. "Gang Green" Guacamole

Serving: Makes about two cups | Prep: | Cook: |Ready in:

Ingredients

- 2 good-sized ripe Haas avocados, peeled and cut into chunks
- 2 ripe tomatoes, peeled, seeded, and cut into chunks (as finding nice tomatoes in the middle of winter is about as easy as kicking a 54-yard field goal into the wind, you can substitute a can of top-quality Italian tomatoes)
- 1 bunch scallions, white part only, sliced and diced
- 1 7-ounce can peeled green chiles, drained, seeded, and finely chopped
- 4 ounces bacon, fried to a crisp and crumbled
- 1/2 lime

Direction

- In a large bowl, summoning the spirit of the Jets' intimidating defensive line, use a potato masher to combine the avocado, tomatoes, scallions, chiles and bacon until mixed, but not totally smooth. Refrigerate until kickoff. Just before serving, squeeze in the juice of the half-lime, stir, scrape into a football-themed crock and serve with veggies and/or corn chips.

7. "Hot Ham"

Serving: Serves 6-8-10 | Prep: | Cook: |Ready in:

Ingredients

- 4-5 pounds fresh ham
- 8 ounces Black Currant jelly
- 1 to 2 cups Port
- 1/2-1 cups dark raisins
- 1 pinch White horse radish
- 2 Garlic medium cloves, minced
- 6 Whole cloves
- 1 tablespoon Whole black peppercorns
- 1/4 cup Sour (Seville) Orange or Meyer lemon juice

Direction

- In a small saucepan over low heat, "melt" the currant jelly. Add the Port, raisins, horse radish, garlic, cloves, peppercorns and juice. Stir and bring to the slightest of a simmer. Remove from heat. Let sit while you do next step. This can be (and is much better) done way ahead of time, but will need to be warmed again before coating the ham.
- Wipe Ham with a damp tea towel or paper towel, then cut away surface fat until no more than 1/4 inch thick. Score fat in any design you wish. I prefer no pattern but, whatever...
- Place Ham in a roasting pan not too much bigger than the meat (you want the glaze and ham juices to collect, not get baked dry) and

slather the thing with the Port/Juice mixture. Shove the raisins and cloves into the score marks. Put in a pre-heated 375 degree oven and baste every 10-12 minutes or so. It should be cooked through in 40-50 minutes. Remember, the ham is already cooked so it's getting the glaze right that you want.

- Remove the ham from the oven, rest and then tent with tinfoil until you are ready to serve. If there is still a lot of liquid "glaze" in the roasting pan, pour into that same small saucepan, reduce and pour over ham just before carving. Serve with any of the additions you like with Ham--for us, ALAS, no mustard!

8. "ONE, TWO, THREE, FOUR, FIVE" SPARERIBS

Serving: Serves 2 or more | Prep: | Cook: | Ready in:

Ingredients

- 1 1/2 pounds meaty pork spareribs
- 1 tablespoon dry sherry
- 2 tablespoons dark soy sauce
- 3 tablespoons cider vinegar
- 4 tablespoons sugar
- 5 tablespoons water

Direction

- Separate the ribs first; then chop each, meat side down, into 3 pieces. (John's note: Asian supermarkets sell pork ribs already sliced flanken-style, which will be much easier for you to chop into pieces. Recommend you seek them out). Put them in a skillet or saucepan and set it over high heat; add the simmering ingredients and stir to mingle. When the liquid comes to a boil, adjust heat to maintain a very gentle simmering, (John's note: not THAT gentle; you want the liquid to mostly evaporate by recipe's end) and cover and simmer for 40 minutes. Stir and turn the spareribs from time to time.

- Uncover and turn heat high to bring the sauce to a sizzling boil. (John's note: when you uncover the pot, the ribs will look unappetizing, but take heart, in just a few minutes they will become gorgeous, worthy of a magazine cover!). Stir rapidly until the sauce is all but evaporated and the ribs are coated in a rich glaze. Arrange ribs on serving platter.
- My personal touch is to sprinkle a thinly sliced scallion over the ribs when you plate them. This dish looks and tastes very impressive. We've all had the experience of being in a Chinese restaurant when a fantastic-looking dish is brought to another table of diners, and you think "Mmmm wonder what that is, wish we had ordered that dish." This is one of those dishes. Try it--you'll see!

9. (Not) Shepherd's Pie: Pork And Sweet Potato Version

Serving: Serves 6-8 | Prep: | Cook: | Ready in:

Ingredients

- 1.5-2 lbs leftover pork shoulder roast, shredded, with the remaining juices.
- 1/3 cup diced carrot
- 1/3 cup diced celery
- 1/3 cup diced parsnip
- 1/3 cup diced fennel
- 1/2 cup frozen pearl onions, thawed
- 1 teaspoon herbes de province
- 3 tablespoons olive oil
- 1 teaspoon carway seeds
- juices from original roast. Add beef broth if necessary to moisten mixture
- 1 diced, peeled granny smith apple
- 1 teaspoon large russet potato, baked, peeled
- 1 fairly large sweet potato, baked, peeled
- 1/3 cup half and half
- leftover potato/sweet potato/apple mixture from roast. If you don't have this, add about

another cup of potatoes and possibly a little bit of applesauce if you want.

- 2 tablespoons butter
- 1/3 cup whole milk or half and half

Direction

- In a large bowl toss together vegetables, herbes de province, and olive oil. Place on a foil lined baking pan and roast at 425, stirring a couple of times, until just beginning to caramelize, about 20 minutes.
- Add vegetables, diced raw apple, caraway seeds, and liquid to shredded pork. Season to taste with salt and pepper. Place in an ovenproof casserole.
- Mash russet potato and sweet potato with whatever is left of the potato/apple mixture left from original roast or increase amount of potato and sweet potato to equal about 2-2 1/2 cups. Add butter, milk or cream, and salt and pepper to taste. Spread evenly on top of meat/veggie mixture.
- Bake at 350 for about 45 minutes. You will want to place a baking sheet on the rack beneath the casserole to catch overflowing juices.

10. A Bowl Of Red

Serving: Serves 6 hungry chiliheads | Prep: | Cook: | Ready in:

Ingredients

- Chile Paste
- 2 ounces dried chile pepper pods, mostly New Mexico with a couple Guajillos tossed in
- Chili
- 1 1/2 tablespoons bacon fat
- 3 pounds chuck (after trimming), neatly diced into 1/2 to 3/4-inch cubes (partially freeze the meat for easier dicing)
- 1/2 pound ground pork
- lots of freshly-ground pepper

- 1 1/2 - 2 cups homemade beef or chicken broth
- 1 gigantic sweet onion (about one pound), diced
- 6 cloves garlic, minced
- 8-10 tablespoons premium commerical chili powder, such as Whole Foods or Gebhardt's
- 2 tablespoons ground cumin, toasted briefly
- healthy pinch oregano
- 1 teaspoon Kosher salt
- 2 cups tomato sauce
- 1/2-ounce square bittersweet chocolate
- Chili paste
- 2 tablespoons brown sugar
- plenty of shredded cheddar, sour cream and lime wedges for serving

Direction

- Chile Paste
- Wearing rubber gloves, stem and seed the chile pods and cover with near-boiling water. Let steep for 30 minutes, then pour off the water and puree the softened pods in a food processor until they form a paste. Pass through a sieve to remove skins and errant seeds. Set aside.
- Chili
- First, pour yourself a shot of tequila and toast legendary chili head Carroll Shelby, who founded the International Chili Society. Then, heat the bacon fat in a really big skillet, and working in batches, sauté the beef and pork until no longer pink. Drain off the fat.
- Place the meat, along with several grinds of pepper, the onions and garlic, in your favorite chili pot and add 1 1/2 cups of the beef or chicken broth. Bring to a boil, lower to a simmer, and cover. Keep the lid on, and your hands off, for 90 minutes.
- After 90 minutes, stir in the chili powder, cumin, oregano, salt, tomato sauce, chocolate and half the chile paste. Cover and cook for another half-hour or so. Chase away your guests, who will no doubt be hovering around, demanding to know when it's going to be ready.

- At this point, check for consistency. If it's too thin, scoop out the meat and reduce the sauce by bringing to a boil, and when you're happy with it, return the meat to the pot. Stir in the brown sugar. (If it's too thick, add some more of the broth.) Smack any guest who gets too close with a wooden spoon.
- Cook, uncovered, for 10 more minutes, and check for seasoning. You can add more salt, chili powder and cumin if you like, or more chile paste if you want to amp it up, or more brown sugar if you like it sweet and hot.
- When it looks as good as it smells, summon the troops and serve with a squeeze of lime and a dollop of sour cream. (But have some cheese on hand anyway for the die-hard cheddar lovers!)

11. A Grilled Pizza Party

Serving: Serves 8 | Prep: | Cook: | Ready in:

Ingredients

- For the pizza dough
- 2 cups warm water
- 2 tablespoons sugar
- 2 packets yeast
- 6 tablespoons olive oil
- 1 cup whole wheat flour
- 2 teaspoons salt
- 5 cups bread flour, or use all-purpose flour
- additional flour as necessary for kneading
- additional olive oil for the bowl
- For the toppings (my suggestions, you can add and subtract as you like)
- 6 cups pizza sauce, homemade or purchased
- 2 cups pesto, homemade or purchased
- 2 cups ricotta, homemade or purchased
- 2 cups roasted garlic cloves, homemade or purchased
- 2 cups sliced sautéed onions
- 2 cups sliced sautéed mushrooms
- 2 cups diced sautéed green peppers
- 2 cups pitted black olives
- 2 cups browned Italian sausage, removed from casings and crumbled
- 2 cups sliced pepperoni
- 4 cups shredded mozzarella
- small bowls of crushed red pepper, fennel seed, and dried oregano
- anything else your heart desires

Direction

- It's much easier to use a mixer to make this large quantity of dough, but of course you can also make it by hand as people have done for centuries. In a stand mixer fitted with the dough hook (or large bowl) combine the water and sugar. Sprinkle the yeast over the water and let it stand until it's foamy, about 10 minutes. Add the oil, then the whole wheat flour and the salt. When those are mixed in, begin adding the white flour, one cup at a time. Mix the dough until it comes together and the sides of the bowl are almost clean. The dough should still be a little bit sticky. If necessary, add a little more flour, but be sure the dough remains elastic.
- Using olive oil, lightly oil a large bowl. Place the dough in it and turn it over so that the whole dough ball is coated with oil. Cover the bowl tightly with plastic wrap. Let it stand in warm draft-free area until the dough doubles, about 1-1 1/2 hours.
- After the dough has doubled in size, gently punch it down and knead it lightly in the bowl for a minute or two. Divide the dough into 8 equal pieces (it helps to use a kitchen scale for this so that everyone gets the same amount of crust to work with).
- Light a charcoal grill, using wood chunks if at all possible, high-quality briquettes otherwise. Let the fire die down to a super-hot glow with no active flames.
- Now, depending on your guests, you can either pre-cook the dough rounds just before they arrive, or let each person work with her own dough. In either case, this is what you

need to do. Roll or pat out each piece on a lightly floured surface to a 9" round.

- Pre-cook the crusts like this: place each crust on the hot grill and cook just until the underside is crisp, about 2-3 minutes. Flip the crust and grill for another minute. The dough should not be burnt, but it will not be cooked all the way through either.
- Now you're ready to top the pizza. I suggest covering the whole dining table (or other very large work surface) in aluminum foil to facilitate cleanup. Place all of the toppings in the center of the table and give each person one of the pre-cooked crusts. Instruct them to place the toppings on the well-cooked side of the crust, because the lightly cooked side will get more cooking once the toppings are in place.
- Using baking sheets to ferry the topped crusts to the grill, let each person grill her own masterpiece. It's best to do this with the cover on the grill, to help melt the cheese and bring the toppings together. Depending on your fire, this last step should take 3-4 minutes per pizza. This means that everyone won't sit down to eat at the same moment, but both those eating and those grilling will be happily occupied, and every pizza will be crafted to the diner's exact specifications. People LOVE to do this, and it's amazing how many people have never made their own pizza before.

12. A Grown Up's Grilled Cheese

Serving: Serves 1 | Prep: | Cook: | Ready in:

Ingredients

- 2 pieces White Bread
- 2 pieces Aged White Cheddar
- 1/2 piece Red Onion
- 2 pieces Bacon Slabs
- 1 tablespoon Culinary Argan Oil
- 2 tablespoons Butter

Direction

- Slice the red onion to make half-moon pieces and sauté them with your favorite oil. Use very little oil as you will add Culinary Argan Oil later. Once they are nice and translucent, put them aside.
- In the same pan you used for the onions, start frying the bacon slab. Little secret: We like to use non-packaged thick slabs from our butcher and think you should too!
- On a separate pan, melt butter and lay both slices of bread to toast. Check under the bread periodically until it is lightly golden. This will be the inside of your sandwich.
- Add butter to the pan as needed. Flip the two pieces of bread on the other side to toast. Immediately place the two slices of cheese on one piece of bread and allow to start melting.
- Mix the Culinary Argan Oil into the caramelized onions and place the whole on top of the melting cheese. Now, place the bacon on top, and close the sandwich with the empty piece of bread.
- Continue to toast until the underside is golden and crispy. Now flip the sandwich and allow the cheese to flow down and fuse the two pieces of bread. Remove from pan and plate. You could also make it a meal by make a side to go along with it :)

13. ARANCINI (RICE BALLS) RECIPE

Serving: Serves 2 | Prep: 0hours10mins | Cook: 0hours40mins | Ready in:

Ingredients

- 1 cup uncooked sticky rice
- 7 ounces finely ground pork
- 1/2 cup finely grated Parmesan cheese
- 7 ounces Cheddar cheese, cut into half-inch cubes
- 1/2 cup frozen green peas

- 1/2 cup carrots, chopped to the size of green peas
- 1 egg
- 3/4 cup all-purpose flour
- 1 tablespoon milk
- 1,5-2 cups water (you should try out boiling chicken stock if possible)
- 4 teaspoons olive oil
- 1 small onion, finely chopped
- 1 clove garlic, crushed
- Salt and pepper
- 1 cup vegetable oil for deep frying

Direction

- Beat the egg and milk in a small bowl until blended.
- Fry rice: Get a frying pan and turn on to high heat. Pour 2 tsp olive oil, then toss in all the sticky rice and give it a cursory fry in about 1 minute. Sprinkle salt into the rice and stir it properly for 2 more minutes.
- Cook the rice with Parmesan cheese: Get the fried sticky rice out into a large pot, spread them evenly to fill all over the bottom's surface. Pour in water (or boiling chicken stock) so as the rice is an inch covered by the water. Turn on the stove to medium high heat in 5 minutes. Pour in Parmesan cheese and stir properly so it melts and marries well with the rice. Put on the lid to cover. Reduce the heat to medium level and keep it that way in 7 minutes. Finally, shut down the stove, remove the pot from heat and let sit so it can cool down a bit.
- Make the filling: Heat the olive oil on a frying pan over high heat. Add garlic and then green peas, stir a bit. After 1 minute, toss the carrot in and keep stirring for 2 more minutes before tossing onion in at last. Stir until fragrant (but make sure the onion slices don't turn brown), then add ground pork. Sprinkle some pinches of pepper and salt, and continue to stir for 3 - 5 minutes based on your usual habit of having meat done to a turn or a bit underdone. Remove the pan from the stove and let chill.

- Make balls: For each ball, get 3-4 tablespoons of cooked sticky rice and use your palm to roll it into a ball. Press to flatten the rice ball, then stuff the filling that has been done at step 3, together with 1-2 cubes of Cheddar cheese right in the center. Finally, roll up to enclose them. Coat each ball with flour, roll in the milk and egg mixture, then a final coat of flour as a finish. Get your rice balls to a large saucepan with plenty of oil and deep fry them. As the oil starts to shimmer, scoop the balls out on paper to drain, then serve immediately while they're still hot.
- Notes: Any batch of Arancini can be stored in the fridge overnight. Next day you take them out, just heat them in the microwave without defrosting first. But, simultaneously, for each batch of Arancini, you should only stick them in and out within 3 days of use for best quality and flavor. So please remember to consider on the yield, as well as the number of your table's mates to prevent overfeeding. Since Arancini is already a sizzling serving, getting a sweet cinch to side is definitely a legit step. A tomato-spearmint cocktail would be wonderful, I suppose.

14. Almond Crusted Salmon Fillets With Roasted Broccolini

Serving: Serves 2 | Prep: | Cook: | Ready in:

Ingredients

- 2 1/2 # salmon fillets, skin removed
- 1 large egg, beaten
- 1 1/2 tablespoons Dijon mustard
- 2 tablespoons extra virgin olive oil
- 1/3 cup Panko bread crumbs or equivalent
- 1/2 cup toasted almond slivers, ground fine
- 1/3 cup white flour
- 2 pinches red pepper flakes
- 1 pinch salt

Direction

- In a dry 10" sauté pan, toast the almond slivers until mostly golden brown; avoid letting them get too dark. Remove them, let them cool a little and grind them fine in a spice grinder or mortar and pestle. Reserve for now.
- 2. Line up 3 shallow bowls or deep plates for dipping the salmon. A. In the first bowl, spread out the flour. B. In the second bowl, combine the egg, mustard and red pepper flakes. C. In the third bowl, combine the bread crumbs and ground almonds.
- Put the olive oil in the sauté pan over low-medium heat until it is warm enough to spatter water drops.
- Dip both sides of the thickest fillet in the flour until pretty well covered. Follow that by dipping both sides in the egg mixture until covered. Then lay both sides of the salmon on the nut mixture until it is thoroughly coated. Immediately place it in the sauté pan over the low-medium heat.
- Repeat for the thinner fillet as quickly as possible.
- Sauté the fillets for 4 minutes; turn over and repeat. Then if necessary, reserve in a 200*F warming oven on the serving plates until the broccoli is ready.

15. Alsatian Charcroute

Serving: Serves 4-8 | Prep: | Cook: | Ready in:

Ingredients

- For the cabbage braise:
- 1 Head of cabbage, shredded
- 1/2 Sweet large onion
- 2 Apples, pealed, cored chopped
- 1 tablespoon Vegetable oil
- 1-2 Bottles of good Pilsner-style beer
- 1 teaspoon Caraway seeds
- 8 Juniper Berries
- 1 Bay Leaf

- Splash of white wine
- Salt and Pepper
- Brats: Here any combination of smoked brats/wursts will do - also smoked ham or other meat will work just fine.
- 1 package of bratwurst
- 1 package of good hot dogs
- 1/2 package of German veal sausage (white)
- 4 Links of sweet Italian sausage (optional)
- 1 Kielbasa cut into large pieces (optional)

Direction

- Pre-heat oven to 325.Sweat onion in a large Dutch oven for until translucent and then add cabbage and rest of ingredients. (Add one can/bottle of beer at first and reserve rest for later) Cook for 5 minutes or so on stovetop and then transfer, covered into oven. Cook for at least an hour - checking periodically to make sure nothing is burning and stirring in more beer if too dry. You can braise this as long as you like, the flavors just get better and deeper.
- After about at 1 or 1 1/2, add a combination of smoked "brats" or "wursts" from your store. I like to cook them until they puff up and the casings start to crack. About a half hour. Again keep stirring and checking pot periodically. After a few hours you have a wonderful dish you can serve with dark bread, a variety of mustards and great beer! PS Fish out Bay and Juniper berries (if you can) before serving.

16. Amorette Casaus' Pork Belly Stew

Serving: Serves 6-8 | Prep: | Cook: | Ready in:

Ingredients

- 1 tablespoon canola oil
- salt and black pepper
- 1 pound pork belly, cut into 1-inch cubes

- 1 1/2 pounds pork shoulder, cut into 1-inch cubes
- 1 medium onion, roughly chopped
- 2 medium carrots, roughly chopped
- 3 large creamer potatoes (about 1 1/2 pounds), roughly chopped
- 4 medium shallots, thinly sliced
- 3 sprigs fresh thyme
- 1 bay leaf
- 1/2 cup red wine
- 2 quarts chicken stock
- 15 ounces can whole tomatoes

Direction

- Heat canola oil in a heavy pot or Dutch oven. Season pork belly and shoulder with salt and black pepper and, starting with the belly, sear in batches till well-caramelized. Remove and reserve.
- Sweat chopped onion, carrot and potato in the rendered pork fat just until onion becomes transparent, then remove and reserve the vegetables.
- In the same pot, sweat shallots, thyme and bay leaf.
- Deglaze with red wine and simmer till reduced by half. Return pork belly and shoulder to pot. Add chicken stock, tomatoes (crushing them in hand as you go) and their juice and bring back up to a simmer. Season with salt and pepper.
- Simmer for 1 1/2 hours, partially covered, skimming fat as needed. Once the pork is nearly as tender as you'd like it, add back in the reserved onion, carrot and potato.
- Simmer until potatoes and carrots are tender but not falling apart, about 20-30 minutes more. Season to taste with salt and black pepper.

17. An American Patzaria Creamy Beet Spread With Blue Cheese And Bacon

Serving: Serves 3-4 | Prep: | Cook: | Ready in:

Ingredients

- 2 medium beets
- 1 cup nonfat Greek style yogurt
- 1.5 ounces blue cheese, finely crumbled
- 2 pieces bacon
- 1 tablespoon chives, finely minced
- 3 pieces pita bread, lightly toasted

Direction

- Scrub the beets, drizzle with olive oil, sprinkle with salt, enclose in a foil packet and roast at 350 degrees for 40 minutes to an hour, or until tender. Let cool and chop into a fine dice.
- Fry the bacon until crisp. Let cool, and chop finely.
- Combine the yogurt and the blue cheese in a small bowl and mash with a fork until the cheese in incorporated into the yogurt.
- Add the chopped beets, bacon and the chives. Mix thoroughly until the entire mixture is a rather alarming magenta hue (this actually helps convince 3 year old girls to eat it, believe it or not). The mixture may be covered and stored in the refrigerator right away, or eaten immediately.
- Serve with toasted pita triangles. Enjoy.

18. Apple & Candied Bacon Upside Down Cake

Serving: Serves 8 | Prep: | Cook: | Ready in:

Ingredients

- Candied Bacon
- 4 pieces thick cut bacon strips
- 2 tablespoons light brown sugar

- 1/2 tablespoon maple syrup
- Upside Down Cake
- 3 apples, peeled, cored & each cut into 8 wedges
- 1 tablespoon lemon juice, freshly squeezed
- 3 teaspoons cinnamon
- 1 1/2 cups all purpose flour
- 1 1/2 teaspoons baking powder
- 1/4 teaspoon salt
- 9 tablespoons butter, room temperature
- 1/2 cup granulated sugar
- 2 large eggs, room temperature
- 1 teaspoon vanilla extract
- 1/2 cup apple sauce
- 1/2 cup milk, 2% or whole
- 2 tablespoons bacon fat (set aside from cooking candied bacon)
- 1/4 cup light brown sugar

Direction

- Candied Bacon
- Preheat oven to 350. Mix light brown sugar and maple syrup into a paste. Put bacon on a parchment lined baking sheet and spread 1/2 of the paste on the top side. Bake for 10 min.
- Remove bacon from oven. Spoon 2 tbsp. of bacon fat into a 9" cake pan & set aside. Flip bacon and slather with remaining sugar-maple paste. Return to oven for 5-7 min, until it takes on a nice dark color, but is still lying flat. (You don't want to crisp the bacon completely since it will cook more in the cake pan.) Remove from oven and set aside, keeping oven at 350.
- Upside Down Cake
- Cut candied bacon into bits and toss with apple wedges, lemon juice, and 1 teaspoon cinnamon. Set aside.
- Whisk together flour, baking powder, salt, and remaining 2 teaspoons cinnamon in a medium bowl.
- In a separate large bowl, beat 8 tablespoons butter and granulated sugar with an electric mixer until light and fluffy. Beat in eggs, vanilla and apple sauce until well incorporated.

- Turn mixer to lowest speed and mix in one third of flour mixture; then half of milk; another third of flour; remaining milk; remaining flour. Set batter aside.
- Add remaining tablespoon of butter to the bacon fat already set aside in your cake pan. Add 1/4 c light brown sugar. Heat over a very low flame until all of the fat is melted and sugar begins to bubble. Remove from heat and spread sugar evenly (approximately!) across bottom of the pan.
- Arrange prepped apples in a pinwheel on top of sugar coating, getting as much bacon onto the bottom of the pan as you can (for crispy bits!).
- Pour batter over apples and spread evenly.
- Bake for 45-50 minutes, until the sides easily pull away from the edge of the pan and a toothpick inserted into the center of the cake comes out clean. Let rest in pan for 15 min before placing a plate on top of the pan and flipping the cake over.

19. Asian Short Ribs

Serving: Serves 6 | Prep: | Cook: |Ready in:

Ingredients

- 14 ounces ramen noodles, fresh or dried
- 10-12 short ribs
- 1 cup flour
- 2 teaspoons salt
- 1 tablespoon black pepper
- 2 tablespoons olive oil
- 2 cups kabocha, not peeled & cut in 1/2 inch slices
- 1 cup lotus root, peeled and cut into 1/2 inch slices
- 1 yellow onion, diced
- 2 tablespoons garlic, diced (about 3 large cloves)
- 1 tablespoon fresh ginger, grated
- 1/2 cup soy sauce

- 1/3 cup brown sugar
- 1/2 cup sake
- 1/4 cup rice wine vinegar
- 2 whole star anise
- 1/3 cup chopped green onions
- orange zest

Direction

- Pat the short ribs dry with a paper towel. Combine the flour with the salt and pepper in a wide bowl or plate. Lightly whisk together using a fork. Dredge the ribs in the flour and set on a plate.
- In a large skillet, heat the oil. When the ribs have been dredged in flour, place them in the hot skillet and brown on all sides, about 1-2 minutes per side. Set aside.
- In the slow cooker, combine the soy sauce, garlic, ginger, onion, brown sugar, sake, rice wine vinegar and star anise. Stir together to dissolve the sugar. Add the short ribs. Layer the kabocha and lotus root on top. Cook on high heat for 7 hours, turning the ribs once about half-way through.
- Prepare the ramen noodles according to the package directions.
- On each plate, place a layer of noodles, top with the short ribs, veggies, and some sauce. Sprinkle with chopped green onions and orange zest. Serve immediately.

20. Asian Slow Cooker Pork With Vegetable & Apple Noodles

Serving: Serves 4 | Prep: | Cook: | Ready in:

Ingredients

- Slow-Cooked Pork
- 2 1/2 pounds pork shoulder
- 1/2 large sweet onion, chopped
- 3 1/2 cups chicken stock
- 1/2 cup low-sodium soy sauce
- 1/4 cup mirin

- 1/4 cup fish sauce
- 2 tablespoons sugar
- 1 tablespoon sesame oil
- 2 teaspoons kosher salt
- 1 teaspoon garlic powder
- 1 teaspoon Chinese five-spice
- Vegetable & Apple Noodles
- 3 large zucchini
- 4 medium carrots
- 2 large apples
- 1 pinch salt
- 1 pinch red pepper flakes (optional)
- 2 tablespoons chopped chives (optional)
- 2 tablespoons sesame seeds (optional)

Direction

- Place the pork and onions into a slow cooker. Pour in the chicken stock, soy sauce, mirin, and fish sauce. Add the sugar, sesame oil, salt, garlic, and five spice. Set the slow cooker on low and the timer to 8 hours. Carry on with your day.
- When the pork is almost done, make noodles out of the zucchini, carrots, and apples using a spiralizer, julienne peeler, or a mandolin slicer. I spiralized the zucchini and apples, and I used a julienne peeler for the carrots.
- Heat a large pan with the olive oil. When the pan is hot, cook the zucchini and carrots for 1 to 2 minutes ONLY. Any longer will cause the zucchini noodles to get too soggy. Season with a tiny pinch of salt, and remove from heat. I immediately plated all the noodles together (including the apples) because I didn't want the zucchini to continue cooking in the hot pan.
- When the pork is ready, take the pieces of pork out of the slow cooker. Using a fork, shred the pork. Plate the pork on top of the noodles and garnish with chives, sesame seeds, and red pepper flakes.

21. Asian Stir Fried String Beans With Pork

Serving: Serves as an addition to a chinese meal | Prep: | Cook: | Ready in:

Ingredients

- 1 pound Fresh string beans (or long beans if available) cleaned
- 2 tablespoons Peanut oil (or canola oil)
- 2 Large cloves of fresh garlic, thinly sliced
- 4 scallions (green and white, divided) chopped
- one half pound ground pork
- 1 teaspoon Chile paste with garlic*
- 1 teaspoon Brown bean sauce*
- 1 teaspoon Hoisin Sauce*
- 2 teaspoons Low sodium soy sauce
- 2 teaspoons Chinese rice wine or dry sherry
- 1 teaspoon Sugar
- one half teaspoon Dark sesame oil (toasted)*
- one half teaspoon LIght soy sauce*
- dash Hot sauce to taste

Direction

- In large pot of boiling water, blanche the string beans for 3 to 4 minutes. Remove to bowl. In wok, heat the oil, add the garlic. Stir fry for one minute. Add the while parts of the scallions to pan, stir fry for one minute. Add ground pork and cook till pork loses its pink color. Add the string beans. Stir fry for one minute. Add the next 9 condiment ingredients and cook for another 4 to 5 minutes. Add sesame oil and light soy sauce and a dash of hot sauce if desired.
- Garnish with green parts of scallion. Heat through and serve over white or jasmine rice. Tip: Have all ingredients ready because the cooking goes very fast once added to the wok. *Found in Asian Markets

22. Aunt Alice's Pepperoni Bread

Serving: Makes 4 loaves | Prep: | Cook: | Ready in:

Ingredients

- Dough
- 4 1/2 cups all purpose flour
- 1 1/2 cups water (warmed to 110 - 115 degrees)
- 1 packet active dry yeast
- 1 tablespoon sugar
- 2 tablespoons olive oil
- 1 teaspoon kosher salt
- Assembly of the bread
- 40 - 50 very thin slices of pepperoni (I used 3 inch diameter slices - you may need more if your pepperoni is narrow)
- 2 cups shredded mozzerella
- 2 cups shredded provolone (if you can't find shredded, use slices (about 10 and break them up into smaller pieces)

Direction

- Dough
- In a large measuring cup, add the warm water, sugar and yeast. Let it proof (or bubble up) for 5 minutes. If your yeast water doesn't bubble - start over because your water may have been too hot or too cold or your yeast bad. Add 1 tablespoon of the olive oil.
- In a large bowl, mix the kosher salt and flour. Make a well in the center and pour in the yeast water. Mix until the dough comes together. Then use your hands to knead the dough for 3 - 5 minutes, until the ingredients are well incorporated and you have a ball. Put the dough in a bowl, pour over the remaining olive oil and let it rise for 2 hours - covered with plastic wrap.
- Assembly of the bread
- Cut your dough into four equal parts. Roll them out into rectangles (8 x 14 inches - approximately) on a floured surface. Cover each rectangle with 10 -12 slices of pepperoni, 1/2 cup mozzarella, and 1/2 cup of provolone.

Starting on of the long sides of the rectangle, roll up the bread like jelly roll. Tuck in the ends of each loaf and pinch the seams together.

- Bake on a cookie sheet in a preheated 350 degree oven for 25 - 30 minutes or until golden brown. Serve with marinara sauce.

23. BAT Wich: Bacon, Arugula, And Tomato Sandwich

Serving: Serves 4 sandwiches | Prep: | Cook: | Ready in:

Ingredients

- 8 slices soft white bread
- extra virgin olive oil
- 2 ounces arugula leaves
- enough tomato slices for four sandwiches
- 8 slices bacon, cooked crisp and drained on paper towels

Direction

- 1. Using a tablespoon, dribble some olive oil on 4 slices of bread. Between one and two tablespoons is about right.
- 2. Layer over the arugula leaves so that they feather over the edge of the bread slice. The finished sandwich will look pretty if you do this.
- Layer the tomato slices over the arugula leaves.
- On top of the tomato slices, place the two slices of cooked bacon. They have plenty of fat so you don't need olive oil on this side of the sandwich.
- Top with the second slice of bread, and slice on the diagonal. It will be juicy and delicious. You will only need to eat one, with a glass of iced tea.

24. BBQ Country Style Spareribs

Serving: Serves 6 | Prep: | Cook: | Ready in:

Ingredients

- 4 pounds country style spareribs
- 1/2 cup soy sauce
- 1/2 cup oyster sauce
- 3/4 cup ketchup
- 3/4 cup sugar
- 1 tablespoon orange marmalade or guava jelly
- 1/8 teaspoon 5-spice
- 1/2" piece of ginger, grated

Direction

- Boil country ribs for 1 hour. Drain well and wash off scum.
- Preheat oven to 350 degrees. Place ribs in large baking pan.
- Combine remaining ingredients. Pour over ribs. Bake 1 1/2 hours.
- Remove from pan and slice across the grain to serve.

25. Baby Back Ribs With Hatch Green Chile BBQ Sauce

Serving: Serves 6 - 8 | Prep: | Cook: | Ready in:

Ingredients

- For the ribs
- 1 rack baby back ribs
- Garlic salt (or garlic powder and salt if you prefer)
- Black pepper
- Cayenne pepper
- water
- Hatch Green Chile BBQ Sauce
- 5 Hatch green chiles, or you can use poblano peppers, Anaheim peppers, etc.
- 2 tablespoons olive oil
- 1 medium onion, chopped

- 2   cloves garlic, chopped
- 1/3 cup Worchestershire sauce
- 1/4 cup cider vinegar
- 1/2 cup beer, your choice, I used lager
- 1/4 cup brown sugar
- 1 teaspoon each salt & black pepper
- 1   29 ounce can tomato sauce

Direction

- For the ribs
- Spread foil out to fit your rack of ribs. Liberally season both sides of the ribs with the garlic salt, black pepper and cayenne. Set aside.
- Build a fire in the fire box of the smoker or on one side of the grill and let it get to 300 degrees. Try to keep it around this temperature throughout cooking.
- Add a little water in the bottom of your foil rib pouch and close up loosely. Place the ribs in the smoker, or on the grill away from the flame. Cook for 2 hours or until tender, turning the package around occasionally when you check the fire.
- Remove the ribs from the foil package and mop with BBQ sauce. Place the rack near the fire or directly over the flame and cook for 5 - 10 minutes or until the sauce starts to caramelize.
- Remove to a platter to cool slightly and cut to eat.
- Hatch Green Chile BBQ Sauce
- Roast the chiles directly over the flames of the fire or in the oven until they blister and char. Remove them to a paper sack to sweat for 10 minutes.
- Wearing rubber gloves, remove the charred skin, stem and seeds. Set aside for now.
- In a large saucepan, heat the olive oil over medium high heat. Add the onions and garlic and cook until tender.
- Add the green chiles and the rest of the ingredients and reduce heat to simmer for about 30 minutes. Remove from the heat to cool slightly.

- In a blender, puree the sauce until smooth. Taste and adjust the seasonings to taste. Refrigerate any unused sauce (should keep a couple of weeks).

26. Baby Back Ribs With Roasted Peach And Smokey Bacon Barbeque Sauce

Serving: Serves 4 | Prep: | Cook: | Ready in:

Ingredients

- Roasted Peach and Smokey Bacon Barbeque Sauce
- 4   large ripe peaches, pitted and cut to quarters (leave the skin on)
- 2 tablespoons brown sugar
- 1/2 cup ketchup
- 2 tablespoons bacon fat (I used 4-6 strips breakfast bacon, rendered ... you can eat the bacon)
- 2 tablespoons balsamic vinegar
- 2 tablespoons soy sauce
- 2   chipotle chili in adobo, chopped
- 1 tablespoon garlic, grated
- 1 tablespoon ginger, grated
- 1 teaspoon Worcestershire sauce
- 1 teaspoon dijon mustard
- Smoked Baby Back Ribs
- 6 tablespoons dijon mustard
- 2 tablespoons ketchup
- 3   medium cloves garlic, minced or pressed through garlic press
- 2 teaspoons ground black pepper
- 1 tablespoon sweet paprika
- 1 tablespoon chili powder
- 1/2 teaspoon cayenne pepper
- 1 1/2 tablespoons kosher salt
- 3 tablespoons brown sugar
- 2   racks Baby back ribs, 2 1/2 to 3 lbs each, trimmed of fat, membrane removed, each rack cut in half

- 1/4 cup Lapsang Souchong tea leaves (finely ground), about 10 tea bags
- 1/2 cup apple juice

Direction

- Roasted Peach and Smokey Bacon Barbeque Sauce
- Preheat oven to 425F. Line a rimmed baking sheet with tin foil to capture the peach juices. Place the peaches in a single layer on the prepared pan and sprinkle with brown sugar. Roast until they start to caramelize, about 20-25 minutes.
- In a large, nonreactive pot, combine roasted peaches and their juices, the ketchup, bacon fat, vinegar, soy sauce, chipotle pepper, garlic, ginger, Worcestershire sauce and mustard and bring to a boil, reduce the heat, simmer for 15 minutes. Remove from heat and let cool for about 10 minutes. Puree in a food processor or blender or using an immersion blender. The BBQ Sauce can be made up to a week in advance and stored in the refrigerator.
- Smoked Baby Back Ribs
- For the Rub: Combine mustard, ketchup, and garlic in small bowl; combine pepper, paprika, chili powder, cayenne, salt, and sugar in separate small bowl. Spread mustard mixture in thin, even layer over both sides of ribs; coat both sides with spice mixture, then wrap ribs in plastic and refrigerate for at least 8 hours and up to 24 hours.
- Heat oven to 500F. Sprinkle ground tea evenly over bottom of rimmed baking sheet; set wire rack on sheet. Place ribs meat side up on rack and cover with heavy-duty foil, crimping edges tightly to seal. Roast ribs at high heat for 30 minutes, then reduce oven temperature to 250F, leaving oven door open for 1 minute to cool. While oven is open, carefully open one corner of foil and pour apple juice into bottom of baking sheet; reseal foil. Continue to roast until meat is very tender and begins to pull away from bones, about 2 hours. (Begin to check ribs after 1 1/2 hours; leave loosely covered with foil for remaining cooking time.)
- After the 1 1/2 to 2 hours, fire up your grill to a medium-hot temperature. Remove ribs from oven and slather on the roasted peach and bacon BBQ sauce. Bring outside and carefully place racks on the grill (at this point, they are very "fall off the bone", so be gentle). Brown ribs until crispy in spots, 5 to 10 minutes. Flip ribs meat side up and cook until well browned and crispy, 5 to 7 minutes more. Cool for at least 10 minutes before cutting into individual ribs. Serve with additional barbecue sauce, if desired.

27. Bacon & Eggs Risotto

Serving: Serves 4 | Prep: | Cook: | Ready in:

Ingredients

- 1/3 pound pancetta
- 2 tablespoons butter
- 1 medium onion, chopped
- 1 cup arborio rice
- 1/2 cup dry white wine
- 3 cups chicken broth (homemade, if possible)
- 1/2 cup Parmesan cheese, grated
- 4 large eggs

Direction

- Bring broth and 1 cup water to a simmer in a saucepan over medium-low heat. Keep it warm throughout the cooking process and gradually add more water if you need more liquid.
- On a cutting board, chop the pancetta into roughly 1/2 to 1-inch pieces. Add the chopped pancetta to a 12-inch skillet, turn the flame to medium heat and cook it until it crisps, about 5 minutes. Transfer to a plate covered with a paper towel to drain.
- Add another 1 tablespoon of butter to the rendered pancetta fat already in the pan, then add in the chopped onion. Cook until the onion softens, about 4 minutes, stirring often.

- Add the arborio rice to the skillet and cook for 1 to 2 minutes until the edges of the rice grains start to become translucent, but the center remains white. Add the white wine and cook until the rice absorbs the liquid, about another 2 minutes.
- Once the rice absorbs the wine, add more liquid to the skillet by spooning in the warmed broth in 1/2-cup increments. Stir each addition into the rice until it is fully absorbed before adding the next 1/2 cup (about 3-5 minutes between each addition). Stir frequently and repeat these additions until the rice is tender and al dente and the sauce develops a creamy texture. This usually takes about 30 minutes and 3-4 cups of liquid. Stir in the cooked bacon and grated cheese. Season with salt and pepper. Keep warm over low heat.
- In another frying pan, heat a small amount of butter over medium-high heat. Crack the eggs into the pan and cook until the whites have fully set but the egg yolks are still a bit runny, about 3-4 minutes. Season with salt and pepper. Flip the eggs over if you prefer over-easy rather than sunny-side-up eggs. Because the egg yolk serves as a sauce for the risotto, be sure not to overcook the egg yolks.
- Plate four servings of risotto into bowls and top each with a fried egg. Season with salt and pepper to taste and serve immediately.

28. Bacon Apple Pie

Serving: Serves 2 | Prep: | Cook: | Ready in:

Ingredients

- Pie Dough
- 1 cup Butter
- 2 1/2 cups Pastry Flour
- 4 teaspoons Sugar
- 2 teaspoons Salt
- 8 milliliters Vanilla Extract
- 60 milliliters Buttermilk or Water
- Filling

- 7-8 pieces Bacon
- 1/3 cup White Sugar
- 1 Lemon
- 3 Grannysmith Apples
- 1/2 cup White Sugar
- 1/4 cup Brown Sugar
- 1 tablespoon Cinnamon
- 1 teaspoon Nutmeg
- 1/2 teaspoon Cloves
- 3 tablespoons Cornstarch
- 2 tablespoons Butter
- 1 Egg

Direction

- Pie Dough
- Mix the pastry flour, salt and sugar together; then sift.
- Cut cold butter into small cubes and blend it in with the flour using a pastry cutter or your fingers. Blend the butter with the dry ingredients until it is pea sized.
- Mixed the buttermilk with the vanilla and pour this mixture into your dry ingredient mixture. Ensure that the buttermilk or water is ice cold.
- Using your hands blend the liquid into the flour until the dough just comes together. Wrap the dough in plastic wrap and put it in the fridge for now.
- Filling
- Preheat oven too 350F
- Cut bacon into 1/2 inch pieces and place into a heated pan.
- After the bacon has started to golden on onside flip and sprinkle 1st sugar over the bacon. Cook until golden brown and remove from pan.
- Juice lemon into a small bowl.
- Peel and slice the Granny smith apples into 1/4 inch pieces. Place the sliced apples immediately in the lemon juice and mix them.
- Add the 2nd white sugar, brown sugar, cinnamon, nutmeg and cloves into the apples. Blend this with the apples and then add the cornstarch and mix it in.

- Get two small ramekins or small dishes of some sort that are oven proof. Get the Pie dough from the previous recipe out of the fridge and divide it into four. Roll all of these out one by one too just a little bigger than the size of your dish. Two of the pieces of dough being the bottom crust and two being the top crust.
- Grease your two dishes and lay the pie dough in each dish one at a time. Ensure to relax the dough and make sure it is resting evenly with the edges of the dish.
- Layer the apple mixture and the bacon in the two small dishes.
- Next, place the butter in pieces in the two dishes, followed by putting the top piece of pie dough on each pie.
- Use your finger to press the bottom piece of dough and the top piece of dough together, sealing it all around the edges. Cut of any excess dough and fold in the edges around the pies.
- Cut 3-4 holes in the top of each pie. Beat an egg and use a brush to egg-wash the top of each pie.
- Place in the oven and bake at 350F for around 45 minutes.

29. Bacon Brussels Spouts ! (AKA: Tiny Cabbages And Bacon)

Serving: Serves 12 | Prep: | Cook: | Ready in:

Ingredients

- 4 pounds Brussels Spouts
- 1 pound bacon (chopped)
- 1/3 cup water (to get drippings from pan)
- 1/2 teaspoon sea salt
- 1/2 teaspoon ground white or black pepper (optional)
- 1 tablespoon vinegar of choice (optional)
- 1 tablespoon sugar (optional)

Direction

- Chop up the sliced bacon. Fry in a large skillet on medium heat until bacon it crisp. Remove bacon from skillet and place in a bowl until needed.
- Using the same large skillet: put Brussels sprouts in and cook on medium heat for about 2 minutes. Add water and spices, cover skillet with lid. Cook for about 10 to 12 minutes longer. Remove lid and add any of the optional ingredients at this time. Gently stir with slotted spoon. Stir in most of the bacon (saving some for optional garnish)*Serve individually or in a large dish.

30. Bacon Nachos

Serving: Serves 1 (or 5, if you're willing to share) | Prep: | Cook: | Ready in:

Ingredients

- 1 package of good quality bacon
- 1/2 cup good cheddar cheese, grated
- 1 farmer's market heirloom tomato, finely diced
- 1/3 cup red onion, finely diced
- 1/2 of one jalapeno, minced
- small handful of cilantro, chopped
- juice of half a lime
- salt and pepper
- 1/3 cup sour cream

Direction

- Preheat oven to 400 degrees. Cut the pieces of bacon in half. On a foil lined baking sheet with a cooling rack placed on top, place the bacon pieces in a "v" formation (so they look a bit like tortilla chips, not so they look like a flock of migrating birds). Bake the bacon for about twenty minutes.
- While the bacon is baking, in a small bowl, make the salsa by combining the finely diced

tomato and red onion with the minced jalapeno, the chopped cilantro, and the lime juice. Salt and pepper to taste (but do remember that the bacon is quite salty, so lots of salt isn't really necessary). Set aside.

- When the bacon looks like it's five minutes from being perfectly cooked, add the grated cheddar and return to the oven. After five minutes or so (checking to make sure the cheese and bacon don't burn), take the bacon out of the oven and allow to cool down slightly for a few minutes.
- Place bacon nachos on a serving dish and give each one a dollop of sour cream and a spoonful of salsa.
- Kick off your shoes, put on some cut off denim shorts, and enjoy your bacon nachos!

31. Bacon Wrapped Pork Loin Stuffed With Walnuts And Rice

Serving: Serves 6 | Prep: | Cook: | Ready in:

Ingredients

- Rice Stuffing
- 1 cup dry brown rice cooked in chicken/beef broth
- 1/2 large onion, chopped small
- 2 small carrots, chopped small
- 1 rib of celery, chopped small
- 6-8 mushrooms of any kind, chopped small
- 2/3 cup walnuts, chopped small
- 1 cup golden raisins (rehydrate if you want)
- 1 apple, cored and chopped small
- 1-2 teaspoons thyme
- 2 teaspoons ground sage
- 1/2 teaspoon ground nutmeg
- butter and olive oil
- salt and pepper
- Pork Roast
- 3 pounds pork roast
- 8-10 sage leaves

- 6-10 slices thick sliced uncured apple wood smoked bacon
- Ground Sage
- 1/2 cup maple syrup
- olive oil
- salt and pepper
- cooking twine

Direction

- Start by making the rice stuffing. Cook the brown rice per package instructions substituting chicken/beef broth for water, be sure and include the butter that directions on the box call for. I cook my rice in the microwave, and it works great.
- While rice is cooking put the onion, celery, and carrot into a pan on the stove with a drizzle of olive oil and cook until the onion is clear. Add the mushrooms and a large pat of butter; cook for about 5 minutes or until the mushrooms are tender. Add the dry spices: thyme, sage, nutmeg, and salt and pepper to taste. Remove pan from heat and stir in the apple, walnuts and raisins. When your rice is ready add it to the veggies as well. Taste and adjust spices as needed. Set aside until you need to stuff the roast.
- Butterfly the roast so it can be stuffed. Start by slicing across the roast about one inch from the bottom rolling the rest of the meat away from your blade. Think of it as un-rolling a rug. Continue across until you have laid open the whole piece of meat. Then rub the inside with olive oil and spice with ground sage, pepper and salt.
- Fill the roast with about 1 cup of the rice stuffing, fill down one side and roll up. As you roll you may need to add more or less stuffing. Secure the roast in 3-4 places with cooking twine. Trim the extra string off close to each knot.
- Next layer the fresh sage across the top of the roast. Then cover with bacon in a single layer tucking the ends under the roast.
- Place the roast into a deep roasting pan and put in the oven at 375 degrees for about 30

minutes a pound. The extra rice stuffing can be put in an ovenproof dish and into the oven for the last 30 minutes of baking to heat it up. Serve the rice on the side of the roast.

- 5-10 minutes before the roast is done drizzle maple syrup over top of the bacon, and return to the oven. When inside temperature of the roast is 160 remove from oven and let rest ten minutes before slicing parallel to the bacon so the spiral stuffing will show in each slice. Serve and enjoy.

32. Bacon Wrapped Roasted Radishes

Serving: Makes 12 single radishes | Prep: | Cook: | Ready in:

Ingredients

- 12 radishes
- 6 slices of bacon, halved
- 1/3 cup prepared BBQ sauce

Direction

- You will need 12 toothpicks or 3 bamboo skewers.
- Place bacon strips on wire rack over cake pan; bake in preheated 400 degree oven until just starts to brown, about 10 to 15 minutes.
- Wrap each radish with bacon strip and secure with skewer. Brush all sides with barbecue sauce. Return to oven and bake until bacon is crisp and radishes are soft; additional 15 to 20 minutes.
- Serve with additional BBQ sauce.

33. Bacon And Cashew Caramel Corn

Serving: Makes 15 | Prep: | Cook: | Ready in:

Ingredients

- 1/2 cup popcorn kernels
- 2 tablespoons vegetable oil
- 8 ounces bacon, chopped
- 3/4 cup unsalted raw cashews, coarsely chopped
- 1 teaspoon coarse kosher salt or coarse sea salt
- 1/4 teaspoon cayenne pepper
- 1/4 cup heavy whipping cream
- 1 Early Grey tea bag
- Nonstick vegetable oil spray
- 1 1/2 cups sugar
- 1/4 cup water
- 2 tablespoons light corn syrup

Direction

- Preheat oven to 300°F. Heat popcorn and oil in covered heavy large pot over medium-high heat until kernels begin to pop. Using oven mitts, hold lid on pot and shake pot until popping stops.
- Pour popcorn into very large bowl.
- Cook bacon in heavy large skillet over medium heat until almost crisp.
- Using slotted spoon, transfer to paper towels to drain; cool.
- Add bacon and cashews to bowl with popcorn. Sprinkle with coarse salt and cayenne; toss to coat.
- Bring cream and tea bag just to boil over medium heat. Remove from heat; let steep 15 minutes, occasionally pressing on tea bag with back of spoon to release flavor. Discard tea bag.
- Line rimmed baking sheet with foil; coat with nonstick spray. Coat 2 wooden spoons or heat-resistant spatulas with nonstick spray; set aside.
- Stir sugar, 1/4 cup water, and corn syrup in large saucepan over medium-low heat until sugar dissolves.
- Increase heat to high; boil without stirring until syrup turns amber, occasionally swirling pan and brushing down sides with wet pastry brush, about 10 minutes. I like my popcorn

pretty dark, but if you like yours lighter, take it off the heat before it reaches this amber color. Remove from heat and immediately add cream (mixture will bubble up). Stir until blended.

- Immediately drizzle caramel over popcorn mixture; toss with sprayed spoons until evenly coated. Transfer to sheet.
- Place caramel corn in oven and bake until caramel is shiny and coats popcorn, tossing mixture occasionally, about 15-20 minutes.
- Cool completely on sheet on rack, tossing occasionally to break up large clumps.
- NOTES: Can be made 2 days ahead. Store airtight in refrigerator.

34. Bacon And Herb Seasoner

Serving: Makes about 1/2 cup | Prep: | Cook: | Ready in:

Ingredients

- 4 slices thick-cut bacon, coarsely chopped
- 2 teaspoons fresh thyme leaves
- 2 teaspoons minced fresh rosemary leaves
- 2 to 3 teaspoons minced, peeled fresh ginger
- 2 to 3 large cloves garlic, minced
- Salt and freshly grated black pepper

Direction

- Combine all the ingredients in a small bowl; season with salt and freshly grated black pepper.
- Get creative with this herb and bacon mix! Use as a seasoner by tucking under the skin of a whole chicken before roasting; or, sprinkle it over cauliflower florets spread on a baking pan and oiled, then roast in a 375 degree oven until cauliflower is caramelized and tender. Or, sprinkle the mixture into long-simmering meat-based soups or stews. The bacon releases its flavorful fat into chicken as it roasts to act as a powerful moistening agent. No extra

butter or olive oil needed. You can vary the herbs, or even add curry powder to taste!

35. Bacon And Tomato Pasta Salad

Serving: Serves 15 | Prep: | Cook: | Ready in:

Ingredients

- 12 ounces Small Shell Pasta
- 1/2 cup milk
- 6 pieces bacon
- 3 medium size tomatoes cut into chunks
- 1/4 cup sour cream
- 1 cup mayonnaise
- 1 tablespoon ground thyme
- 3 dashes salt
- 3 dashes black ground pepper

Direction

- Cook pasta in a pot of oil and salted water. Drain pasta and stir in milk
- Cook bacon and until brown and crisp. Remove from pan and drain on a paper towel over a plate.
- In pan that the bacon cook, add the tomatoes and thyme until the tomatoes are warm. Season the tomato and thyme mixture with salt and pepper.
- Break apart the bacon and set aside 1/4 cup of bacon bits.
- Stir in tomato and thyme mixture and bacon in with the pasta.
- Stir in the mayonnaise and sour cream into the pasta until well mixed. Pour pasta into an 8 inch by 12 inch pan. Put the 1/4 cup of bacon on top of the pasta.

36. Bacon, Cheddar, Spinach And Tomato Strata

Serving: Serves 4-6 (can be multiplied) | Prep: | Cook: | Ready in:

Ingredients

- butter for pan
- 6 ounces day old bread, cut into cubes
- 4 ounces bacon, cut into small pieces
- 1/2 cup finely chopped onion
- 3 plum tomatoes, peeled, seeded and chopped into small pieces (canned tomatoes are OK)
- 1 cup (ish) baby spinach, roughly chopped
- 6 ounces extra sharp cheddar cheese (use your favorite), grated
- 4 large eggs
- 1 cup whole milk
- 1 tablespoon Dijon mustard (mustard haters can leave this out)
- 1/2 teaspoon fresh ground black pepper
- salt to taste (depends on how salty your bacon is)

Direction

- Butter an 8 inch square baking dish (or one of equivalent size).
- Cook bacon in a large skillet over medium heat until the fat is rendered and the bacon is crisp. Drain the bacon on a plate lined with paper towels.
- Pour off all but 1 tablespoon of bacon fat. Sauté the onions in the bacon fat until they begin to soften and become translucent, about 3-5 minutes. Add the tomatoes, raise the heat, and cook the onions and bacon together, scraping up any browned bits, until they are somewhat caramelized and any liquid has evaporated. Stir in the spinach till wilted. Remove from heat.
- Place half of bread in baking dish. Top with half the tomato-onion-spinach mixture and top that with half the bacon, and 1/3 of the cheese. Layer on the rest of the bread followed by tomato-onion-spinach mixture and 1/2 of the remaining cheese.
- Whisk together milk, eggs and mustard in a large bowl and pour evenly over strata. Sprinkle remaining cheese over top, and grind about 1/2 teaspoon of black pepper over the cheese. Chill strata, covered with foil at least 1 hour and up to overnight (for bread to absorb custard).
- In the morning, remove strata from refrigerator and heat oven to 350. Bake uncovered 40-45 minutes until cooked through and lightly browned on top. Let rest about 5 minutes before serving.

37. Bagels To Go.

Serving: Makes 12 | Prep: | Cook: | Ready in:

Ingredients

- Red salmon filling:
- 12 plane, stale mini bagels
- 2 cups milk
- 2 cups caned red salmon, drained
- 1 medium white onion (fine diced)
- 2 hard-boiled eggs (fine diced)
- 3/4 cup prepared mayonnaise mixed with juice and zest of 1 large lemon and 2 teaspoons fresh dill (chopped)
- 1 cup shredded cheese (optional)
- Sausage and Sun-Dried Tomatoes filling:
- • 4 Bratwurst or Italian sausages, casings removed
- • 1 medium onion, chopped
- • 1/4 cup chopped sun-dried tomatoes (if very dry, soaked in hot water and drained first)
- • Coarse salt and freshly ground pepper
- • 1 large egg beaten
- • 1 cup shredded mozzarella cheese
- • 2 tablespoons freshly chopped parsley

Direction

- In a large glass baking dish lay out the bagels in one layer. Pour the milk over the bagels and soak them until puffed. Turn bagels a few times or press down. Meanwhile make the filling. In a mixing bowl steer eggs, onion, mayonnaise until well combined.
- To make the sausage filling: In a large skillet over medium-high heat, cook sausage, stirring occasionally, and breaking up meat with a spoon, until browned, 8 to 10 minutes.
- Add onion; cook stirring, until soft, 8 to 10 minutes. Stir in sun-dried tomatoes and parsley. Transfer to a plate; let cool to room temperature. Mix in the beaten egg to bind the filling.
- To assemble with red salmon filling: Preheat oven to 375 degrees F. Cover a large baking sheet with parchment paper, spray with cooking spray, and lay out the bagels. In the center mount 1 heaping tablespoon salmon mixture and sprinkle with cheese. If not using cheese, cover the filling with about 1 teaspoon mayonnaise or bread crumbs sautéed in butter. Bake for about 10- 15 minutes or until golden brown.
- To assemble with Sausage filling: In the center mount 1 heaping tablespoon Sausage mixture and sprinkle with cheese. Bake for about 10- 15 minutes or until golden brown.

38. Baked Clams Amatriciana

Serving: Makes 12 baked clams | Prep: | Cook: | Ready in:

Ingredients

- For the Clams
- 1 tablespoon butter
- 1 clove of garlic, crushed
- 12 littleneck clams, rinsed in cold water to remove grit
- 1 cup white wine
- 1 bay leaf
- For the Sauce
- 1/3 pound pancetta, finely diced (or guanciale)
- 1 tablespoon butter
- 3 cloves minced garlic
- 1/2 teaspoon red chile flakes
- 1 small red onion, finely diced
- one 14 1/2-ounce can crushed tomatoes
- 2 tablespoons finely grated Pecorino Romano
- 2 tablespoons finely chopped fresh parsley
- Olive oil

Direction

- Set a large skillet over medium heat and add 1 tablespoon of butter and 1 crushed clove of garlic. When the butter is melted and foaming, add the clams and the white wine. Adjust the heat to high, bring the white wine to a boil, and cover the clams with a lid. Check the clams every few minutes, stir them, and remove any open clams to a mixing bowl. Removing the clams as they open will prevent them from overcooking. When all of the clams have opened, turn off the heat and do not discard the remaining cooking liquid from the clams. When the open clams are cool enough to handle, remove the meat from the shell. Save the clam meat and the shells separately. Strain the leftover cooking liquid from the clams and reserve ¼ cup. The rest can be discarded.
- Separate the top of each empty shell from the bottom. Rinse the empty shells to remove any grit. Store the empty shells in the refrigerator until ready to use. Finely dice the clam meat and store it in the refrigerator.
- Set a large pot over medium heat and add the pancetta. Stir regularly until the bottom of the pot is coated with rendered pancetta fat. When the bottom of the skillet is coated with rendered fat, you can stir less frequently. Cook the pancetta until it looks brown and crispy. Using a slotted spoon, remove the pancetta from the skillet. Keep the rendered pancetta fat in the pot.
- Add 1 tablespoon of butter to the pot with the rendered pancetta fat. Adjust the heat to

medium. When the butter is melted and bubbling, add 3 cloves of minced garlic, along with the chile flakes and the red onion. Stir regularly, until the onion and garlic are soft and beginning to caramelize. Add the cooked pancetta back into the pot. Add the crushed tomato. Add the reserved ¼ cup of clam cooking liquid to your amatriciana sauce and stir to incorporate. Allow the tomatoes to cook for 20 minutes, stirring occasionally.

- Mix ¼ cup of the amatriciana sauce with the diced clam meat. Reserve the rest of your amatriciana sauce for another use. If you are making this dish immediately, begin to fill the clam shells with a dollop of the clam mixture. You can also store the clam mixture in your refrigerator for up to 48 hours before completing and serving this dish.
- Preheat the oven to 450° F. Top each clam with a small pinch of Pecorino Romano and a small pinch of finely chopped parsley. Drizzle the smallest about of olive oil over the top of each clam. Bake the clams for 3 to 5 minutes, until the sauce is bubbling inside the clam shell. Serve and enjoy.

39. Baked Jalapeno Poppers

Serving: Makes 10 pieces | Prep: | Cook: | Ready in:

Ingredients

- 5 large jalapeno peppers, split lengthwise and seeded with the white ribs removed
- 1/3 cup cooked bacon, cut small or use prepackaged Bacon Bits
- 1/3 cup green onions, chopped small
- 1/4 cup fresh cilantro, chopped small
- 6 slices Pepper Jack cheese, chopped small
- 4 slices Pepper Jack cheese, cut to fit jalapenos
- 3/4 teaspoon dried cumin
- 1/2 teaspoon dried oregano

Direction

- Cut off the top of the peppers close to the stem. Then split the peppers lengthwise and scoop out the seeds and white ribs; a grapefruit spoon works pretty well for this.
- Cut 4 pieces of the cheese to fit over the 10 stuffed poppers. Chop the rest into small pieces for the filling.
- Mix all of the chopped and shredded ingredients together and fill the pepper halves. Place a piece of cheese on top of the filling on each popper.
- Place all of the peppers, filling/cheese side up on a lightly oiled baking dish and bake at 375*F for 20 minutes or until the cheeses is thoroughly melted but not burned and the pepper looks cooked.
- Allow to cool then arrange on a bed of shredded iceberg lettuce or cilantro sprigs placed on a white serving plate. Enjoy the color, texture and taste of these delicious little treats. If you really like poppers dipped in a sauce, then we suggest that you dip these in a lite Ranch Dressing.

40. Bar Style Double Tortilla Pizza

Serving: Serves 2 | Prep: | Cook: | Ready in:

Ingredients

- 2 flour 10 inch tortillas
- ¼ red onion
- ½ white onion
- 1 cuptomato sauce
- 5 cherry tomatoes halved
- 1 slice pulled of prosciutto
- 5 small slices of salami
- 1 cupgrated Mozzarella
- 1 teaspoonItalian spices
- 2 mushrooms thinly sliced
- 1 tablespoonvegetable oil

Direction

- Preheat the oven at 400°F / 200°C

- Heat a saucepan and some vegetable oil
- Bake the halved cherry tomatoes until soft
- Add the sieved tomatoes and stir. Now add the Italian spices. Set aside
- Heat the skillet on medium heat. Brush the skillet with the olive oil and brush the pan
- Put the first tortilla in the pan
- Spread two to three tablespoons of tomato sauce across the tortilla all the way to the edges
- Now add 1/3 of the Mozzarella on the pizza and put the second tortilla on top
- Repeat spreading the tomato sauce on the tortilla
- Sprinkle the red and white onions
- Now add the mushrooms and finally cover with cheese
- Bake in the oven for 8 minutes until cheese is melted

41. Barbecue Glazed Pork Shoulder Butt & Beer

Serving: Serves about 8 | Prep: 0hours30mins | Cook: 6hours0mins | Ready in:

Ingredients

- For the Pork Shoulder Butt:
- 6 pound pork shoulder butt – bone in
- Lawry's seasoning salt
- black pepper (fresh ground)
- 1 medium onion – chopped
- ½ cup cherry tomatoes (or regular) – chopped
- extra virgin olive oil
- 1 bottle (12 ounce) dark beer (we used San Miguel)
- 2 tablespoons white distilled vinegar
- 2 teaspoons soy sauce
- For the Barbecue Glaze:
- 2 cups of your favorite barbecue sauce (we used Chris & Pitts)
- ½ cup port
- 2 tablespoons sherry

- ½ cup red wine
- juice of one orange
- juice of 2 limes
- juice of 2 tangerines
- 1 tablespoon Worcestershire sauce
- 1 teaspoon sea salt
- 1 teaspoon black pepper
- 1 teaspoon smoked paprika
- 1 tablespoon soy sauce
- 2 tablespoons white (distilled) vinegar

Direction

- Preheat oven to 325 degrees.
- Place pork shoulder butt in roasting pan. Sprinkle liberally with seasoning salt, black pepper and drizzle olive oil over top. Surround with onions and tomatoes. Add vinegar. Pour beer around all. Place in preheated oven. Cook for one hour.
- Meanwhile, mix all ingredients for barbecue glaze in medium bowl. Set aside.
- After an hour, turn the roast over.
- After half an hour, turn roast over again and baste with thick layer of glaze. Continue to do this every half hour (turning and basting...turning and basting) for a total of about 6 hours cooking time, or until roast is tender and falling off the bone.
- Slice and serve with thick sauce on the side.

42. Barbecue Sans The Grill

Serving: Serves 12 | Prep: | Cook: | Ready in:

Ingredients

- 2 pounds pork shoulder
- 2 cups catsup
- 1 gallon water
- 1 hot sauce to your liking

Direction

- Place pork shoulder and catsup in pot and cover with water. Boil until meat is cooked.
- Remove meat. Allow to cool. Do not discard remaining water in pot.
- Once meat has cooled, remove excess fat Return to the pot of water.
- Bring to a second boil, allow to simmer until you can shred the meat with a fork.
- As water dissipates, if needed, add more catsup.
- When you have what looks like BBQ, add hot sauce to your liking.
- Serve!

43. Barley Salad With Apples, Walnuts, And Deep Fried Sage

Serving: Serves 4 large salads | Prep: | Cook: | Ready in:

Ingredients

- 1 cup hulled barley (purple if you can find it)
- 3 cups water
- 6 fronds of sage leaves (divide use)
- 1 lemon (divided use)
- 1/2 cup chopped walnut pieces
- 1 medium sized celery root
- 1 firm apple, such as a honey crisp
- 4 strips of bacon
- 1 teaspoon Dijon mustard
- 1/2 teaspoon honey
- 1 small head of lettuce or 4 big handfuls of salad greens

Direction

- Soak the barley overnight. The next day, drain and add 3 cups of fresh water, 2 fronds of sage leaves and a generous amount of salt. Use a vegetable peeler to make a long strip of lemon rind and add this to the pot. Bring the water to a simmer and cook gently, partially covered, over low heat until the barley is tender but still has a lot of bite, about 90 minutes. Adjust seasoning and discard the lemon rind and sage leaves. You can cook the barley ahead and reheat it before finishing the salad.
- Peel the celery root (reserve any celery leaves for your salad) and chop into about ¼ inch dice. Peel the apple and chop into about ½ inch dice.
- Heat a skillet big enough to cook the bacon. When it is warm, toast the walnut pieces until they are fragrant but be sure not to burn them. Reserve.
- Now cook the bacon until it is nice and crisp. Drain on paper towels.
- Over medium heat, submerge the remaining 4 sage fronds, stem side up, into the hot rendered bacon fat and let them cook for a minute. Rescue them out of the vat of oil by their stems, and let them recover from their adventure on the paper towels. They will crisp up into crunchy treats.
- Reserve 1 tsp of rendered bacon fat for your dressing, and pour off all but about 1 Tbsp. of the fat from the pan. Over medium heat, add the diced celery root and sauté for a minute. Now add the diced apple and sauté for a minute longer. You want these to be flavored by the bacon fat but still have some crunch. Transfer the sautéed celery root and apple to a large bowl. Stir in the warm barley and the toasted walnuts. Taste and adjust the seasoning.
- Mix up a dressing for your lettuce by combining juice from one lemon, mustard and honey and then whisking in the reserved 1 tsp of bacon fat. Toss your lettuce leaves, and celery leaves if you have some, with the dressing and arrange on four plates. Top with a quarter of the barley mixture. Crumble a piece of bacon over each mound and top with the deep fried sage leaves. Enjoy warm.

44. Bean And Ham Stew With Roasted Vegetable Garnish

Serving: Serves 6 | Prep: | Cook: | Ready in:

Ingredients

- 2 cups anasazi beans or a similar variety, rinsed
- 1 ham bone from a bone-in ham, ham shank, or ham hock
- 1 small or 1/2 regular sized cabbage, finely chopped
- 1 onion, chopped
- 2 carrots, peeled and sliced
- 2 celery stocks, sliced
- 5 garlic cloves, finely chopped
- 1 serrano pepper, seeded and finely chopped (optional)
- 2 bay leaves
- 7 cups water, or more as needed
- 6 parsnips, peeled and chopped into ~1 inch chunks
- 6 small golden beets, peeled and chopped into ~1 inch chunks
- 2 tablespoons olive oil
- salt and pepper to taste

Direction

- In a slow cooker or soup pot, combine all of the stew ingredients (up to the water in the ingredient list). Cook on low for about 4 hours until the beans are tender, stirring occasionally. If cooking on the stovetop you may need less time and more water to maintain a thick stew consistency. Remove the ham bone or hock from the pot, shred the ham from the bone, and return the meat to the pot. Adjust seasonings to taste.
- About 45 minutes before you plan to serve the soup, preheat the oven to 450 degrees. Peel and chop the parsnips and beets. In an oven safe dish, toss the vegetables in olive oil, salt, and pepper. Roast for 30 to 40 minutes, stirring occasionally, until soft and browned. Serve the stew with a spoonful of roasted vegetables on top.

45. Beanie Weenies

Serving: Serves 4-6 | Prep: | Cook: | Ready in:

Ingredients

- 1 package little smokies cocktail sausages
- 1 tablespoon olive oil
- 1 shallot, minced
- 1 teaspoon cumin
- 1 teaspoon chili powder
- 2 tablespoons white vinegar
- 1/4 cup stout beer
- 1 can Bush's Baked Beans (I used Maple Cured Bacon)
- large handful of spinach
- salt and pepper to taste

Direction

- Heat a large skillet under medium heat and add sausages. Cook until browned, about 5 minutes or so. Set aside on a plate.
- In same skillet, add olive oil and shallots. Cook until shallots begin to soften, about 2-3 minutes. Add cumin and chili powder and mix well. Add vinegar, beer, and beans. Bring to a boil and then lower heat to a simmer.
- Return sausages to pan and allow to simmer for at least 10 minutes to let all of the flavors blend together.
- A couple minutes before serving, stir in the spinach and allow to wilt. Mix well and serve in bowls!

46. Beer Braised Carnitas Tacos

Serving: Makes enough for about 12 tacos | Prep: | Cook: | Ready in:

Ingredients

- for the beer braised carnitas
- 3-4 pounds boneless pork shoulder
- 1 yellow onion (diced)

- 6 cloves garlic (sliced)
- 1 4 ounces can diced green chilies
- 1 can beer
- 1 1/2 cups chicken broth (homemade or low sodium)
- spices (cumin, coriander, paprika, ancho powder, chipotle powder, Mexican oregano)
- 1 bay leaf
- 1 lime (zest & juice)
- grapeseed or canola oil
- salt and pepper
- for the pickled red onion
- 1/4 red onion (thinly sliced)
- 1/2 cup rice vinegar
- 1/4 cup water
- 1 pinch salt
- 1 pinch sugar

Direction

- For the beer braised carnitas.
- Preheat oven to 300 degrees. Let the pork come close to room temperature before cooking, for about 1 hour. Make sure to trim excess fat off of the pork before you start. Save a little bit of that excess fat. Salt and pepper the pork generously on all sides.
- In a large Dutch oven, turn the heat to low and drop in a few pieces of that pork fat with a tbsp. of oil and let the fat melt. Once melted, crank up the heat to high. Drop the pork in, with the fattiest side down and let it sizzle away for about 4 minutes, until browned. Repeat the process on all sides of the meat. Once done, remove from heat. Your kitchen will probably get super messy from splattering oil, unless you have a splatter screen. Get one.
- Lower heat to medium and add onion, garlic and green chilies. Let cook for about 5 minutes, until onions are soft. Deglaze the pan with the can of beer, scraping any leftover bits on the bottom of the pan. Now add a healthy dash of each spice (not too much of the chipotle though), the chicken broth, bay leaf, lime zest and juice, salt and pepper. Bring to a simmer.

- Once simmering, drop the pork with all the accumulated juices into the simmering sauce. Cover and pop into the preheated oven. Turn the pork over in the juices once or twice during the cooking process. Let the pork cook for 3 hours, covered the whole time.
- Remove from oven and bring pork to a cutting board. Remove any large pieces of unpleasant looking fat, and shred the rest with a fork. Spoon some of the liquid onto the pork, and you're ready for taco assembly.
- For the pickled red onion
- Bring vinegar, water, salt and sugar to a slow simmer, and turn off heat once simmering. Pour liquid over sliced onions and pop into the fridge for 30 minutes.
- Assemble tacos using your favorite toppings. I made mine with fresh cilantro, Greek yogurt, pickled onions and a squeeze of fresh lime.

47. Beer Braised Pork Butt Or Shoulder

Serving: Serves 4 | Prep: | Cook: | Ready in:

Ingredients

- 6 pounds Pork butt or shoulder
- 3 Onions
- 2 pounds Carrots
- 2 pounds Sweet potatoes
- 1 Celery root
- 3 Parsnips
- 2 to 3 Bottle of dark beer
- Chicken stock

Direction

- Sauté pork add onions carrots and rest of vegetables all vegetables cut to same size. Add beer and chic stock to cover and cover pot. Low fire for 3 hours

48. Beer Braised Pork Chops With A Kick

Serving: Serves 2 | Prep: | Cook: | Ready in:

Ingredients

- 2 tablespoons olive oil
- 2 boneless pork chops, 1-inch thick
- 3 cloves garlic, minced
- 1 shallot, chopped
- 1 whole jalapeno pepper, minced
- chili powder to taste
- salt & pepper to taste
- 1 can beer (I prefer Budweiser)

Direction

- Trim pork chops of any fat. Season both sides with salt, pepper, and chili powder.
- Heat up a deep sided, medium size pan (that has a lid). When pan is hot enough that a few drops of water dance across the surface, add the oil. Place the pork chops in the pan, hear that beautiful sizzle, and let sit for 3-4 minutes to allow optimal browning. Flip and brown the other side for another 3-4 minutes. Once both sides are browned, remove pork chops from pan.
- If needed, add some more olive oil. Add garlic, shallot, and jalapeno into pan and allow to sweat and cook until soft and slightly brown, infusing the flavors of the vegetables into the oil, about 3-4 minutes.
- Pour about half of the beer into the pan, and scrape up any brown bits. Bring to a boil. Nestle the pork chops back in the pan, and cover, bringing heat to low. You want the liquid level to hit around halfway up the pork chop. Let braise in the beer for 10-15 minutes. If you have any beer leftover, no one's judging- finish that bad boy while the meat's cooking.
- After chops are done simmering, plate each chop and top with some of the jalapeno-shallot-beer sauce. Oh yeah, and enjoy!

49. Besotes Caliente "Hot Kisses"

Serving: Makes 2 dozen | Prep: | Cook: | Ready in:

Ingredients

- 24 medium to large fresh jalapenos
- 24 medium (21-25) peeled & deveined shrimp
- 24 slices apple smoked (or other slightly sweet) bacon
- 8 ounces goat cheese

Direction

- Plan to pre-heat the grill or the broiler about 15 minutes before finishing the preparation. Medium heat for grill and not too close broiler element.
- Cut the goat cheese into 24 small oblong pieces, ~1" long. Place in freezer while preparing shrimp & jalapenos.
- While wearing latex kitchen gloves, just barely cut the stem top off & core the fresh jalapenos. To do this, you will need to cut a single slice almost the length of the pepper on only one side, but stopping just short of the pointy bottom. An easy way to core the jalapenos without special tools, is to hold it in one hand and rotate a butter knife down the center of the pepper.
- Stuff & wrap each pepper: Tuck a piece of goat cheese and one shrimp in each pepper; then wrap a slice of bacon around covering the whole pepper. Anchor bacon in place with two toothpicks as skewers.
- Cook ~10 minutes, turning several times. The time is very imprecise, because of the variance in grill or broiler temp. You want it hot enough to cook quickly, but slow enough to cook, not blacken the bacon. They are done when the bacon is nice and caramelized.
- These are hard to let cool enough to eat, but are good at room temp. Hot, creamy, smoky and a little sweet, no-one can eat just one.

50. Bibigo Asian Sliders

Serving: Serves 2-4 | Prep: | Cook: | Ready in:

Ingredients

- 4 Mini Buns
- 200 grams Ground Beef
- 50 grams Ground Pork
- 1 Tomato
- 1 Onion
- 1 Head of Lettuce
- 1 teaspoon Minced Garlic
- Salt & Pepper

Direction

- Thinly slice tomato and onion
- Mince onion and garlic with salt and pepper. Mix with beef and pork
- Heat oil in a non-stick pan and cook patties
- Mix Go-Chu-Jang sauce and mayonnaise
- Serve on the buns with mustard green/lettuce, tomato, patties, onion and gochujang mayo sauce

51. Black Bean And Chorizo Chili

Serving: Serves 4 | Prep: | Cook: | Ready in:

Ingredients

- 1 tablespoon cooking oil
- 1 onion, chopped
- 1/2 pound ground Mexican chorizo, casing removed
- 1 pound ground beef
- 3 cloves garlic, minced
- 1 green bell pepper, chopped
- 16 ounces can black beans, drained
- 16 ounces can kidney beans, drained
- 16 ounces can diced tomatoes (preferably fire-roasted)
- 16 ounces can tomato sauce
- 2 hot chillies, minced (serrano, jalapeno, etc.)
- 1 tablespoon chili powder
- 1 tablespoon dried oregano
- 1 teaspoon cumin
- 1 teaspoon coriander
- 1/4 teaspoon salt
- 1/4 can good beer (optional)
- cilantro, for garnish

Direction

- Add the oil to a large frying pan over medium-high heat, then brown the onion, beef, and chorizo for about 3-4 minutes. Don't stir too often, allowing the onions and meat to brown on one side. Break apart any large clumps of ground meat.
- Add the meat and onions to a heavy-bottomed pot, along with all the remaining ingredients. Make sure to wear latex gloves when handling the hot peppers!
- If using beer (I recommend Guinness), pour just enough to cover the ingredients with liquid -- no more than half a can should be needed.
- Cover the pot and simmer over low heat for about 45 minutes. If you find a lot of liquid forming on top of the chili, stir the chili and continue to cook with the lid removed. Serve garnished with chopped fresh cilantro.
- Variations: Since the chorizo sausage is naturally spicy and flavorful, you can easily make this recipe without the hot chillies. An alternative is to add a few squirts of Sriracha sauce when combining the ingredients. Other beans can be substituted, such as pinto beans, but make sure at least one can is black beans!

52. Black Magic Marinade

Serving: Makes about 1/2 cup | Prep: 0hours15mins | Cook: 0hours0mins | Ready in:

Ingredients

- 3 tablespoons Freshly ground, medium roast coffee
- 1.5 tablespoons Brown Deli Mustard
- 3 tablespoons Apple Cider Vinegar
- 1/2 tablespoon minced garlic
- Zest of 1/2 medium orange
- about 1/2 cups Fresh Breadcrumbs
- 1 tablespoon brown sugar
- 1.5 teaspoons Salt
- 1/2 teaspoon Black pepper
- Good, strong olive oil

Direction

- Combine everything from the coffee grounds through the black pepper in a small bowl.
- Add enough olive oil to make a spreadable paste. If you get olive-oil-glug-happy, just add more breadcrumbs to adjust the consistency.
- Season your protein with additional salt and pepper if desired, and then generously slather with the marinade. While you can cook your protein immediately, the marinade has a chance to work that signature magic if it sets for several hours, or even overnight.
- Cook your protein until almost at the right temperature, and then uncover and broil to create a crust that'll keep them coming back for more!

53. Borlotti Beans And Speck

Serving: Serves 4 | Prep: | Cook: | Ready in:

Ingredients

- 18 ounces borlotti beans
- 5 ounces fresh pasta
- 3 ounces onion
- 1.75 ounces speck (or bacon)
- 1.75 ounces peeled tomatoes ("pomodori pelati"from the can)
- 1.4 ounces olive oil
- vegetable broth
- salt&pepper

Direction

- Take a can of borlotti beans (you can also use the dry kind) and put them in a pan of boiling water for about 5 minutes to soften them up and then put them in a food mixer or grinder to create a type of creamy bean paste.
- Prepare a medium-sized saucepan of vegetable broth. We use the Knorr stock, just add it to boiling water and in 5 minutes it's ready.
- Grate the onion and cut about two thirds of the speck into small pieces
- Heat the oil in a large pan (I would suggest a deep pan like a wok) and let the onion and speck cook for about 2 minutes.
- Add the tomatoes, borlotti beans paste and add a good bit of the vegetable broth.***The trick to know much broth to use is that you have to think that the pasta is going to cook in this pan for about 6 mins so there should be enough water for this but also to make a creamy sauce.***
- Add the pasta to the pan and cook for as long as necessary (We use fresh pasta because it cooks quicker and is ideal for this dish). If the sauce is beginning to dry up add some more vegetable broth.
- When the pasta is cooked take the pan off the flame and add salt and pepper and let it cool for a few minutes
- Serve with the remaining speck pieces sprinkled on top

54. Braised 5 Spicepork Belly With Roasted Eggplant, Scallions, Hoisin And Edamame

Serving: Serves 6 to 8 | Prep: | Cook: | Ready in:

Ingredients

- 3.5 pounds pork belly
- 5 chineese eggplant

- 5 bunches scallions
- 1 1/2 packets soba noodles
- ginger
- garlic
- 1 bottle bunches soy sauce
- 1 small bottle mirin
- 3 tablespoons rice wine vinegar
- 2 tablespoons fish sauce
- 2 cups water
- 5 spice
- salt and pepper
- 1 bag edamame
- hoisin
- 1 1/2 packets wide soba noodles
- sesame oil
- toastes sesame seeds (optional)
- oil of your choice

Direction

- Preheat oven to 350. Season the pork belly with the skin on with salt, pepper, and 5 spice. Sear in a hot deep pan in some oil.
- Make a braising liquid with 2 cups soy sauce, 2 cups mirin, 3 tablespoons of rice wine vinegar, 2 tablespoons fish sauce,
- Add braising liquid to pork, take some scallion tops, some ginger and some crushed garlic. Bring up to a boil, cover and place in the oven for 1 hr. and 45 minutes.
- Next, slice the scallion bottoms (the white and the light green), and caramelize in a little oil and butter till nice and golden brown. Set aside. Save the dark green tops, and slice them for garnish
- then peel some of the skin off the eggplants, then cut in small chunks, toss in a little salt and let some of the moisture and bitterness drain out for 1/2 hr. after that, toss in a little olive oil and roast for 30 minutes. Make sure you check it every so often and move the eggplant around so it doesn't burn.
- Once the pork is fork tender, set aside to cool. Once cool, remove the pork and strain the liquid. Do not throw out the liquid, you will use it for the sauce. Remove the skin and any bones (my butcher left some pork ribs in) and

then shred the pork in large chunks, adding a bit of the braise to prevent it from getting dry.
- Boil a pot of water for your soba noodles. While the water is coming up, take a deep pan, and add water, a tablespoon of oil and the frozen edamame. Heat on a high setting until the water is evaporated. Add caramelized scallions, roasted eggplant, and braising liquid. Heat on a high till the eggplant and scallion melt into the sauce, thickening it up a bit. Add 3 tablespoons of hoisin.
- Cook noodles as directed on the bag. When you drop your pasta, add the pork to the eggplant and heat through. Take some of the pasta water and add it to your pork sauce in case it's too thick. Finish with the juice of one lemon
- When the pasta is done, strain, place in the bowl of your choice. Add the pork ragu. Garnish with scallion tops and toasted sesame if you wish.

55. Braised Leek And Bacon Bisque

Serving: Serves 4 | Prep: | Cook: |Ready in:

Ingredients

- For the Bisque
- 1/4 pound bacon, diced (about 4 slices)
- 3 large leeks
- 3 cups chicken stock, homemade if available
- 1 garlic clove, smashed and peeled
- 1 tablespoon lemon thyme (or regular thyme)
- kosher salt and freshly ground black pepper
- 1/3 cup heavy cream
- 1 tablespoon lemon juice
- For the Fried Leek Garnish
- leek trimmings, leftover from making the bisque
- 2-4 tablespoons all purpose flour
- 1/4 cup olive oil

Direction

- For the Bisque
- Preheat the oven to 325 degrees.
- Prepare the leeks. Trim the root and dark green ends and set the trimmings aside- you'll use them for the garnish. Cut the leeks in half lengthwise, but do not cut all the way through the root end- the leek halves should still be connected at the base. Rinse the leeks under running water, fanning out the layers to rinse away any dirt that might be trapped there. Set the leeks aside.
- Fry the diced bacon in a small Dutch oven (3-4 quart) over medium-low heat, until crispy. Remove the bacon with a slotted spoon and drain on paper towels.
- Transfer 1-2 teaspoons of the rendered bacon fat to a 9x9 inch baking or gratin dish and use a pastry brush to grease the pan with the hot bacon fat. Save the remaining bacon fat for another day.
- Add one cup of chicken stock to the empty Dutch oven and turn the heat up to high. Bring to a boil and scrape up the good crusty bits from the bottom of the pot with a wooden spoon. Turn off the heat. Stir in the smashed garlic clove and chopped lemon thyme.
- Place the cleaned leeks in the greased baking dish. Sprinkle with kosher salt, pepper, and the crispy bacon. Pour the chicken stock mixture over the leeks. Cover the baking dish with foil, and place in the oven to braise for 30 minutes.
- After the first 30 minutes, use tongs to flip the leeks over to the other side and recover with foil. Braise for an additional 30 minutes, or until the leeks are very tender.
- Meanwhile, make the fried leek garnish (recipe below).
- Remove the baking dish from the oven and let cool briefly. During the cooling time, add the remaining two cups of stock to the Dutch oven you used earlier and bring to a simmer over low heat.
- Puree the leeks and braising liquid in a blender along with a ladleful of the stock from the Dutch oven. (You stand with the dish trembling in your hands, your face aghast:

"surely she doesn't expect me to puree the bacon too?!". Yes. Yes, I do. And friend, it will be delicious. Your bisque will be flecked with dancing particles of bacon-y goodness.) Transfer the puree to the Dutch oven with the rest of the simmering stock. Bring the soup to a simmer, and then remove from heat. Stir in the heavy cream and lemon juice, and add salt and pepper to taste. Garnish with fried leeks.
- For the Fried Leek Garnish
- While the leeks are braising, prepare the fried leek garnish.
- From the tops of the leeks that you trimmed earlier, remove the outer layers until you get to the lighter green, more tender center. Slice these tender bits thinly, lengthwise, so that you're left with little strips of leek. These should be about 2 inches in length, so cut them in half if need be. Rinse these to get rid of any sand, then pat dry.
- Heat the oil in a small skillet over medium-high heat until shimmery. Toss the leeks and the flour in a small bowl. Shake off any excess flour and drop the leeks into the hot oil. Fry until the leeks just begin to turn golden- they should still be mostly green. Remove from the skillet and drain on paper towels, and sprinkle immediately with salt.

56. Braised Pork Roast With Onion Jus, Pears, Turnips And Potatoes

Serving: Serves 4 | Prep: | Cook: | Ready in:

Ingredients

- 2 1/2 pounds bone-in pork butt or sirloin roast with good marblization
- 4 onions, trimmed, peeled and julienned
- 3 tablespoons unsalted butter
- 5-7 bay leaves depending on their size
- 6 sprigs of thyme, tied in a bundle with kitchen twine

- 6 garlic cloves, trimmed, peeled and sliced
- 2 cups dried white wine
- kosher salt and fresh ground white pepper
- 2 or 3 bosc pears, ripe but firm ripe
- 2 or 3 turnips
- 2 or 3 russet potatoes
- canola oil

Direction

- Season the roast liberally with salt, place in on a rack over a sheet tray and place it in the fridge for two hours or overnight.
- Remove the pork roast from the fridge. Season it with white pepper. Heat a large enameled Dutch oven over medium high heat. Once the pot is very hot but not smoking add a glug of canola oil just to coat the bottom. A tablespoon or so. Add the roast and brown it on all sides adjusting the heat as necessary.
- Once it is deeply browned remove it from the pot and add butter and the onions. Season the onions with a two finger pinch of salt and a couple of grinds of white pepper. Add the bay leaves, thyme and garlic.
- Once the garlic becomes aromatic snuggle the roast into the onions and add the wine. Let the wine come to a boil then cover the pot and reduce the heat to low and season again with a pinch or two of salt and some white pepper. Keep an eye on the liquid in the pot and if it becomes too low add water as necessary. Simmer at a lazy bubble for two hours or until the roast is very tender but not fall apart.
- Towards the end of the roast is simmering time slice the pear, turnip and potatoes lengthwise to get two 1/2 inch pieces from each vegetable and the fruit. You may only need two veggies or fruit each to do this the third is just backup.
- You will need to do this in batches so turn the oven to 350F. Place a non-stick skillet over medium high heat. Pour in enough oil to coat the pan and add 1 tablespoon of butter. Sear the turnips and potatoes until they are nicely browned then remove them to a sheet tray. Then do the same with the pears, depending on the firmness of the pears you may want to put them on separate tray so you can cook them separately and for less time.
- Time this so they can come out of the oven at the same time you are slicing the pork so you may want to wait to put them into the oven till the roast is done.
- When the roast is done remove it from the pot. Turn the heat to high and reduce the jus by half. I like to use an immersion blender and puree and thicken the sauce. You could do the same with a blender just be careful of hot liquid in a blender it likes to explode out the top. Or you could just leave the onions as they are and keep the dish rustic.
- Slide the potatoes, turnips and pears into the oven till tender. Slice the pork, plate it to a sauced platter or to individual sauced plates and serve.

57. Breakfast Kolaches

Serving: Makes 8 kolaches | Prep: | Cook: | Ready in:

Ingredients

- Dough:
- 1 cup whole milk
- 8 tablespoons (1 stick) unsalted butter
- 1 tablespoon (1 packet) active dry yeast
- 1/4 cup sugar
- 1/2 teaspoon kosher salt
- 3 to 4 cups all-purpose flour
- 2 tablespoons vegetable (or neutral) oil
- 3 egg yolks
- Fillings: (I liked egg-chorizo, jalapeno-cheese, or jalapeno-egg-cheese, but you can mix and match)
- 2 chorizo sausages, casings removed, browned in skillet and cooked through
- 6 to 8 eggs, scrambled
- 3/4 cup grated cheddar cheese
- 2 to 3 whole pickled jalapeños, thinly sliced

Direction

- Over medium heat, warm the milk and the butter until the milk is just beginning to steam, but is not boiling, and the butter is melted. Remove from the heat.
- In a large mixing bowl, whisk together the yeast, sugar, salt, and 1 1/2 cups of the flour. Pour in the warm milk mixture and stir until a sticky dough has formed. Cover the dough and let it rest for 30 minutes.
- Once the dough has rested, beat together the oil and egg yolks in a separate bowl. Pour the eggs into the flour mixture and blend until fully incorporated. Slowly stir in enough of the remaining 1 1/2 to 2 1/2 cups flour until the dough comes together and is soft but not sticky. Turn the dough out onto a floured surface and knead for about 10 minutes, or until it is smooth.
- Place the kneaded dough in a lightly oiled bowl and cover. Allow to rise until doubled in size, about 1 hour.
- Line a baking sheet with parchment paper. After the dough has risen, punch it down and divide into 8 even-sized pieces. Using your hands, roll the pieces of dough into balls, flatten the balls into disks, and then pull the disks into oblong rectangles. (The rectangles, in my experience, held more filling than circles, creating a better dough-to-filling ratio.) Stretch the rectangles to about 1/3-inch thickness, then divide the scrambled eggs, chorizo, cheese, and jalapeños among the eight kolaches. While you don't want to overstuff, don't be shy, either—otherwise you'll end up with a sad little tunnel of filling in a mass of bread. Once you've filled, fold one side over the other, like a burrito. They'll likely feel a little too buttery and a little too soft. It will all work itself out in the oven, I promise. Place kolaches on the lined baking sheet 1 inch apart, seam side down. Cover and allow to rise for 45 more minutes.
- Preheat the oven to 375° F.
- Bake, uncovered, for 15 to 18 minutes, or until lightly browned. Serve warm, with hot sauce or mustard, if you'd like. They are best on the day they are made, but they can be tightly wrapped and then reheated, up to 2 days after baking. They can also be frozen and reheated in a 350° F degree oven.

58. Breakfast Sandwich

Serving: Serves 1 | Prep: | Cook: |Ready in:

Ingredients

- Pesto Mayo (makes about 1 cup)
- 2 cups fresh basil leaves
- 1/3 cup walnuts
- 3 cloves garlic
- 1/2 cup extra virgin olive oil
- 1/3 cup grated Parmesan-Reggiano cheese
- Pinch salt and pepper to taste
- 4 tablespoons mayonnaise
- Assembling the sandwich
- 1/4 cup canola oil
- 1/4 red onion
- 2 rashers smoked bacon
- 1 Ciabatta roll (sliced in half)
- Bunch watercress leaves and tender stems
- 1/2 tablespoon unsalted butter
- 1 large brown egg
- crumbled blue cheese

Direction

- Pesto Mayo (makes about 1 cup)
- In a food processor, pulse the walnuts. Add fresh basil leaves and garlic and pulse a few more times.
- Slowly add the olive oil in a constant stream while processor is on, ensuring that the sides of the processor are scraped down.
- Add the grated cheese and pinch salt and pepper and continue to pulse until all ingredients are well blended. Pesto should be thick (adjust olive oil portion to suit personal tastes).

- Combine approximately two tablespoons of the pesto with the mayonnaise and set aside.
- Assembling the sandwich
- Heat canola oil in a non-stick skillet. The stove should be on high. While heating, slice the onion, flat side down, to make thin strips. When the oil is hot, but not smoking, add the onion strips and cook on medium low until the onions are glistening and have reached a dark, rich brown color (~15 minutes).
- Heat a cast iron skillet on medium heat and add bacon. Allow bacon to crisp in its own fat. Cooking times vary, so after turning it over a few times, remove when it reaches your desired crispiness and darkness. Drain on paper towel and set aside.
- Depending on the amount of fat leftover in the pan used to cook the bacon (you may want to remove some before proceeding) lightly fry both slices of the Ciabatta roll (flat side down) until slightly brown. Remove and spread pesto mayo on both sides. Place bunch watercress on bottom slice and set aside.
- Place a small non-stick pan on low heat and add butter. Let it slowly melt, making sure it doesn't foam and is not sizzling.
- Crack the egg in a small bowl, or ramekin, and when all the butter has melted, gently slide the egg into the frying pan and cover with a lid.
- Cooking eggs (whether frying, poaching, or whatever) can be tricky, but continue cooking for approximately 5 minutes, or until the egg white solidifies from its transparent, original state. The yolk should thicken slightly as it heats, but do not flip (the satisfaction of this sandwich is the runny egg!)
- When the egg is done, slide onto the bed of watercress (bottom bread slice) and season with salt and pepper. Top with crispy bacon, and garnish with caramelized red onions and crumbled blue cheese. Enjoy!!

59. Breakfast Sunshine Platter (Chilaqueles With Tomatillo Sauce)

Serving: Serves 6 | Prep: | Cook: | Ready in:

Ingredients

- Roasted Tomatillo Sauce
- 1 poblano pepper, large
- 1 yellow onion
- 1/2 red onion
- 3-4 garlic cloves (up to a 1/2 head)
- 12 tomatillos, husks removed & washed & quartered
- oil, salt & pepper
- Chilaqueles
- 8 corn tortillas cut into 6 triangles (each)
- oil for frying
- tex-mex seasoning: 1 T. kosher salt and 1/2 t. each of cumin, coriander and chili powder with 1/4 t. of cayenne
- 1/2 pound ground chorizo, browned and well drained
- 6 ounces refried beans
- 3 ounces cream cheese
- 4 ounces queso fresco (or substitute chevre/ goat cheese)
- 1 avocado, sliced
- 1/2 bunch cilantro
- 1 lime, quartered
- 6-8 poached eggs

Direction

- Prep the tomatillo sauce: Slice off top of pepper, discard seeds (unless you like it really hot) cut lower part of pepper in half lengthwise. Chop onions into large hunks. You can use as much as a half head of garlic, just slice off the top of the bulb and let it roast. Toss with oil, salt & pepper, roast in a 400 degree oven for 1 hour.
- Discard top/stem of poblano pepper. Pulse/process in a blender or food processor to achieve a chunky sauce.
- Brown chorizo. Drain well.

- Warm refried beans and cream cheese in microwave, half power, 1-2 minutes to make a smooth, softened mixture.
- If possible, let tortillas sit out overnight. This will allow some of the moisture to escape and make a crispier tortilla. You can substitute flour tortillas.
- Fry tortillas (in batches) in 1 inch of oil, drain on paper towels and immediately sprinkle tex-mex seasoning salt on top.
- Prepare pan/ water for egg poaching. If you made everything the night before, warm beans, warm tomatillo sauce
- On a platter, heap a layer of chips, then spread bean mixture and tomatillo sauce on top... sprinkle chorizo and flake cheese with a fork to make crumbles. Garnish with sliced avocado, cilantro and lime wedges.
- Poach eggs and place on top. Enjoy!

60. Bricktop

Serving: Serves 4-6 | Prep: | Cook: | Ready in:

Ingredients

- 1 pound ground rib eye or comparable cut (we like a bit of fat)
- 1 pound ground pork (shoulder or loin)
- 3 eggs (hold one egg back for the wash)
- ¼ cup fresh pistachio nuts
- 1 tablespoon fresh thyme
- 6 ounces chanterelle mushrooms (see note to cook)
- 1 large garlic clove peeled and chopped
- ¼ cup unseasoned bread crumbs (there is a time for panko and a time for not, now is not the time)
- White truffle oil
- Sea salt and pepper
- 1 sheet puffed pastry cut to fit your terrine

Direction

- With soft brush clean off dust from the mushroom. In a large bowl mix the beef, pork and eggs (lightly beaten) with your hands--- yes really. Season lavishly with sea salt and coarse ground pepper. Squish in the bread crumbs, and of course include the pistachio nuts and garlic. Make sure everything is evenly distributed.
- Heat up your oven to 350 (no two ovens are calibrated exactly, so work with that). Meanwhile press half your meat loaf mix into a lubricated terrine. On top of this layer your chanterelles. Drizzle with truffle oil. Spread fresh thyme over this and follow with another layer of meat. Yes, I said "meat" vegan horde.
- Press it down as hard as you can. I've discovered that a bottle of Absolut vodka wrapped in cling wrap or foil works really well. We are after something like a pate` texture here. Smooth as opposed to coarse. This is why you grind your own meat.
- Drizzle a bit more truffle oil. Top with your puffed pastry sheet. Brush that with an egg wash of one egg and bit of water---you didn't forget that other egg did you? Child safety warning: do not bake with the vodka bottle on top, something really terrible could happen.
- Into the oven it goes. It will need to cook for at least 1 hour to 1 1/2. The outside "croute" should be brown and crisped and the inside temperature should be about 150 when tested with an instant read.
- This is good either hot or cold. Serving cold, a little dressing works well with some olives or cornichons on the side.
- * Okay, I know you have your Kitchen Aids. Go buy the grinder attachment. You will thank me later. Note you can make this identical dish by substituting dried and reconstituted porcini mushrooms for the chanterelles. For me they were in season and available for a reasonable price.

61. Broccoli Salad With Maple Bacon And Caramelized Apple Vinaigrette

Serving: Serves 3-4 as a main, or a crowd as a side | Prep: | Cook: | Ready in:

Ingredients

- For the dressing
- 4 ounces apple cider vinegar, divided
- 2 ounces brown sugar
- 1 apple, peeled, cored and diced into medium-sized pieces (preferably Pink Lady or another sweet/tart apple variety)
- 1 clove garlic, minced
- 1 teaspoon fresh thyme
- juice of half a lemon
- 1 teaspoon maple syrup
- sea salt
- 4-6 ounces olive oil
- For the salad
- 1/2 cup sliced almonds
- 6 strips thick-cut bacon
- maple syrup
- 1/2 small red onion, chopped small
- 1 pound broccoli, chopped into bite-sized pieces
- 1 Pink Lady apple, sliced thin and chopped
- 3/4 cup shredded carrots
- 1/2 cup dried cranberries
- 1/4 cup golden raisins
- salt

Direction

- For the dressing
- In a small skillet over medium heat, add the 3 oz. of vinegar and the sugar. Let it reduce and thicken. It should turn a dark caramel color and foamy bubbles should form on the surface.
- Add the apple and garlic, cooking until the apple gets soft, about 5 minutes. Remove from the heat to let it cool for a few minutes.
- In a blender or food processor, add the apple mixture with the rest of the vinegar, thyme, lemon juice, maple syrup, and a pinch of salt. Pulse until combined and only small chunks remain.
- Add 4 oz. of olive oil and pulse again. Add more olive oil until you reach your desired consistency. I ended up using about 5 oz., which made a dressing closer to the consistency of a thin apple sauce.
- Add salt to taste and set aside.
- For the salad
- Preheat the oven to 350ºF. Spread the almonds on a baking sheet and toast for 5 minutes or until golden brown. Set aside.
- Lay bacon slices on a rimmed baking sheet with parchment paper, leaving room between each slice. Drizzle the bacon with maple syrup. Bake in the oven for 15-20 minutes or until it reaches your desired crispness. Place finished bacon on a paper towel-lined plate to drain. (While the bacon cooks, this would be a good time to do some chopping)
- Place the chopped onion in a small bowl with 1/2 cup of the dressing. Let that sit for at least 5-10 minutes.
- In a large bowl combine the broccoli, apple, carrots, cranberries, raisins and almonds. Chop the bacon into bite-sized pieces and add it to the bowl. Add the dressing-soaked onions to the bowl.
- Mix everything around and add more dressing as desired. I ended up using all of my dressing. (This salad was not overly-dressed. If you prefer your salad with a heavier dressing, you may want to double the dressing recipe and enjoy the leftovers on something else throughout the week.) Add salt to taste.

62. Brussels Sprout Salad

Serving: Serves 2 | Prep: | Cook: | Ready in:

Ingredients

- half pound Brussels Sprouts (small)
- 4 pieces Bacon

- 1 Fresh Carrot
- 1 Avocado
- some Parmesan Shavings
- 3 tablespoons Olive Oil
- 1.5 tablespoons Balsamic Vinegar
- half Lemon
- Pepper

Direction

- Cut up the Brussels sprouts in half or in quarters depending on how long you'd like the sprouts to cook. Set aside. Stack the 4 pieces of uncooked bacon and cut them into small pieces.
- Heat a non-stick pan and toss the bacon pieces in. Cook the bacon until crispy, or 5 minutes then add the cut Brussels sprouts. Let the Brussels sprouts absorb the bacon grease and remove from heat when the sprouts becomes brown on their cut side.
- Pour the bacon and sprouts into a salad bowl. Clean your carrot, shave the outer layer if you prefer then shave the carrot down completely into the bowl. Remove skin from the avocado and cut into half inch pieces. Toss the pieces into the bowl. Squeeze roughly half a lemon into the bowl (or to taste), and follow with olive oil and balsamic vinegar. Toss the ingredients until everything is coated. The avocado will melt slightly due to the heat of the sprouts/bacon giving the salad a creamy texture. Put onto a plate, or bowl, and top with bits of shaved parmesan and corse pepper. Salt is not recommended as the bacon and lemon will create a salty taste but it can be added if you prefer a rather salty taste. Serve.

63. Bucatini Carbonara With Cremini Mushrooms And A Warm Poached Egg

Serving: Serves 1 (with leftovers) | Prep: | Cook: |Ready in:

Ingredients

- 8 ounces bucatini pasta
- 2 tablespoons olive oil
- 4 ounces pancetta, sliced into strips
- 4 ounces cremini mushrooms, thinly sliced
- 2 cloves garlic, minced
- 3 eggs, divided use
- 1/2 cup grated Parmesan or Pecorino Romano cheese
- Kosher salt
- Freshly ground black pepper
- 1 tablespoon vinegar
- 2 tablespoons finely chopped chives

Direction

- Bring a large pot of salted water to a boil. Add the bucatini and cook until al dente, according to package directions.
- Start making the sauce while the pasta is cooking so that you will be able to add the hot pasta to the sauce as soon as it's done cooking. Heat the olive oil in a large sauté pan over medium high heat. Add the pancetta and cook until browned. Add the mushrooms and cook until just softened, about 3-4 minutes. Add the garlic and cook another minute until fragrant. Drain the bucatini and add the hot pasta to the pan. Toss well to coat all of the pasta with the fat. Reserve 1 cup of the pasta water. Bring the water back to a simmer to use for the poached egg.
- Beat 2 eggs and the cheese together in a medium bowl. Remove the sauté pan from the heat and pour the egg and cheese mixture into the pasta, stirring it constantly with tongs until the eggs thicken and form a creamy sauce. Keep the pasta in constant motion so that the eggs don't scramble (the heat of the pasta will cook the eggs). Add some of the pasta water to thin out the sauce until it reaches the desired consistency (it will take ½ to 1 cup). Season the pasta with salt and freshly ground black pepper to taste.
- To make the warm poached egg, add the vinegar to the pot of hot water and bring it to a

simmer (just below boiling, 185-200 degrees F). Crack the remaining egg into a ramekin or small cup. Once the water reaches a simmer, pour the egg into the water. The egg will sink to the bottom of the pot and then float to the top. Cook until the white is coagulated and the yolk is partially set (slightly thickened but still flowing), 3-4 minutes. Remove the egg with a slotted spoon and blot it on a paper towel to remove excess water. Trim the edges if they are ragged.

- To serve, place a mound of pasta in a bowl and top with the warm poached egg. Garnish with fresh chives. Save the remaining pasta for leftovers!

64. Bucatini Pasta With Pork Ragu

Serving: Serves 6 to 8 | Prep: | Cook: |Ready in:

Ingredients

- 1/4 cup extra virgin olive oil
- 1 pound ground pork
- 1 pound sweet Italian sausage
- 4 ounces pancetta or bacon (optional, but recommended)
- 1 large carrot
- 2 celery ribs
- 1 medium onion (or half a large one)
- 4 large garlic cloves (or more if they are small)
- 1/4 cup plus 2 tablespoons chopped fresh parsley
- 1 tablespoon chopped fresh oregano (or 1/2 tablespoon dry oregano)
- 2 to 3 anchovies
- 2 dry hot Calabrian chile peppers, crumbled (or 1/4 teaspoon regular hot pepper flakes)
- 1 tablespoon tomato paste (preferably Italian, from San Marzano tomatoes)
- 28 ounces can of San Marzano tomatoes (can use regular, but it won't be the same!)
- 1/4 cup dry red wine

- 1 pound bucatini pasta
- 1/2 cup grated fresh Parmesan cheese (plus more for serving)
- 1/3 cup grated fresh pecorino cheese (can just use Parmesan if not available; just add an extra 1/3 cup)
- 2 or more cups water
- Kosher salt and freshly ground black pepper to taste
- Very high quality balsamic vinegar to taste (optional)

Direction

- Slice the pancetta or bacon into strips if using. Alternatively, you can cube a slab of either as well. Remove the sausage from the casings.
- Heat 3 tablespoons of the olive oil in a large Dutch oven over medium-high heat. Add the pancetta or bacon first. Cook about 3 minutes, stirring frequently until browned and crispy; remove with a slotted spoon to a bowl and set aside. Add the ground pork and sausage, breaking up the meat and mixing it with the back of a spoon or the tip of a spatula. Try to break the meat into even pieces.
- Remove half of the meat from the pan and make sure heat is on high. Now cook the first batch without touching and let it sizzle for a 3 minutes. You want to get the meat nice and brown and get some "brown bits" on the bottom of the pan. This is FLAVOR for the sauce! Repeat with second batch. Remove meat with slotted spoon, leaving as much fat as possible in the pan. Add the meat to the pancetta/bacon.
- Prepare the vegetables: Chop the onion, carrot, and celery. Thinly slice the garlic and chop the Calabrian hot peppers. Note: Don't worry about being perfect with the chopping because you will be puréeing all the vegetables anyway with an immersion blender. This is just so they cook evenly. Also chop the parsley, fresh oregano, and anchovies.
- Heat leftover meat fat in the pan over medium heat and add the last tablespoon of olive oil. Add the onion, carrot, celery, garlic and hot

pepper to the pan. Cook on medium heat until vegetables are soft and onions are translucent, about 8 minutes. Lower heat to medium-low if the vegetables are browning. While they are cooking, season with 1/4 teaspoon kosher salt (or a little regular salt) and a few grinds of fresh black pepper.

- While the vegetables cook, mix 1 tablespoon tomato paste with 1 cup of water. Open the can of San Marzano tomatoes (yes, you can use regular tomatoes...but it just won't be the same!), pour into a bowl and use your hands to crush them. Make sure your hand is submerged in the sauce when crushing or you'll get tomato sauce flying everywhere! Again, don't worry about them being perfect, since you will puree them anyway.

- Add the chopped anchovies, parsley, and oregano to the vegetables. Cook for 2 minutes more, stirring well. Turn up the heat and add the 1/4 cup red wine, scraping the bottom to release the caramelized meat bits. Let the alcohol cook off for a few minutes, then add the tomato paste and water mixture. Stir and let the mixture boil for 5 minutes.

- Add the crushed San Marzano tomatoes to the pan, mix, and cook 2 more minutes. Now use an immersion blender to blend everything into a smooth, creamy sauce. Add a couple of pinches of sugar and kosher salt and 2 more grinds of black pepper. We're building flavor here... slowly.

- Now add the meat to the pan and stir to combine. Raise the heat to high and bring to a boil. Then lower heat to as low as you can get it so the pot barely bubbles. Cover with lid leaving just a little gap and let it simmer for the next few hours. 3 and a half hours does the trick, but 4 is better and 5 is perfect. You want to stir the sauce every 45 minutes if you can, and add some water when the sauce gets so thick that the meat is poking out. After a few hours, your sauce should be perfect and you won't be able to stop tasting it! Now is the time to add a little balsamic vinegar if you're using it.

- Fill a large pot with water, add a couple of dashes of salt, and bring to a boil. Cook the bucatini about 8 minutes. You want the pasta to be slightly underdone. As it gets close to being done, scoop out 2 cups of the pasta water.

- Drain the bucatini and add to the sauce, along with about 1/2 cup of the pasta water. Simmer for 4 minutes until pasta is perfectly done and the sauce has thickened. The starch in the pasta water helps thicken the sauce.

- Turn off heat, add the other 2 tablespoons chopped fresh parsley and 1/2 cup grated Parmesan and 1/3 cup grated pecorino (or just 3/4 cup Parmesan). Mix everything together.

- Carefully scoop the bucatini into bowls, adding some sauce on top. Sprinkle with more freshly grated cheese and a little chopped parsley for some color. Give it a few grinds of fresh pepper if you'd like.

65. Bucatini All'Amatriciana

Serving: Serves 2-4 | Prep: | Cook: | Ready in:

Ingredients

- 1 handful bucatini pasta, or substitute perciatelli
- Olive oil, about 2 tablespoons or enough to coat the bottom of your pan
- 1 large shallot or the equivalent amount of chopped onion
- 1 dried hot pepper, coarsely chopped and seeds separated. Alternatively, ½ teaspoon red pepper flakes (separate the seeds with the point of a knife).
- 4 ounces guanciale, chopped (or substitute pancetta or bacon)
- 14 ounces chopped, canned tomatoes (in summer by all means substitute fresh)
- Freshly grated pecorino cheese
- Salt and pepper

- A chiffonade of two basil leaves or alternatively a small handful of finely chopped parsley for garnish; very optional

Direction

- Heat the olive oil until it's shimmering but not smoking. Sauté the shallot, the guanciale and the pepper flakes until the onion is only lightly colored.
- Turn down the heat to low and add the tomatoes. Simmer this while the pasta is cooking. Add salt and pepper.
- When the pasta is cooked drain it saving a few tablespoons of pasta water (if needed). Add the drained pasta directly to the sauce and stir to combine. Make sure the sauce is "tight" but if it's too tight flick in a little bit of the pasta water.
- To plate: using tongs portion out the pasta on warm plates. Grate the pecorino cheese over each. If using the garnish sprinkle it over the top.
- Notes to cook: it's worth your trouble to source real guanciale even if it is domestic. You can substitute pancetta but we are talking nose to tail here, so we want you using face parts. Bucatini is a long, relatively thick strand of round pasta with a pinhole running through it. Latini is a good brand as is Rustichella D'abbruzzo. But perciatelli works just fine. Focus on the guanciale.
- Find the guanciale. Make me proud. You can do it.
- Note to cook: You can up the amount of red pepper if you like but we're not going all' arrabbiata here.

66. Bucatini All'Amatriciana

Serving: Makes 4 generous portions | Prep: | Cook: | Ready in:

Ingredients

- 14 ounces (400 grams) bucatini, spaghetti, or rigatoni
- 7 ounces (200 grams) guanciale (cured pork jowl)
- 14 ounces (400 grams) tomato passata (puréed tomatoes)
- 1 dried or fresh red hot chile, sliced finely
- 1/2 cup (50 grams) grated pecorino cheese (or parmesan), plus more for garnish

Direction

- Put a large pot of water on to boil the pasta and when it starts boiling, salt it with 2 teaspoons of salt.
- In the meantime, prepare the guanciale. Cut off the tough layer of rind (the "cotenna," in Italian), if present, then slice the rest of the guanciale (which should be mostly fat with a thin streak of flesh through it) thinly, then into sticks about 1/4 inch (5mm) wide.
- Heat a large skillet over medium heat and fry the guanciale pieces until the fat has melted and sizzled to a golden brown. Add the tomato and chile and bring back to a simmer over low-medium heat. Let cook 10 minutes, stirring occasionally. Just before taking off the heat, add the pecorino cheese and stir through, until the sauce is creamy. Set aside until pasta is ready.
- Meanwhile, add the pasta to the boiling water and cook until al dente—I recommend looking at the timing instructed on the packet and taking off a minute or so. Drain the pasta, saving about a cup full of the pasta's cooking water. Add the pasta directly to the skillet with the amatriciana sauce, along with a splash of the cooking water, to help loosen the sauce. You want the sauce to easily coat the pasta but still be quite thick. Toss well until the pasta is coated (if the sauce has gone cold, reheat it before tossing) then serve immediately, with more pecorino over the top if desired.

67. Bánh Mì Inspired Breakfast Sandwich

Serving: Makes 1 sandwich (just scale up to make more than 1!) | Prep: | Cook: | Ready in:

Ingredients

- Bánh Mì-Inspired Breakfast Sandwich
- 1 tablespoon mayonnaise
- 1 teaspoon Sriracha
- 1 teaspoon miso
- 1 toasted English muffin
- 2 pieces cooked bacon (preferably Sriracha Maple Bacon: https://food52.com/recipes...)
- Bacon grease or butter for frying the egg
- 1 large egg
- Salt and pepper
- Pickled veggies (see below)
- 1 handful chopped cilantro
- Pickled Veggies (makes enough for a few sandwiches)
- 1 very large carrot, washed and julienned
- 1/2 English cucumber, washed and julienned.
- 1/2 daikon radish, washed and julienned (if you can't find daikon, you can use a couple thinly sliced regular radishes)
- 1/2 cup rice vinegar
- 2 tablespoons sugar
- 1/2 tablespoon sea salt

Direction

- Bánh Mì-Inspired Breakfast Sandwich
- Stir together the mayonnaise, sriracha, and miso, then spread as much as you want to use (i.e. a generous smear!) on your toasted English muffin. Cut the two pieces of bacon in half and layer them onto the muffin (cutting the bacon in half is not necessary, but it makes it fit the muffin better.)
- Use either bacon grease or a bit of butter to fry the egg -- with a pinch each of salt and pepper -- to your liking, then put this on top of the bacon. Add pickled veggies and cilantro to taste, close up the sandwich, and go to town!

- Pickled Veggies (makes enough for a few sandwiches)
- Put the carrot, cucumber, and radish into a bowl. Put the vinegar, sugar, and salt in a small saucepan. Bring just to a boil, stirring to dissolve the salt and sugar. Take off the heat and pour over the vegetables. Toss the vegetables, then refrigerate them. Let them rest at least 30 minutes (stirring occasionally) before using. These will keep in an airtight container in the fridge for a couple weeks.

68. Bánh Xèo Vietnamese Crepes With Nuoc Cham Dipping Sauce

Serving: Makes six crepes | Prep: | Cook: | Ready in:

Ingredients

- For the crepe batter
- 1 1/2 cups rice flour
- 1 cup unsweetened coconut milk
- 1 cup water
- 1 teaspoon powdered turmeric (for color)
- 4 thinly sliced green onions
- pinch of salt
- oil for the frying pan
- For the filling
- 8 ounces of pork shoulder, thinly sliced
- 8 ounces of peeled and deveined shrimp
- bean sprouts
- grated carrot
- cilantro
- butter leaf lettuce
- oil for frying, if needed

Direction

- For the crepe batter
- In a blender, put the rice flour, coconut milk, water, turmeric and blend together until the mixture looks like pancake batter. If the batter is looking too thick, add more water a bit at a

time and continue to blend. When you're satisfied with the batter's consistency, pour it into a mixing bowl and whisk the scallions vigorously into the batter and set aside while you make the dipping sauce and marinate the pork.

- After you've made the batter, it's time to make the Nuoc Cham, dipping sauce. (Also the marinade) In a mixing bowl, add 2 tablespoons fish sauce, 1 cup water, 3 tablespoons lime juice, a pinch of sugar, red pepper chile flakes and two smashed garlic cloves. Whisk together and set aside 1/2 of the Nuoc Cham for dipping, place it into the fridge and the other half of the Nuoc Cham, place into a separate bowl and toss the pork into. Let the pork marinate for at least 1/2 hour.
- For the filling
- Heat your pan to high and fry the pork until mostly cooked through and then add the shrimp, cooking until the shrimp are done. After the pork and shrimp are cooked, set them aside in a bowl and make the crepes.
- Returning the same pan to the heat, add another tablespoon of oil (if needed) and ladle in the crepe batter and cook the crepe until bubbly around the edges and turn over, like you would a pancake.
- Spoon the shrimp and pork mixture onto the crepe and place the crepe on the lettuce leaf. Finish them with some grated carrot, cilantro and bean sprouts and enjoy with the dipping sauce!

69. CHOCOLATE COVERED BACON ON A STICK WITH MARCONA ALMONDS AND DRIED CHERRIES

Serving: Serves 12 | Prep: | Cook: | Ready in:

Ingredients

- 12 slices of thick-sliced apple or hickory wood smoked bacon, skewered lengthwise
- 2 cups high quality semi sweet chocolate chips
- 6 tablespoons butter
- 1/8 teaspoon sea salt
- 1/2 cup finely chopped marcona almonds
- 1/2 cup finely chopped dried cherries
- demerara or turbinado sugar for sprinkling

Direction

- COOK BACON: Preheat the oven to 400. Place skewered bacon on a broiling pan. When oven is ready, bake the bacon until crisp, about 20 - 25 minutes in the top third of your oven. When done, set the pan aside and let the bacon cool. Meanwhile, line a baking sheet with wax paper and set aside.
- PREP YOUR ASSEMBLY LINE: Place bowl of finely chopped almonds and bowl of finely chopped cherries next to the bacon. Place Demerara sugar next to that. When your chocolate is done, you will have an assembly line of bacon, melted chocolate, cherries, almonds, and Demerara sugar.
- PREP CHOCOLATE: Place semi-sweet chocolate and butter in a shallow microwaveable bowl and microwave for 1 minute. Stir. Continue to microwave in 15 second increments, stirring after each one, until the chocolate and butter have melted. When melted, add the sea salt and stir to combine.
- COVER BACON IN CHOCOLATE: Using a pastry brush, coat both sides of each piece of bacon with melted chocolate and place on baking sheet. If your bowl of chocolate sauce cools and hardens before you are finished brushing it onto the bacon, just stick it back into the microwave for 20 seconds or so.
- SPRINKLE WITH ALMONDS, CHERRIES, AND SUGAR: When all of the bacon is covered in chocolate, work with one piece at a time and cover with toppings. While the chocolate is still warm, place some of the chopped cherries over the chocolate on one

side of a piece of bacon. The cherries are sticky so it is a bit of work. Sprinkle that side with the almonds and a pinch of Demerara sugar. Flip that piece over and do it again so that both sides are sprinkled with cherries, almonds, and Demerara. Do this for each piece of chocolate covered bacon. Refrigerate until hardened. Serve.

70. CHORIZO CORN SOUP

Serving: Serves 4 servings | Prep: | Cook: | Ready in:

Ingredients

- 1 pound Spanish Chorizo, chopped
- 2 tablespoons Extra Virgin Olive Oil
- 1 Baking Potato, peeled and diced
- 6 Ears of Corn, kernels removed or 3 to 4 cups frozen corn
- 1 Red Bell Pepper, chopped
- 1 medium Onion, chopped
- 3 large Garlic Cloves, chopped
- 4 - 5 sprigs Sprigs Thyme, leaves removed and chopped
- 1 Dry Bay Leaf
- 1 28-oz can Fire-roasted Tomatoes
- 1 quart Chicken Stock
- 1 Large Bunch Kale, thick stems removed, leaves roughly chopped (about 4 cups)
- Bread, for dipping

Direction

- Place a large pot over medium-high heat with 2 turns of the pan of olive oil, about 2 tablespoons. Add the chorizo and cook stirring every now and then for 2-3 minutes. Add the potatoes and corn, and brown that up a little bit, then add bell pepper, onions, garlic, thyme, bay leaf, salt and pepper, and cook for 5 minutes. Pour in the tomatoes and chicken stock, and bring up to a bubble. Simmer for 5 minutes. Add the kale and simmer for 5 more minutes. Garnish soup with parsley or cilantro

and lime juice and serve with lots of bread for dipping alongside.

71. CREAMY LEEK, ASPARAGUS, AND BACON TAGLIATELLE

Serving: Serves 3-4 | Prep: | Cook: | Ready in:

Ingredients

- 2 tablespoons butter
- 6 ounces bacon, finely diced
- 1/2 of a leek, washed and finely sliced
- 7.5 ounces (1/2 bunch) of asparagus, cut on the bias
- 1 clove garlic, minced
- 1 dash salt, to taste
- 1.5 cups heavy cream
- 3 egg yolks
- 1 cup freshly grated parmesan
- 8 ounces Tagliatelle pasta

Direction

- Get a large pot of water going for the pasta. In a large cast iron skillet set over medium-low heat, fry the bacon until crispy. Remove to a bowl and set aside.
- Turn heat up to medium. Add 2 tablespoons of butter to the pan. Once melted, add the leek and asparagus. Season with salt. Cook, stirring occasionally, until tender, about 7-10 minutes. Add the garlic and cook 1 more minute. Remove all to a bowl and set aside.
- Cook pasta according to package instructions, making sure to generously salt the water.
- Meanwhile, pour the cream into the skillet (set on low heat) and whisk until hot. Slowly ladle half of the cream into the egg yolks, whisking constantly. Return to pan and cook, whisking, until slightly thickened. Stir in the parmesan until melted. Add the vegetables, pasta and bacon. Serve immediately with extra parmesan.

- Serve your finished lobster over fresh cooked pasta with a few pinches of parmesan cheese and a sprinkle of chopped green onions over the top.

72. Cajun Lobster Pasta

Serving: Serves 5 | Prep: | Cook: | Ready in:

Ingredients

- 3 Strips of Bacon
- 3 Cloves of Garlic, Minced
- 1 Bell Pepper, Chopped
- 3 Green Onions, Chopped
- 3/4 cup Broth (seafood, veggie or chicken will work)
- 1 teaspoon Cajun Spice
- 1 teaspoon Old Bay Seasoning
- 1/2 teaspoon Onion Powder
- 1/2 teaspoon Garlic Powder
- 1/2 teaspoon Lemon Pepper
- 1/2 teaspoon Oregano
- 1/8 teaspoon Pepper
- 1 pound Lobster, Cooked
- 1/4 cup Heavy Cream
- Salt to Taste

Direction

- Cook up your bacon in a small frying pan over medium heat. Remove the bacon and drain off the fat, reserving about a tablespoon.
- To the pan add in your garlic and pepper. Cook it up on medium heat for about two to three minutes.
- Add in the green onions. Let cook for an additional minute.
- Chop up your bacon and add it to the pan along with the broth.
- Now add in your spices; the Cajun, old bay, onion powder, garlic powder, lemon pepper, oregano, and pepper.
- Allow the mixture to heat back up and then turn your heat down to medium low. Add in your lobster and allow it about three to five minutes to heat up completely.
- Last up, add in your cream.

73. Cajun Shrimp Alfredo

Serving: Serves 4 | Prep: | Cook: | Ready in:

Ingredients

- 1 pound andouille sausage, diced
- 2 tablespoons olive oil
- 1 medium onion, chopped
- 3 garlic cloves, minced
- 1 tablespoon red pepper flakes
- 8 tablespoons worcestershire sauce
- 1 cup milk
- 2 cups half and half
- 3 tablespoons Cajun or Creole seasoning
- 1 teaspoon chili powder
- 1 stick butter
- 1 cup parmesan cheese, grated
- 1 pound raw shrimp, peeled and deveined
- 1 pound long pasta of your choice

Direction

- In a large, deep skillet, render the diced Andouille in one tablespoon of olive oil over medium-high heat.
- Add the chopped onion and cook for four or five minutes.
- Add the chopped garlic and red pepper flakes and continue to cook so the Andouille starts to caramelize.
- Meanwhile, put the pasta water on to boil.
- Coat the peeled shrimp with two tablespoons of Cajun seasoning and set them aside.
- Deglaze the sausage/onion/garlic pan with the Worcestershire sauce and cook for two minutes, stirring.
- Add the milk and half-and-half to the pot and continue to stir and cook.

- Add the butter and parmesan cheese and lower the heat on the sauce to simmer.
- Cook the pasta according to the directions.
- In a separate skillet over medium heat, sauté the shrimp until they turn pink.
- Toss the drained pasta in the sauce and serve the cooked shrimp on top. Garnish with some parsley and serve with crusty bread.

74. Canal House's Pork Belly With Gingery Rhubarb Compote

Serving: Serves 6 | Prep: | Cook: | Ready in:

Ingredients

- Pork Belly
- 3 pounds pork belly, skin removed, fat intact
- 2 tablespoons fresh thyme leaves
- 2 tablespoons sugar
- 2 tablespoons kosher salt
- 2 teaspoons freshly ground black pepper
- 1   medium onion, sliced into 1/2-inch rings
- 1   cup dry white wine
- Gingery Rhubarb Compote
- 1 cup packed light brown sugar
- 1/2 cup golden raisins
- 1/2 cup red wine vinegar
- 1/4 cup finely chopped crystallized ginger
- 1 tablespoon drained capers
- 1 pinch crushed red pepper flakes
- 1 pinch freshly ground black pepper
- 1 pound rhubarb, trimmed, sliced 1/2-inch thick

Direction

- Using a sharp knife, score pork belly fat in a crosshatch pattern at about 3/4-inch intervals, taking care not to cut into meat.
- Mix thyme, sugar, salt, and pepper in a small bowl. Rub thyme mixture on both sides of pork. Place pork in a large resealable plastic bag, seal bag, and chill at least 8 hours and up to 1 day.

- Preheat oven to 250°. Arrange onion in bottom of a large heavy pot with a lid. Rinse pork and place fat side up on top of onion; add wine.
- Cover pot; place in oven and braise pork, basting occasionally, until fork-tender, 2 1/2 to 3 hours. Increase oven temperature to 400°. Uncover pot and cook until meat is very tender and fat is crisp and golden brown, about 1 hour longer. If the onions are starting to get dark before the pork, add a bit more wine.
- To make compote: Combine brown sugar, raisins, vinegar, ginger, capers, red pepper flakes, and black pepper in a medium skillet. Cook over medium heat, stirring often, until liquid is reduced by half, about 5 minutes.
- Add rhubarb to skillet and stir to coat. Cook, swirling pan occasionally, until rhubarb is tender and liquid is syrupy, about 15 minutes.
- Note: Compote can be made 5 days ahead. Let cool; cover and chill. Reheat before using.
- Slice pork and serve with Gingery Rhubarb Compote.

75. Cauliflower Gratin With Ham

Serving: Serves 4-6 | Prep: 0hours5mins | Cook: 0hours5mins | Ready in:

Ingredients

- 1 large head cauliflower , cut into florets
- 1/4 cup unsalted butter
- 3 tablespoons all-purpose flour
- 1 1/2 cups whole milk (can substitute part of it with heavy cream for an even richer, creamier result)
- 1/4 cup grated Parmesan cheese
- 1 teaspoon salt
- 1/8 teaspoon freshly ground nutmeg
- 2 large egg yolks
- 6 ounces smoked ham , diced
- 1/2 cup grated Jarlsberg or Swiss cheese

Direction

- Butter a 2 quart baking dish and sprinkle a little bit of flour in the bottom (less than a tablespoon).
- Preheat the oven to 350 degrees F.
- Boil cauliflower florets for 3-4 minutes just until barely softened. Do not overcook. Drain thoroughly while you're making the bechamel sauce.
- To make the bechamel sauce: Melt the butter in a medium saucepan over medium heat. Add the flour and use a wire whisk to blend it with the butter. Let the mixture bubble for 2 minutes until just barely lightly golden, continually whisking.
- Gradually add the milk while continually whisking to prevent lumps and whisk until smooth. Let it simmer, whisking continually, until thickened. Add the Parmesan cheese, salt and nutmeg and whisk until smooth. Let the sauce simmer for a couple of minutes, whisking continually. Remove from heat and let the sauce cool for 5 minutes then whisk in the egg yolks followed by the diced ham. Add more salt and pepper to taste.
- Place the cauliflower florets in the prepared baking dish. Sprinkle lightly with a little salt. Pour the sauce over the cauliflower then even sprinkle over the cheese. Bake uncovered for 30-40 min or until the top is golden and the mixture is bubbly. Let sit for 5 minutes before serving.
- NUTRITION
- Calories: 251kcal | Carbohydrates: 13g | Protein: 14g | Fat: 16g | Saturated Fat: 9g | Sodium: 928mg | Potassium: 581mg | Fiber: 2g | Sugar: 5g | Vitamin C: 67.5mg.

---

76. Cauliflower Sausage Bake

Serving: Serves 8-10 | Prep: 2hours0mins | Cook: 0hours30mins | Ready in:

Ingredients

- 1 very large head cauliflower, cut into 6 1-inch slices (or two smaller heads)
- 1 pound sweet Italian sausage, crumbed and browned in EVOO
- 1 pound hot Italian sausage, crumbed and browned in EVOO
- 4 large red peppers, diced
- 2 large Vidalia onions, diced
- 4 tablespoons minced garlic
- 1 pound thick sliced mozzarella
- 1 cup crumbled feta
- 2.5 cups Italian red sauce (see notes)
- 1 cup shredded asiago (or parmesan)
- 1-3 tablespoons fennel seeds
- 1-3 tablespoons rosemary leaves
- 1-3 tablespoons crushed black pepper

Direction

- Cut the stem from a very large head (or two smaller heads) of cauliflower and remove the leaves. Slice as best as you can into 6 ca. 1-inch slices. I can usually get 4 full slices to hang together and then the remaining pieces just need to be collected.
- The slices and pieces are laid out on a baking pan covered with oiled parchment, then sprayed with oil and dusted with ground black pepper. Roast at 450 F for 15-20 minutes on one side. Use a large spatula and turn over all of the pieces, spray with oil and roast another 15-20 minutes, until tender and golden brown. Remove and reduce the heat to 350 F.
- Brown the Italian sausage. Near the end of the browning, add and mix the garlic, then add fennel seeds, and rosemary leaves. Heat for a few moments until aromatic and then reserve (use a slotted spoon and keep the fat in the pan).
- Caramelize the onions in the hot sausage fat. About half way through the process add the red pepper. Add more herbs as desired. Near the end, combine with the sausage. Heat and mix thoroughly. Reserve.
- My Italian red sauce is posted elsewhere. Caramelize two diced sweet onions with a

diced red pepper. Add these to a food processor with a large can of DOP San Marzano tomatoes, a roasted red pepper, a can of tomato paste, EVOO, herbs and spices to preference. Process together and simmer on low for an hour.

- Carefully remove the cauliflower to line the bottom of a 9 x 13 inch baking dish. Coat the cauliflower with tomato sauce.
- Place the pieces of mozzarella in a layer. Then sprinkle the open spots with the feta.
- Top with the sausage mixture.
- Bake at 350 F for 25-30 minutes until the liquid is bubbly. Top with some shredded asiago about 5 minutes before the end.
- Remove and let sit for a few minutes. Plate your serving with some added asiago and a sprinkle of Italian seasonings.

---

77. Cavatelli With Bacon, Corn, Mushrooms, And Parmesan, A La The Red Hen

Serving: Serves 4-6 | Prep: 0hours30mins | Cook: 3hours0mins | Ready in:

Ingredients

- For the roasted mushrooms, the parmesan broth, and the corn brodo:
- 1 pound shiitake mushrooms
- olive oil, for roasting
- salt, pepper, and chopped fresh thyme to taste
- 6 ears sweet corn, husked and de-silked (or 4 cups frozen sweet corn kernels, defrosted)
- 3 tablespoons unsalted butter, divided
- 1 head garlic, halved, plus 1 garlic clove, halved
- 1 medium-large onion, chopped
- 2 or 3 carrots and celery stalks (each), chopped (combined, they should roughly equal the quantity of onion)
- 1/4 ounce dried mushrooms (porcini, shiitake, mixed wild...go nuts)

- 1 bay leaf
- 1 pinch black peppercorns
- a few (each) parsley and thyme sprigs
- 1 pound parmesan cheese rinds
- 1 cup dry white wine
- 2 quarts water, brought to a simmer
- 1/2 cup yellow onion, diced
- 2 garlic cloves, chopped
- creme fraiche, to taste
- For the finished pasta:
- 1/2-1 pounds cavatelli (the Red Hen uses housemade whole wheat cavatelli, but regular pasta is fine, too; use the lesser amount of pasta if you want a more equitable ratio of pasta to the rest of the components, otherwise use the whole box)
- olive oil, for sauteing
- 4 ounces bacon, preferably double-smoked, diced
- 8 green onions, thinly sliced
- roasted shiitakes, reserved corn kernels, and corn brodo (see above)
- 2 tablespoons unsalted butter, for finishing
- 1 cup freshly grated parmesan cheese
- chopped fresh parsley and thyme, for garnish

Direction

- For the roasted mushrooms, the parmesan broth, and the corn brodo:
- Heat oven to 500F. Stem the shiitakes, reserving the stems. Slice the caps 1/8" thick. Toss with olive oil, salt, and pepper to taste, and roast 5-7 mins. Remove to a bowl. Using a micro plane, grate 1/2 a clove of garlic (or more/less to taste) over, and season with fresh thyme and more salt and pepper if necessary. Toss and set aside until ready to use.
- Cut the kernels from the 6 ears of corn. (You should get ~4 1/2 - 5 cups.) Set two cups kernels aside for the brodo, and the rest for the pasta. Scrape the cobs over the reserved brodo kernels with the back of your knife to extract the sweet corn "milk." Reserve the cobs. (NOTE: If fresh corn is out of season, skip this step and use defrosted frozen kernels--2 cups for the brodo and 2 for the pasta--instead.)

58

- Heat a little olive oil and 1 tbsp. butter in a large pot over medium heat. When the butter melts, add the scraped corn cobs and reserved shiitake stems, along with the halved garlic head, onions, carrots, celery, mushrooms, herbs, and spices. Let the aromatics soften, 8-10 mins, stirring occasionally. (Look for browning of the garlic and translucence of the onions.) As in the Cowgirl recipe, add the cheese rinds next, allowing them to sit at the bottom of the pot for short periods of time (10 seconds between scrapes) to get some nice browning going. Deglaze with white wine, stirring to scrape up all the good stuff stuck to the bottom of the pan, and reduce by half, then add the 2 quarts of simmering water. How long you let it go on the stove depends how robust a flavor you want--about two hours at a gentle simmer will reduce the broth by half, yielding a quart. A shorter simmer (say an hour), will yield a less-concentrated quart and a half. In either case, be sure to stir often (every five minutes, give or take), as the rinds will stick to the bottom and scorch otherwise. When reduced to the desired amount, strain and cool. Season to taste with salt. If making far enough in advance, refrigerate overnight so a fat cap forms and is easily removable. Otherwise, do your best to skim fat from the surface once the broth has cooled. You will only need 2 cups broth for the corn brodo; reserve the rest for another use.
- Next, make the corn brodo. Melt the remaining 2 tbsp. butter in a large saucepan over medium heat, and sauté the 2 cups reserved corn kernels with 1/2 cup chopped onion and 2 chopped garlic cloves until corn is tender. Remove from heat and let cool, then puree with 2 cups of the parmesan broth until smooth. Put through a fine-mesh sieve, then whisk in a few tbsps. of crème fraiche and season with salt to taste. Set aside till ready to use.
- For the finished pasta:
- Bring a pot of well-salted water to a boil, and cook the cavatelli according to package directions, draining it just shy of the recommended cook time, as it will finish cooking in the sauce. (Reserve some of the cooking water--a cup should do.)
- While the pasta is cooking, film a large skillet with olive oil and sauté the bacon and green onions over medium heat, until bacon starts to brown and crisp at the edges. Add the remaining reserved corn kernels and roasted shiitakes--about a 1/2 cup of each per person. (You may have some leftover mushrooms.) Toss. Add corn brodo and lower to a simmer.
- When pasta is ready, toss it in the sauce with a little of the pasta water and allow it to finish cooking. Add more water if too dry. Remove from heat and stir in butter and parmesan. Garnish with parsley, thyme, and a little extra parmesan, and serve.

78. Cavolo Nero Al Guanciale (Kale With Guanciale)

Serving: Serves 4 | Prep: | Cook: | Ready in:

Ingredients

- 1 bunch dinosaur kale, stems removed, roughly chopped
- 1 bunch dandelion greens, roughly chopped
- 1 small handful celery leaves
- 1 medium apple, cut into thin wedges
- 1/2 lemon, juiced
- 2 tablespoons extra-virgin olive oil
- 4 ounces guanciale, cut into lardon
- salt, to taste
- a generous amount of freshly ground black pepper
- 2 tablespoons finely chopped italian parsley

Direction

- In a small saucepot, render the guanciale over low heat.
- Combine greens, celery and apple in a large bowl. Season with salt, and add lemon juice and oil. Toss and distribute onto plates.

- Add black pepper and parsley to the pot with the guanciale. Immediately bring the pot to the table and spoon the guanciale and fat over each plate, and serve.

79. Cesare Casella's Pontormo Salad With Pancetta And Egg

Serving: Serves 1 | Prep: | Cook: | Ready in:

Ingredients

- 1 tablespoon olive oil
- 2 1/2 ounces diced pancetta
- 1 1/2 tablespoons chopped parsley
- 1 1/2 tablespoons chopped fresh marjoram
- 1 1/2 tablespoons chopped fresh thyme
- 2 eggs
- 1 ounce mesclun or other delicate lettuce, cut into 3/4-inch strips
- 1 tablespoon red wine vinegar
- 1 tablespoon balsamic vinegar
- Salt and black pepper, to taste

Direction

- In a small skillet over medium-high heat, combine the oil, pancetta, and herbs. Cook to render some of the fat from the pancetta, but do not brown. Crack the eggs into a bowl, but do not whisk. Pour the eggs into the pan and cook, stirring over medium-low heat with a rubber spatula, until the eggs are lightly scrambled and still very soft. Season with salt and pepper.
- Remove the pan from heat to keep the eggs from overcooking. In a bowl, toss the lettuce with a drizzle of both vinegars. Add the eggs and toss. Season with salt and pepper, and serve immediately.

80. Challah And Wild Mushroom Stuffing With Pancetta

Serving: Serves 6-8 | Prep: | Cook: | Ready in:

Ingredients

- 1 Loaf of Challah Bread without Poppy Seeds
- 12 Slices of Pancetta
- 4 Celery Stalks
- 1 Shallot
- 1/2 cup Butter
- 2 teaspoons Freshly Grated Nutmeg
- 6 Sprigs Fresh Thyme
- 2 teaspoons Salt
- 2 teaspoons Pepper
- 2 cups Vegtable Stock
- 6 ounces Alba Clamshell Mushrooms
- 5 ounces French Horn Mushrooms
- 4 ounces Chanterelle Mushrooms
- 3 ounces Cremini Mushrooms

Direction

- Side Note: I make my own challah and for this recipe I only used 3/4 of the loaf, because it is so large, if you buy a loaf they are usually a little smaller so use the whole loaf then.
- Cut challah loaf into small cubes and place on a baking sheet in a 250 degree oven until crispy and dry. About 30 minutes
- In broiler in two batches broil pancetta until crispy, when cool break into little pieces, set aside. In a large sauté pan melt butter and add chopped celery, and sliced shallots and crispy pancetta. Add a pinch of salt and pepper and sauté for about 10 minutes. Stirring occasionally.
- While mixture is sautéing, slice mushrooms and set aside. I sliced the French Horns into half and all the other varieties are sliced into medium size. Add mushrooms and Nutmeg, thyme and the salt and pepper to celery and shallot mixture, Sauté for about 15 minutes or until mushrooms have shrunk a little in size and are tender.

- Measure 2 cups of stock into a bowl and set aside. In a large bowl add mushroom and bread mixture and toss, pour the stock over bread mixture and mix to combine. Lightly butter a 9x13 pan and pour mixture into it. Do not pack it in. Turn oven to 350 and cook until crispy and warm. About 30 minutes. Test after 30 to make sure it is crispy and perfect enough for you. Enjoy!

81. Char Siu Pork

Serving: Serves 4 | Prep: | Cook: | Ready in:

Ingredients

- 2 to 3 pounds pork roast
- 1/2 cup hoisin sauce
- 1/2 cup sherry
- 1/4 cup honey
- 2 tablespoons toasted sesame oil
- 2 tablespoons Sriracha sauce (or other hot sauce)
- 1 tablespoon freshly grated ginger
- 1 tablespoon minced garlic
- 1 tablespoon five-spice powder
- 1/4 onion, grated
- red food coloring, optional

Direction

- Mix all ingredients but the pork in a bowl to create the marinade. The red food coloring is optional, but traditional.
- Place the pork in a zip-lock bag and pour in the marinade. Squeeze out as much of the air as you can, seal the bag, and marinate the meat overnight in the refrigerator.
- Preheat the oven or grill to 300°F.
- Place the pork roast onto a rack over a sheet pan. Reserve the left-over marinade. Don't forget to line the pan with aluminum foil or you'll be very sorry when clean-up time comes.
- Roast for 1 hour.

- While pork is roasting, place the reserved marinade in a saucepan and boil vigorously for 5 to 10 minutes until thickened. Set aside.
- After the 1 hour roasting time, baste the pork with the thickened glaze. Place back into the oven for 10 to 15 minutes to set the glaze.
- Let rest 10 minutes. Slice the pork thinly and serve over noodles or rice.

82. Charles Phan's Lo Soi Pork Shoulder

Serving: Makes 1 pound pork shoulder (plus a big batch of lo soi) | Prep: | Cook: | Ready in:

Ingredients

- 1 3-inch piece cinnamon stick
- 3 star anise pods, whole (or their equivalent)
- 10 whole cloves
- one 2-by-1 inch piece ginger, crushed
- 1/2 teaspoon five-spice powder
- 2 tablespoons fish sauce
- 2 cups light soy sauce (if you only have standard soy sauce, that's fine)
- 2 tablespoons light brown sugar
- 1 pound pork shoulder, cut in two equal pieces

Direction

- Toast the cinnamon, star anise, and cloves in a dry frying pan over medium heat for 30 seconds, or until fragrant. Place in a large pot along with the ginger, five-spice powder, fish sauce, soy sauce, and brown sugar. Add 7 cups of water. (Yes, seven cups.) Bring to a boil, stirring occasionally. Reduce to a simmer.
- With the liquid at a low simmer, add the pork shoulder. Cook for 20 minutes. Then turn off the heat and let the pork sit in the pot for another 30 minutes. Remove the pork and let cool; slice thinly. Serve with rice, soft-boiled eggs, and plenty of sauce.

- To preserve the lo soi (the flavored liquid): skim off the scum and fat and strain into a large container. Then refrigerate or freeze until next use. Before using it again, add fresh spices (the first four ingredients above); tinker with the soy sauce or sugar as needed. If you refrigerate the lo soi and do not use it for a month, return it to the stove and boil for five minutes, then refrigerate again; it should keep up to a year.

83. Cheese Scrambled Eggs With Bacon And Jalapeno Cheddar Cheese Roll

Serving: Serves 2 | Prep: | Cook: | Ready in:

Ingredients

- 4-6 organic, pasture raised eggs
- Splash of milk
- 1 green jalapeno, seeded and chopped medium
- 1 tomato, seeded and chopped medium
- 2 green onions, whites and greens, sliced ¼"
- 1 cup sharp cheddar cheese, grated large
- 1/2 red bell pepper, chopped medium
- 1 pinch red pepper flakes
- 1 pinch salt and pepper
- 4-6 slices of bacon

Direction

- With a whisk, mix the milk in with the eggs and whisk until blended.
- Grate the cheese and add to the egg mixture. Set aside to warm while cooking veggies.
- Chop the jalapeno, tomato, green onions, and red Bell pepper.
- Heat a lightly oiled 10" cast iron pan then add the veggie mixture and red pepper flakes and sauté over medium low heat until starting to soften, about 3-4 minutes.
- Add the egg mixture and the salt and pepper. Cook until the eggs have the desired stiffness.

- Serve on heated plates with fried thick cut bacon and toasted jalapeno-cheddar rolls or what have you on hand. Of course any bacon and toast can be substituted.

84. Cheesy BBQ Pulled Pork Bombs

Serving: Serves 16 bombs | Prep: | Cook: | Ready in:

Ingredients

- 16 ounces can refrigerated biscuits
- 1 1/2 cups Curly's BBQ Pulled Pork
- sharp cheddar cut into 16 1-inch cubes
- 3 tablespoons butter, melted
- 2 cloves garlic, minced
- 1 tablespoon dried parsley
- salt and pepper to taste
- extra BBQ sauce for dipping

Direction

- Preheat oven to 375°F
- Turn biscuits onto a lightly floured surface and cut each biscuit in half to get 16 pieces. Flatten each into a round with your palm.
- Place a spoonful of Curly's BBQ Pulled Pork and 1 cube of cheddar on each biscuit round.
- Bring the edges up and over, pressing them together and being sure to leave no gaps for the filling to leak out. Arrange the bombs in an oiled cast iron skillet or cake pan. If you have leftover cheddar cubes, arrange them in between a few of the bombs for extra cheesiness.
- Combine melted butter, garlic, salt and pepper, and dried parsley in a small bowl. Brush the butter mixture onto each bomb.
- Bake at 375 for 20-25 minutes, until browned.
- Serve warm with your favorite BBQ sauce for dipping.

85. Cheesy Mushroom & Pork Enchiladas

Serving: Makes 4 | Prep: | Cook: | Ready in:

Ingredients

- Filling:
- 1 tablespoon olive oil
- 1 onion, finely chopped
- 1 teaspoon crushed garlic
- 1/2 teaspoon cumin
- 1/4 teaspoon paprika
- 1 pinch chilli flakes
- 200 grams pork mince
- 1/2 red pepper, chopped
- 200 grams mushrooms, chopped
- 1 tablespoon tomato puree
- 1/2 cup chicken stock
- salt
- pepper
- small bunches coriander, chopped
- Sauces and to assemble:
- 2 teaspoons olive oil
- 1/2 teaspoon crushed garlic
- 100 milliliters tomato puree
- 50 milliliters water
- 1/4 teaspoon paprika
- 1/4 teaspoon cumin
- 1/4 teaspoon Italian herbs
- salt
- pepper
- 2 teaspoons butter
- 2 teaspoons flour
- 100 milliliters milk
- 1/3 cup grated cheddar cheese
- 4 20cm flour tortillas
- 1/4 cup grated cheddar cheese
- fresh coriander leaves, to garnish

Direction

- To make the filling: heat the olive oil in a deep saucepan. Gently cook the onion over a low heat until soft and translucent. Add the garlic, cumin, paprika and chili flakes and toss everything together.

- Add the pork mince and cook for a few minutes to brown. Add the red pepper and mushrooms and cook for a further 3 minutes.
- Add the tomato puree, chicken stock and season with salt and pepper. Simmer for 10-12 minutes until most of the liquid has reduced. Check the seasoning, remove from the heat and stir through the coriander. Set aside.
- To make the tomato sauce: heat the olive oil in a frying pan. Sauté the garlic for a few minutes, then add the tomato puree, water, paprika, cumin, Italian herbs and season with salt and pepper. Allow to simmer for 5 minutes, then take off the heat and set aside.
- Make the cheese sauce by melting the butter in a small saucepan. Add the flour and whisk into the butter. Allow to cook for a minute then remove the saucepan from the heat. Gradually add the milk while whisking. Return the saucepan to the heat and continue to whisk until the sauce has thickened slightly. Take the saucepan off the heat and add the cheese. Whisk until smooth. (The sauce can also be made in the microwave.)
- Preheat your oven to 180°C. Divide the mushroom and pork filling between the 4 tortillas and roll each one up like a cigar. Arrange the rolled tortillas next to each other in an ovenproof dish.
- Spread the tomato sauce over the tortillas. Then spread the cheese sauce over the top. Sprinkle with the remaining cheese and bake the enchiladas for 30 minutes. Garnish with fresh coriander and serve while hot!

86. Chestnut Pasta With Pear, Brussels Sprouts And Mascarpone Sauce

Serving: Serves 2 | Prep: | Cook: | Ready in:

Ingredients

- Chestnut pasta for 2 people

- 200g mascarpone
- 1 handful chopped parsley
- 1 large pear
- 2 tablespoons olive oil
- 2 handfuls shaved Brussels sprouts
- Salt and pepper
- 1 handful hazelnuts, chopped
- shaved Pecorino
- 1-2 slices of prosciutto, cut into bite-size pieces

Direction

- Cut the pear into dices. Shave the Brussels sprouts. Cook the pasta
- In the meantime, heat the mascarpone, parsley and 5 tbsp. of water on low heat. Season with salt and pepper
- Heat some olive oil in a pan and cook pear on low-medium heat. Season with some pepper. Right before serving, add the Brussels sprouts. Cook for no more than 2 minutes (I like to keep the Brussels sprouts crispy)
- Arrange the pasta on two plates and top with mascarpone sauce, pear and Brussels sprouts. Finally add hazelnuts, prosciutto and shaved pecorino.

87. Chickpeas With Blood Sausage, Pine Nuts, & Raisins

Serving: Serves 4 | Prep: | Cook: | Ready in:

Ingredients

- Chickpeas with Sausage, Pine Nuts, & Raisins
- 1 pound cooked chickpeas
- 1/4 cup seedless raisins
- 1/4 cup pine nuts
- ~ 4 ounces blood sausage, casing removed, crumbled into small pieces (more if you wish)
- 1 cup onion confit (refer to recipe below)
- 3 tablespoons extra-virgin olive oil, mixed with large pinch hot smoked paprika
- 3 tablespoons fresh flat-leaf parsley, chopped

- Coarse sea salt
- Onion Confit
- 2 large onions, peeled, cut in half, thinly sliced
- 2 tablespoons unsalted butter
- 1 1/4 teaspoons sugar
- 3 sprigs thyme
- 1 cup red wine
- 1/8 cup red wine vinegar
- 1/8 cup sherry vinegar
- salt and pepper to taste

Direction

- Chickpeas with Sausage, Pine Nuts, & Raisins
- Heat 2 tablespoons of the paprika infused oil in a large skillet or wok over medium-high heat. When hot add the onion confit and stir. Add the blood sausage and stir to incorporate. Add the raisins and pine nuts. Stir to incorporate. Add the cooked chickpeas and parsley. Stir until the chickpeas are well incorporated and hot.
- Serve with a drizzle of paprika infused olive oil and sprinkle of coarse sea salt.
- Onion Confit
- Brown the butter in a large pan over medium heat.
- Add the onions, season with salt and pepper. Cover and cook for 5 minutes, until onions soften.
- Stir in the sugar and cook, covered, a few more minutes to allow the sugar to caramelize slightly.
- Add the thyme sprigs, red wine, and vinegars. Turn down the heat to medium-low and simmer, uncovered, for ~1 to 1 1/4 hours, until the liquid is cooked down to a syrup. You can prepare ahead of time.

88. Chicons Au Gratin

Serving: Serves 6 | Prep: | Cook: | Ready in:

Ingredients

- 12 endives
- 4 tablespoons butter
- 5 tablespoons flour
- 1 liter warm milk
- 1 1/4 cups grated cheese (Edam, Swiss Cheese Gruyère)
- 1 pinch nutmeg
- 12 slices of dry-cured ham

Direction

- Remove the base of the endives and discard any browned outer leaves. Steam the whole endives for 15 minutes and drain.
- Preheat the oven on 400F. Wrap each endive with one slice of dry-cured ham and arrange the endives in a single layer in buttered oven dish.
- For the béchamel: Melt the butter on medium heat then stir in the flour and mix slowly with a wooden spoon until smooth and brownish. Remove from heat. Add one cup of hot milk at a time, whisking constantly and let the béchamel thicken. Put back on heat until the mixture thickens some more. Remove from heat again, add half of the cheese, salt, pepper and a pinch of nutmeg. The cheese will melt.
- Add the béchamel on top of the endives. Top with the rest of the cheese and bake for 25-30 minutes on 400F, until golden.

89. Chili Verde Totchos

Serving: Serves 6 to 8 | Prep: | Cook: | Ready in:

Ingredients

- For the baked tater tots:
- 2 pounds (about 2 large) Russet potatoes
- 1 teaspoon salt
- 1/2 teaspoon black pepper
- 1 tablespoon chopped flat-leaf parsley
- 3 tablespoons peanut oil
- For the chili verde and nacho béchamel:
- 1 tablespoon olive oil

- 1/2 pound ground pork (substitute ground chicken if you prefer)
- 1 small can green chilies
- 1/2 medium onion, diced
- 3 tomatillos, husked and cut in half
- 2 cloves garlic
- 1/4 cup chicken stock
- Salt and pepper, to taste
- 2 tablespoons butter
- 2 tablespoons flour
- 1 1/4 cups milk
- 1 1/2 cups shredded sharp cheddar cheese, divided
- 1/4 cup grated Parmesan cheese
- 1 to 2 tablespoons pickled jalapeños, depending on heat preference
- 1 pinch salt
- 2 tablespoons sour cream, for garnish
- 1/2 tablespoon piment d'espelette, for garnish
- 2 tablespoons chopped cilantro, for garnish

Direction

- For the baked tater tots:
- Place potatoes (skin and all, they are super easy to peel after boiling) in a pot of water, bring to a boil, and boil for 30 minutes (if your potatoes are small, check after half the time). Turn off the heat and let the potatoes sit in the water 10 to 15 minutes.
- Drain potatoes over a colander and run under cold water. Peel potatoes with your hands: The skin literally rubs off and there is very little wasted potato. Preheat oven to 450° F.
- When potatoes are cool, grate on the medium size hole of a box grater into a medium bowl. To the bowl add salt, pepper, and parsley and combine with hands. The natural starch in the potatoes will hold the mix together. When well blended, shape into "tots." I used about 1 1/2 teaspoon of the mixture for each tot, but I stopped measuring halfway through and eyeballed the rest.
- Place peanut oil on a Silpat- or parchment-lined half sheet pan, place in oven for a minute or two. Place the tots on the hot pan, then bake

15 minutes, turn the tots, and bake another 15. They should be golden brown and crunchy.

- For the chili verde and nacho béchamel:
- Start by making the chili verde: Add olive oil to a skillet and brown the ground pork over medium-high heat, until golden.
- In a blender or processor, add green chilies, onion, tomatillos, and garlic. Blend until you form a thick salsa, then add to pork, cook until bubbly, add stock, reduce heat to medium-low, and let simmer for 20 minutes, frequently stirring and add salt and pepper to taste. While it simmers, prepare béchamel.
- Make béchamel by heating butter in a saucepan over medium-high heat. Add flour then stir and cook for about 2 minutes. Reduce heat to medium and slowly whisk in milk, cooking until thick and bubbly.
- Add 1/2 cup cheddar and the Parmesan, stir until melted, then add jalapeños. Check for salt and add a pinch if needed. Turn heat down to low.
- Preheat broiler. Place baked tater tots on a broiler-safe tray or platter, drizzle béchamel over the top, add chili verde, and top with 1 cup remaining shredded cheddar. Broil until golden.
- Top with sour cream and sprinkle with piment d'espelette and cilantro. Enjoy this with cerveza while watching football with friends.

90. Chili Al Pastor

Serving: Serves 6 (or less if you're really hungry!) | Prep: | Cook: |Ready in:

Ingredients

- Chili al Pastor
- water
- 3.5 lb boneless pork shoulder
- 2 valencia oranges
- 1 tablespoon ground cumin
- 2 teaspoons kosher salt
- ½ teaspoon coarsely ground black pepper

- ¼ teaspoon ground cloves
- 3 tablespoons canola or vegetable oil
- 5 dried guajillo chiles (about 1 oz)
- 1 large dried ancho chile (about 1 oz)
- 1 large or 2 medium yellow onions
- 4 medium cloves garlic
- 14.5-oz can diced tomatoes
- 2 large or 3 medium bay leaves
- 1 tablespoon dried Mexican oregano
- 1 to 2 tablespoons lime juice
- coarsely chopped cilantro (garnish)
- finely diced onion or sliced green onion (garnish)
- lime wedges (garnish)
- Polenta and Caramelized Pineapple
- 3 cups water
- 1 teaspoon kosher salt
- 1 cup polenta
- Small pineapple
- ½ teaspoon sugar
- 1 tablespoon canola or vegetable oil

Direction

- Chili al Pastor
- Preheat oven to 350° F. Start a pot of water to boil.
- Trim excess fat from the pork shoulder, and cut into approximately 1-inch chunks. Transfer the chunks to a medium to large bowl. Zest one of the oranges. Sprinkle the orange zest over the pork chunks, and set the 2 oranges aside. Sprinkle the cumin, salt, pepper, and cloves over the pork chunks. Toss well to evenly coat with the seasonings; allow to rest at room temperature for 45 minutes.
- Remove and discard the stems and seeds from the chiles. Roast the chiles in the oven for 4 to 5 minutes, until you can start to smell them. Remove from the oven and place in a bowl. Cover with 2 to 3 cups of water, and allow to steep for 15 or more minutes to soften. Turn off the oven.
- Dice the onion and set aside (you should have 2 to 2 ½ cups of diced onion.) Mince the garlic and set aside (you should have about 4 teaspoons.) Juice the oranges into a 2 cup

glass measure and set aside (you should have between ¾ and 1 cup.)

- Heat oil in a 6-quart Dutch oven or stock pot over medium-high heat until shimmering. Add the pork chunks, and cook stirring every 3 or so minutes until nicely browned with no pink remaining. Reduce heat to medium, and add diced onion and minced garlic. Cook, stirring occasionally until the onion is translucent. Add the diced tomatoes (including the juice), bay leaves, and oregano. Reduce heat to maintain a simmer.
- Remove the chiles from the soaking water, and transfer them to the blender. Add enough of the soaking water to the orange juice to make 2 cups total, then add the juice mixture to the blender. Pulse several times, then blend until smooth, scraping down the sides of the blender once. Pour the chile purée into the pork mixture.
- Gently simmer the chili until the pork is tender, stirring occasionally. This will take about 2 hours. At this point you can cool and refrigerate the chili until you are ready to serve it, then gently reheat. Otherwise lower heat as much as possible, and proceed with making the polenta and caramelizing the pineapple. Season to taste with salt, pepper, and lime juice, and thin with water if needed just before serving.
- To serve: Place a wedge of polenta into each bowl. Divide chili evenly amongst bowls. Divide caramelized pineapple evenly amongst bowls (you should have about ¼-cup per serving.) Garnish with cilantro, onion, and lime wedges. Enjoy!
- Polenta and Caramelized Pineapple
- Bring 3 cups of water and 1 teaspoon kosher salt to a boil. Gradually stir in the polenta and reduce the heat to low. Partially cover the pan to help prevent spattering. Stir frequently until the polenta mixture is thick and cooked through, about 20 to 30 minutes. Oil a medium bowl, and transfer the cooked polenta to the bowl. Immediately spread into an even layer. Allow to set up at least 10 minutes, then turn onto a cutting board and slice into 6

wedges. (NB: because polenta brands vary, make sure to check your package's instructions. Follow them for using 1 cup dried polenta if the proportions are much different from the directions I've given.)

- While the polenta water is coming to a boil, trim the pineapple, then cut it into quarters and remove the core. Cut each quarter lengthwise into thirds, then crosscut into ½-inch thick chunks. Toss the pineapple chunks with sugar. Once the polenta is cooking, heat 1 tablespoon of canola oil in a 12-inch skillet over medium-high, until it shimmers. Add the pineapple chunks to the skillet in a single layer. Cook, stirring occasionally until the chunks have softened and caramelized, about 7 to 8 minutes. Transfer to bowl, and set aside.

91. Chinese Barbecued Pork

Serving: Serves 4 | Prep: | Cook: | Ready in:

Ingredients

- Chinese Barbecued Pork
- 4 pounds Boneless Pork Butt
- 1/2 cup Sugar
- 1/2 teaspoon Soy Sauce
- 6 tablespoons Hoison Sauce
- 1/4 cup Sherry Vinegar
- 1 tablespoon Grated Fresh Ginger
- 1 tablespoon Sesame Oil
- 2 Cloves Chopped Garlic
- 1 tablespoon Five Spice Powder
- 1/3 cup Honey
- 1/4 cup Tomato Paste
- 1 pinch Salt and Pepper
- Perfect Rice
- 1 cup Basmati Rice
- 1 1/2 cups Water
- 2 pieces Star Anise

Direction

- Chinese Barbecued Pork

- Cut the Pork Butt lengthwise, turn on its side and cut lengthwise into equal parts. Prick the Butt with a fork and place in ziplock bag or Vacuum bag "if you have one" Combine Sherry, oil, garlic, spice powder, and pepper and put half in bag and set the other half aside. Seal bag and put into fridge for at least an hour or more.
- Combine Tomato Paste and Honey with the reserved marinade and reduce in small sauce pan till thick and syrupy
- At this stage you can do one of two things.1: Turn oven onto 300 Degrees place marinaded pork on wire rack in a Baking sheet lined with Foil. Put 1/4 Cup of water in the bottom and wrap the sheet with foil to create an airtight seal. Cook for 20 minutes, uncover and cook for another 40 minutes, till edges are brown. Heat broiler and coat meat with glaze and cook for 3 to 5 minutes each side until you get a nice even brown color.2: I have a sous vide set up and Vacuum bags. Sous vide Meat in 145 Degrees water bath for 3 hours, cool bags in ice bath the remove meat form bag and set aside. You can either broil as directed above or if you have a grill. Open the bottom vent and light briquettes and when they are ashed over close grill and heat for 5 Minutes. Cook as broiled instructions above
- Perfect Rice
- Rinse Basmati Rice under cold water to release any extra starch. The water should look clear. Put the rice in medium sauce pan with Star Anise, and Pinch of Salt and Pepper into rice. Pour water over rice and place the lid on. Bring to boil as fast as you can and turn down heat. Place a towel over the pan and replace lid and cook for an additional 8 to 10 Minutes. The water should have evaporated. Remove Anise and fluff up with fork. There you have perfect rice.

92. Chinese Sticky Rice Stuffing With Cantonese Sausages

Serving: Serves enough for a medium-sized turkey | Prep: | Cook: | Ready in:

Ingredients

- 1 pound glutinous (sticky) rice
- 2 tablespoons dried shrimp
- 3 tablespoons Shaoxing rice wine
- 6 shiitake mushrooms (dried or fresh)
- Boiling water as needed
- 10 shelled chestnuts (fresh, frozen, or dried)
- 2 Chinese sausages (try duck liver and Cantonese sausages)
- 1/2 cup roasted sesame oil
- Hot chicken stock, as needed
- 2 tablespoons vegetable or peanut oil
- Turkey giblets
- 1/2 cup edamame (green soybeans)
- 2 tablespoons light soy sauce
- 1 teaspoon sugar
- Freshly ground pepper
- More soy sauce, rice wine, salt to taste

Direction

- Place the rice in a large bowl and cover with cool water. Soak the rice overnight, or at least 8 hours. Steam the rice until done. Rinse the hot, cooked rice in a sieve to break up the clumps and cool down the rice. Drain the rice thoroughly and place it in a large, clean work bowl.
- Place the dried shrimp in a small, heatproof bowl and cover the shrimp with boiling water. Let them soak until they are pliable. Drain the shrimp, pick them over for any debris, and then soak them in the rice wine until you're ready to use them.
- If you're using dried mushrooms and/or chestnuts, cover them with boiling water for at least an hour to plump them up. Remove the stems from the fresh or reconstituted mushrooms and slice the caps into thin pieces; set aside. Pick over the chestnuts and remove

any brown skin that remains. Roughly chop the chestnuts so that they are still at least 1/2 inch across; add to the mushrooms.

- Remove the casings from the sausages and cut the sausages lengthwise into four strips. Cut across the strips to form 1/4 inch cubes. Heat the 2 tablespoons oil in a wok over medium-high heat until it starts to shimmer and add the sausages. Gently stir-fry the sausages until they start to render their fat, and then add the mushrooms and chestnuts. Lightly fold the ingredients while they fry so that they don't break up. As soon as the sausages are lightly browned, add the roasted sesame oil and heat it until it shimmers before adding the drained rice. Once again, gently toss everything together for about 5 minutes. Remove everything to your large work bowl.

- Clean and dry the turkey giblets and cut them into 1/4 inch pieces. Heat the vegetable or peanut oil in the wok over medium-high heat and add the giblets to the wok. Gently stir-fry the giblets until they are lightly browned. Pour the giblets and any fat in the wok into the bowl with the rice.

- Drain the shrimp and add both the shrimp and the edamame to the rice, along with the sesame oil, soy sauce, sugar, and pepper. Toss the rice well and add enough hot stock so that the rice is slightly soupy. (It will absorb the stock as it steams in the turkey.) Taste the rice and adjust the seasoning with more soy sauce, rice wine, or salt as needed.

- Stuff the turkey very loosely, as the rice will swell, and place any extra stuffing in a greased casserole dish. Truss up the turkey and baste with a combination of soy sauce, rice wine, and sesame oil; bake it as you normally would. Cover the casserole with an oiled piece of foil and bake it after you take out the turkey; it will need around 30 minutes, depending upon the amount of stuffing and the size of the dish, so just taste it to see if it's done.

93. Chinese Dumplings

Serving: Serves 4-5 | Prep: | Cook: |Ready in:

Ingredients

- The dumpling
- 2 cups flour (apf is best, but white whole wheat can work, too)
- 1/2 teaspoon fine sea salt
- 1/2 cup cold water, divided
- 6 ounces ground beef
- 6 ounces ground pork
- 1 egg white
- 1/2 cup water chestnuts, chopped
- 1/2 cup finely minced napa cabbage
- 3 ounces scallions bulbs, finely chopped
- 2 ounces chopped chives
- 1 ounce fresh grated ginger, peeled
- 1 teaspoon rice vinegar
- 1 teaspoon soy sauce
- grapeseed, rapeseed, peanut or canola oil suggested for frying
- Dipping sauce
- 6 ounces soy sauce
- 2 ounces rice vinegar
- 1 ounce finely grated ginger
- 2 tablespoons chopped green scallions

Direction

- The dumpling
- In a large bowl add the flour and salt together. I find all-purpose flour is easiest and tastiest (but I have just used 1 2/3 white whole wheat flour with 1/3 cup spelt flour for a healthier version). Make dent in the middle and pour in 1/4 cup of the water. Mix in. Add more water a spoonful at a time until you have a firm smooth dough; do not let this get sticky by adding too much water. Some days you might need a little more water, other days less. Knead this and create a ball shape. Cover with a kitchen towel and let this rest for 30 minutes.
- Mix all the remaining ingredients together for the filling using clean hands.

- After the dough has rested, divide the ball into 3 pieces; roll each of these out as thinly as possible on a lightly floured surface. Thin is key. Cut or stamp out 3 three inch diameter circles from the rolled dough. Add a tablespoon of filling into each circle. Fold in half, then fold and pleat the edges, sealing with your fingers using just a little water to seal the edges; create the pleated or fluted pattern with your fingers.
- Boiling method option: In a large pot, boil water. One batch at a time, add about a third of the dumplings to the boiling water; cook for about 7 minutes. Remove and set aside. Continue until all the dumplings have been cooked. You can eat them this way or proceed to pan fry them. Another alternative is to steam them for about 10 minutes instead of boiling them. Or, you can also skip this step and just fry them, making sure the meat cooks inside.
- Fry method: Heat some oil (with a high smoke point) in a large skillet or wok, just enough to cover the bottom of the pan until sizzling. Add the dumplings (boiled, steamed, or raw) and cook until golden brown. Drain on paper towels if needed.
- Dipping sauce
- Mix the ingredients together and serve as a dipping sauce with the hot dumplings. Some folks might like to add a tad of salt and sugar to season this sauce, but I am happy without these additions. I favor plenty of fresh greens instead.

94. Chipotle Corn With Bacon

Serving: Serves 4 | Prep: | Cook: | Ready in:

Ingredients

- 2 strips bacon, diced
- 6 ears corn, shucked and silked
- 1/2 medium sweet onion, diced fine
- 2 cloves garlic, minced
- 1 or 2 chipotles in adobo, minced
- 1/2 cup water

Direction

- Sauté the bacon until crisp; remove and set aside.
- Dice onion and sauté in bacon fat until translucent and soft. Add garlic and sauté for about 90 seconds.
- Cut kernels off corn and add to skillet. Sauté over medium high heat until some of them begin to brown lightly.
- Add minced chipotles as well as a little adobo and stir.
- Add 1/2 cup water and cover. Reduce heat to medium low and simmer for about 10 minutes. Remove cover and continue to cook until water has evaporated.
- Stir bacon back in to corn immediately before serving.

95. Chorizo Borracho

Serving: Serves 4 (or more for appetizer option) | Prep: | Cook: | Ready in:

Ingredients

- 1 pound cured Chorizo (Spanish salchicha, or Portuguese linguisa or salpicao are other delicious options - just NOT the fresh Mexican style chorizo which is not precooked)
- 2 cloves garlic, thinly sliced
- leaves from one large sprig rosemary, finely chopped
- 1 cup spicy red wine (such as Rioja, Garnacha, or Tempranillo)
- 1 tablespoon honey

Direction

- Heat a drizzle of olive oil in a large Dutch oven with a lid (big enough so that your sausage can cook in a single layer) over medium heat. Slice the links of chorizo into

1/2 - 3/4 inch rounds on the diagonal and cook 5 minutes, stirring occasionally, until just starting to brown and render some fat and brown bits in the bottom of the pan.

- Add the sliced garlic and rosemary to the sausage and cook, stirring constantly, for about one minute.
- Add the red wine, stirring up the bottom of the pot to deglaze all the brown deliciousness. Bring to a simmer, then reduce the heat to medium low and braise the sausages in the wine for 10 minutes, flipping the rounds about halfway through so both sides really take on the red color.
- Remove the lid, raise the heat to medium high, and stir in the honey. Cook uncovered for another 4-5 minutes until the wine is reduced to a thin glaze (if you're using a large Dutch oven, this happens fast so keep an eye). Taste for salt and pepper - I'd recommend not adding any until you've checked, as a very flavorful chorizo or other cured sausage often has just the seasoning you need (this is probably the only dish I make that I do not salt and pepper). Enjoy!

96. Chorizo, Onion And Potato Tacos With Salsa Verde

Serving: Serves 4-5 | Prep: | Cook: | Ready in:

Ingredients

- Vegetable or olive oil or bacon fat
- 1 pound Portuguese chorizo*, cut in half lengthwise and sliced into ¼ " slices
- 20 ounces Yukon gold potatoes, cubed, skin on
- 10 ounces Yellow Onion, peeled and chopped in 1/3 inch dice
- 15-20 ounces Salsa Verde (Trader Joe's brand is great)or Tomatillo Sauce
- 2 packages (12 each) Corn Tortillas, from refrigerated case in the market (Trader Joe's

are excellent and better than the Whole Foods brand)
- 2 1/2 - 3 cups Plain yoghurt; about 1/2 cup per person
- Chopped cilantro - optional
- no salt You are not likely to want salt for this recipe.

Direction

- Place potatoes in a single layer in a 2 tiered steamer** with a few inches of hot water in the bottom. Cover and turn heat to high. In a few minutes, once steam begins to rise, cook 3-4 minutes until just tender when skewered. Remove domed lid and set tiers on empty pots and/or in front of open windows to cool. Do not rinse. (Retain the covered steamer with hot water in case you want to add more potatoes to the recipe after tasting the mixture.)
- Sauté chorizo in a little hot oil over medium heat until browned and some fat has been released. Remove from the pan, leaving the fat in the pan. Sauté onions in that fat over medium high heat until soft and translucent or lightly browned. Add cooked potatoes and stir to coat. Add chorizo and salsa verde. Simmer 5-10 minutes to blend flavors. Don't let it be too dry or too soupy. Taste and adjust ingredients as needed. (It will be very salty from the salsa verde and the chorizo, but the yoghurt will counter that nicely.)
- One at a time, toast tortillas over a wire rack over a medium flame- on both sides. Keep them warm, wrapped in a kitchen towel. (Or heat ¼" vegetable oil till hot, briefly sauté tortilla on each side till slightly crispy but still pliable, drain on paper towels.)
- When all tortillas are toasted, fill each with about 1/3 cup of the hot chorizo mixture, top generously with plain yoghurt and chopped cilantro, and serve. The tangy yoghurt counters the salty spiciness perfectly.
- We allow 3-4 chorizo tacos per hungry adult. Makes 6 cups filling (about 18 tacos)

- Notes*: I do not care for the cinnamon notes in Mexican chorizo. For this recipe, I prefer Portuguese chorizo, like Gaspari.
- Notes**: I have become a major fan of steaming instead of blanching or boiling. It is quicker, uses less water and fuel, requires no dangerous boiling water, and is far more nutritional, as the steamed food retains its nutrients rather than discharging them into a big pot of water. I love my 2- tiered aluminum Chinese dome-topped steamers which I bought in a Chinatown restaurant supply store. The tiers are flat (think 'flat colander" or 'cake pan with holes all over') and they are so space efficient, both for setting over another pot to cool, and for stacked storage. They have an interior diameter of 10" and hold a lot of food in a single layer. They also have a good rim around each tier, making it easy to grasp them. You can improvise a steamer by placing a disposable aluminum pan (that you have punctured all over with a skewer tip) over a water filled can or a cake rack -into a larger pot with a few inches of water in the bottom, and a tight fitting lid. Or you can use the standby fold-up 'steamer basket', opened up as wide and flat as possible, to hold more food.

97. Chorizo, Red Pepper And Feta Frittata

Serving: Serves 4 | Prep: | Cook: | Ready in:

Ingredients

- 1/2 pound baby potatoes, unpeeled and left whole
- olive oil
- 5 ounces chorizo sausage, thinly sliced
- 1 red onion, thinly sliced
- 2 cloves garlic, roughly chopped
- 2 red peppers, roasted, skinned and roughly chopped (or use well-drained jarred roasted peppers)
- 8 eggs
- salt and freshly ground black pepper
- 5 ounces feta cheese, cubed or crumbled
- green salad, to serve

Direction

- Preheat the oven to 350°F.
- Bring a pot of water to a boil. Place the potatoes in the pot and boil for about 5 minutes, or until just cooked and fork tender — do not overcook them or they won't keep their shape when sliced. Drain. When they're cool enough to handle, slice thinly and set aside.
- Heat a splash of olive oil in a large ovenproof, nonstick frying pan over a medium heat. Add in the sliced chorizo and cook for about 5 minutes, until the chorizo has released its oils into the pan and has browned slightly. Scoop the chorizo out of the pan with a slotted spoon and set aside to drain on a paper towel-lined plate. If there's an excessive amount of oil now in the pan, drain some off until only 1 or 2 tablespoons remain.
- Reduce the heat to low, add the onion to the oil left behind in the pan and cook gently for 7 to 10 minutes, until softened. Add in the garlic and cook for 1 minute more, then remove from the heat. Add in the chopped roasted red peppers and set aside.
- Whisk the eggs in a large bowl with a pinch of salt and some freshly ground black pepper (don't use too much salt, since the chorizo and feta are also quite salty). Stir in the potatoes and chorizo. Using a slotted spoon, transfer the onion and peppers from the pan to the egg mixture and give everything a good stir.
- Wipe out the frying pan and add 2 tablespoons of fresh olive oil (you can use less oil if you have a really good nonstick pan). Heat the oil in the pan, then pour in the egg mixture, making sure the chorizo and vegetables are evenly distributed throughout the pan. Top with the feta cheese.
- Transfer the pan to the oven and cook for 25 to 35 minutes, or until set in the center. Remove

from the oven and allow to cool a little before sliding it out of the pan onto a large serving platter or cutting board. Serve warm or at room temperature with a green salad on the side.

98. Chorizo Endives Tart Tatin

Serving: Serves 6 people | Prep: | Cook: |Ready in:

Ingredients

- 6-7 endives
- 7 tablespoons butter
- 2 tablespoons brown sugar
- 2 shallots
- 1 puff pastry or shortcrust pastry
- Salt and pepper
- slices of shorizo

Direction

- Clean the endives, trim the ends and cut in half. Peel and mince the shallots
- Peel and mince the shallots. Preheat the oven to 350F
- In a frying pan, cook the endives and shallots in 5 tbsp. of butter for about 15 minutes, until the sugar melts and turns golden. Season to taste.
- Put the brown sugar in a baking pan with 2tbsp of diced butter. Lay the endives on top, cut side down and in a tight even layer. Drape the puff pastry/shortcrust pastry over the pan and tuck the edges in around the filling. Bake for 30 minutes until golden and risen
- 5-10 minutes before the tart tatin is baked, cook the chorizo slices in a frying pan. Take the tatin out of the oven, Remove from the oven, let cool then delicately turn it onto a plate. Place the chorizo slices on top and press gently. Let cool for another 2-3 minutes to let the chorizo "infuse". Serve with a side salad.

99. Cider Braised Pork Shoulder With Caramelized Onion And Apple Confit

Serving: Serves 4 | Prep: 0hours10mins | Cook: 3hours0mins |Ready in:

Ingredients

- 2 1/2 pounds pork shoulder (butt), boneless and tied
- 2 pinches salt and freshly ground black pepper
- 2 tablespoons olive oil
- 4 large yellow onions, halved, thinly sliced
- 1/4 cup Calvados brandy
- 1 large Granny Smith apple, peeled, cut in 1/2-inch cubes
- 2 garlic cloves, chopped
- 1 teaspoon dried thyme or 1 tablespoon fresh thyme
- 1 cup apple cider
- 1 cup chicken stock
- 1 tablespoon Dijon mustard

Direction

- Preheat oven to 400° F.
- Pat the pork dry and season with salt and pepper.
- Heat oil in a large oven-proof pot or Dutch oven with a lid. Brown pork on all sides, turning with tongs, 6-8 minutes per side. Transfer pork to plate.
- Pour off excess fat from pot. Add onion and 1 teaspoon salt. Sauté over medium heat, stirring occasionally, until onions are very soft ad deep golden brown, 18-20 minutes.
- Add Calvados and stir to deglaze pan. Add apple, garlic and thyme. Cook, stirring, 30 seconds.
- Return pork to pot, nestling it down in the onions. Add cider and chicken stock. Cover pot and place in oven. Reduce heat to 325 F. Braise until meat is very tender, 2 1/2-3 hours.

- Return pot to cooktop. Transfer pork to a cutting board and remove kitchen strings. Boil onion and apples until thickened and liquid slightly reduced, 1-2 minutes. Stir in mustard. Season to taste with salt and pepper.
- Cut pork in serving pieces and arrange on serving platter or individual dinner plates. Spoon onion apple confit over and around the meat.

100. City Chicken

Serving: Makes about 12 sticks | Prep: 0hours20mins | Cook: 2hours0mins | Ready in:

Ingredients

- 1 1/2 pounds pork shoulder meat, cut into 1 1/2 inch cubes
- 1 1/2 pounds veal stew meat (use all pork if you can't find veal)
- Salt and pepper for seasoning the meat
- 2 eggs beaten with 3 tablesppons water
- 2 cups seasoned dry bread crumbs
- Flour for dusting the skewers
- 12 to 15 wooden skewers, 4 to 5 inches long
- Vegetable oil for browning
- 1/2 cup water

Direction

- Thread each skewer with alternating veal and pork cubes. Season liberally with salt and pepper.
- Dust the skewers with a little flour. Shake off excess.
- Coat the skewers with the egg mixture and the thoroughly bread them with the seasoned bread crumbs.
- In batches, brown the skewers in a large frying pan in the vegetable oil reaching to almost an inch.
- Place the skewers in a 9 x13 inch baking dish and pour the 1/2 cup water or chicken broth into the dish.

- Cover tightly with foil and bake at 325F for 1 hour. Uncover, raise the temp to 350F and bake 15 to 20 minutes more.
- The water in the baking dish keeps the meat moist and creates a little sauce to dress the meat and the must have mashed potatoes!

101. Convection Oven Old Meatloaf

Serving: Serves 6-8 | Prep: 0hours45mins | Cook: 1hours30mins | Ready in:

Ingredients

- 1 cup fresh bread crumbs(soft white bread)
- 1/3 cup milk
- 1 1/2 pounds ground chuck (85/15)
- 1/2 pound ground pork (not lean)
- 2 tablespoons butter
- 1 large onion, diced
- 2 celery stalks, diced
- 1 medium carrot, diced
- 2 garlic cloves, minced
- 1/2 cup creme fraiche
- 2 eggs, beaten
- 2 teaspoons Worcestershire sauce
- 1 teaspoon dry mustard powder
- 1 teaspoon paprika
- 2 tablespoons fresh parsley, chopped
- 1 1/2 teaspoons kosher salt
- 1 teaspoon freshly ground black pepper
- 6 slices bacon
- 1 cup ketchup
- 2 tablespoons brown sugar
- 1 tablespoon Dijon mustard
- 1/4 teaspoon freshly grated nutmeg

Direction

- Preheat oven to 350°F.
- In a small bowl place bread crumbs and drizzle the milk over the top. Set aside.

- Melt the butter in a large skillet, add the onion, celery and carrot. Sprinkle with a pinch of salt and cook, stirring occasionally until vegetables are soft, but not browned. Add garlic and cook for another 2-3 minutes. Remove from heat, scrape into a small bowl and allow to cool to room temperature (about ten minutes).
- In another bowl, whisk together the beaten eggs, crème fraiche and Worcestershire sauce.
- In a large bowl place the beef and pork, add the breadcrumb mixture, vegetables, egg mixture and the rest of the ingredients except the bacon, ketchup, brown sugar and mustard. Use your hands to thoroughly combine the meatloaf ingredients and then place into a large ovenproof baking dish. Lay five strips of bacon lengthwise over meatloaf; cut the remaining bacon strip in half and place at each end of loaf.
- Place in oven and set timer for 45 minutes. Meanwhile combine Ketchup, Brown Sugar, Mustard and Nutmeg and set aside. At the end of 45 minutes, set oven to convection and cook meatloaf for another 15 minutes. When completed, remove meatloaf from oven and pour or brush glaze all over the surface of the bacon (it's ok if some drizzles down into the pan). Place back in over and bake for an additional 15 minutes until the glaze is bubbling. Remove from oven and let sit for 15 minutes. Serve!

102.   Corn Bacon Blueberry Skillet Cake

Serving: Makes 10" cake | Prep: | Cook: |Ready in:

Ingredients

- 1/2 pound smoked bacon, in lardons
- 1-3 tablespoons butter
- 1.5 cups corn, leftover, cut from the cob (I'm sure fresh would be great and frozen would be acceptable)
- 1 cup AP flour
- 1 cup corn meal, I prefer a coarse grind, but fine makes a nice crumb
- 1 teaspoon baking powder
- 1/2 teaspoon baking soda
- 1/2 teaspoon salt
- 2 eggs
- 1 teaspoon vanilla
- 1-1/4 cups buttermilk
- 1/4 cup maple syrup
- 1-1/2 cups blueberries

Direction

- Preheat the oven to 375°.
- In a 10" or 11" well-seasoned cast iron skillet, cook the lardons slowly until very crisp. Remove lardons and set aside.
- Pour off the bacon fat to measure. You need five tablespoons of fat - so add melted butter as necessary to get to 5T. Put the skillet back into the oven to get piping hot.
- Puree 3/4 c of corn, the buttermilk, maple syrup, eggs and vanilla in a blender. (Every good beach house has a blender.)
- Whisk together dry ingredients, make a well and pour in puree. Add the bacon fat and butter. Stir quickly with a fork. Fold in remaining corn, bacon and blueberries.
- Remove the skillet from the oven. Brush the oils remaining in the skillet up the sides and around the bottom. Pour/spoon the batter into the hot skillet and bake for 25-30 minutes. The cake will be deep golden and will be pulling away from the sides of the pan.
- Serve with maple syrup, honey, jam or just by itself, a small slice cut off the cake in the late afternoon when you get back from the beach, famished.

103.   Cornmeal And Chorizo Pancakes

Serving: Makes 8 pancakes | Prep: | Cook: |Ready in:

Ingredients

- 1 cup sour cream
- 1 large egg
- 1 tablespoon maple syrup
- 1/4 teaspoon fine sea salt
- 1/2 cup fine cornmeal or corn flour
- 1/4 cup all-purpose flour
- 1 teaspoon baking powder
- 1/2 teaspoon baking soda
- 1/2 cup diced dried chorizo
- Toppings! Might I recommend either maple syrup and peaches or blueberries OR salsa/tomatoes and avocado with sea salt and maybe some cilantro or lime or sour cream or pickled onions...

Direction

- Preheat your oven to 250° F (Optional: This is to keep your first batch of pancakes warm while you cook the second). In a medium mixing bowl, whisk together the sour cream, egg, and maple syrup. In a separate bowl, combine the salt, flours, baking powder, and baking soda. Add the dry ingredients to the wet ingredients and fold them in until you have a lumpy mixture free of dry streaks. Fold in the chorizo just until mixed in.
- Heat a large skillet over medium heat. Add a large pat of butter and let it melt and foam. Add the batter in about 1/4-cup spoonful, leaving space between each pancake so they can spread.
- Cook on the first side until they are a deep golden brown on the bottom, forming bubbles, and dry around the edges. Then flip and cook on the second side until browned and cooked through. Transfer the finished pancakes to a baking sheet and keep them warm in the oven while you cook the remaining pancakes.
- Serve the pancakes with a variety of toppings, sweet or savory. They go well with maple syrup and tart fruits; they also go well with taco-style toppings.

104.   Country Meatloaf

Serving: Serves 2-3 | Prep: | Cook: |Ready in:

Ingredients

- 1/2 pound ground beef
- 1/2 pound ground pork
- 1/2 medium onion, finely chopped
- 2 gloves garlic, finely chopped
- 1-2 tablespoons chopped fresh parsley
- 1 teaspoon cumin
- 1 teaspoon ground coriander
- 1 teaspoon ground allspice
- 1/2 teaspoon salt
- 1 tablespoon tomato paste
- pepper to taste
- 1/2 cup panko crumbs
- 5 dashes worchestershire sauce
- 1 egg
- 2 1/2 tablespoons heavy creme
- 2 tablespoons freshly grated pecorino romano
- 1/4 cup shelled whole pastachios
- 4-6 strips of bacon

Direction

- I usually start with my ground meat first and make a well in the middle of the meat, then I start adding each ingredient one by one. Add all the ingredients on list, stopping at pistachios and bacon. Just a note: This time I used pecorino Romano cheese, but I generally use whatever hard cheese I have on hand. It tastes great with parmesan cheese as well.
- Mix together well. I like to mix my meatloaf in a wide shallow bowl. My mom does it right on the chopping block. I cannot imagine mixing meatloaf without getting my hands right into it. I have also made this meatloaf with ground veal and pork combination with great success.
- After meat mixture is mixed well, add in the pistachios and blend throughout.
- Form into a loaf shape and place in baking dish.
- Wrap loaf with strips of bacon. Sometimes I like them to completely cover the loaf and

other times I like to leave some space in between so that I can see the meatloaf. It depends on my mood and how much bacon I have.

- Place in a 350F preheated oven for about 40 minutes. Sometimes, I like to crisp up the bacon more by sticking under the broiler for a minute. Other times, it does not feel necessary.

105. Cowboy Cocktail

Serving: Serves 2 | Prep: 1hours0mins | Cook: 1hours0mins | Ready in:

Ingredients

- Leftover pulled pork, chopped brisket, or grilled chicken.
- BBQ'd beans
- cole slaw
- your favorite BBQ Sauce
- 2 slices cooked bacon (optional)
- 1 chopped green onion (optional)
- 1 pickled jalepeno, seeded and chopped (optional)

Direction

- The size of the serving containers determines the amount of ingredients. For a main dish I use beer mugs. For an app, small glasses or bowls.
- Warm leftover chopped brisket, pulled pork, or grilled chicken. In another pan, warm beans.
- Fill the serving vessel one third full of warmed beans. The next layer should be another third filled with your meat. Top with BBQ sauce to taste.
- Cover with coleslaw. I like to place another dab of BBQ sauce on top of the slaw because it looks pretty and makes my wife happy. Serve while meat and beans are still warm.
- Any optional ingredients can be added at any layer you choose. Make it your own.

- I like to have slices of bread on the side. Garlic bread works well for us.

106. Creamy Sausage And Spinach With Whole Wheat Rotini

Serving: Serves 2-4 | Prep: | Cook: | Ready in:

Ingredients

- 2 garlic and herb pork sausages
- 1 tablespoon grapeseed oil
- 1 tablespoon butter
- 2 tablespoons all purpose flour
- 1 cup milk
- 1 clove of garlic, smashed
- 1/2 cup grated Parmesan cheese in two, 1/4 cup portions
- 1 pinch fresh ground pepper (to taste)
- 1 pinch salt (to taste)
- 3 cups frozen chopped spinach (thaw and squeeze off most of the liquid if it's in a brick, or add frozen if it's in a bag and not stuck together)
- 2 cups whole wheat rotini

Direction

- Preheat your oven to 400 degrees Fahrenheit.
- In a medium sized pot, cook the rotini in salted water and drain when al dente. In the duration of time it takes to bring the water to a boil and then cook the pasta, you should have enough time to make the sausage and spinach sauce.
- Drizzle the tablespoon of grape seed (or any other high-heat oil) into a skillet on medium-high heat and add the sausages. Once the sausages start to brown turn the heat down to medium-low and let the sausages cook for about 5 more minutes so that they will be almost cooked through. Take the sausages off of the skillet and let rest on a plate for about 5 minutes then slice them diagonally into ~1/4"

slices. Heat up the pan to medium-high, and add the sausage back to the pan to brown the cut surfaces. This should take about 5 minutes.

- In a small sauce pan, melt the butter over medium-low heat. Once the butter is melted, add the flour to make a roux. Stir the flour into the butter and keep stirring for a minute or two. Add the cup of milk and smashed garlic clove. The clove will come out later, so don't smash it to oblivion. Season with salt and pepper. Keep stirring the sauce over medium heat until it thickens, which will take around 5-7 minutes (it should have a similar viscosity to glue...but doesn't taste like glue! I promise!).
- Once the sauce is thick, take out the garlic clove, stir in the first 1/4 cup of Parmesan cheese, then stir in the spinach and heat on low for another minute or two to reheat the sauce incorporate the spinach. Stir in the sausage, and some of the pan drippings if you want to add a little extra meatiness to the sauce.
- Drain the pasta and mix in the spinach and sausage mixture until all of the pasta is coated. Pour into an oven safe dish, top with the remaining 1/4 cup of Parmesan cheese, and bake in the oven for 12-15 minutes until the pasta on top browns a little. I baked mine in a 10" cast-iron skillet, which I had used to brown the sausages. I wiped out the remaining fat and oil before adding the coated pasta.

---

107. Crispy Pork Cutlets And Peach Salsa

Serving: Serves 4 | Prep: | Cook: |Ready in:

Ingredients

- 2 peaches, peeled, pitted and cut into 1/2" dice
- 1/2 red bell pepper, 1/4" dice
- 1/4 cup red onion, 1/4" inch dice
- pinch of salt

- 1/2 teaspoon lime zest
- 2 tablespoons freshly chopped parsley
- 1 tablespoon julienned basil (add basil just before serving)
- 1 1-lb pork tenderloin
- 1 egg, lightly beaten
- 1/2 cup all purpose flour
- 1 teaspoon salt
- 1/2 teaspoon black pepper
- 1 cup panko breadcrumbs
- 8 slices of thinly sliced Prosciutto Di Parma

Direction

- In a small bowl combine the peaches, bell pepper, red onion, lime zest and parsley. Toss to combine. Don't add the basil until you're ready to serve. It wilts and discolors quickly, so to retain the freshness, add it at the last minute. Set aside.
- Preheat the oven to 200°.Cut the pork into 3/4" medallions, cutting across the tenderloin crosswise. Lay the pork pieces on a cutting board and use the flat side of a meat mallet to pound the cutlets to about 1/4" thick. Set aside.
- In a shallow bowl, add the flour, salt and pepper, stir to combine. Add the egg to a shallow bowl and whisk lightly with a fork. Add panko to a third shallow bowl. Coat the pork cutlets in assembly line fashion, dipping and coating both sides of the pork first in the flour mixture, then in the egg and finally in the panko. Transfer the cutlets to a platter.
- Place a cast iron or other heavy skillet over medium to medium high heat. Add enough canola oil to reach about 1/4" up in the pan. When the oil is hot but not smoking, test it by adding 1 or 2 breadcrumbs to the oil. If they sink to the bottom, continue to heat the oil. If they float immediately, the oil is ready.
- Carefully transfer the pork tenderloins a few at a time to the skillet - but don't crowd the pan, the cutlets should not touch one another. Cook for 2-3 minutes per side or until the cutlets are a golden brown. Transfer to a baking sheet lined with paper towels to soak

up the excess oil. Keep the pork warm in the oven while you cook the remaining cutlets.

- Cut each slice of the prosciutto in half, lengthwise. Place the cutlets on a serving platter and top each with a piece of prosciutto. Add the basil to the salsa and serve the salsa alongside the pork cutlets.

---

108. Crock Pot Brown Sugar & Balsamic–Glazed Pork Tenderloin

Serving: Serves 6 | Prep: 0hours15mins | Cook: 8hours0mins | Ready in:

Ingredients

- 1 teaspoon ground sage
- 1/2 teaspoon salt
- 1/4 teaspoon pepper
- 1 garlic clove, crushed
- 1/2 cup water
- 2 pounds pork tenderloin
- 1/2 cup brown sugar
- 1 tablespoon cornstarch
- 1/4 cup balsamic vinegar
- 1/2 cup water
- 2 tablespoons soy sauce

Direction

- Mix together the seasonings: sage, salt, pepper and garlic, and rub over the tenderloin.
- Place 1/2 cup water in slow cooker, followed by the tenderloin, and cook on low for 6 to 8 hours.
- 1 hour before the roast is finished, mix together the ingredients for the glaze in a small saucepan: brown sugar, cornstarch, balsamic vinegar, water, and soy sauce.
- Heat over medium and stir until mixture thickens, about 4 minutes.
- Brush roast with glaze 2 or 3 times during the last hour of cooking. (For a more caramelized crust, remove from crock pot and place on aluminum lined sheet pan, glaze, and set under broiler for 1 to 2 minutes, until bubbly and caramelized. Repeat 2 to 3 more times until desired crust is achieved.)
- Serve with remaining glaze on the side.

---

109. Crockpot Hawaiian Kalua Pork

Serving: Serves 12 | Prep: | Cook: | Ready in:

Ingredients

- 3-4 pounds pork shoulder blade roast
- 1 yellow onion, sliced
- 2 tablespoons oregano
- 2 tablespoons powdered garlic
- 31/2 tablespoon red Hawaiian salt (alea)

Direction

- Remove pork roast from packaging and cut off as much visible fat as possible.
- Mix oregano and garlic powder together and rub all over roast.
- Slice yellow onion. Place a large square of heavy duty foil on a board, and put the onion rings in the center.
- Put the pork roast on top of the onion, and rub the salt all over the roast. Close up the foil tightly. Hawaiian red salt is available online, gourmet stores or at Cost Plus.
- Set the crockpot temperature to low, and cook roast for 10-12 hours or overnight, until pork is tender and shreds easily.
- Serve on Hawaiian sweet rolls with coleslaw, or add your favorite BBQ sauce. Use for tacos, quesadillas, pizzas, or wherever else pulled pork sounds good.

110. Croque Madame Burger

Serving: Serves 5 | Prep: | Cook: |Ready in:

Ingredients

- Peppered Bechamel
- 2 1/2 tablespoons butter
- 2 1/2 tablespoons all-purpose flour
- 2 cups whole milk
- 1 teaspoon salt
- 1 teaspoon pepper
- 1/4 teaspoon grated nutmeg
- Burger
- .75 pounds 90-10 ground beef
- 3/4 cup cured, smoked fatty pork shoulder, very finely chopped
- 1 teaspoon salt
- 1 teaspoon fresh ground black pepper
- 2 tablespoons extra virgin olive oil
- 4 emmental cheese slices
- 4 large eggs
- 4 hamburger buns
- spicy brown mustard

Direction

- In a bowl, use your fingers to gently combine the ground beef, pork shoulder, salt and pepper. Make 4 patties by lightly forming 4 equal-size balls of meat and softly patting them until ¾ inches thick. Chill the patties for 1 hour in the fridge.
- For the peppered béchamel sauce, heat a saucepan over medium heat and the butter. When melted, add the flour and stir with a whisk until smooth. Cook while constantly stirring until the roux (combination of flour and fat) becomes a golden blonde color. Meanwhile, in a separate pan, heat the milk until it is almost boiling. Whisk the milk into the roux 1 cup at a time until very smooth. Bring the mixture to a boil and cook for 10 minutes while constantly stirring. Remove from heat and gently stir in the salt, pepper, and nutmeg. Set aside.

- Heat a cast-iron skillet over medium-high heat and coat it with 1 tablespoon of the oil. Sear and cook the patties until a crust forms, or about 4 minutes per side. Top each patty with a slice of cheese during the last minute.
- In another pan, fry the eggs in 1 tablespoon of olive oil over a medium-low heat to desired doneness. Personally, I'm a runny yolk kinda gal, but to each their own. In a third pan over medium-high heat, toast the inside of the buns until lightly brown.
- To assemble, spread spicy brown mustard on the buns to taste. Layer the burger, béchamel sauce, and fried egg.

111. Crustless Quiche

Serving: Serves 6-8 | Prep: | Cook: | Ready in:

Ingredients

- 2 tablespoons butter
- 1 large leek finely chopped
- cooking spray
- 1/4 pound ham, diced
- 1 cup shredded gruyere cheese
- 4 eggs
- 2 cups whole milk
- 1/2 cup biscuit mix
- 1/2 teaspoon ground mustard
- 1/2 teaspoon kosher salt
- 1/8 teaspoon pepper

Direction

- Preheat oven to 350 degrees. In a frying pan melt the butter over medium heat. Add the leeks and saute until softened, 5-7 minutes.
- Spray a 10 inch pie plate with cooking spray. Sprinkle the leeks, ham and cheese evenly over the bottom.
- In a medium bowl beat the eggs. Add the remaining ingredients and stir to combine. Pour into the pie pan.

- Bake until golden brown and center is set, 45-50 minutes. Remove from oven and let stand 5 minutes before cutting and serving.

112. Curried Ham

Serving: Serves 4 | Prep: | Cook: |Ready in:

Ingredients

- 1 Bone in Ham (small)
- 4 medium Russet Potatoes
- 1 onion - medium diced
- 2 tablespoons Curry Powder
- 2 teaspoons Ginger
- 540 ml can diced tomatoes
- 3 lime leaves or bay leaves

Direction

- Put all ingredients into slow cooker, cook on low for 8 hrs. Remove ham, and rest. Add frozen peas. Serve.

113. Curried Meatballs

Serving: Serves 4 | Prep: | Cook: |Ready in:

Ingredients

- 1 pound ground pork
- 2 onions
- 1 big apple
- 1 egg
- 1/2 liter milk
- 3 tablespoons butter
- 2 tablespoons breadcrumbs
- 2 tablespoons flour
- 3 tablespoons yellow curry powder
- 1 teaspoon dried sage
- salt
- pepper

Direction

- Start by mixing the meat for the meatballs: Put the ground pork in a bowl, add salt, pepper, the dried sage and grate haft an onion. Stir - then add one egg, the breadcrumb, salt and pepper and a little milk just a tablespoon or two. Stir again - the meat mixture needs to come together as a dough almost. It needs to be able to hold a shape. Set aside for at least one hour.
- Chop the remaining onion (1 1/2) and cut the apple into smallish chunks.
- Bring a pot of salted water to the boil - meanwhile shape the meat mixture into balls. I prefer small meat balls - I usually use a teaspoon to shape them.
- Once the water is at a boil - dump 6-7 meatballs into the water - don't crowd the pot. They are done, when they float to the top - about 3-4 minutes. Boil them in batches and set aside - and save the liquid.
- In a heavy pot - I use an enameled pot - melt the butter and then add the curry, onion and apple. Give it a good stir and gently fry for 4-5 minutes being careful not to brown the onion.
- Then add the flour and stir for a short while to start cooking it like a roux. Then start adding cooking liquid from the meat balls one ladle at a time while stirring vigorously until a thick sauce forms - then switch from the cooking liquid to milk until you have a fairly thin sauce. Add salt and pepper and the meat balls. Let the dish gently cook for about 5 minutes - it's alright to cook it longer, as long as it does not burn at the bottom which this kind of sauce has a tendency to do.
- Serve in a deep dish with white rice cooked with raisins, sliced tomato and mango chutney.
- For a dessert my Lemon Half-moons and a cup of strong Earl Gray tea would be wonderful.

114. Dairy Free Bacon Broccoli Slaw

Serving: Serves 4 | Prep: | Cook: |Ready in:

Ingredients

- 1/3 cup vegan grapeseed mayo
- 1 tablespoon worcestershire sauce
- 1 tablespoon maple syrup
- 1 teaspoon dijon mustard
- 1/8 teaspoon garlic
- 12 ounces broccoli slaw
- 4 ounces shredded carrots
- 1/2 cup dried cranberries
- 1/2 cup cashews
- 4 pieces uncured natural nitrate free bacon

Direction

- Combine first five ingredients into a smooth sauce.
- Combine broccoli slaw, shredded carrots, cashews and cranberries.
- Mix sauce into veggie mixture, garnish with bacon crumbles and serve!

115. Deep Fried Pork & Potato Balls

Serving: Makes 15-20 balls | Prep: | Cook: |Ready in:

Ingredients

- 2 cups garlic mashed potatoes
- 1/2 pound ground pork
- 1 shallot, diced
- 1/4 cup button mushrooms, diced
- 2 teaspoons sugar
- 2 teaspoons fish sauce
- 2 teaspoons soy sauce
- salt and pepper to taste
- 1/4 teaspoon chinese 5 spice
- 2 tablespoons flour
- 1-2 eggs, lightly beaten

- 1 cup panko bread crumbs
- vegetable oil, for frying

Direction

- In a medium bowl, mix the ground pork, shallot, mushrooms, sugar, fish sauce, soy sauce, salt, pepper, and Chinese 5 spice.
- Heat a large skillet under medium high heat and add 1 tablespoon olive oil. Cook pork mixture until browned and broken up. Turn off heat and set aside to cool.
- Once the pork mixture is cooled, mix in with mashed potatoes. Season with salt and pepper, if needed.
- Shape the mixture into small to medium sized balls, about 1 to 1 & 1/2 inch in diameter should be fine. Dip each ball into the flour, shaking off any excess. Then dip in eggs, and roll in panko.
- Heat a large Dutch oven under medium high heat and fill with about 3 inches of oil. When temperature is about 350 F, start heating balls in batches, about 5 balls per batch should do it. Fry until golden brown, about 3 minutes or so, and drain on paper towels.
- Serve with sriracha sauce!

116. Diana Kennedy's Carnitas

Serving: Serves 4 to 6 | Prep: 0hours5mins | Cook: 2hours40mins |Ready in:

Ingredients

- 3 pounds pork shoulder, butt, or country-style spare ribs, skin and bone removed
- Cold water to barely cover
- 2 teaspoons salt, or to taste

Direction

- Cut the meat, with the fat, into strips about 2 x 3/4 inches. Barely cover the meat with water in a flameproof dish, add the salt, and bring it to a boil, uncovered.

- Lower the flame enough to bring down to a simmer. Let the meat continue simmering until all the liquid has evaporated -- about 1 hour and a half, depending on the shape of your pot. By this time the meat should be cooked through but not falling apart.
- Lower the flame a little more and continue cooking the meat until all the fat has rendered out of it. Keep turning the meat until it is lightly browned all over -- about 1 hour and 10 minutes.
- Notes: The meat will get more evenly cooked if the dish is rather large and shallow. Do not add too much water at the beginning or the meat will fall apart at the frying stage. If the meat is still fairly hard when the water has evaporated, then add a little more water and continue cooking. Choose pork that has a fair amount of fat or you will have to add some lard for it to brown properly.

117.   Dipping Sauces For Vietnamese Spring Rolls

Serving: Serves 4 | Prep: 24hours20mins | Cook: 0hours0mins | Ready in:

Ingredients

- For the fish sauce dipping sauce:
- 3 tablespoons fish sauce
- juice of 1 lime
- 3 tablespoons sugar, or to taste
- 1/2 tablespoon minced ginger
- 1/2 teaspoon thinly sliced fresh Thai chiles
- 1/3 cup water
- Salt and pepper, to taste
- For the hoisin peanut dipping sauce:
- 5 tablespoons hoisin sauce
- 3 tablespoons pork broth
- 1 tablespoon peanut butter
- 1 tablespoon minced garlic
- 1 teaspoon vegetable oil
- 1 tablespoon sugar

- chopped peanuts, optional

Direction

- For the fish sauce dipping sauce:
- Mix together all of the ingredients and refrigerate. Store for 1 day prior to serving in order to let the chile flavor infuse.
- For the hoisin peanut dipping sauce:
- Whisk together the hoisin, pork broth, and peanut butter.
- In a small fry pan, heat the garlic and oil and sauté until fragrant. Add the hoisin sauce mixture and the sugar, then simmer for 1 to 2 minutes until thick. Let cool.
- Top with peanuts, if desired.

118.   Early Bird Breakfast Tacos

Serving: Serves 2 to 4 | Prep: | Cook: | Ready in:

Ingredients

- For the carrot esabeche
- 1 yellow onion, sliced
- 1 (10-ounce) bag of matchstick carrots
- 1 garlic clove
- 2 tablespoons unsalted butter
- 1 (4-ounce) can diced jalapeños, juices drained
- 1 cup white vinegar
- For the roasted poblano cream sauce
- 1 large fresh poblano chile
- 2 tablespoons chopped white onion
- 1 small garlic clove, minced
- 1/2 tablespoon unsalted butter
- 3/4 cup heavy cream
- 1/4 cup whole milk
- Kosher salt and freshly ground black pepper, to taste
- To assemble the tacos
- 1 packet (10-count, 6-inch) flour tortillas (trust us)

- 1/2 pound ground pork (not sausage)
- 1/2 pound chorizo (the fresh Mexican kind, not cured Spanish chorizo)
- 6 eggs
- 1 (8-ounce) package shredded cheddar cheese
- 1 bunch cilantro, for garnish

Direction

- Make the carrot escabeche: Sauté the onion, carrots, and garlic in the butter for 5 minutes. Combine the sautéed mixture with the jalapeños and vinegar and store in a sealed jar for at least 24 hours.
- Make the roasted poblano cream sauce: Char the chile over a gas flame until blackened in spots, seal in a plastic bag, and let cool. Peel, seed, and chop coarsely. Sauté the onion and garlic in butter until soft, then add the chile. Add cream and milk and bring to boil, whisking constantly. Reduce heat to low and simmer until reduced. Transfer to a blender, purée until smooth, and season to taste with salt and pepper.
- Assemble the tacos: Heat the tortillas in the oven or microwave, according to package directions. Sauté the meat in a pan until browned and cooked through, scramble the eggs with cheese, top with the carrot escabeche and roasted poblano cream sauce, then garnish with cilantro. You're good to go—best breakfast tacos ever!

119.   Easy Dumplings

Serving: Makes 16 dumplings | Prep: | Cook: | Ready in:

Ingredients

- Flour, Water, Salt
- 2 cups Flour
- 3/4 cup Water
- 1/2 teaspoon Salt
- Pork Chorizo, Chopped Onion, Cilantro, Chopped Lettuce, Thin carrot sticks

- 1 packet Pork Chorizo
- 5 handfuls Chopped Onion
- 2 handfuls Cilantro
- 2 handfuls Chopped Lettuce
- 2 handfuls Thin carrot sticks

Direction

- Flour, Water, Salt
- In a medium bowl, mix the flour and salt.
- Then, slowly add the water.
- Mix first with a wooden spoon and then knead the dough with your hands.
- Roll out onto a lightly floured surface and cut out a circle about 6 inches in diameter.
- Pork Chorizo, Chopped Onion, Cilantro, Chopped Lettuce, Thin carrot sticks
- In a medium bowl, put in the pork chorizo.
- Add the chopped onion and cilantro and give it a quick mix.
- Then add the chopped lettuce and thin carrot sticks until combined.
- Add a tablespoon to each dumpling wrapper.
- Add the filled dumpling wrappers to a hot oiled skillet and cook until browned on both sides.
- Let the finished dumplings dry on a paper towel and cool for about 10 minutes.

120.   Eat Your Peas & Carrots Quinoa Pasta (with Bacon!)

Serving: Serves 2 - 3 | Prep: | Cook: | Ready in:

Ingredients

- 3 slices bacon, cut crosswise into 1/2-inch pieces
- 2 medium carrots, peeled and finely chopped
- 1 leek (white and light green part only), halved lengthwise then cut crosswise into thin slices
- 1/4 teaspoon kosher salt
- 1/4 teaspoon freshly ground black pepper
- 1/2 cup half-and-half

- 1 teaspoon finely chopped fresh rosemar
- 8 ounces quinoa spaghetti or regular spaghetti
- 1/2 cup grated Parmesan cheese
- 1/3 cup frozen or fresh green peas

Direction

- In medium saucepot, cook bacon over medium heat 5 to 7 minutes or until crisp, stirring occasionally. Add carrots, leek, salt and pepper and cook 6 to 8 minutes or until carrots are softened, stirring occasionally. Add half-and-half and rosemary; heat to boiling. Reduce heat to medium-low and simmer 5 to 7 minutes or until sauce has thickened (should coat the back of a spoon); stirring occasionally. Remove from heat but keep in a warm place on the stove.
- Meanwhile, cook the pasta in salted water as the box instructs for al dente. Drain the pasta, but save about 2 cups of the cooking water.
- Add Parmesan, peas, pasta and 1 cup of pasta cooking water to sauce. Heat over medium heat, stirring constantly, until sauce completely coats pasta and peas are warmed through. Add more pasta cooking water as needed.

121.	Egg Souffle With Bacon And Asparagus

Serving: Serves 2 | Prep: | Cook: | Ready in:

Ingredients

- 3 strips thick-cut bacon
- 1/2 medium onion, minced
- 6 asparagus stalks, tips reserved and stalks cut into coins
- 4 large eggs
- 3/4 cup heavy whipping cream
- 1/2 cup Parmesan cheese, grated
- 1/2 teaspoon salt
- 1/2 teaspoon pepper

Direction

- Preheat oven to 350 degrees. Lightly grease a 16-ounce ramekin or two 8-ounce ramekins.
- In a nonstick frying pan, cook bacon over medium-high heat until crispy. Place bacon strips on a paper towel-lined plate to drain. When bacon is cooled, cut into bite-sized pieces and set aside.
- Drain all but 2 teaspoons of bacon fat from pan. Add minced onion and sweat for 3 to 4 minutes, until onions are almost translucent. Add asparagus and cook for about a minute more. Remove pan from heat.
- In a small bowl, whisk together eggs, heavy cream, Parmesan, salt and pepper, until ingredients are incorporated. Stir in onions and asparagus.
- Line bottom of ramekin(s) with bacon pieces. Pour egg mixture over bacon. Arrange reserved asparagus tips on top of the egg mixture and place ramekin on a parchment-lined baking sheet. Bake in oven for 35 to 40 minutes, until center slightly jiggles and top of soufflé is somewhat browned. Serve immediately, before it falls!

122.	Eggs & Hash Browns With Home! Made! Bacon!

Serving: Serves 2-4 | Prep: | Cook: | Ready in:

Ingredients

- 4-6 Eggs
- 4 Yukon Gold potatoes (3-4 c. when cubed)
- 3 Leeks, white and light green parts only
- 1/2 pound fresh bacon, sliced in 1/4 inch thick slabs and then cut again width-wise into 1/4 inch by 1 inch batons
- 1 tablespoon Unsalted butter
- Olive oil
- Salt & pepper to taste

Direction

- In a large skillet over medium-medium high heat, heat 1 Tbsp. olive oil, add the bacon and fry the until the fat has rendered out and your desired crispness level has been achieved. For me, that's on the burnt side. Hell, I've even eaten bacon that has been on fire, who am I kidding? Most people would cook this a little less.
- While your bacon is cooking, chop your potatoes–you're looking for a size somewhere between a store-bought frozen "country-style hash brown" and "country potatoes" in a restaurant–1/2 to 3/4-inch rough cubes.
- After your bacon has crisped, remove to paper towels to drain. Depending on how much fat has rendered out of your bacon, you may need to add some fat to the pan. Add or subtract until you have roughly 3 Tbsp. of fat left in the pan.
- Add the potatoes to the skillet and add salt & pepper to taste. Sautee 5 minutes, stirring frequently to avoid sticking as much as possible.
- While your potatoes are cooking, slice the leeks in 1/4-inch rings. Rinse either under running water or in a water bath, separating rings, until all grit is removed. Drain and add to pan with the potatoes. Cook, stirring often, until leeks are soft and potatoes are crispy in spots on the outside and done in the middle, about 8 minutes more. If your potatoes are sticking too much and look dry, add a little olive oil to loosen things up again. I usually start off with a wooden spoon to stir and then switch to a heavy spatula, as my pan loves to cling to potatoes. That's ok. Just stir frequently and scrape the bottom of the pan as you go. You'll get tasty little curls of crispy potato crust. Taste for seasoning and add if needed.
- Remove to your serving vessel of choice and top with the bacon.
- Turn the heat on your pan down to medium/medium-low and add 1 Tbsp. butter. Crack the eggs in the pan, salt & pepper to taste and cook to your desired doneness.
- Add cooked eggs to the hash browns & bacon and serve. Revel in the bacony, eggy goodness.

123. Eggs+Ham On English Muffins With Greek Goddess Dip And A Radish Salad

Serving: Serves 1 | Prep: | Cook: |Ready in:

Ingredients

- 1 teaspoon Butter or olive oil
- 1   English muffin (whole wheat), split
- 4-6 Ham slivers
- 2   Boiled eggs, peeled, and sliced
- Kosher salt and fresh-ground pepper
- 3 tablespoons Melissa Clark's Greek Goddess Dip (or other dip or dressing)
- 1 cup Sliced mixed fresh vegetables: 3-4 radishes, some zucchini, yellow peppers, cucumber, etc.
- 1/2 teaspoon Sherry vinegar
- 4-6   Cherry tomatoes, sliced

Direction

- Heat the butter or oil in a small skillet over medium flame and place the English muffins in face down along with the ham slivers. Let cook several minutes or until browned and crispy.
- Place the muffins on a plate and add the sliced eggs along with the ham. Sprinkle with salt and pepper. Drizzle with Greek Goddess (or other) dip.
- Add the sliced vegetables to the plate and season with a few grains of salt and pepper. Drizzle with sherry vinegar. Garnish with cherry tomatoes. Serve warm or at room temperature.

124. Enfrijoladas With Chorizo And Greens

Serving: Serves 6 | Prep: | Cook: | Ready in:

Ingredients

- 1 tablespoon olive oil
- 1 bunch (6-8) scallions, thinly sliced
- 2-3 garlic cloves, minced
- 1 jalapeno or serrano peppers, seeded and minced
- 2 teaspoons ground cumin
- 1 teaspoon chili powder
- 1 teaspoon dried oregano
- 2 (15 oz) cans black beans, drained and rinsed
- 3 cups water
- 1 bay leaf
- Salt to taste
- 1 pound Mexican (soft) chorizo
- 3 cups fresh spinach, radish greens, or beet greens
- 12 corn tortillas
- Crumbled queso fresco for garnish (optional)

Direction

- Heat olive oil in a large saucepan over medium heat. Add about 3/4 of the scallions and a pinch of salt, and sweat for about 3 minutes, or until the scallions are translucent. Add garlic, jalapeno or serrano pepper, cumin, chili powder, and oregano, and cook, stirring frequently, for another 30 seconds to a minute, or until the mixture is fragrant. Add beans, water or cooking liquid, bay leaf, and salt, and bring to a boil. Reduce the heat to medium-low, cover, and simmer for 20-30 minutes, or until the beans are very soft and the liquid is richly flavored.
- While the beans are simmering, wash, stem, and roughly chop the greens. Heat a large heavy skillet over medium heat. Add chorizo and the remaining scallions, using a wooden spoon to break up the meat into chunks (it may just flatten into a squishy mass, which is fine). Cook, stirring occasionally, for 10-12 minutes, or until the chorizo is completely cooked through. Add greens, a handful at a time, and continue to cook, stirring frequently, for 3-5 minutes, or until the greens are wilted and tender. Reduce the heat to low and keep warm.
- Once the beans are cooked, remove the bay leaf and discard. Transfer the mixture to a blender (or use an immersion blender) and puree until thick, creamy, and not quite smooth. Return the sauce to the pan and bring it back to a simmer over medium-low heat. Taste and adjust the seasoning; add water as needed to keep the sauce at a thick but still liquid consistency. Reduce the heat to low and keep warm.
- Place a serving platter or deep-sided dish next to the stove. Using a pair of tongs, dip one of the corn tortillas into the warm bean sauce, flipping gently to coat each side. Place the tortilla on the serving platter or dish, and place a spoonful of the chorizo mixture into the center. Fold the tortilla in half over the filling. Repeat with the remaining tortillas.
- Once all of the tortillas are filled and folded, spoon any remaining bean sauce over the top. Garnish with queso fresco (if using). Serve immediately.
- The bean sauce can be prepared ahead of time; it will keep in an airtight container in the fridge for up to 3 days, or in the freezer for up to a month. Make the filling and assemble the enfrijoladas right before serving.

125. Espresso Ancho Dry Rub Ribs

Serving: Makes 4 servings | Prep: | Cook: | Ready in:

Ingredients

- 2.5 -3 pounds baby back ribs
- 2 tablespoons espresso powder
- 2 tablespoons ancho chili powder

- 2 tablespoons hot smoky paprika
- 1 1/2 tablespoons garlic powder
- 1 1/2 tablespoons cumin
- 1 tablespoon dried oregano
- 3 tablespoons kosher salt
- 1 tablespoon black pepper

Direction

- Preheat oven to 250 degrees. Mix together all the spices. You'll have about double what you need. Take the meat out of the fridge about 20 minutes before you cook them to let them come closer to room temp.
- Pat the ribs dry and spread the dry rub all over. Be generous. Cut the ribs so that there are 3 - 4 bones per piece. I ended up with 4 pieces.
- Add water to a deep baking pan, about 1/2 inch high. Place a wire or slotted rack on top of the pan and put ribs on top. Cover the ribs in foil and pop in oven for 4 1/2 hours. Add a cup of water to the bottom of the pan if it ever looks like it's getting low.
- With 30 minutes remaining, remove the foil and finish the ribs uncovered. This will allow the crust on the ribs to really dry up and get crusty as if they were in a smoker.
- Last step, toss them on the grill or grill pan over medium high heat. Get a good char on the outside of those delicious ribs. It will only take about 5 minutes. I serve these ribs without any BBQ sauce, but a good mustard sauce would be a-okay on these babies.

---

126.   Fabada (Asturian Fava Bean Stew)

Serving: Serves 4-6 | Prep: | Cook: | Ready in:

Ingredients

- 1 pound dry fava beans
- 1 pound pork shoulder
- 1/4 pound pancetta or bacon

- 2 pieces morcilla
- 2 pieces chorizo
- 3 cloves garlic, minced
- 1 Spanish onion, diced
- 2 tablespoons olive oil
- 1 handful flat-leaf parsley, for garnish
- 1 piece lemon, for finishing (optional)

Direction

- DO AHEAD: cover beans in water and soak overnight or until tender.
- Add olive oil and garlic to a cold, Dutch oven. Turn heat to medium low. When garlic is translucent, add onion, stir occasionally.
- In a separate large pan over medium heat, add a glug of olive oil and brown bacon. Add to onion mixture with 1/2 of the drippings.
- Time to strain the beans and toss them in with the rest of your pork products. Cover all ingredients with cold water. Bring to a boil and then turn heat down. Cover and simmer for at least an hour.
- Test pork products for doneness. Cut into the morcilla and chorizo to see if they're fully cooked.
- When ready to serve, chop parsley. Cut morcilla and chorizo into quarters and serve a couple pieces in each bowl with some pork shoulder too. Serve the fabada hot, with parsley and slices of lemon for squeezing on top.

---

127.   Fall Apart Mango Habanero Ribs

Serving: Serves 2-3 | Prep: | Cook: | Ready in:

Ingredients

- 1 Rack Pork Loin Baby Back Ribs
- 1.5 cups Home-made or store bought BBQ Sauce
- 2 tablespoons Liquid Smoke
- 1/4 cup Mango Juice

- 1-2 Habaneros - cut in half
- Salt
- Pepper
- 2 teaspoons Garlic Powder
- 2 teaspoons Onion Powder
- 1-2 teaspoons Habanero Powder
- Aluminum Foil

Direction

- Season the ribs with salt, pepper, garlic powder, onion powder, and habanero powder. Make sure to be generous with the seasoning, some will fall off when searing.
- Get a pan really hot and sear both sides of the ribs so that they are a dark brown. I use a big griddle pan that came with my oven, but it works equally well to chop the ribs in half or even 3 pieces if you do not have a pan that is big enough.
- Once each rib is seared, mix the BBQ sauce with liquid smoke, mango juice and habaneros. I've used fresh or canned mango juice and it tastes great either way.
- Place the seared ribs on a large piece of foil. Typically I fold two pieces of foil together before putting the ribs on it. The goal is to make sure that the ribs and sauce are trapped in the foil with no place to escape. I think this is the trick to making them fall off the bone.
- Pour the BBQ sauce mix all over the ribs, make sure they are covered really well. The sauce will thicken when it is cooked.
- Bake ribs in the oven for 1 hour at 375. Turn down the oven to 250 and cook for another 3 hours. No need to check on them, as long as they've got plenty of BBQ they will be perfect when you open them!

128.	Fiendishly Tasty Bacon Turkey Burgers

Serving: Makes 4 burgers | Prep: 0hours20mins | Cook: 1hours0mins | Ready in:

Ingredients

- For the bacon turkey burgers:
- 1 pound thickly sliced peppered bacon
- 1 extra-large yellow or sweet onion
- Salt
- 1 pound ground turkey (about 90% lean)
- 4 pub or brioche hamburger buns
- 4 slices swiss cheese (if they're especially thin slices, double up)
- 4 bun-sized butter lettuce leaves (preferably crisper inner leaves)
- For the smoky burger spread:
- 1/2 cup mayonnaise (homemade is excellent, but store-bought works well)
- 2 tablespoons finely minced pickled peppers (sweet or spicy -- your choice)
- 1 1/2 tablespoons Dijon mustard
- 1/2 teaspoon smoked paprika
- 1/4 teaspoon ground cumin

Direction

- Preheat oven to 400° F, with a rack in the lower middle position. Lay slices of bacon onto a rimmed half-sheet pan without any overlap. Bake the bacon 15 to 18 minutes -- it should be cooked but still a little pliable. Remove the bacon to a paper towel-lined plate. (Do not eat more than one slice!) Pour the bacon fat through a strainer into a jar or other suitable receptacle.
- While the bacon is cooking, prep the onion. Cut the root and leaf ends off, then remove the papery outer skin. Cut the onion in half lengthwise (from cut end to cut end). Cut each half into thin, lengthwise slices.
- Transfer 2 tablespoons of bacon fat into a large sauté pan and heat over medium-low. Add the onions, and stir to coat. Cook over medium-low, stirring occasionally, until golden brown and lightly caramelized. It will take about 45 minutes. Lightly season with salt.
- Combine the burger spread ingredients in a small bowl. Mix until homogenous.
- Coarsely chop or crumble the bacon, and transfer to a food processor. Pulse until finely

chopped. Combine the chopped bacon, ground turkey, and 1 tablespoon bacon fat in a medium bowl. Mix, using your hands, until bacon is well-distributed through the meat. Divide the mixture into 4 equal portions, and form into patties that are about 5/8-inch thick and between 1/2 and 3/4 inch larger in diameter than the buns. Refrigerate if you will be 30 minutes or longer until you grill the burgers. Season the burgers with salt just before cooking them.

- Heat the grill to high, with coals to 1 side if using charcoal. Clean and oil the grates. If using a gas grill turn off one burner. Assemble the burger ingredients. Brush the insides of the bun with a thin layer of bacon fat (or spread it on if the fat has solidified). Grill the burgers over direct heat, for 3 to 4 minutes per side until cooked through. Watch closely and remove the burgers to indirect heat briefly as needed if more than minor "flare-ups" occur. Grill the buns over indirect heat, until lightly toasted, about 3 minutes. When the burgers are a minute or so from being done, apply a slice of cheese to each patty and put the cover on the grill to allow the cheese to soften and start to melt.
- Assemble the burgers: Spread the burger spread on both sides of each bun. Place the patties on the bottom buns. Divide the caramelized onions between the burgers. Cap with the butter lettuce leaves concave side down. Place top buns on. Dig in!

---

129.   Fiery Korean Tofu Soup With Pork Belly And Kimchi

Serving: Serves 1 to 2 | Prep: | Cook: |Ready in:

Ingredients

- It's all about that (soup) base
- 8   dried anchovies (head and guts removed)
- 5 ounces radish (peeled, washed and thinly sliced)
- dried kelp (6 x 4 inch pieces)
- Fiery Paste
- 2 tablespoons Korean hot pepper flakes (gochugaru)
- 1 teaspoon sesame oil
- 1 teaspoon vegetable oil
- 1/2 cup pork belly (cut into small pieces)
- 1/4 cup onion (chopped)
- 1   garlic clove (minced or chopped finely)
- 1   green pepper (roughly chopped)
- 350 grams well-fermented kimchi (chopped)
- 1 pinch salt (to taste, but roughly about 1 teaspoon)
- 1/2 teaspoon sugar
- 1   package soft tofu (cut in medium sized cubes)
- 1   tube silken tofu (cut tube in half)
- 1   egg
- 1 tablespoon soybean paste (doenjang)
- 2 sprigs spring onion (finely chopped)

Direction

- It's all about that (soup) base
- To make the anchovy/kelp stock, place the dried anchovies, radish and dried kelp in a pot and add 4 cups of water. Cover the pot and boil over a medium heat until it starts boiling. Then reduce the heat to the low and boil the stock for another 20 minutes or so. Remove the stock from the heat and strain the stock. Leave this to the side and start making the fiery paste.
- Fiery Paste
- Heat up earthenware pot for a couple of minutes until the pot is hot. Add the vegetable oil, onion and garlic and fry with a wooden spoon until fragrant (about 1 minute, but make sure not to burn the mixture). Add the pork belly and stir until the pork is no longer raw. Add the kimchi, the soybean paste and half of the stock you've made earlier. Cover the pot and cook on medium heat for another 7 or 8 minutes. Add the salt, the sugar and stir well. Add the soft tofu, the silken tofu (squeeze out the two halves of the tube). Gently stir (try not to mush the tofu) and then

add the rest of the pre-made stock. If the pot looks too dry, add a bit of water. Separately mix the hot pepper flakes with some sesame oil in a bowl and then add to the tofu pot that is bubbling away. Crack an egg right before serving and let it sizzle for 1 minute. Add some whole dried chilies. Sprinkle some spring onion over the pot and this little hot pot is ready to be enjoyed!

130. Filipino Adobo A Family Recipe

Serving: Serves 5-6 | Prep: 0hours15mins | Cook: 3hours0mins |Ready in:

Ingredients

- 3/4 kg chicken pieces, skin on
- 1/2 kg pork belly, cubed
- 2 heads of garlic, chopped
- soy sauce
- white or cane vinegar
- whole peppercorns
- bay leaves
- rock salt (optional)

Direction

- Put the chicken and pork in a medium-sized pot with a lid. Add the garlic, peppercorns, and soy sauce and vinegar, which should make enough liquid just to cover some of the meat (some pieces will still be above the liquid and that's ok). There should be twice as much vinegar to the soy sauce. If you're not using soy sauce, salt the meat well and add enough vinegar just to cover. You can also dilute the vinegar just a bit with about 1/4 cup of water. Give the meat mixture a quick but thorough stir.
- Add about 5 bay leaves and then in medium-high heat, bring the adobo to a boil. Turn heat down to low and then cover. Simmer gently until meat is tender (at least an hour, up to

three), and the soy-vinegar mixture has somewhat reduced.

- Turn the heat off and let the adobo rest, covered, at room temperature, until no longer piping hot. You can actually serve the adobo at this point or do as we do and move on to the next step.
- Carefully transfer the chicken and pork (which should be really tender) to a non-stick frying pan this time, but one that's big enough to hold all of the meat in one layer. Pour in a bit of the oil from the first pot and gently fry the adobo over medium heat. The point is to cook the chicken and pork further down to a crisp, turning the pieces once to brown on both sides.
- Once all the meat is done to your liking you can choose to pour the rest of the adobo sauce into the frying pan to heat. Serve with hot rice and enjoy. Or if you are making ahead, cool the adobo before keeping in the fridge and reheat gently on the stove before serving the next day.

131. Flexible Chili

Serving: Serves 6-8 | Prep: | Cook: |Ready in:

Ingredients

- 100 grams chopped bacon (about 6 slices, chopped)
- 4 cloves garlic, minced
- 2 onions, chopped into 1/2 inch cubes
- 2 bell peppers (I usually use one yellow and one green), chopped into 1/2 inch cubes
- 4 tablespoons chili powder (or less, depending on the heat of your chili powder and your taste for heat)
- 1 tablespoon ground cumin
- 1 tablespoon paprika (I like Hungarian paprika, but normal paprika does the trick as well)
- 2 teaspoons dried oregano
- Salt and pepper, to taste

- 500 grams/1 pound ground meat (I usually use ground pork because the only thing cheaper than ground pork in Denmark is snow). You can increase the amount of meat to 750 grams/1 1/2 pounds if you so desire
- 1 cup red wine
- 1 can (400 grams/15 oz.) black beans, rinsed
- 1 can (400 grams/15 oz.) pinto beans, rinsed
- 1 can (400 grams/15 oz.) navy beans, rinsed
- 1 can (400 grams/15 oz.) kidney beans, rinsed
- 3 cans (400 grams/15 oz. each) chopped tomatoes

Direction

- Heat a large heavy-bottomed pan, like a Dutch oven, over medium heat. Add the bacon and cook until brown. Add the garlic, onions, bell peppers, chili powder, cumin, paprika, oregano, salt, and pepper and stir to coat everything with bacon fat at the spices. Cook on medium heat until vegetables start to soften, 5-7 minutes. Don't worry about the spices sticking to the bottom of the pot… the liquid from the meat will help release everything from the pot.
- Make a well in the middle of the pot, pushing the vegetable mixture to the sides of the pan. Add the ground meat and brown the bottom. Then break up the meat with your wooden spoon, mix with the vegetable mixture, and cook until the meat is no longer brown.
- Once the meat is cooked through, add the wine. Turn the heat up to high and, scraping the bottom of the pot and stirring, reduce the liquid by half, about 10 minutes. (If you are making this ahead of time and want to use a crock pot, follow the above instructions up to this step. Then add the cooked meat and vegetable mixture to your crock pot along with the canned tomatoes and rinsed beans. Stir and cook on high for 4 hours or on low for at least 6 hours. Season to taste before serving)
- When the liquid has reduced, add all of the beans and canned tomatoes (with the tomato juice!). Stir to combine everything, lower the heat to low, partially cover, and cook for at least 90 minutes, though longer is better. After 90 minutes, taste and add more salt and pepper if needed.
- Serve with crème fraiche, cheddar cheese, vinegar, and crusty bread on the side.

---

132.   Freedom Pork With Sticky Greens And Mop Sauce

Serving: Serves 4-6 | Prep: | Cook: | Ready in:

Ingredients

- For the pork:
- 3 - 31/4 pounds Boneless Boston-butt
- 1/4 cup dark brown sugar
- 2 tablespoons kosher salt
- 2 pounds collard greens, ends trimmed
- For the mop sauce:
- 1 tablespoon unsalted butter
- 1/2 cup shallots, minced
- 1 1/2 tablespoons minced garlic
- 3/4 cup cider vinegar
- 1/2 cup dry white wine
- 2 teaspoons whole grain Dijon
- 1 teaspoon Dijon
- 2 teaspoons tomato paste
- 2 teaspoons honey
- 1 tablespoon Italian parsley, minced
- 1 tablespoon chives, minced
- 3 tablespoons unsalted butter, cold, cut into small cubes

Direction

- Combine the brown sugar and kosher salt. Mix it well breaking up any clumps of brown sugar. Rub the mix over the entire Boston butt. Set in a container with sides, cover with plastic wrap and place in the fridge for 4 to 6 hours.
- Preheat the oven to 275 degrees. Remove the pork from the fridge and give it a very quick rinse, like one time under from end to end, under cold water and then pat it dry. Place it, fat side up, into an 8 quart enameled Dutch

oven. Place it in the oven. Set the timer for 1 1/2 hours. When the timer sounds off bast the pork roast with the juices. Set the timer for another hour.

- Meanwhile trim the ends of the greens and then roll a bunch up and cut them into 1/2 inch ribbons and then cut the ribbons into half inch squares. I used a salad spinner, but you could use a colander also, but rinse the greens and spin them dry.
- When the timer goes off remove the pork from the oven and place the pork on a plate. Turn the oven to 325 degrees. Place the Dutch oven onto a burner over medium heat. There should be about two tablespoons of fat in the bottom. If there is not add some canola oil. If there is more remove some.
- Add the greens and turn them with some tongs to coat them with the fat. Cook them until they just begin to wilt. Place the pork roast on top of the greens, cover the pot with a lid and place it back into the oven. Set the timer for 50 minutes.
- Place a small sauce pan over medium high heat. When hot add 1 tablespoon of butter. When it melts add the shallot and sauté until they start to soften. Add the garlic and sauté for a minute. Add the wine and let the alcohol burn off. Then add the vinegar, mustards, tomato paste and honey. Simmer until the sauce is thick.
- When the timer goes off remove the pot from the oven. Remove the pork roast to a cutting board. Stir the greens and taste for seasoning. Add salt and pepper if needed. Place the sauce pan over medium low heat and bring to a simmer. Add the parsley and chives. Remove from the heat and whisk in the butter until just melted. Set it aside.
- To serve. Place the greens on a platter. Slice the roast into 1/2 inch thick slices and place attractively on the greens. Serve the sauce on the side.

| 133. | French Toast Kabobs |

Serving: Serves 4 | Prep: | Cook: | Ready in:

Ingredients

- 4 one-inch-thick slices challah
- 2 eggs
- 1/4 cup half-and-half
- 1/4 teaspoon cinnamon
- 1/8 teaspoon nutmeg
- 12   strips thin-sliced bacon
- 4 tablespoons butter
- 4 tablespoons canola oil

Direction

- Cut each challah slice into thirds, and thread lengthwise onto a skewer. Beat eggs, half-and-half and spices, and dip each skewer. Melt butter on a grill pan and fry toast skewers over medium high heat, turning to brown on all four sides. Set aside.
- Fry bacon to done-but-still-limp stage. Drain. When cool enough to handle, wind one bacon strip around each toast skewer, securing with toothpicks if necessary.
- Heat canola oil over high heat in a very shallow pan and give kebabs a final flash-fry (maybe 30 seconds on a side) to crisp everything up.
- Let cool just slightly, so bacon will hold its shape, and remove toothpicks. Serve with honey, syrup or fruit preserves for dipping. (B Side sprinkles theirs with powdered sugar, but I can't bring myself to do it.)

| 134. | Fried Pork Tenderloin Sandwich |

Serving: Makes 4 giant sandwiches | Prep: | Cook: | Ready in:

Ingredients

- 1 to 1 1/4 pounds pork tenderloin, trimmed of excess fat
- 2 cups buttermilk
- 2 large eggs
- 1/4 cup pickle juice (from a jar of dill pickles)
- 2 teaspoons kosher salt
- 1 teaspoon freshly ground black pepper
- 1 cup all-purpose flour
- 1 sleeve soda crackers (about 40 crackers
- peanut oil, for frying
- potato buns (such as Martins)
- Suggested toppings: mayonnaise, dill pickles, tomato, onion

Direction

- Trim the pork tenderloin of any excess fat or silver skin. Cut the pork tenderloin into 4 equal pieces (about 2- to 3-inches in length). Butterfly each piece by slicing almost all of the way through vertically; open the pork like a book and flatten it with your hands on a cutting board. Cover each piece of pork with plastic wrap or wax paper, and pound into a thin cutlet with a meat mallet or heavy frying pan until about 1/4-inch in thickness.
- In a shallow bowl or pan, whisk together the buttermilk, eggs, pickle juice, kosher salt, and pepper. Add the pork (it should be fully submerged in the brine); cover and refrigerate for at least 4 hours or overnight.
- Take the pork out of fridge about 20 to 30 minutes before you plan to fry it. (Frying cold pork will cause the oil to drop in temperature.) Pulse the crackers in a food processor, aiming for a mix of finer and coarser-sized crumbs.
- Set up a breading station by placing the cracker crumbs in a wide, shallow dish, and the flour in another dish. Remove each piece of pork from the brine, letting any excess drip off. Dredge both sides of the pork in the flour, then place back in the buttermilk brine, then fully coat with cracker crumbs.
- Meanwhile, fill a large skillet with high sides with at least one inch of peanut oil and heat to 350 degrees F.

- Place each piece of pork in the skillet (one at a time is recommended) and fry on the first side until golden, about 3 minutes. Carefully flip the pork, and fry on the second side until golden, crispy, and cooked through, another 3 minutes. Drain on paper towels or on a wire cooling rack set over a baking sheet. (You can transfer the fried pork to a baking sheet in a 220 degree F oven to keep it warm while frying the rest.) Make sure the oil is at 350 degrees F before frying each piece of pork.
- Place the fried pork on the buns, garnish with condiments of choice, and serve immediately.

135.   Frugal Moroccan Paella

Serving: Serves 4 | Prep: | Cook: | Ready in:

Ingredients

- olive oil for pan
- 4 small chicken breasts or thighs, skin and bone in
- 1/2 pound chorizo
- 1 red bell pepper, cored and cut into 1/2 inch lengths
- 1 large yellow onion, chopped
- 1 small leek, sliced into rounds
- 6 cloves garlic, peeled, minced
- 2 heirloom tomatoes, grated, skinned, seeded, and drained
- 1/2 cup dry white wine
- 1 teaspoon hot paprika
- 2 teaspoons ground cumin
- 1 teaspoon ground coriander
- 2 teaspoons fresh lemon zest
- fresh milled pepper to taste
- kosher salt to taste
- 4 1/2 cups homemade seasoned chicken broth
- 10 threads of Spanish saffron
- 1 1/2 cups Bomba or other short grain rice
- 10 black mussels, cleaned
- 1/2 pound butternut squash, peeled and cut into long 1/2 inch wide by 6 inch long lengths

- 1 parsnip, peeled and cut into thin long lengths
- 1 small turnip, peeled and cut into thin strip lengths
- 1 small carrot, peeled and coarsely julienned
- 10 ounces chick peas, cooked
- 2 ounces dried apricots, sliced thin
- 1 ounce dried white currants or yellow raisins
- 1 tablespoon hot red pepper flakes
- 2 tablespoons olive oil
- fresh chopped flat leaf parsley and cilantro for garnish
- 8 lemon wedges for garnish

Direction

- Heat the oil in the paella pan. Brown the chicken breasts seasoned with salt and pepper very well with the chorizo. Remove to a plate for later. When cool, cut up the chicken into smaller pieces. Cook the red pepper until limp in the paella pan. Remove that to a plate as well.
- Add the garlic, chopped onions, and leek to the paella pan and saute until translucent. Add the grated tomato to make the sofrito. Cook until it turns darker. Add the wine and reduce until it reaches a compote consistency for the sofrito. Add the paprika, cumin, coriander, and lemon zest. Season with salt and pepper.
- Heat the chicken stock in a sauce pan. Remove a small quantity, a half a cup or less and parboil the squash, turnip, parsnip and carrot in it. Add the saffron and let stand. Pouring the saffron-infused broth back to the sauce pan, set the parboiled vegetables aside. Make sure the broth is seasoned with enough salt and pepper.
- Add the rice to the sofrito base in the paella pan. Distribute the rice evenly in the pan. Arrange all the vegetables, chicken, sausage, mussels, and fruit on top in the pan. Pour 4 1/4 cups of the heated stock on top, reserving the rest for later. Bring to a vigorous simmer on medium high. When the rice reaches the same level as the liquid, about 10 minute,

reduce the heat to medium low. Continue to simmer gently rotating the pan if necessary. When the liquid is absorbed test a grain of rice. It should be al dente with a tiny dot in the center. If it is not quite done, then add the remaining broth to the pan and cook a few more minutes.
- To make the socarrat, increase the heat to medium high and rotate the pan. Cook for about 2 minutes until the bottom layer of rice caramelizes. If you smell burning, remove the pan from heat right away. Then when the rice has become crusty, remove the pan from heat, cover and let rest for about 5 minutes.
- Meanwhile heat a small pan. Add the hot pepper flakes. Add the olive oil and stir. Take off the heat and pour into a tiny bowl. Put this harissa in the center of the paella pan. Add some fresh chopped herbs and lemon wedges around the paella dish and invite your company to the table.

136.   Fuschsia Dunlop's Ma Po Tofu

Serving: Serves 4 | Prep: 15hours0mins | Cook: 15hours0mins |Ready in:

Ingredients

- 1 pound firm tofu cut into cubes
- peanut oil
- 6 ounces ground pork
- 2 garlic cloves minced
- 2 leeks thinly sliced, sans green bits
- 2.5 tablespoons chili bean paste
- 1 tablespoon fermented black beans
- 2 teaspoons Szechuan whole peppers, pounded into coarse powder or ground into finer powder
- 1 cup chicken stock
- 2 teaspoons white sugar
- 2 teaspoons light soy sauce

- 1 tablespoon corn starch dissolved in some water
- 1 scallion diced
- salt to taste

Direction

- Soak the cubes of tofu in some salted hot water.
- While the tofu soaks, pour the oil into a deep skillet or wok over high heat. Stir fry the pork. Turn the heat down a bit and throw in the garlic and leeks. When it starts to smell delicious, add in the chili bean paste, black beans, and Sichuan pepper. Stir the mixture some, and let the flavors meld.
- Pour in the stock.
- Drain the tofu and dump that in ... but don't stir! You'll break up the beautiful cubes. Use the back of your ladle to move the pieces around gently.
- Add the sugar, soy sauce, and salt (if needed). Let the mixture simmer some more (~5 mins).
- Now put in the cornstarch mixture, but bit by bit. You may not need all of it. The sauce should be thick enough to coat the back of your ladle.
- Serve while it's still hot, fresh off the burners, with some white rice, garnished with scallions and a bit more Szechuan pepper powder...if you dare.

---

137.   Giddy Swamp SC Hash

Serving: Makes 6 quarts | Prep: 0hours30mins | Cook: 2hours30mins | Ready in:

Ingredients

- 5 pounds Pork shoulder/Boston butt
- 2 pounds onions peeled and chopped coarsley
- 1 pound potatoes peeled and cut into small dice
- 1 cup cider vinegar
- 9 ounces yellow mustard

- 1 tablespoon salt
- 2 tablespoons black pepper
- 1 teaspoon red pepper flakes
- 1 splash water to cover

Direction

- Cut pork into 2 inch pieces (include whole bones if available)
- Cover with water by 2 inches and bring to rolling boil for 3 minutes.
- Drain meat discarding water and rinse to remove grey blood scum.
- Return meat to pressure cooker, add water to cover by two inches, close lid and bring to pressure for 20 minutes.
- Release pressure. Remove and discard bones. Add onions. Cover cooker and bring back to pressure for 15 minutes.
- Release pressure. At this point you have several options. You can use an immersion blender, food processor or blender to grind meat and onions into a slurry like consistency. There may still be identifiable pieces of meat left but they will continue to cook down in the final cooking.
- Add potatoes, vinegar, mustard, salt, pepper and red pepper flakes and continue to cook on low heat for at least another hour or two. Continue to stir occasionally and add water when it appears too thick.
- Check seasonings after first hour... you might have to add more vinegar. Hash should have a sharp bite and the black pepper should be pronounced. Add butter for the last hour. I know it seems strange, but the butter gives a slick texture to the hash that it needs. (And my original recipe would call for a pound of butter).
- Serve over white rice or toast with a side of greens or cole slaw; as a side dish to BBQ ribs, chicken or pulled pork; or on a toasted bun, like a hash sloppy joe.

138.   Gingery Congee With Pork And Crispy Shallots

Serving: Serves 4 | Prep: | Cook: | Ready in:

Ingredients

- Gingery Congee
- 1 chicken drumstick
- 1 tablespoon vegetable oil
- 1/2 pound ground pork, 1/3 for congee, 2/3 for topping
- 2 slices of fresh ginger
- 2 cups cooked rice (almost any type)
- 3-4 cups water
- salt
- 8 napa cabbage leaves, sliced
- Pork and Crispy Shallots
- 4 teaspoons soy sauce
- 1 teaspoon cooking sherry or rice wine
- 1/2 teaspoon brown sugar
- 2/3 of the 1/2 lb of ground pork listed above
- 4-5 tablespoons vegetable oil
- 4 shallots, sliced thinly
- 1 clove garlic, minced
- 1 green onion, sliced thinly

Direction

- Gingery Congee
- Put large pot on medium to high heat. Add chicken thigh and brown (you can also just use chicken stock instead of including the thigh).
- Add oil and about 1/3 of ground pork and ginger slices. Fry until pork browns.
- Add 3 cups water and rice and about 1/2 tsp salt. Stir to mix.
- Heat to boiling, then turn to simmer. Cook for ~30 minutes on a simmer, stirring the pot occasionally to prevent sticking. In the meantime, prepare the toppings.
- Pork and Crispy Shallots
- Add 2 tsp soy sauce, sherry, and sugar to the remaining pork. Mix together well (hands work well here).
- Add oil to medium size pan or wok.

- When oil is very hot, add about 1/3-1/2 of the shallots. Fry until deep brown and crispy. Using a slotted spoon remove shallots and drain oil from them back into the pan. Then place shallots on paper towels. Repeat with remaining shallots.
- Once all shallots have been fried, add green onions and garlic to the remaining oil.
- Add pork and toss around the pan. Cook meat through.
- Add 2 tsp of soy sauce and 1 Tbsp. of water. Mix and let liquid reduce slightly. Remove to a bowl.
- Add napa cabbage and 1/2 cup more water to congee. Stir and simmer about 10-15 minutes or until the rice is done to your desired consistency.
- For serving, ladle congee into bowls. Add pork and shallots on top, serving the remaining on the side.

139.   Gramma Russo's Gravy

Serving: Serves a big family | Prep: | Cook: | Ready in:

Ingredients

- 1 pound Boneless Pork Country Style Ribs
- 1 pound Hot Italian Sausage
- 1 pound Sweet Italian Sausage
- 1 tablespoon Olive Oil
- 1/2 cup Yellow Onion/small dice
- 1/4 cup Shredded Carrot
- 1 tablespoon Tomato Paste/Concentrated style paste in a tube such as Amore or Cento
- 1 cup Italian Red Wine
- 3 15 ounce cans tomato sauce
- 15 ounces Beef Stock
- 1 tablespoon Dried Oregano
- 1 teaspoon Dried Fennel Seeds/Anise
- Salt and pepper to taste
- Red Pepper Flakes to taste
- 2 Dried Bayleaves

Direction

- In a large stock pot, heat olive oil on medium high. When oil is hot add the Boneless Pork Country Style Ribs and the Sweet and Hot Italian Sausage. Cook on medium high heat until nicely browned.
- Once meat is browned add the diced onion and shredded carrot. Cook until onion is just becoming soft and translucent.
- Add tomato paste, working it around the pan with the other ingredients, cooking the paste for a 2-3 minutes
- Turn the heat up just a touch to make sure the pan is hot and add the wine. *NOTE: You should always cook with a wine you would like to drink. * The wine should bubble up and steam. Using a wooden spoon stir and scrape up the brown bits on the bottom of the pan left over from browning the meat and cooking the tomato paste. Allow to bubble for 3-4 minutes.
- Add 3 x 15 ounce cans of tomato sauce. Fill 2 of the empty cans with water and add to pan. Fill the third empty can with beef stock and add to pan.
- Stir in remaining ingredients (all the spices and herbs).
- With heat turned up, let this boil with the lid on for approximately 1/2 hour. Keep an eye on it, you want a pretty good boil going without boiling over.
- Reduce the heat to low and let simmer for a few hours. Take the lid off the pot and let the gravy reduce to the consistency you and your family like. My Gramma Russo started this in the wee hours of the morning and let it simmer almost all day. The house was full of the savory smell by the time sat down to the mid-afternoon Sunday meal. *NOTE: If the gravy gets too thick, add some liquid. If it's too thin, let it reduce a bit. This is the beauty of true old fashioned Italian Spaghetti Gravy. It's an all-day affair.*The Pork Ribs should fall apart in the gravy but if they need some help, just pull them apart using two forks.
- Serve over your favorite pasta. Or just dip in with some crusty bread.

Serving: Serves 4 | Prep: | Cook: |Ready in:

Ingredients

- 2 pounds Pork Loin, Cut Into 1-inch Pieces
- 1 Large Onion, Finely Chopped
- 1 14.5 oz Can Diced Tomatoes
- 2 Green Peppers, Seeded and Cut into 1/2 Inch Strips
- 4 tablespoons Salted Butter
- 1/2 teaspoon Hot Hungarian Paprika
- 1 pinch Salt (to taste)
- 1/4 teaspoon Caraway Seeds, crushed w-back of spoon
- 1/2 cup Water

Direction

- In 3 qt covered flame-proof casserole, sauté onion in butter over medium-high until it wilts (about 3 minutes.) Remove from pan and place in a large bowl.
- Return pan to stove-top and add the pork. Cook until pork is browned on all sides, then remove the pork from the casserole and add to the bowl with the onions.
- Add 1/2 cup water to pan and scrape-up the juices and cooking detritus.
- Add the salt, paprika and caraway seeds. Stir. Put meat and onions back into casserole, then add enough water to just-barely cover the meat. Simmer on low, covered for 30 minutes.
- Add green pepper strips, tomatoes and their juices to casserole. Cover and simmer for an additional 60 minutes, adding water whenever needed, to keep the meat just barely covered with sauce.
- Remove from heat, let cool and skim fat from surface of the sauce. Taste and correct

seasonings to taste. (A pinch of red pepper flakes can kick this up a notch!)

- Place spaetzle or egg noodles in bottom of individual bowls, then spoon the stew over these and enjoy.

---

141.   Grandy's Sausage Stuffing

Serving: Makes one 10 x 14- inch casserole dish, plus 5 cups for stuffing the turkey | Prep: 0hours10mins | Cook: 1hours30mins | Ready in:

Ingredients

- For the sage sausage
- 2 1/2 pounds ground pork shoulder, chilled (or any mix of cuts that is 70% lean to 30% fat)
- 1   tablespoon plus 1 teaspoon kosher salt
- 2 teaspoons freshly ground black pepper
- 1 1/2 teaspoons dried sage, ground
- 1 splash white wine (about 1/8 cup)
- 1/4 cup ice water
- For the stuffing
- 1 pound sliced white sandwich bread (the cheaper the better!), cut into 1/2-inch cubes
- 1/2 cup (1 stick) unsalted butter, cut into pieces
- 3   medium yellow onions, chopped
- 1/2 pound button mushrooms, sliced thin
- 4   large celery ribs, chopped
- 3   green bell peppers, cored and diced
- 4   cloves garlic, minced
- 1 teaspoon kosher salt (you may want to adjust this is you're using a particularly salty stock)
- 2 1/2 pounds sage sausage (recipe above)
- 1 cup chicken or turkey stock

Direction

- For the sage sausage
- A note before starting: Make sure your pork is cold! Meat binding breaks down at 64° F, so if the meat gets warm, it's going to be a lot

harder to make it bind together, and your sausage will be a crumbly mess.

- TO MAKE THE SAUSAGE IN A STAND MIXER: Place the ground pork shoulder in the bowl of an electric mixer fitted with a paddle attachment. Turn the mixer to the lowest speed and add the salt, pepper, and sage. Mix for exactly 1 minute (set a timer!), then add the white wine and mix for another timed minute, then add the ice water (just the water, not the ice) and mix for one more timed minute.
- TO MAKE THE SAUSAGE BY HAND: Add the pork and spices to a large bowl and knead the meat like you would knead bread, for about 5 minutes, until the mixture is tacky. Add the wine and the water and continue to knead until the surface is no longer outwardly wet -- about 1 more minute. The sausage should resist slightly when you try to pull a chunk out. A good way to test if the sausage is done is to take a medium-sized piece of it and stick it to the palm of your hand. If the mixture stays stuck to your palm for 10 seconds when you hold your palm up in the air, you're good to go!
- For the stuffing
- Pre-heat oven to 350° F and lay the bread cubes out in an even layer on two baking sheets. Bake until bread has dried out, rotating sheets halfway through—about 10 to 12 minutes.
- Melt butter in a large skillet and add onions, mushrooms, celery, bell peppers, garlic, and salt. Cook until onions are translucent and the mushrooms and peppers are soft. Set aside to cool.
- Once the vegetables have cooled enough to handle, transfer them to a very large bowl and add the toasted bread cubes and sausage to the bowl. Roll your sleeves up and mush the mixture together with clean hands, until everything is mixed evenly throughout (this was my favorite part as a kid).
- Reserve 5 cups of sausage for stuffing your turkey. Transfer the remaining stuffing to a large casserole dish (10 x 14 inch, or 2 quarts), cover with aluminum foil, and bake on the

middle rack of the oven for 40 minutes, basting with chicken stock every 20 minutes or so.

- After 40 minutes, uncover the pan and roast until internal temperature reaches 140° F, about 25 more minutes (if you aren't sure about the quality of your pork, cook it until the internal temperature is 160° F).
- Stuff your turkey with the remaining 5 cups of sausage. Cook your stuffed bird until the thickest part of the inner-thigh reads 175° F — the stuffing should reach at least 140° F.

---

142. Greek Meatballs In Spiced Tomato Sauce

Serving: Serves 4 | Prep: | Cook: | Ready in:

Ingredients

- Meatballs
- 10 ounces ground pork
- 10 ounces ground beef
- 2.5 ounces panko breadcrumbs
- 1 handful fresh parsley, finely chopped (extra to garnish)
- 2 cloves garlic, minced
- ½ medium white onion, grated
- 1 egg
- ¾ teaspoons ground cumin
- ½ teaspoons ground cinnamon
- ½ teaspoons ground paprika
- 1½ teaspoons kosher salt
- ½ teaspoons ground black pepper
- 1 tablespoon light olive oil, for greasing
- Tomato Sauce
- 2 tablespoons light olive oil
- ½ medium white onion, finely chopped
- 2 cloves garlic, minced
- 1 15-ounce can diced tomatoes
- 3 tablespoons tomato paste
- ½ teaspoons dried thyme
- 1 pinch ground cinnamon
- ½ teaspoons ground cumin
- ½ teaspoons paprika
- 1 bay leaf
- 1 teaspoon sugar
- ½ teaspoons kosher salt
- ½ teaspoons ground black pepper
- 1 handful chopped parsley, to serve
- 1 splash extra-virgin olive oil, to serve

Direction

- Begin by preparing the tomato sauce. Heat 2 tablespoons of light olive oil in a medium saucepan, add the onion and then gently fry over a medium heat for about ten minutes, or until they are soft. Add the garlic and fry for another few minutes. Add the rest of the ingredients, stir well and cover. Leave to simmer for 20 minutes.
- Place all the ingredients for the meatballs in a large bowl and mix them together with your hands. Lightly grease a large baking tray with a light olive oil and, roll meat into about 20 1-oz balls and transfer them to the tray.
- Preheat the oven to 425F. Brush the meatballs with a little more olive oil and then pop them in the oven and cook for around 10-12 minutes, turning frequently, until they are browned.
- Add the meatballs to the tomato sauce and simmer for 5 minutes so the meat absorbs the flavors of the sauce.
- Just before serving, sprinkle with some chopped parsley and a drizzle of extra virgin olive oil.

---

143. Green Chile And Chorizo Potato Pancakes

Serving: Serves 2 | Prep: | Cook: | Ready in:

Ingredients

- 1 large Russett potato
- 1/4 pound chorizo (I use 1/2 of a large link)
- 1 Jalapeno pepper

- 1/2 Anaheim, Poblano, or Hatch chile
- 2 tablespoons sour cream
- 1 large egg
- 1 tablespoon flour
- 1 good squeeze of lemon juice

Direction

- Boil potato until cooked through--about 25 minutes depending on size. Remove from water, let cool, and peel. Put in refrigerator for up to three days.
- Cook chorizo in a pan. I like the sausage to be in small bits so when it is cooked I run it over with a pastry cutter until it is almost in crumbles. Can be put aside in fridge overnight.
- Finely chop chiles. Add to pan with chorizo fat and sauté until softened, 4-6 minutes. Mix with chorizo (make sure both chorizo and chiles are the same temperature if you are going to put them in the fridge. If using immediately you can add hot chiles to cool sausage).
- Everything until this point can be done in advance.
- Grate cold potato over paper towels. Squeeze lemon juice over grated potatoes and let sit for a minute. I find that cold potatoes don't give off nearly as much water as warm.
- Put grated potatoes in large bowl. Stir in sour cream, egg, and flour until well mixed. Add salt and pepper to taste. Stir in chorizo and chile mixture.
- Add oil to chorizo fat (if still available) until pan is well coated. I use vegetable oil that was used to fry chicken, but think that any vegetable or canola oil is preferable to olive oil here. Heat oil.
- Form potato mixture into small pancakes (should make 5-8), compacting the pancakes so they stick together, and add to the pan in small batches. Fry pancakes until golden brown turning only once--1-3 minutes per side depending on your stove.

- Let pancakes drain on a paper towel. Serve warm with a dollop of sour cream and your favorite hot sauce.

---

144.   Green Curry With Eggplant, Bacon And Cashews

Serving: Serves 4 | Prep: | Cook: | Ready in:

Ingredients

- Curry Paste
- 1 tablespoon coriander seeds
- 1 teaspoon cumin seeds
- 2 cardamom pods
- 1/2 teaspoon curry powder
- 1 poblano pepper
- 1 serrano pepper
- 1 jalapeno
- 1 large sweet onion
- 9 cloves of garlic
- 3-4 wide strips of lime zest
- 3 tablespoons brown sugar
- Everything Else
- 1 1/2 cups cashews
- 1 medium eggplant
- 1/4 cup salt
- 3 strips of bacon
- 1 14 oz can of coconut milk
- 1 1/2 teaspoons fish sauce
- 2 tablespoons lime juice

Direction

- Begin charring your poblano in a cast iron skillet over medium-high heat, turning the pepper occasionally so it is cooked on all sides. This will take about ten minutes. The skin of the poblano should look blistery and blackened in some places (you might want to open a window). Once done, let the poblano cool on your cutting board.
- While the poblano cooks, place your cashews in a small bowl and cover with water. Let them soak for about fifteen minutes until

softened a bit. Once softened, drain the cashews. Heat up one tablespoon of veggie oil in a cast iron skillet and stir fry your cashews for about five minutes or until they gain a bit of color. Set these aside.

- Peel your eggplant and chop into one inch cubes. Place these in a colander set over a bowl. Cover evenly with salt and let sit for about fifteen minutes. This will suck some of the moisture and bitterness out of the eggplant. Then rinse off salt and set aside.
- Place cardamom pods, cumin seeds and coriander seeds in a grinder. Pulse until smooth.
- Chop poblano, serrano, jalapeno and onion roughly and place these in the bowl of a food processor. Add lime zest, garlic, brown sugar, curry powder and other ground spices in food processor. Blend until smooth. This is your curry paste.
- Cook your bacon until crispy. I used a cast iron Dutch oven, but a big pot would also work. Remove the bacon and let it cool on your cutting board.
- Add your curry paste to the bacon grease and heat for a few minutes over medium-high heat until boiling lightly.
- Add coconut milk about a third at a time, stirring. Let the mixture heat up in between adding the coconut milk. You should see some oil separating on top of the curry.
- Continue stirring occasionally but reduce the heat to medium-low.
- Toss in eggplant and cook until it is as soft as you like. I let my eggplant cook for about ten minutes which resulted in very soft pieces. If you want crispy eggplant chunks then stir fry them in a tablespoon or two of veggie oil, in a separate pan- then add them when your curry is finished.
- Stir in fish oil.
- Once eggplant is cooked stir in cashews, chopped up bacon pieces and lime juice. Remove from heat and let sit for five minutes. Serve with rice and garnish with left over bacon, cashews, cilantro or basil.

---

145. Green Eggs And Ham Quiche

Serving: Serves 8 | Prep: | Cook: | Ready in:

Ingredients

- Pie Crust
- 1 2/3 cups All Purpose Flour
- Pinch salt
- Pinch Sugar
- 2 tablespoons Chives, Chopped
- 8 tablespoons butter
- 1   Egg plus One Egg Yolk
- 2-3 tablespoons Ice Water
- Quiche Filling
- 1 tablespoon Unsalted Butter
- 2 tablespoons Olive Oil
- 2   Garlic Cloves, minced
- 1   Leek, Chopped, white and light green parts only
- 2   Scallions, chopped
- 2 cups Baby or Regular Spinach, chopped
- 1/4 teaspoon Nutmeg, Freshly Grated
- 2 ounces Proscuitto, chopped
- 4   Eggs
- 1 1/2 cups Heavy Cream
- 1/2 teaspoon Kosher Salt
- 1/4 teaspoon Freshly Ground Pepper
- 1/2 cup Italian Fontina, Grated

Direction

- First make pie dough: In a food processor pulse flour, salt, sugar, and chives. With machine running add butter 1 tablespoon at a time. Then add egg and egg yolk. Add water a tablespoon at a time until dough just comes together. Pat into a disc, wrap in plastic wrap and refrigerate until firm.
- Roll out dough to 1/8 inch thick and fit into a 10 inch deep dish tart pan. Cut away excess dough. Prick bottom with a fork. Put in freezer until firm. Preheat oven to 400 degrees. Line the tart with parchment and fill with pie

weights. Bake for 15 minutes until the edges are starting to brown. Take off parchment and pie weights and cook for another 10 minutes. Set aside to cool.

- In a large pan heat butter and 1 tablespoon olive oil over medium heat. Add garlic, leeks, and scallions and sauté until softened. Add spinach and cook until just wilted. Stir in nutmeg. Transfer mixture to food processor and puree.

- In another pan heat remaining tablespoon olive oil and add prosciutto until crisp. Drain on paper towels.

- In a large bowl whisk together eggs, cream, salt, pepper, and spinach puree. Stir in prosciutto. In the bottom of the tart pan sprinkle the fontina evenly. Pour in the egg filling. Bake for 30 minutes until slightly puffed. Let quiche rest for about 15 minutes before cutting. Enjoy!

146. Grilled Autumn Pizza

Serving: Makes 1 pizza | Prep: | Cook: | Ready in:

Ingredients

- 1 store bought medium thick pizza crust
- olive oil
- 3 ounces pancetta
- 1/2 cup sliced yellow onion
- 1 pinch sage leaf
- 2 tablespoons butter
- 1 apple (sliced thin)
- 1/2 pound smoked gouda cheese
- shredded mozzarella
- shredded parmesan
- honey to taste

Direction

- Place onions and pancetta with 2 tablespoons of butter and a pinch of sage leaf in a skillet. Sauté the onions until they are caramelized.

-) Olive oil your pizza crust on both sides. Sprinkle mozzarella on the crust first. Then place your caramelized pancetta/ onion mixture on top of the mozzarella cheese. We dumped the wonderful grease from the skillet right on the pizza. A little grease won't hurt anyone! After all, it's where all the flavor lives!

- Now crumble some of the smoked gouda on top of the onions/ pancetta. Place your thinly sliced apples on next. We did not use the whole apple, just enough slices to cover the pizza. Put more of your crumbled Gouda on top of the apples. Drizzle honey on top.

- Place that pretty autumn festive pizza on the grill and cook until crispy. We used an electric GMG wood pellet grill and grilled on 400 degrees for about 20 minutes or so.

147. Grilled Pears With Arugula, Prosciutto And Balsamic Reduction

Serving: Serves 8 | Prep: | Cook: | Ready in:

Ingredients

- 7 ounces baby arugula
- 10 seckel pears or any other tiny variety, about 12oz
- 5 ounces prosciutto, shaved
- 4 ounces pecorino romano, shaved
- 3/4 cup aged balsamic vinegar
- Salt and pepper
- Extra-virgin olive oil

Direction

- Put the balsamic in a small skillet or sauce pan, and bring to boil over medium heat. Lower the heat and simmer until reduced to about a third of the original volume.

- Cut the pears in quarters and remove the center. Light a grill or preheat a broiler. Brush the pears with oil. Season with salt and pepper. Grill over high heat, cut sides up, until lightly charred, about 7 minutes. Let cool.

- Place a layer of arugula on individual plates. Top with prosciutto, pears, and pecorino. Drizzle with olive oil, and again season with pepper. Spoon the balsamic reduction on top and serve immediately.

148. Grilled Pizza With Figs, Prosciutto, Gorgonzola And Arugula Pesto

Serving: Serves 6-8 | Prep: | Cook: | Ready in:

Ingredients

- 1 small garlic clove
- 2 cups arugula leaves, tightly packed
- 1/4 cup toasted walnuts
- 1/3 cup extra virgin olive oil
- salt and pepper, to taste
- 1 pound pizza dough
- 6 fresh black figs
- olive oil (for grilling)
- 4 ounces gorgonzola crumbles
- 4 ounces prosciutto, thinly sliced

Direction

- Mince the garlic clove in a food processor until fine. Add arugula leaves, walnuts, and a bit of the olive oil and process, continuing to drizzle in olive oil until a pesto texture is achieved. Add salt and pepper to taste and set aside.
- Spread or roll pizza dough to the desired thickness and set aside to rest a few minutes.
- Slice off stems of figs and cut into quarters. Brush lightly with olive oil and grill over medium high heat until grill marks appear, about 3 minutes. Remove to a plate and set aside.
- Brush pizza dough lightly with olive oil and place oiled side down on the grill. Cook over medium low heat until first side is lightly browned, about5-8 minutes, checking every

couple of minutes for bubbles that need to be popped in the crust.

- Flip crust over to the other side, and spread crust with most of the arugula pesto. Layer with prosciutto slices and place grilled figs on top. Sprinkle Gorgonzola crumbles over the top and dot with remaining arugula pesto, and continue to grill until the crust is fully cooked and the cheese has melted, about 5-10 minutes. (If the crust is becoming too dark on the bottom but isn't cooked through, move the pizza to a side of the grill that is turned off and allow it to cook from indirect heat from the remaining side that is turned on.)
- When pizza is cooked through and cheese has melted, remove from the grill and slice and serve.

149. Grilled Pork Tenderloin With Pickled Blackberries And Shallot

Serving: Serves 4-6 | Prep: | Cook: | Ready in:

Ingredients

- 1.5 lb. Pork tenderloin
- 1 Pint blackberries
- 1 Large shallot, sliced
- 1/2 c. White wine vinegar
- 1 T. Sugar
- Kosher salt & pepper
- Olive oil

Direction

- Rub a grill pan with a tablespoon or two of olive oil, so that it's nicely coated. Bring the pan to high heat and season the pork with salt and pepper.
- Once the pan is searing hot, add the tenderloin. Turn it over on each of its four sides for about five minutes per side.
- While the pork tenderloin is cooking, add the blackberries, sliced shallot, white wine

vinegar, and sugar to a sauce pan. Turn the heat on high until the vinegar begins to boil. Reduce the heat to medium and let the berries and shallot simmer for five minutes. Remove the pan from heat.

- Once the pork is grilled on all sides, let it rest for about five minutes before cutting into it. Meanwhile, drain all of the liquid from the sauce pan. To serve, slice a few pieces of tenderloin and top them with the pickled blackberries and shallot. Season with any additional salt and pepper to taste.

150.   Grilled Pork Tenderloin With Roasted Red Pepper Sauce

Serving: Serves 4 | Prep: | Cook: | Ready in:

Ingredients

- 1 1/4- pounds pork tenderloin
- Sea salt and freshly ground pepper
- 1 tablespoon butter
- 1 cloves garlic, peeled
- 2 ounces Pecorino cheese
- 1/4 cup toasted pumpkin seeds
- 1 roasted red bell pepper, (fresh or from a jar), peeled and seeded
- 1 teaspoon Sherry vinegar
- 1 teaspoon paprika
- Pinch cayenne
- 1/4 cup extra virgin olive oil

Direction

- Preheat the oven to 400°F or the grill to medium high heat. Season the pork with salt and pepper.
- If cooking in the oven, heat a large ovenproof skillet over medium-high heat. Add the butter. Add the pork to the skillet. Cook until browned, 3 to 5 minutes. Turn and repeat until browned on all sides. Transfer to the oven and cook until a thermometer inserted into the center reaches 135°F, about 20 minutes.

Transfer to a cutting board and let sit for 5 minutes.

- If grilling, put the pork on the grill over direct heat, cover and cook for 6 minutes. Turn, cover and cook for 6 minutes. Turn again, cover and cook 6 more minutes. Until a thermometer inserted into the center reaches 135°F. Transfer to a cutting board and let sit for 5 minutes.
- While the pork is cooking, put the garlic in a food processor and pulse until chopped. Add the pecorino and pulse until finely chopped. Add the pumpkin seeds and pulse until finely chopped. Scrape down the sides with a spatula. Add the pepper, vinegar, paprika and cayenne. Pulse until almost smooth. With the machine running, gradually add the olive oil. Season to taste with salt.
- Slice the pork and arrange on a platter. Serve with the red pepper sauce on the side.
- To roast a pepper: Place the red pepper under the broiler and cook until the skin begins to brown. Turn and cook until all of the sides are browned. When it's cooked on all sides, put in a plastic bag and seal it. Let rest 20 minutes before peeling.

151.   Grilled Shrimp & Bacon Wrapped Pineapple Skewers

Serving: Serves 4 | Prep: | Cook: | Ready in:

Ingredients

- 1 pound Large Shrimp
- 1 Pineapple peeled and cut into 2 inch cubes
- 10 slices thick cut bacon
- 1/4 teaspoon Garlic Powder
- 1/4 teaspoon Onion Powder
- 1/4 teaspoon Chili Powder
- 1/4 teaspoon Dried Chipotle Powder
- 1/2 teaspoon Smoked Paprika

Direction

- Combine spices for seasoning and set aside. Soak skewers in a large bowl with water for 20 minutes to 1 hour.
- Wrap 1 piece of bacon tightly around each piece of pineapple. Working on a hot grill, lay a piece of aluminum foil down and arrange bacon wrapped pineapple on the foil. Make sure to lay them with the seam side down, so as the bacon cooks it adheres to itself and stays in place.
- Dust each piece of shrimp with the seasoning mixture and arrange 3 or 4 on a skewer, being careful not to over crowd the skewer. Stretch the shrimps out slightly so each part cooks evenly. Lay on the hot grill and cook until the meat turns pink, about 2 minutes on each side.
- Once the bacon is fully cooked, arrange 1 shrimp and 1 pierce of bacon wrapped pineapple on a skewer to serve.

---

152. Gyoza Dumplings: The Pretty Feed

Serving: Makes 40-50 | Prep: | Cook: | Ready in:

Ingredients

- 4 tablespoons rice vinegar
- 4 tablespoons soy sauce
- 2 garlic cloves pressed of finely chopped
- 1 teaspoon finely chopped or grated ginger
- 1 green onion finely sliced
- 1 teaspoon sesame oil
- 1/4 teaspoon chili flakes
- 1 pound of pork
- 1 tablespoon of minced garlic
- 1 head of napa cabbage
- 1 teaspoon grated ginger
- 3 minced scallions

Direction

- Make sure you chop the cabbage as small as you can (use of food processor if needed). Then salt it and let it sit for 15 minutes.

Squeeze it in a towel to wring out ALLLLL excess moisture. This is an arm workout. As for the ratio of meat to cabbage, technically it's up to you, but we've found that we use about a pound of cabbage for every pound of pork. Combine ginger, garlic, scallions, cabbage and pork in a bowl using your hands. Work the ingredients together to help release all of the flavors.

- Place about a tsp of your filling into the 'wrapper' and dampen the edges of it with water. Then use your index finger and thumb to crimp the edged together and seal the gyoza. Honestly, this part is the fun part! We are definitely not experts at this, but we had a great time laughing at the failed ones and pointing out our favorites. This is a case where you just need to practice. Once this is done, place the finished gyoza's on the parchment paper. If you want to freeze some, use another tray with parchment paper and place the whole thing in the freezer. Let them harden so they maintain their shape and then transfer them into a ziplock bag or container.
- For the sauce, all you have to do is whisk everything together. You can also just dip it in soy sauce or tamari. We usually prepare the sauce first so that the flavors have time to really develop.

---

153. Hachis A La Turque

Serving: Serves 6-8 | Prep: | Cook: | Ready in:

Ingredients

- 8 ounces butter, divided
- 3 tablespoons olive oil, divided
- 4 sprigs fresh thyme
- 6 medium yellow onions
- salt (to taste)
- 5 large sweet potatoes, cut in 1/4 inch slices
- 5 large russet potatoes, cut in 1/4 inch slices
- 3 garlic cloves, minced
- 1/2 pound ground pork

- 1/2 pound ground beef
- pepper (to taste)
- 1 small red pepper, diced
- 1 1/2 teaspoons herbes de Provence/ Provence herbs (dried)
- 1/4+1/8 teaspoons ground cinnamon, divided
- 1/4 teaspoon ground cumin
- 1/8-1/4 teaspoons hot chili pepper flakes
- 1/4 cup toasted pine nuts
- 1/4 cup fresh parsley, chopped
- 1 egg, beaten
- 1/2 cup heavy cream
- 1-2 tablespoons low sodium chicken broth
- 8 ounces goat cheese crumbles
- 1 cup swiss cheese, gratted
- 1/2 cup shaved (or shredded) parmesan
- 3/4 cup roasted and unsalted pistachio nut meat, ground to a coarse grind
- 1/4 teaspoon dried sweet basil
- 1/4 teaspoon garlic powder

Direction

- Slice the onions in half lengthwise and then in thin slices. In a large skillet, on medium-low heat, melt 2 tablespoons of butter with 1 tablespoon of olive oil. Add the thyme sprigs to the melted butter, and add the onion slices. Add a couple pinches of salt and pepper (to taste). Stir to coat the onion slices with the butter. Simmer uncovered for 30 minutes, allowing the onions to turn "brown" in color but stirring them occasionally to prevent burning. Remove the skillet from the heat and transfer the caramelized onions to a bowl. Set aside.
- Wash, peel, and slice the sweet potatoes and the potatoes. In a medium saucepan, add water to cover the sweet potatoes slices by about 1-2 fingers. Bring the water to a boil. Lower the heat to medium, making sure to maintain the water at a low boil, until the sweet potatoes are fork tender, about 30 minutes. Repeat in a different pot/saucepan with the potato slices.
- While the potatoes and the sweet potatoes cook, chop the garlic. In the skillet previously used to caramelize the onions, heat 2 tablespoons of olive oil on medium heat. Add the chopped garlic. When the garlic becomes fragrant, add the ground pork and the ground beef to the pan, breaking the meat in small chunks with a wooden spoon. Add salt and pepper to taste. As the meat begins to brown, add the chopped red pepper, the herbes de provence, 1/4 teaspoon of the cinnamon, the cumin, and the hot chili pepper flakes. Stir well until the spices are well incorporated into the meat. Cook the meat about 5 minutes, until fully browned. Remove the meat from the heat, add the pine nuts and the chopped parsley to the meat mixture, and set aside to cool for 5 minutes. Once cooled, in a separate bowl, beat the egg and add it to the meat mixture. Stir well to distribute the egg evenly.
- Preheat the oven to 350 degrees Fahrenheit.
- Drain the potatoes. Add them back to the empty pot where they were cooked. Mash them coarsely, adding 2 tablespoons of butter to the potatoes as you mash them. Add the heavy cream until you reach the consistency you like. Add the garlic powder, salt and pepper to the potatoes. Set aside.
- Drain the sweet potatoes. Add them back to the empty pot where they were cooked. Mash them coarsely, adding butter as you mash. Add the chicken broth (or water if you prefer) to the sweet potatoes until the sweet potatoes reach your preferred consistency. Add 1/8 teaspoon of cinnamon and salt and pepper to taste. Set aside.
- Spray a large casserole dish with butter, or use 1 tablespoon of butter to butter its sides. Start by spreading the sweet potato mash in an even layer at the bottom of the pan. Sprinkle the goat cheese crumbles evenly on top of the sweet potatoes. Make another layer on top of the goat cheese using half of the caramelized onions. Add the meat mixture on top, and then cover the meat layer with the remaining half of the caramelized onions. Finish with the mashed potato layer.

- In a separate mixing bowl, prepare the crumble topping. Add the Swiss, the parmesan, the ground pistachio meat and the basil to the mixing bowl. Stir well to mix. Sprinkle the topping evenly throughout the top of the mashed potato layer.
- Bake in a preheated oven for 30 minutes. Remove from the oven when the topping is "golden" and the cheese is melted. Cool for 10 minutes before serving. Serve hot.
- (Accompany with a Belgian endive and pomegranate salad with balsamic vinaigrette for an additional twist!)

154.   Ham Balls With A Pineapple And Chipotle Drizzle

Serving: Serves 6 | Prep: | Cook: | Ready in:

Ingredients

- 2 eggs, beaten
- 3/4 cup homemade breadcrumbs
- 1 cup minced ham, cooked
- 2 tablespoons minced onion
- 3/4 cup panko breadcrumbs
- 1 1/2 cups canola oil
- 1/4 cup Swiss cheese, small cubes
- 4 ounces crushed pineapple
- 1/2 cup water
- 1 whole chipotle pepper, chopped
- 1 pinch salt

Direction

- Begin by adding the ham, eggs, onion, and homemade breadcrumbs to a large bowl. Mix well. Add the panko breadcrumbs to a plate. Take enough of the ham mixture and form it into a golf ball size shape. Once formed, press it down a bit with your thumb. This is where you will take a cube of the Swiss cheese and place it in the middle of the ham ball. Form it back into a ball, and roll it into the panko

breadcrumbs. Place on a separate plate. Repeat.
- Once all of the balls are formed, place the plate of balls into the freezer and let them form and solidify, approximately 30 minutes.
- During this time, make the glaze. Add the pineapple, water, and chipotle pepper to a sauce pan. Bring to a simmer, and cook for about 10 minutes. Set aside and let cool. Add the mixture to the blender and pulse it down to a nice puree. A bit of texture is just fine. Heat the oil in a pot on the stove. Heat it on medium high heat until you reach about 375 degrees. Take the ham balls out of the freezer and add a few to the heated oil, moving them around until they are all nice and golden brown. This will only take about 5 minutes, if that.
- Remove the balls with a slotted spoon onto a paper lined plate, and sprinkle them with a pinch of salt. Repeat. When you are ready to plate and serve, add the balls to a serving plate, and add the sauce in a small bowl. This plating allowed for a nice drizzle of the sauce on the ham ball. Pure delight through and through. A great crunch on the exterior, while nice a fluffy on the inside, this ham ball when perfect with the sweet heat from the sauce.

155.   Harry's Meat Balls

Serving: Serves six | Prep: | Cook: | Ready in:

Ingredients

- see below
- 1 pound ground pork
- 1 pound ground veal (or turkey)
- 1 pound ground lamb (or beef)
- see below
- 2 eggs
- 6 tablespoons bread crumbs
- 1 large onion--grated
- 2 tablespoons mustard
- 2 tablespoons worcheshire

- 1/2 cup currants
- 2 tablespoons chopped parsely
- 2 tablespoons spicy ketchup (optional)
- 1/2 prserved lemon (totally optional)

Direction

- wash your hands and in a big bowl mush all together/chill /Make a da meatballs--you should make about 24 of them in a big heavy frying pan heat 2 tablespoons olive oil and put bit of onion slice carefully add the meatballs (do not crowd --do this in at least two batches) and cook for about ten minutes total as you carefully use a spoon to move them around and brown on all sides. Remove to a plate. Deglaze the burned onion and bits with two tablespoons of balsamic vinegar. Remove from heat. Add to tomato sauce.
- For tomato sauce. In a large pot add two large cans of good crushed tomatoes,1/3 cup red wine /two tablespoons brown sugar, a few chopped cloves of garlic/ three tablespoon of chopped herbs (oregano/basil/parsley) Simmer sauce until reduced by about half. Salt /pepper/ brown sugar to taste. Add meat balls to sauce and cook for 1/2 hour. Serve with al dente pasta and freshly grated parmesan. Be prepared to be loved....xoxox

---

156.   Hearty Quiche

Serving: Serves 4 to 8 | Prep: | Cook: |Ready in:

Ingredients

- 1- 9" unbaked pie shell
- 6 strps bacon, cooked crisp, crumble and set aside
- 1 large onion, chopped fine
- 1-1/2 cups grated natural Swiss cheese (6 oz.) or Gruyre
- 1/2 cup chopped ham
- 1 medium potato, cut to 1/4 to 1/2 inch cubed

- 1/2 cup sliced mushrooms
- 1-10 ounces box frozen chopped spinach, very well drained
- 2 tablespoons flour
- 4 eggs
- 2 cups Half & Half
- 1 teaspoon salt
- 1/4 teaspoon pepper
- 1/2 teaspoon Oregano
- 1/2 teaspoon Rosemary
- 2 tablespoons Sour Cream
- 4 tablespoons grated Parmessan Cheece

Direction

- In pan bacon was cooked in, drain off all but one tablespoon of bacon drippings. Cook onion and potatoes until soft. Add ham and mushrooms and heat through, remove from heat.
- Mix together in a large bowl, 2 tablespoons flour, 4 eggs, 2 cups Half & Half, 1 teaspoon salt, 1/4 teaspoon pepper, 1/2 teaspoon oregano, 1/2 teaspoon Rosemary, mix well. Add the grated cheese, bacon, ham, onion, potatoes, mushrooms, grated Parmesan cheese, sour cream and well drained chopped spinach. (Drain spinach by squeezing it very well with your hands.) Mix all ingredients well and pour into unbaked pie shell.
- Bake at 350º for 40 to 45 minutes, or until puffed and brown. Cool 30 minutes before cutting into 8 wedges.

---

157.   Holiday Shaped Sausage Cookies

Serving: Serves 6 | Prep: | Cook: |Ready in:

Ingredients

- 1 packet Jimmy Dean® Regular or Hot Flavor Pork Sausage Roll
- 2-3 pinches Garnishes to decorate sausage: assorted shredded cheeses such as cheddar

and mozzarella, chopped green onions, chopped tomato, red and green bell pepper strips, fresh herbs such as rosemary, thyme, parsley, etc.
- 2 Holiday Cookie Cutters (for best results use metal) such as star, holiday trees, etc.

Direction

- Remove sausage from roll and flatten onto a large sheet of parchment or plastic wrap. Top sausage with second piece of parchment paper. Roll sausage evenly to about ¼-inch thickness. Place on a large baking pan and cover. Freeze for about 1 hour until firm but not a hard freeze.
- Remove sausage from freezer and cut sausage with cookie cutters into fun holiday shapes.
- Cook sausage shapes in a large skillet over medium heat for 8 to 10 minutes or until a minimum temperature of 160°F is reached. Decorate with garnishes to serve, if desired.

---

158. Homemade Knife Cut Noodles With Simple Pork Chao Mian

Serving: Serves 4 | Prep: | Cook: |Ready in:

Ingredients

- For the knife-cut noodles:
- 4 cups bread flour, plus more as needed
- 1 cup plus 2 tablespoons cold water, divided
- For the pork chao mian stir-fry:
- Cooking oil, as needed (Canola or peanut oil both work well)
- 1/2 cup shredded carrot
- 1/4 head napa cabbage, white and pale green parts thinly sliced and separated
- 1 cup fresh shiitake mushroom, sliced thinly
- 4 garlic cloves, minced
- 1 slice fresh ginger, thinly chopped
- 4 Thai chile peppers (chopped if you want more heat)

- 1/4 pound ground pork
- Knife-cut noodles (see recipe above)
- 2 tablespoons sugar
- 1 1/2 tablespoons light soy sauce
- 2 tablespoons dark soy sauce
- 1 teaspoon oyster sauce
- 1 tablespoon Shaoxing wine
- 1 dash white pepper, plus more to taste
- 2 tablespoons chopped scallions
- 4 eggs, scrambled lightly
- Salt, to taste
- 1 teaspoon sesame oil
- Green part of scallions, to garnish

Direction

- For the knife-cut noodles:
- In a large bowl, add the bread flour and make a well in the center. Add 1 cup water in roughly 1/8 cup increments, mixing it in with chopsticks, until all the water has been added. It will look rough.
- Once all of the water has been added, use your hands to mix it in, kneading it to form a rough dough inside the bowl. The dough should be dry, but if it's falling apart, add more water 1 tablespoon at a time. Knead until there are no residual clumps of dough in the bowl or on your hands. Once it resembles a rough dough, turn it onto a dry surface and knead for 5 to 6 minutes. Its surface should start to become smooth.
- Wrap it in plastic wrap and let it rest for 15 minutes, to allow the flour to hydrate.
- Remove dough from plastic wrap and knead it on dry surface for another 5 to 6 minutes. Wrap it in plastic and allow it to rest for another 15 minutes. After each rest, the dough should become visibly smoother and easier to work with.
- Remove dough from plastic wrap and knead for another 5 to 6 minutes. Form a long oval shape and fold it into thirds, with the two ends overlapping, so that there are three layers. Knead it into a long oval shape again, and repeat this process another two times. Form it into a long oval shape once more and wrap it

in plastic. Allow it to rest in the refrigerator for 30 minutes. At this point, the dough's surface should be very smooth, or "guan hua ti shi" in Chinese.

- After 30 minutes, bring a pot of salted water to a boil and begin to cut the dough into noodles, using one of two methods: For the traditional method, use a very sharp knife and have a pot of boiling water ready. With your left hand, hold the oval dough pointed downward at a 30° angle, with the downward-facing edge resting on a cutting board. This will help you make smooth, even cuts. With your right hand, shave the knife down the dough to create thin noodles. There's a Chinese saying to help you visualize this technique, "Knife doesn't leave the dough, and dough doesn't leave the knife." It should be a continuous loop. This technique is tricky, which is why I opted to do the second, less traditional but easier technique: Place the oval dough flat on the cutting board. Use a sharp knife to slice off noodle pieces, as if it were a vegetable. This makes it easier to control the thickness and length. If the cut noodles begin sticking together, flour them with bread flour.
- Add the noodles into the boiling water and stir to prevent clumping. If you're using the noodles for the stir-fry below, remove the noodles as soon as the water returns to a boil. Rinse with cold water and set aside. If you are using these noodles for soup, cook them completely through, about 8 minutes. Either way, they should be used immediately to ensure freshness.
- For the pork chao mian stir-fry:
- Heat up a wok with some cooking oil.
- Add in the carrots, white parts of cabbage, and shiitake mushroom, and cook until softened, about 1 to 2 minutes. Remove from the pan and set aside.
- Add garlic, ginger, and Thai chile peppers to the wok, and stir-fry until lightly brown and fragrant.
- Add in the pork and cook, breaking up the pieces, until browned on all sides and halfway

cooked. Add the carrot/shiitake mixture back into pan.

- Add in the knife-cut noodles, sugar, and sauces (light soy sauce, dark soy sauce, oyster sauce, and Shaoxing wine). Add the white pepper.
- Add in the scallions, green parts of cabbage, and egg. Stir until noodles are completely covered in sauce and the egg is scrambled in and cooked through. Add salt and white pepper to taste, and mix until well combined.
- Drizzle in some sesame oil and serve hot. Garnish with scallions.

---

159. Hot Sour Salty Sweet Minted Pork Salad

Serving: Serves 2 entrees | Prep: | Cook: |Ready in:

Ingredients

- Minted Dressing
- 1/4 cup fish sauce
- 1/4 cup water
- 1/8 cup sugar
- 1/2 teaspoon chili garlic sauce
- juice of one lime (zest saved)
- 1/2 cup mint, chopped
- Salad
- 2 small zucchinis, julienned
- 1 cup carrots, thinly sliced
- 1 cup radishes, thinly sliced
- 1 cup sugar snap peas, julienned
- 2 green onions, green parts sliced, rest saved for another use
- 1/4 red onion, thinly sliced
- 1 tablespoon uncooked glutinous rice
- 1 tablespoon vegetable/canola oil
- 1 medium shallot, minced
- 1 serrano (or jalapeno), minced
- 2 garlic cloves, minced
- zest from lime
- 3/4 pound ground pork
- 1 tablespoon black sesame seeds

- 6-8 basil leaves
- 1/4 cup cilantro

Direction

- Put zucchini in a strainer, toss liberally with salt and allow to drain in sink or over bowl. Soak onion in cold water. Allow to rest until wilted while you prep the rest of the dish.
- Mix all dressing ingredients together until sugar has dissolved. Can be made a day or so ahead of time.
- Toast rice in a dry skillet over medium heat, shaking often, until light brown. Put into spice grinder and allow to cool completely before grinding to a fine powder.
- Add oil to pan and brown shallots over medium heat.
- Rinse zucchini and red onion and pat dry. Toss with carrots, radishes, peas, green onions. Add about half of dressing and toss to coat. Allow to sit for at least 5-10 minutes while you cook the pork for any liquid to be extracted from the veggies.
- Add lime zest, garlic and chili (to taste) to shallots. (We shared this with a kid who does not eat spicy food and just added raw chiles to our own bowls, but you can add them here adjusting to your heat tolerance). Stir until fragrant and add pork. Cook until pork is no longer pink and some liquid has formed in pan. Add toasted rice powder and cook a bit longer until starting to brown. Remove from heat and set aside.
- Toss salad again and pour off excess liquid. Toss with sesame seeds and pork adding more dressing to taste. Garnish with basil and cilantro.

---

160.   Hungarian Pork Paprikash

Serving: Serves 4 | Prep: | Cook: |Ready in:

Ingredients

- 1 1/2 pounds boneless pork shoulder, trimmed of fat and cut into large chunks
- 2 tablespoons sunflower oil, plus extra if needed
- 1 large onion, finely chopped
- 1 1/2 pounds baby bella mushrooms, sliced
- 1 tablespoon smoked paprika
- 1 tablespoon dry dill
- 1 tablespoon cornstarch
- 1 cup condensed cream of mushroom soup, low sodium
- 2 red bell peppers, halved lengthwise, seeded, and diced
- 4 tablespoons Greek yogurt
- 10 ounces dry egg noodles
- 2 tablespoons butter
- salt
- fresh ground black pepper
- chopped chives, to serve

Direction

- Season the pork with salt and pepper. Heat the oil in a large skillet over high heat. Lower the heat to medium, add the pork and fry 3 to 5 minutes until brown on all sides, working in batches to avoid overcrowding in the pan, and adding extra oil if necessary. Use a slotted spoon to transfer the pork to the slow cooker as it browns.
- Add the onion to the skillet and fry, stirring, 3 to 5 minutes until soft. Add the mushrooms, sprinkle with salt, and fry 5 to 8 minutes until all the liquid is absorbed. Sprinkle the paprika and dill over the mushrooms and stir 30 seconds.
- Put the cornstarch and 2 tablespoons cold water in a small bowl and whisk until smooth. Add the cornstarch paste and mushroom soup to the pan and bring to a boil, scraping the bottom of the pan. Pour the mixture into the cooker and stir well. Season lightly with salt and pepper.
- Cover the cooker with the lid and cook on LOW 8 hours. Stir in the peppers and yogurt. Switch the cooker to HIGH, re-cover and cook

30 minutes until the pork and peppers are tender.

- Twenty minutes before serving, bring a large pot of salted water to boil, add the egg noodles and cook to package directions. Drain well, shaking off any excess water, then return the noodles to the hot pot, add the butter, and stir until it melts.
- Spoon the paprika over the noodles and season with a little more salt and pepper, if you like. Sprinkle with chives and serve.

161.   Incredible Italian Ham And Cheese Sandwich

Serving: Makes 2 sandwiches | Prep: | Cook: | Ready in:

Ingredients

- 4 thick slices good country bread
- 2 large strips prosciutto (I used prosciutto di san daniele by principe)
- 2 ounces Taleggio
- 2 ounces Asiago fresco

Direction

- In a small, heavy-bottomed pot (I used a 1.5 quart Staub) set over medium-low heat (I used my simmer burner and had it on medium), put the cheeses and let cook until melted, lowering the temp if things in the pot get too active. You want it at a steady melt.
- Meanwhile, toast the bread and when they're crispy and warm, put the prosciutto strips on each of two bread slices. On the other bread slices, spoon the melted cheese. Press the two sides of each sandwich together and enjoy immediately!

162.   Inside Out Egg Sandwich (with Spinach, Tomato, Cheddar, And Canadian Bacon)

Serving: Serves 2 | Prep: | Cook: | Ready in:

Ingredients

- 2 English muffins, separated into halves (I used sourdough English muffins)
- 2 large organic eggs
- 1 tablespoon milk, any type
- 2 cups organic baby spinach
- 2 slices cheddar cheese
- 2 slices Canadian bacon (approx. 1/4" thick)
- 1 small to medium tomato (I used Roma)
- olive oil for cooking
- salt and pepper to taste

Direction

- Prepare muffins as you would French toast: Whisk eggs, milk, a pinch of salt, and a pinch of pepper in a shallow bowl. Lie English muffin halves in egg mixture while preparing other ingredients, turning every five minutes or so until the bread is saturated.
- Wilt the spinach: place greens plus 1 tablespoon of water in a small saucepan. Cover and place on medium heat. Every 3 minutes turn the spinach and check the amount it has cooked/wilted. Remove from heat and transfer spinach to plate covered with paper towels (to absorb excess moisture). Do not overcook the spinach!
- Heat a frying pan to medium. Brush slices of Canadian bacon lightly with olive oil and place them in dry, hot pan. Turn after five minutes or so, lightly browning both sides of the meat. Transfer to plate.
- Brush heated frying pan with a light layer of olive oil. Place saturated English muffin halves outer/flat side down in the pan. Spoon any remaining egg mixture into the nooks and crannies of the muffins. Cook for at least five minutes, reducing heat if necessary so as not to brown them too fast.

- Assemble as you wish: I layered in the following order: greens, tomato, Canadian bacon on the un-cheesy muffin half, then popped the cheesy side of the 2nd muffin half on top of those layers.
- Serve warm.

163. Instant Pot Pork Vindaloo With Cauliflower Rice

Serving: Serves 4 | Prep: 0hours10mins | Cook: 0hours50mins | Ready in:

Ingredients

- Pork Vindaloo
- 1 jar Masala Mama Vindaloo Simmer Sauce https://food52.com/shop...
- 1 tablespoon ghee or oil
- 1½ pounds pork shoulder, cut into 4 pieces
- 1 onion, chopped
- ½ teaspoons red pepper flakes, more for additional heat (optional)
- Salt and pepper
- Cauliflower Rice
- 1 tablespoon ghee or oil
- 1 10 oz. bag frozen or fresh riced cauliflower
- 1 lime, juiced
- Fresh cilantro, for garnish
- Salt and pepper

Direction

- Add oil to Instant Pot and select Sauté setting. Once the oil is hot, add the pork and cook until golden brown on each side. Add the onion to the Instant Pot and sauté for an additional 2-3 minutes.
- Cancel the Sauté function on the Instant Pot and add Masala Mama Vindaloo Simmer Sauce, red pepper flakes and the brown sugar. Stir well and lock the Instant Pot lid in place and turn the steam release valve to Sealing. Select Manual/Pressure Cook and cook on high pressure for 35 minutes.

- When cooking is complete, turn the Instant Pot off and allow steam to release naturally for 5 minutes before turning the valve to Vent. Remove the Instant Pot lid and shred the pork with a pair of forks.
- Adjust salt and pepper to taste and serve with cauliflower rice. (Recipe as follows)
- While Vindaloo Pork is cooking, heat oil in a large skillet over medium-high heat. Add the riced cauliflower to the pan. Stir the cauliflower so the oil coats it evenly and season with salt and pepper.
- Cook, stirring a few times, until the cauliflower rice starts to turn lightly golden brown, about 5-8 minutes.
- Squeeze lime over the top of the cauliflower rice and garnish with cilantro to serve.

164. Italian Pork And Pepper Stew ~ Crock Pot Style

Serving: Serves 6-8 | Prep: | Cook: | Ready in:

Ingredients

- 1 Yellow Onion
- 1 Jar of Roasted Red Peppers
- 1 splash Olive Oil
- 2 pounds Pork Loin, Cubed
- 1 Lg. Can of Diced Tomatoes
- 3/4 cup Red Wine
- 1 teaspoon Rosemary
- 1 dash Red Pepper Flakes
- 1/2 teaspoon salt
- 1/4 teaspoon pepper
- 3 tablespoons Flour
- 1/4 cup Water

Direction

- 1. Layer the onion, roasted red peppers and garlic in the slow cooker.
- 2. In a large skillet over high heat, warm the splash of olive oil until very hot. Add the meat (don't overcrowd, you may want to do this in

batches.) Sear the meat on all sides. Don't worry about cooking the middle, you are just trying to get some browning on the outside edges.

- 3. Once all of the meat is browned and removed from the pan, add in the tomatoes, peppers and wine to the skillet and bring to a gentle boil. Be sure to scrape up all of those bits of goodness from the bottom of the pan.
- 4. Add the spices and pour everything from the skillet into the slow cooker. Cook and cover on low until the pork is tender~ about 7 hours. (Chicken will probably take less time.)
- 5. In a small bowl, whisk together the flour and water until smooth. Whisk this slurry into the slow cooker and stir to incorporate into the stew. Increase the heat to high and cook, uncovered, about 15 minutes.
- 6. Serve either in a bowl with some rustic, crunchy bread or on top of pasta, polenta or mashed potatoes.

---

165. Italian Sausage And Tomato Soup With Tortellini

Serving: Serves 4-6 | Prep: 0hours5mins | Cook: 0hours50mins |Ready in:

Ingredients

- 1 tablespoon Olive Oil
- 1 pound Ground Sweet Italian Sausage
- 1 cup Diced Onion (1 med. onion)
- 2 tablespoons Minced Garlic
- 28 ounces Crushed Tomatoes with basil (non-basil works too)
- 32 ounces Chicken Broth
- 4 tablespoons Fresh Chopped Basil
- 1.5 teaspoons Salt (or to taste)
- 1/2 teaspoon Pepper (or to taste)
- 1 tablespoon Italian Seasoning
- 9 ounces Refrigerated Tortellini
- 4 cups Packed Fresh Spinach (or chopped kale)

- 5 Parmesan Cheese to taste

Direction

- In a large pot, heat olive oil until hot. Add diced onions and sauté until onions are soft (roughly 5-7 mins)
- Add Italian Sausage and garlic with the onions. Crumble the Italian Sausage and cook until sausage is no longer pink (roughly 10 mins)
- Stir in Crushed tomatoes, broth, basil, Italian seasoning, salt and pepper. Bring to a boil, reduce heat to low, and cover. Let soup simmer for 30 minutes
- Add tortellini and spinach and simmer for about 10 minutes, until pasta is tender
- Top with Parmesan cheese (if desired) and serve immediately or let cool and freeze for another occasion
- For a healthier or gluten free option, supplement the tortellini for cauliflower and carrots. Chop 1 small head of cauliflower into 1 to 1.5-inch pieces and 1 chop 1 cup of carrots into quarter size pieces. Add cauliflower and carrots to the soup with the crushed tomatoes rather than with the spinach

---

166. Jacinta's Duck Rice Arroz De Pato Da Jacinta

Serving: Serves 6 - 8 | Prep: | Cook: |Ready in:

Ingredients

- 4 1/2 pounds whole duck, cut up in 8 pieces
- 2 1/2 cups medium grain rice
- 5 cups duck broth (from cooking the duck)
- 1/2 Chourizo
- 2 medium yellow onions peeled and left whole
- 1 medium carrot
- 1 medium leek – white part only
- 1 celery stalk, trimmed
- 2 garlic cloves, peeled and left whole

- 2 bay leaves
- 3 cloves
- 6 sprigs fresh parsley
- 3 sprigs fresh thyme
- 1 teaspoon Black whole peppercorns
- 2 tablespoons Extra Virgin Olive Oil
- salt

Direction

- Peel the garlic and the onion and leave whole. Insert the cloves in the onion by pressing them in.
- Wash the leek very well to remove any earth attached.
- Peel the carrot. Trim and wash the celery stalk. Wash the parsley and the fresh thyme leaving the stalks.
- Wash the whole duck and cut in 8 pieces.
- In a big pot over high heat, add the duck, onion with cloves, leek, celery stalk, carrot, garlic, bay leaves, parsley, thyme, peppercorns and cover with water. Season with salt. Bring to a boil, reduce the heat and simmer, covered with lid, for 1 hour. Remove the lid and allow to cook for a further 45 minutes until duck is very tender and almost falling of the bones.
- Remove the duck from the broth and let it cool. Remove the flesh, shred it in big pieces. Discard the skin and all the bones – be very thorough because the duck has some very small bones.
- Sieve the duck broth and reserve – you will need 5 cups. The broth will be very rich and have a lot of fat from the duck which will give the rice its special flavor.
- In a big pan with a tight fitting lid, over medium heat, add the olive oil and fry the rice until it's well coated in olive oil and almost sticking to the pan.
- Add the duck broth, stir and scrape any rice attached to the pan. Check the salt, bring to a boil, reduce the heat and simmer, covered, for 17 minutes. During this time DO NOT uncover or stir the rice.

- Remove from the heat and allow to rest for 5 minutes without uncovering the pan or stirring the rice.
- Fluff up the rice so you don't have any lumps.
- Pre-heat the oven to 375'°F with rack in the middle position.
- In a deep oven proof serving dish, spread half the fluffed up rice. Spread with the shredded duck on top. Cover with the remaining rice.
- Slice the chorizo and add slices on top of the rice.
- Bake in the oven for 8 to 10 minutes until the top layer of the rice is lightly golden and the chorizo is crispy. Serve immediately.

167. Jamon Serrano With Marinated Red Peppers And Boquerones

Serving: Serves 4 | Prep: | Cook: | Ready in:

Ingredients

- 4 red bell peppers
- 2 large garlic cloves
- 4 tablespoons your best extra virgin olive oil
- 2 tablespoons chopped fresh savory
- about 20 boquerones
- about 24 black pitted niçoise oilves
- 1 loaf rustic crusty bread
- 1/4 pound jamon serrano

Direction

- Roast the peppers over a gas flame until the skins are charred and blistered and place them in a covered bowl for 20 minutes or so to steam the skins off. (Alternatively, you can roast them in the oven, if preferred).
- Mince the garlic as fine as possible while the peppers are steaming in the bowl.
- Cut the tops off the peppers and peel and seed them. Blot them dry with a paper towel and

cut in half lengthwise and then into inch wide strips.

- Preheat oven to 250 and pour a tablespoon of the olive oil into a gratin pan to grease it. Arrange the strips of peppers across the bottom of the dish until covered and then layer the pepper strips with the minced garlic and savory, olives and then, the Boquerón's. Cover the Boquerón's with another layer of pepper strips and the remaining olive oil. Salt and freshly grind pepper to taste.
- Place in the oven and heat for about 15 minutes until warm. Serve with the sliced bread and a layer of jamon seranno.

---

168.   Jeffrey Alford And Naomi Duguid's Luang Prabang Fusion Salad

Serving: Serves 6 to 8 | Prep: | Cook: | Ready in:

Ingredients

- For the salad
- 3 to 4 large or extra-large eggs, preferably free-range
- 2 medium heads leaf or Bibb lettuce, washed and dried
- 4 scallions, trimmed, smashed flat with the side of a cleaver, cut lengthwise in half or into quarters, and then cut crosswise into 2-inch lengths
- 1 cup cilantro sprigs
- 1 cup loosely packed, coarsely chopped or torn Chinese celery leaves, or substitute flat-leaf parsley sprigs
- For the lime juice dressing and the cooked dressing
- 1 tablespoon minced ginger
- 2 bird or serrano chiles (optional), minced
- 3 tablespoons Thai fish sauce
- 2 tablespoons fresh lime juice
- 9 to 10 cloves garlic, minced (divided)

- 2 tablespoons peanut or vegetable oil or minced pork fat
- 1/2 pound ground pork
- 1 teaspoon salt
- 1 tablespoon sugar
- 3/4 cup hot water
- 1/2 cup rice or cider vinegar
- 2 to 3 tablespoons dry-roasted peanuts, coarsely chopped

Direction

- Put the eggs in a saucepan with cold water to cover. Bring to a boil, then reduce the heat and cook at a gentle rolling boil for 10 minutes. Drain and set aside to cool.
- Tear the salad greens into large coarse pieces. Place all the greens, including the scallions and herbs, in a large bowl and set aside.
- Peel the hard-cooked eggs and cut crosswise in half. Transfer the yolks to a small bowl and mash; set aside. Slice the whites crosswise and set aside.
- In a medium bowl, mix together the ginger, chiles, fish sauce, lime juice, and 1 to 2 cloves' worth of minced garlic; set aside.
- When you are ready to proceed, put the remaining dressing ingredients near your stovetop. Heat a wok or heavy skillet over high heat. Add the oil or fat and heat for 20 seconds, then add the remaining 8 cloves' worth of minced garlic. Stir-fry briefly, until the garlic starts to change color, about 20 seconds, then toss in the pork. Use your spatula to break up the pork into small pieces as you stir-fry. Once all the pork has changed color completely, after 1 to 2 minutes, add the salt and sugar, then add the hot water and bring to a boil. Add the vinegar, add the reserved mashed egg yolks, and stir to blend.
- Pour the hot liquid and pork over the prepared greens and toss gently. Pour the lime juice dressing and toss. Transfer the salad to a large flat platter (or to individual dinner plates) and mound it attractively. Sprinkle on the chopped roasted peanuts, arrange slices of

egg white attractively on top, and serve immediately.

169. Kimchi Jjigae (Kimchi Stew) 김치찌개

Serving: Serves 4-6 | Prep: | Cook: | Ready in:

Ingredients

- 2 tablespoons vegetable or canola oil
- 1 pound pork belly, loin, or shoulder, sliced thinly
- 1/2 teaspoon sea salt
- 1/4 teaspoon ground black pepper
- 4 cups ripe kimchi
- 3.5 cups water
- 1 tablespoon sesame oil
- 1 bunch green onion, chopped finely

Direction

- In a large, heavy-bottomed pot, heat the oil on medium-high heat.
- Add pork slices, and sauté with the salt and black pepper until golden and cooked through.
- Add the kimchi and stir together until kimchi has cooked through, around 3-5 minutes.
- Add water, just enough to barely cover the kimchi and pork. Cover, and reduce heat to medium and simmer for 40-45 minutes.
- Turn off the heat and add sesame oil and green onion and stir to combine.
- Enjoy with a bowl of hot, white rice.

170. Kimchi, Pork + Scallion Pancake With Watercress Radish Relish

Serving: Serves 4 | Prep: | Cook: | Ready in:

Ingredients

- 2 cups store-bought kimchi, chopped
- 1 cup chopped scallions (from 1 bunch)
- 1 1/2 cups cups chopped watercress, divided (from 1 large bunch)
- 8 ounces ground pork
- 1 garlic clove, finely grated
- 1/2 teaspoon ground cayenne pepper
- 1 cup all-purpose flour
- 2 large eggs, lightly beaten
- 1/4 cup soy sauce
- 2 tablespoons rice-wine vinegar
- 1 tablespoon sesame oil
- 1/2 cup sliced radishes (from about 8 halved radishes)

Direction

- In a large bowl, combine kimchi, scallions, 1 cup chopped watercress, pork, garlic, cayenne, flour, egg, and 6 tablespoons water. Stir to combine.
- Meanwhile, heat 2 tablespoons oil in a large nonstick skillet over medium-high heat. Add half of pancake mixture, pat it into a large pancake, and cook until browned on the underside, about 4 minutes. Slide the pancake onto a plate, then carefully flip it back into the skillet to brown the other side, about 4 minutes. Repeat with remaining pancake mixture and oil. Transfer both pancakes to a cutting board to cut each cake into 4 wedges.
- While pancake cooks, whisk together soy sauce, vinegar and sesame oil. In a small bowl, toss remaining 1/2 cup watercress and radish together with salt and pepper. Serve wedges of pancake topped with watercress relish; spoon sauce over top or serve alongside.

171. Kristen Kish's Stuffed Cabbage Rolls

Serving: Serves 6 to 8 | Prep: | Cook: | Ready in:

Ingredients

- Cabbage Rolls
- 1 or 2 large green cabbages, enough for 12 to 15 large leaves
- 4 cups of your favorite sauerkraut
- 2 cups tomato juice
- 5 smoked bacon slices (optional)
- Stuffing
- 1 pound ground pork shoulder (Boston butt)
- 1 pound ground beef
- 1 tablespoon sweet, smoked, or hot paprika (I like a mix)
- 2 teaspoons ground fennel seeds
- 1/2 teaspoon crushed red pepper flakes
- 1/2 teaspoon ground coriander
- 1 teaspoon freshly ground black pepper
- 2 garlic cloves, finely grated
- 1/4 cup grated white onion
- 1 1/4 cups uncooked white rice
- Kosher salt
- Grapeseed or other neutral oil

Direction

- Cabbage Rolls
- You'll need 12 to 15 nice large leaves to make these rolls. Gently peel off the outer leaves of the cabbage, then steam these over a pot of boiling water until pliable, roughly 15 minutes. Lay them out on a kitchen towel to cool and dry. Chop up the remaining cabbage (up to 1/2 head) into medium chunks.
- Stuffing
- In a large bowl, mix together with your hands the pork, beef, paprika, fennel seeds, red pepper flakes, coriander, black pepper, garlic, onion, and rice, adding a generous sprinkling of salt. Shape a very small patty of the mixture and, in a hot small frying pan lightly coated with oil, cook it for 2 minutes on each side. Taste for salt and adjust your overall mixture accordingly.
- Preheat the oven to 350°F.
- Roll up 1/4 cup of the stuffing into each steamed cabbage leaf, like you'd roll a burrito, and tuck each roll into a deep baking dish,

seam-side down. Pour a light layer of the sauerkraut juice and all of the tomato juice over the rolls. Insert small pieces of the cabbage heart(s) in between each roll, then top with the sauerkraut and more of its juices: the overall amount to liquid should come three fourths of the way up the cabbage rolls. I like to add some slices of smoked bacon over the top to add flavor while the dish cooks, but it's your choice. Cover tightly with a lid or buttered foil, and bake for 2 1/2 to 3 hours, until tender.

172.	Lao Crispy Rice Salad Nam Khao

Serving: Serves 6 | Prep: | Cook: | Ready in:

Ingredients

- 3 cups Jasmine rice, cooked, and cooled
- 2 whole eggs, beaten with 1 tbsp soy sauce
- 2 cups ground pork, cooked and cooled
- 3 tablespoons Thai red curry paste
- 1 cup unsweetened coconut flakes
- 1 tablespoon palm sugar
- 1 teaspoon salt
- 1/2 cup shallots, thinly sliced
- 1 whole lime
- 1/2 cup roasted peanuts
- 1 head of green cabbage, leaves removed
- 1/2 cup fresh mint leaves
- 1/2 cup fresh cilantro leaves
- 1 tablespoon red chili flakes
- 1/2 cup Nam, fermented pork, chopped
- 2 Thai bird chilies, optional
- 2 cups canola oil

Direction

- Start by combining your cooled rice, the eggs with soy sauce, curry paste, salt, sugar, cooked ground pork, and coconut into a mixing bowl. Making sure everything is combined, form into baseball sized balls.

- Next, heat the oil and let it come up to about 350 degrees. Add one ball at a time, and cook until completely golden brown. Remove with a slotted spoon, and let it rest on a paper lined plate to drain any excess oil.
- Repeat with the remaining balls. During this time, prepare the remaining ingredients into a serving bowl. Take the crispy rice balls, and break apart into bite-sized pieces, adding them into the mixing bowl. Once all of the balls have been taken apart, mix everything together.
- To plate, add a mound of the nam khao to a serving plate, and serve alongside cabbage or lettuce leaves, fresh lime, and whole Thai bird chili peppers.

173. Lavender Chicken

Serving: Serves 4 | Prep: | Cook: |Ready in:

Ingredients

- 4 pieces chicken breast
- 12 pieces bacon
- 12 pieces fresh lavender flower
- 1/4 cup grated cheese
- 1 tablespoon red pepper flakes
- 1/4 cup olive oil

Direction

- Wrap the chicken breast with the bacon and put between the bacon and the chicken a lavender flower (3 bacon strips/3 lavender flowers per breast)
- Add the red pepper flakes, the grated cheese and the olive oil over the chicken. Let marinate for 2 or 3 hours
- Then to the Oven for 20 to 25 and serve.

174. Leek, Prosciutto, And Egg Tart

Serving: Serves 3 or 4 small tarts or 1 larger tart | Prep: | Cook: |Ready in:

Ingredients

- For the crust:
- 3/4 cup all-purpose flour
- 1/2 cup whole wheat flour
- 1 teaspoon salt
- 8 tablespoons cold butter, cut into cubes
- 3 tablespoons ice water, or more as needed
- egg wash, as needed
- For the toppings:
- 2 tablespoons olive oil
- 6 ounces prosciutto, diced
- 1 bunch leeks, thinly sliced
- 2 cloves garlic, minced
- 1/2 cup Boursin (or other soft cheese)
- 1 teaspoon red pepper flakes
- salt and pepper, to taste
- 4 eggs

Direction

- For the crust:
- Preheat the oven to 375° F. Combine the flours and the salt in a medium bowl. Toss the butter in the flour. Use your hands to "shingle" the butter with the flour. Do this by flattening the butter between the palms of your hands. The larger the pieces of butter, the flakier the final dough. The smaller the pieces of butter, the mealier the final dough. For this tart, a flakier crust is better since the toppings are light and won't weigh down the tart.
- Finish the dough by adding ice water one tablespoon at a time until the dough begins to come together. When the dough is finished, bring it together into a disc and cover it with plastic wrap and refrigerate for at least 15 to 20 minutes.
- When the dough is chilled, take it out of the refrigerator and divide it into two pieces. Roll each piece into a ball and roll out on a lightly-

floured surface using a rolling pin. Roll the dough into a circle about 1/4-inch thick. Transfer to a baking sheet. Dock (poke holes into) each piece of dough all over the base with a fork. [Editors' note: You can also make one larger tart: Either shape it free-form or transfer it to a tart pan.]

- Apply egg wash to the edges to the tart shell. Bake in the oven until just starting to brown, about 7 to 8 minutes. Remove from oven and allow to cool.
- For the toppings:
- Preheat the oven to 375° F.
- In a small sauté pan, heat the olive oil over medium-high heat. Add the prosciutto and sauté until it begins to become crispy. Add the leeks and garlic and continue to cook until the leeks are soft.
- Remove from the heat and add the Boursin. Mix to combine, season with red pepper flakes, salt, and pepper. Set aside until needed.
- Spread the leek mixture across the par-baked crusts or crust. Gently top with the raw egg.
- Bake the tart in the oven until the egg white is set and the crust is fully browned, about 5 to 6 minutes. If a less runny egg is desired, add an additional 2 to 3 minutes Remove from the oven and serve on warm plates.

---

175. Lemongrass Grilled Pork Salad

Serving: Serves 4 | Prep: | Cook: | Ready in:

Ingredients

- pork and marinade
- 1.5 pounds pork tenderloin, sliced into bite sized 1/4 inch slices
- 6 sprigs lemongrass, white parts only, sliced thin
- 1 tablespoon light brown sugar
- 1 tablespoon Chili Garlic Sauce
- 1 tablespoon sesame oil

- 2 tablespoons chinese vinegar
- .25 cups soy sauce
- .25 cups fish sauce
- 1 tablespoon minced garlic
- .5 pieces small red onion,sliced
- .5 cups chopped thai basil
- .5 cups chopped cilantro
- 1 lemon,juice and zest
- .5 teaspoons salt
- .5 teaspoons fresh ground pepper
- For the Salad and garnish
- 1 pound rice stick (thin rice noodles)
- 2 cups sliced green onion
- 2 cups bean sprouts
- 2 cups cilantro, roughly chopped
- 2 cups thai basil,torn
- 4 limes, quartered
- 2 jalapeno pepper, thinly sliced
- .5-1 cups rice wine vinegar
- 1 tablespoon toasted sesame seeds
- 1.5 tablespoons sesame oil
- salt and pepper to taste
- Garnish:spring roll fish sauce, chili garlic sauce and Sriracha sauce

Direction

- Combine marinade ingredients with pork in large resealable bag, mix, place in bowl and refrigerate at least one hour.
- Add rice stick to large pot of salted, boiling water for 5-7 minutes. Strain and place in large bowl. Add rice wine vinegar, sesame oil and sesame seeds. Reserve.
- Preheat grill to medium high. Brush grate and wipe on vegetable oil. Remove pork from marinade and pat dry. Grill pork so that outside chars and inside remains moist, about 1-3 minutes per side, depending on grill. Remove to warm plate, loosely cover with foil and reserve.
- Assemble: divide noodles into 4 large bowls. Add bean sprouts, green onions, cilantro, basil, jalapeno slices and lime quarters equally. Gently toss adding additional rice wine vinegar as necessary. Salt and pepper to taste. Add equal portions of pork slices to each

salad. Have bowls of fish sauce, chili garlic sauce and sriracha sauce for garnish.

the inside (approximately 3-5 minutes each side).

- Top pork chops with minted cherry salsa, sprinkle on a bit of feta cheese, and enjoy.

176. Lemongrass Pork Chops With Minted Cherry Salsa

Serving: Serves 4 | Prep: | Cook: |Ready in:

Ingredients

- Lemongrass Pork
- 4 pieces pork chops
- 1 teaspoon salt
- 1 teaspoon cracked black pepper
- 4 garlic cloves
- 2 tablespoons lemongrass paste
- 2 tablespoons MSG-free soy sauce
- 1 tablespoon sugar
- 2 tablespoons olive oil
- Minted Cherry Salsa
- 1 cup sweet red cherries
- 1 tablespoon white vinegar
- 1 pinch salt
- 1 pinch pepper
- 1 handful fresh mint
- 2 sprigs parsley
- 1/4 cup feta cheese

Direction

- If pork chops are more than ½ inch thick, use a butcher knife to flatten by pounding. This will allow pork to cook faster. Salt and pepper the pork chops. Then mince garlic into a fine paste. Add garlic, lemongrass paste, soy sauce, and sugar to pork chops and marinade for 10 minutes.
- Meanwhile, pit and cut cherries in half. Add vinegar, salt, and pepper. Finely chop mint and parsley then add to cherries and let marinade for 5 minutes.
- Pan fry pork chops in olive oil on medium heat until a caramelized crust forms on the outside and the meat is cooked but juicy on

177. Lentil & Chorizo Stew With Saffron & Cinnamon

Serving: Serves 8 | Prep: | Cook: |Ready in:

Ingredients

- 2 tablespoons extra virgin olive oil
- 1 large onion, medium dice
- 2 large garlic cloves, minced
- 1/2 pound Spanish chorizo, thinly sliced
- 1/4 teaspoon pure saffron, crushed with a mortar and pestle
- 1 teaspoon ground coriander
- 1/2 teaspoon ground cinnamon
- 1/2 teaspoon ground ginger
- 1 14-ounce can fire-roasted tomatoes, preferably Muir Glen, or regular canned diced tomatoes
- 1 red bell pepper, medium dice
- 1 yellow bell pepper, medium dice
- 2 cups brown Spanish lentils (padrina) or French green lentils (puy), cooked until tender
- 2 cups dried chickpeas, soaked overnight and cooked until tender, or 2 14-ounce cans, rinsed and drained
- 5 to 6 cups low-sodium commercial chicken stock
- extra virgin olive oil, for drizzling
- cilantro leaves, for garnish
- crusty bread, for serving

Direction

- In a soup pot, over medium heat, add the olive oil. Add the onion and saute' about 3 to 4 minutes, or until onion has softened. Add the garlic, stir for 30 seconds, and add the chorizo. Sauté for another minute or two, then add the saffron, coriander, cinnamon and ginger. Stir to combine. Add the tomatoes, red and yellow bell peppers, lentils and chickpeas. Stir to combine. Add 5 cups chicken stock, cover and cook over medium-low heat for 20-25 minutes to allow the flavors to meld. If the stew seems too dry, add a little more stock.

- To serve, ladle into warm soup bowls, drizzle with olive oil and top with cilantro leaves. Serve hot with warm crusty bread

178. Linguine With Blistered Sungold Tomatoes, Smoked Sausage, And Basil

Serving: Serves 4 | Prep: | Cook: | Ready in:

Ingredients

- 2 tablespoons olive oil
- 1 rope (13 1/2 ounces) smoked sausage, diced
- 3/4 pound linguine
- 1 pint baby sungold or cherry tomatoes
- 2 cloves garlic, thinly sliced
- 1/4 cup grated Pecorino cheese, plus more to serve
- Small handful of torn basil, about 4-5 leaves

Direction

- Bring a large pot of water to a boil.
- While the water comes to a boil, start the sauce: Heat the oil in a 12-inch skillet over medium heat. Add the sausage and cook until it begins to brown, about 7 minutes. Remove and set aside.
- Add 2 tablespoons of the salt and bring back to a rolling boil. Add the pasta and cook until al dente according to package directions.
- While the pasta cooks finish your sauce. Add the tomatoes to the skillet and cook until they begin to burst, about 6 minutes. Add the garlic and cook until pale golden, about 2 minutes. Add the sausage back to the skillet with its drippings and toss the mixture together.

- Add the pasta directly to the skillet and toss, adding in ¼ cup of pasta water or more (up to 1 cup) as needed to loosen up the sauce. Add in the Pecorino cheese and toss again. Season with salt and pepper.
- Plate in bowl and top with basil. Pass Pecorino at the table, if desired.

179. Linguini With Chorizo, Clams, Shrimp And Calamari

Serving: Serves 4 | Prep: | Cook: | Ready in:

Ingredients

- 1 tablespoon garlic, finely minced
- 1 cup onion, medium dice
- 1/2 cup olive oil
- 1 cup dry white wine
- 5 ounces (1/2 - tube) Mexican pork chorizo
- 1/2 pound calamari, cut into bite sized pieces
- 1/2 pound clams in their shells, approx 12 - 15
- 1/2 pound shrimp, deveined and shells removed
- 1 pound linguine
- 1/4 cup parsley, roughly chopped

Direction

- Cut, chop and measure out all ingredients and set aside.
- Set the pot of salted water for the pasta on the stove to bring to a boil.
- While the pasta water is coming to a boil, pour the olive oil into a large frying pan over medium high heat. Add the onions to the hot olive oil and sauté until they are translucent, about 5 to 7 minutes.
- At this point, the pasta water should be boiling so add the linguine to the pot and stir well. Reduce heat slightly and allow to boil for 9 - 10 minutes.
- While the pasta is cooking, add the garlic to the onions and toss quickly to heat, but do not brown.

- Add the chorizo to the onions and garlic and cook until the chorizo is just cooked through, breaking the meat up as it cooks.
- Add the white wine to the chorizo mixture and simmer about 5 minutes.
- Add the clams to chorizo/wine sauce and cook just until they open, about 2 to 3 minutes. Remove the opened clams from the pan and set aside. Discard any clams that did not open.
- Add the shrimp to the chorizo/wine sauce in the pan and cook no more than 3 minutes.
- Add the calamari and cook about 2 minutes more. Turn off the heat
- By now, your pasta should be cooked al dente. Drain the pasta and place in a large serving bowl.
- Add the parsley to the sauce and stir well. Add the clams back into the sauce and mix well. Immediately pour the sauce over the linguine and serve.

---

180.   Lip Smackin' Neck Bone Gravy And Rice

Serving: Makes about 8 servings | Prep: 1hours0mins | Cook: 2hours0mins |Ready in:

Ingredients

- 2 tablespoons vegetable oil
- 1 1/2 pounds fresh pork neck bones , seasoned with salt and pepper
- 1 pound smoked pork neck bones
- 1 large onion, diced
- 1 large green bell pepper, diced
- 2 stalks celery, diced
- 4 cloves garlic, minced
- 1/4 teaspoon cayenne pepper(or a little more for more lip smackin!)
- 1 teaspoon black pepper
- Approximately 8 cups water
- 1 cup AP flour which you have lightly toasted in a saute pan over medium heat, stirring all the while until a light tan color

- 3 tablespoons Worcestershire sauce (or more if you like)
- Salt for seasoning (I needed 1 tablespoon)
- 1 cup thinly sliced green onions
- 8 to 10 cups hot cooked white rice
- More sliced green onions for garnish

Direction

- In a large soup pot or Dutch oven, heat 1 tablespoon of the oil and brown the fresh neck bones on all sides. Remove from the pot and set aside.
- Add the second tablespoon of oil to the pot and add the onion, bell pepper, celery, garlic, cayenne and black pepper. Sauté until everything softens up and becomes fragrant.
- Return the browned neck bones along with the smoked bones to the pot and add enough water to cover. Bring up to the boil and then simmer for about an hour or until the meat is ready to fall off the bones.
- Remove the bones from the pot and let cool a bit. Once cool enough to handle, remove the meat from the bones either with a knife or your clean hands, returning the meat to the pot. Be careful not to let any small bone return to the pot.
- Make a slurry of water and about 1/2 cup of the toasted flour and add it to the simmering pot. Once it boils again, check for the thickness of your gravy. If it's too thin you may want to make another slurry with some or all of the remaining flour.
- Stir in the Worcestershire sauce and then taste. Add salt as needed...this will depend not only on your taste, but on how salty your smoked bones were.
- At this point, if you're making ahead you can cool and refrigerate the pot. When ready to serve, bring back up to the boil, stir in the green onion.
- Place about a cup of the cooked rice into each bowl, ladle some gravy over and garnish with more green onion. Get out the greens and corn bread!

181.   Lucy's Cuban

Serving: Serves 2 | Prep: | Cook: | Ready in:

Ingredients

- 1/4 pound or more, leftover seasoned pork tenderloin, porchetta, or Cuban pork
- 4 slices Black Forest Ham
- 4 sliced un-smoked provolone or baby Swiss cheese
- 6 pepperoncini peppers or sweet red cherry peppers, seeded and cut in half
- 6 slices kosher dills
- Butter and olive oil
- 2 Cuban rolls, or Bolillos

Direction

- Cuisinart Griddler is perfect for this sandwich using the flat plates. I prep the rolls; slice in half brush a little olive oil over and spread with a little butter, toast on open grill plates until light golden. Remove and spread with a little mustard. Layer the pickles, ham, peppers, cheese, and pork. Drizzle with a little olive oil and grind a little pepper over the top layer of pork. Sandwich top on and butter the top, turn it over and butter the bottom. Place on heated griddle plates and press down, grill until hot, toasted and oozing cheese. Slice and serve.

182.   Lumpia (Filipino Egg Rolls)

Serving: Makes about 60 | Prep: | Cook: | Ready in:

Ingredients

- 1 package square wonton wrappers
- 1/2 small onion, finely chopped
- 2 cloves of garlic, minced
- 1/4 cup minced bok choy (optional)
- 1/3 cup minced carrots (optional)
- 1/3 cup soy sauce
- 1 tablespoon rice wine vinegar
- 2 teaspoons black pepper
- 1 teaspoon salt
- 1 teaspoon sugar
- 1 pound ground pork
- 1/2 cup vegetable oil, using more/less as needed

Direction

- Make the lumpia filling by placing all of the chopped vegetables, soy sauce, rice vinegar, pepper, salt, and sugar in a medium-sized bowl. Stir well to combine, and then add pork. Mix to ensure that all ingredients are evenly combined. Editors' note: We par-cooked the filling. To do this, brown the meat mixture lightly in a pan over medium heat, until it's no longer pink, about 6 to 7 minutes. (No need to add any oil to the pan.) Set aside to cool. When cool, proceed with step 2. (This will make the pork a bit crumbly and the lumpia harder to roll—but this way, you won't have to pan-fry them as long, ensuring you don't burn them.)
- Fill a small ramekin with room temperature water and set aside. Open the package of wonton wrappers and set up work station using a cutting board or other clean surface for assembly. To roll, place a very small amount of filling to the far left side of wonton wrapper (approximately 2 teaspoons) and tightly roll it toward you. (Editors' note: We didn't fold the edges.) Seal the rolled end by brushing the wrapper with water and pressing down. Continue rolling until you're out of filling! (You may have some leftover wonton wrappers.)
- Heat a large pan on medium heat, and coat pan with vegetable oil (about 2 tablespoons or more, depending on the size of your pan). Once oil is hot, place 6 to 7 rolled lumpia on the pan. Be careful not to overcrowd the pan. If you didn't par-cook the filling, cook lumpia for approximately 4 to 6 minutes on one side

before flipping to the other side; if you did par-cook, 2 to 3 minutes should do the trick. The cooked side should be golden brown and crispy. Once flipped to the other side, add more oil if needed, and cook for another 4 to 5 minutes, or until golden brown and crispy. Filling should be cooked all the way inside.

- Serve with a dipping sauce of your choice. We've used a sweet and sour pre-made sauce, or a simple sauce made with soy sauce, vinegar, and minced garlic.

183. Maple Horseradish Marinade With An Hors D'oeuvres Suggestion

Serving: Serves 6 | Prep: | Cook: | Ready in:

Ingredients

- Marinade
- small pinch of kosher salt
- 3-4 teaspoons peeled and grated fresh horseradish root, to taste
- 1/2 cup grade B maple syrup
- 1 teaspoon Dijon mustard, recommended for tang
- Bacon and scallop, or water chestnut, hors d'oeuvres
- 30   tooth picks
- @6   slices Black Forest bacon, or applewood cured excellent bacon
- 30   bay scallops, or water chestnut halves, patted dry

Direction

- Marinade
- Add a pinch of salt to the peeled, grated horseradish and let that sit for about 10 minutes.
- Whisk the mustard in with the maple syrup. Then whirl the grated horseradish into the maple syrup; let the combination mingle

together for at least half an hour together in a cup.

- Bacon and scallop, or water chestnut, hors d'oeuvres
- Soak the toothpicks in cold water for about 20 minutes. Meanwhile stretch the bacon slices as long as you can. If they measure 10 inches, you can probably make them 15 inches. Cut each stretched slice into lengths that will wrap around each scallop, water chestnut or chicken piece. I got 5 new pieces out of each slice. Wrap each item with a bacon slice and then secure with a toothpick. Preheat the broiler.
- Swirl each bacon-wrapped hors d'oeuvres gently in the maple horseradish marinade and place on a broiler rack with a pan below. Let these rest for a few minutes, so the marinade soaks in. With the oven rack about 4 inches from the element, broil these for about 2 minutes on one side, then turn over for another 2 minutes. Watch carefully to avoid any flames. Serve while warm.

184. Maple Glazed Bacon & Apple Breakfast Custard

Serving: Serves 4 | Prep: | Cook: | Ready in:

Ingredients

- 4 thick slices of good bacon, 1/2" dice
- 1 large or 2 small shallots, 1/4" dice
- 2 teaspoons fresh rosemary, minced
- 2 ounces dark amber maple syrup, grade B
- ?2 red apples, peeled, cored, 1/2" dice?
- 1 tablespoon dark amber maple syrup, grade B
- 4 large eggs?
- 8 ounces heavy cream?
- Few grinds of pepper?
- Soft butter?
- Crème fraîche for garnish (optional)?
- Pinches of smoked paprika

Direction

- I always cook bacon in the oven. It crisps uniformly, and it doesn't make an unholy mess of the stovetop. Too, the oven is ready to bake the custards. Preheat oven to 375 degrees.
- Cut bacon strips into 1/2" slices and place in a mixing bowl. Add diced shallots, minced rosemary, and maple syrup. Toss with tongs or with your hands so that everything carries a coat of syrup. Arrange everything on a baking sheet lined with parchment. When bacon is browned and crisp, shallots will also be caramelized, 20-25 minutes. Remove from oven and allow to cool slightly (stick the baking sheet in the fridge for a couple of minutes if you need to). Reduce oven heat to 350 degrees.
- While the bacon is cooking, peel, core, and dice the apples. Rinse out the bowl you used for the bacon, shallots, and syrup, and use it to whisk together the eggs, cream, and pepper. Stir the diced apples.
- When bacon and shallots are done and slightly cooled, stir them into the custard mixture along with their juices/syrup.
- Run a pastry brush over some soft butter and brush the insides of 4 4-ounce ramekins.
- Use a large spoon or a ladle to divide custard among the ramekins. Set ramekins on a baking sheet with a lip all the way around. Fill a large measuring cup or pitcher with very hot tap water. Set the baking sheet in the oven with the front edge hanging off the edge of the rack by an inch or so. Pour hot water into the baking sheet until it almost reaches the lip. You are creating a water bath that will ensure that the center of your custards will be done at the same time as the perimeter. Gently slide the baking sheet the rest of the way into the oven.
- Oven should still be set to 350 degrees. Bake custards for 30-40 minutes. Custards are done when puffed and golden on top, and slightly tender when you tap the surface.
- I use a canning jar lifter to remove custards from a water bath. Remove the custards to a cooling surface. Allow to cool for 5-10 minutes before serving. If you wish to gild the lilly, top

each with a spoonful of crème fraîche and pinches of smoked paprika just before you serve. Serve with some good grilled bread and a fruit salad.
- A note about the water bath: the safest way to remove the baking sheet from the oven is to turn off the heat, and leave the door ajar so that the water can cool. When it reaches a temperature that you feel comfortable handling it, go ahead and carefully carry it to a sink.

---

185. Marinated Grilled Peaches With Sliced Pork

Serving: Serves 4 | Prep: | Cook: | Ready in:

Ingredients

- 3 firm-ripe peaches (about 1 1/4 pounds)
- 1/2 cup granulated sugar
- 2 tablespoons fish sauce
- 1 tablespoon freshly squeezed lime juice
- 1/4 teaspoon freshly ground black pepper
- 1 teaspoon minced garlic
- 1 teaspoon grated fresh ginger
- 1 serrano or jalapeño chile, very thinly sliced crosswise
- 1 1/2-2 pounds bone-in or boneless pork loin chops about 1 inch thick
- Kosher salt
- Whole lettuce leaves, such as Little Gem, for serving
- Sprigs of mint and cilantro, for serving
- Lime wedges, for serving

Direction

- Bring a medium pan of water to a boil. Place a bowl of ice water next to the stove. Slip the peaches into the boiling water for 15 seconds. Transfer the peaches into the ice water bath with a slotted spoon. When cool enough to handle, slip the skins from the peaches. (If the skins do not remove easily, dip them back into the boiling water for 10 seconds more and then back into the ice water bath.)

- Cut each peach into quarters, discarding the pit. Transfer them to a bowl and add the sugar, fish sauce, lime juice, black pepper, garlic, ginger and chile; stir gently to combine.
- Preheat a charcoal or gas grill to medium-high. Season the pork chops with salt and grill for 4 to 4 1/2 minutes; turn and cook for 4 to 4 1/2 minutes more or until firm to the touch. Transfer to a cutting board to rest.
- Use a slotted spoon to lift the peaches from the marinade, leaving as much of the marinade as possible in the bowl. (Reserve the marinade for serving.) Place peaches on grill over medium heat and grill until the moment you smell sugar beginning to burn, 3 to 3 1/2 minutes. Turn them using a thin-bladed metal spatula and grill for 3 to 3 1/2 minutes more. Put the peaches back in the bowl with the marinade and set aside until the juice turns caramel colored, about 5 minutes.
- Slice the pork into 1/4-inch-thick strips. Spoon the peaches over the pork and serve with a platter of lettuce, mint and cilantro, along with the extra marinade as a dipping sauce. Let guests make their own bundles of peach, pork and herbs to dip into the sauce.

---

186.   Matilda, Maple, And Garlic Pork Shoulder With Crispy Skin

Serving: Serves up to 8 | Prep: 0hours10mins | Cook: 18hours35mins | Ready in:

Ingredients

- 6 pounds bone-in, skin on pork shoulder (up to 8 pounds for more servings)
- 3 tablespoons fennel seeds, toasted, crushed
- 14 pieces garlic cloves, crushed
- 3 tablespoons kosher salt
- 1/2 cup olive oil

- 1 teaspoon cayenne pepper
- 1 teaspoon black pepper
- 3/4 cup grade b maple syrup
- 1 big bottle of Matilda, or another malty fruity ale
- 2 teaspoons malt vinegar

Direction

- After allowing the meat to come to room temperature, use a sharp knife to score the skin, making 1/2 inch stripes over entire surface. Preheat oven to 450. Toast fennel seeds in a skillet over medium heat, until fragrant (3 minutes); crush using mortar and pestle, set aside. Place garlic and salt in empty mortar and grind together to make a paste. Slowly add olive oil, then sprinkle in cayenne, black pepper, and fennel.
- Rub about 1/3 of the paste over the skinless side of the meat, then place skin side down on a roasting pan in lower third of oven. Cook for 30 minutes. Meanwhile stir the syrup and vinegar into the remaining paste.
- Turn the oven down to 225. Carefully flip the shoulder (use a clean towel), then use a rubber spatula to spread the remaining paste over the shoulder, pushing it into the scored skin.
- Return to oven and cook for 18 hours or longer (you can put it in the oven at bedtime and leave it in until you serve it as an early supper the next day, which is what I did; I just turned it all the way down to 150 for a couple of hours late in the afternoon), pouring 1/3 of the bottle of beer over it at several intervals, and basting with the drippings 2-3 times. Seriously. Before serving, turn up the heat to 450 for ten minutes if the skin is not crispy enough. Put it on a platter, and let people pull off pieces, like wild animals. They will fight over the skin.
- Serve with my Fresh Fennel and Red Pepper Chow-Chow (under "condiments"), and mashed sweet potatoes with apples. Leftover pork, Chow-Chow, and spicy mayo sandwich on ciabatta: very good idea.

187. Meatballs With Chinese Celery Over Noodles In Lemongrass Miso Sauce

Serving: Serves 2 to 4 | Prep: | Cook: | Ready in:

Ingredients

- 2 pieces lemongrass
- 4 scallions, green tops only
- 1/4 cup finely chopped Chinese celery, divided, plus 1/2 cup coarsely chopped stems (for the stock)
- 3 cloves garlic, 2 crushed and 1 minced
- one 1/2-inch slice ginger
- 3 tablespoons finely chopped cilantro, divided
- 1 tablespoon minced or grated fresh ginger
- 2 tablespoons soy sauce
- 1 tablespoon mirin
- 1/2 pound ground pork
- 1/2 pound ground turkey (dark meat)
- 2 carrots, julienned
- 1 cup sugar snap peas or snow peas, sliced diagonally in half
- 1 pound fresh thin lo mein noodles (or dried noodles, if you can't get fresh)
- 2 tablespoons peanut or other vegetable oil, for frying
- 1 tablespoon white miso (see note below)
- 1 to 2 tablespoons toasted sesame seeds, for garnish

Direction

- Cut off the hard root ends of the lemongrass and finely chop the innermost portion, discarding the tough outer layers and using only the most tender pieces close to where you cut off the end. You should have about 1 tablespoon of chopped lemongrass.
- Coarsely chop what remains of the lemongrass. Put it in a stock pot with the scallions, coarsely chopped Chinese celery stems, crushed garlic, slice of ginger, and about 6 cups of water. Over medium heat,

bring the mixture just to a boil, then turn it down to an active simmer, i.e., not quite a boil. Let it simmer, partially covered, while you marinate the meat.

- In a medium bowl, combine the finely chopped lemongrass with 2 tablespoons of the finely chopped Chinese celery, 1 tablespoon of the chopped cilantro, the minced ginger, the minced garlic, the soy sauce, and the mirin. Stir well.
- Gently pull the pork and turkey apart into small pieces and drop the pieces, a few at a time, into the bowl, using a fork carefully to combine the meat with the herb and soy marinade. Cover and refrigerate for at least an hour.
- Strain the stock, discard the solids, and transfer the stock to a large glass measuring cup. Return the stock to the soup pot with the heat on medium-high. When the stock boils, blanche the carrots for two minutes, then add the snap peas for another minute. Promptly remove the vegetables from the stock with a slotted spoon.
- Cook the noodles in the stock according to the instructions on the package but for about a minute less than suggested and adding only as much water as is necessary to equal the amount recommended for cooking. Reserve about 2 cups of the cooking liquid to use in the sauce. Drain the noodles, rinsing briefly with cold water to keep them from sticking together. (I typically start this step while the meatballs are browning.)
- When ready to cook the meatballs, form the meat into balls about the size of walnuts, and put them on a plate next to the stove. It helps to keep your hands wet while shaping the meatballs.
- Heat a very large skillet (one that you have a lid for), then add the oil. It will get hot very quickly. As soon as it starts to shimmer, add the meatballs and cook them for a few minutes, then turn them over and brown them on the other sides, for a total of about 5 or 6 minutes. Pour a cup of the reserved lemongrass stock (the noodle cooking liquid)

in the pan and put the lid on. Simmer gently for about 5 minutes.

- Push the meatballs to one side. Stir the miso and the remaining reserved stock into the sauce that's in the pan and mix to combine. (below.) Add more of the reserved stock if you want a bit more sauce.
- Add the noodles and the blanched vegetables; use tongs or chopsticks to toss it all together. Sprinkle on the remaining 2 tablespoons of chopped Chinese celery and cilantro and the sesame seeds, and gently toss again.
- Serve in large flat bowls, arranging the meatballs on top, with plenty of cold Chinese beer to wash it down.
- Enjoy!! ;o)
- Note: Start by adding a teaspoon of miso, then taste. If you want more, add it gradually. The recipe calls for 1 tablespoon, but that's for people who really like miso. It's always possible to add more, but not to subtract, so do add it gradually, to taste. ;o)

| 188. | **Mediterranean Pressed Picnic Sandwich** |

Serving: Serves 6-8 | Prep: | Cook: | Ready in:

Ingredients

- 1 loaf of good, round rosemary bread, or olive bread - about 12 inches across
- 1/4 cup sun dried tomatoes in olive oil, drained and julienned - reserve oil.
- 8 oz. jar of marinated artichoke hearts, drained, reserving marinade, chopped
- 2 tablespoons balsamic vinegar
- 2 teaspoons fresh lemon juice
- 1 tsp Dijon Mustard
- salt and pepper to taste
- 1/2 cup of purchased black olive tapenade
- 10 oz. of good, high quality, prosciutto slices
- 1 cup (large handful) of baby spinach and / or arugula leaves

- 8 ounces jar of roasted red peppers, drained and cut into strips for layering.
- 6 oz. of crumbled goat cheese
- 10-12 whole, large basil leaves

Direction

- Slice the loaf of bread in half horizontally, like a sandwich or hamburger bun, and remove the inside crumb from the top and bottom, leaving a 1/4 inch border all around. Save the crumbs for bread crumbs.
- Drain the artichokes and sun dried tomatoes, save their oils / marinades, and combine them together. To the marinade, add the balsamic vinegar, lemon juice, Dijon, and salt and pepper. Whisk well to incorporate and taste for seasoning - set aside. If the dressing is too strong, add a few teaspoons of olive oil as needed. You can also add some dried basil, oregano or rosemary if you like.
- Spread the inside of the TOP of the loaf with the olive tapenade, and lay the prosciutto slices in the BOTTOM, covering thoroughly.
- Layer the spinach, artichoke hearts, red pepper, goat cheese, basil leaves, and sun dried tomatoes on the prosciutto in that order. Make sure to cover the sandwich all the way to the edges as evenly as possible with every layer.
- Whisk the dressing well and carefully spoon in about 4 Tablespoons over the layers in the bread boule. Save the rest of the dressing for another use.
- Place the top with the tapenade back on top of the loaf and press down well to secure the top.
- Wrap the loaf securely in wax paper and butcher's twine, and then wrap again securely in aluminum foil. Place in the refrigerator overnight with a heavy cast iron pan or brick on the sandwich to weigh it down.
- When ready to serve, simply unwrap the sandwich and cut into wedges with a serrated knife. It will go quickly. Can be unrefrigerated for up to 4 hours as long as it isn't blazing hot, but I normally keep it in the cooler until about 1/2 hour before it's needed.

189. Melissa Clark's Crispy Salt & Pepper Pork

Serving: Serves 2 to 4, depending on hunger | Prep: | Cook: | Ready in:

Ingredients

- 1 pound boneless pork shoulder (butt), cut into 1-inch cubes
- 1/2 teaspoon fine sea salt
- 1 tablespoon black peppercorns
- 2 teaspoons Sichuan peppercorns (or more black pepper if you can't find them — it just won't be as tongue-tingling)
- Pinch of red chile flakes
- 1 tablespoon peanut oil (make sure it's refined for high heat), or grapeseed or safflower oil
- 1 teaspoon flaky sea salt, like Maldon
- 1/2 cup soft herbs, such as cilantro, mint, chives, and/or basil
- 1 small jalapeño or other chile, seeded and sliced or chopped
- Crisp lettuce leaves, torn and/or sliced cucumbers, for serving
- Lime wedges, for serving

Direction

- In a large bowl, toss the pork cubes with the fine sea salt. Using a spice mill or a mortar and pestle, coarsely grind together the black peppercorns, Sichuan peppercorns, and the red chile flakes. If you've gone electric, be careful not to overdo it; you want some texture here. Add the spices to the pork, tossing well. Let it rest for 20 minutes at room temperature.
- Heat a large, heavy skillet (preferably cast iron or stainless steel, not nonstick) over high heat until it is very hot. Add the oil and let it heat until it is shimmering. Then add the pork and sprinkle it with the flaky sea salt. Stir-fry until the pork cubes are golden brown all over, 5 to 7 minutes. Do this in a couple batches if

needed to be sure not to crowd the meat in the pan, or it will steam, rather than brown. (To get a good sear on the meat and avoid sticking, it helps to leave it alone in the pan for a minute or two before stirring, then leave it alone again, repeat. It should be nice and brown on the bottom each time you do this.)
- Transfer the pork to a platter and top it with the herbs and chile. Serve with the lettuce and/or cucumbers, with lime wedges on the side.

190. Mexican Meatballs

Serving: Makes makes 20-25 meatballs | Prep: | Cook: | Ready in:

Ingredients

- for the meatballs:
- 1 pound ground beef (80/20 or 85/15)
- .5 pounds ground pork
- 3 eggs
- 1/4 cup cream or half and half
- 3/4 - 1 cups panko bread crumbs
- 2 chipotle chilies + 2 tbsp adobo sauce (diced)
- 1/2 yellow onion (minced)
- 4 cloves garlic (minced)
- 1/2 4.5oz can diced green chilies (mild)
- 1 tablespoon cumin
- 1 tablespoon dried oregano
- 1/2 tablespoon coriander
- salt and pepper
- olive oil
- for the sauce:
- 1/2 yellow onion (minced)
- 4 cloves garlic (minced)
- 1/2 4.5oz can diced green chilies (mild)
- 1 28 oz can whole peeled tomatoes
- 1 1/2 cups chicken stock (low sodium or homemade)
- 1/2 cup adobo sauce (from chipotle pepper can)
- 1/2 tablespoon cumin

- 1/2 tablespoon dried oregano
- 1 teaspoon coriander
- salt and pepper

Direction

- Start with the meatballs. In a large sauté pan with high sides, heat olive oil over medium heat. Add onions, garlic, just a dash each of cumin, coriander, and oregano, salt and pepper. Cook for 5 minutes. Remove to a large mixing bowl.
- Add the remainder of the meatball ingredients to the onions and garlic. Mix everything together with your hands. The mixture will be fairly moist, but this ensure a tender meatball. Roll the mixture into golf ball sized meatballs and set on a plate.
- In the same sauté pan, keep the heat at medium and drop in the meatballs. You will likely have to do this in two batches. Sauté on all sides, about 6 minutes total, until a brown crust has formed. Remove and set aside.
- Add a dash more olive oil to what is left in the pan. Add the onion, garlic, chilies, salt and pepper. Sauté for 3 minutes and add the rest of the ingredients. Make sure you break up the whole tomatoes with your hand or the back of a wooden spoon. Cover and bring to a simmer.
- Once sauce is simmering, drop in meatballs. Cover and lower heat to low. Let simmer for 20-30 minutes.
- Serve with cilantro rice, Greek yogurt or sour cream, and fresh cilantro.

---

191.   Mile High Alpine Quiche

Serving: Serves 12 | Prep: | Cook: | Ready in:

Ingredients

- Quiche Filling
- 1/2 pound bacon, chopped
- 2 pounds mushrooms, thinly sliced
- Salt and Pepper
- 4 Green onions, chopped
- 1 teaspoon dried thyme
- 1/2 pound Swiss cheese, shredded
- * Pastry Shell
- 4 cups half and half
- 6 eggs, beaten
- *Pastry Shell
- 2 cups flour
- 1 teaspoon Kosher salt
- 1/2 pound butter, cold, unsalted, cut up
- 1/4 cup ice water

Direction

- Quiche Filling
- Preheat the oven to 325. Cook bacon in a large skillet over moderately high heat until crisp; remove bacon to paper towel. Keep heat at moderately high and cook mushrooms in bacon fat about 5 minutes, stirring occasionally. Reduce the heat to medium; add onions and thyme and cook, stirring often, until the mushrooms are tender, about 10 minutes. Season vegetables with salt and pepper; cool.
- Sprinkle 1/4 cup of the cheese over bottom of the Pastry Shell. Combine half and half and eggs; season with 1 teaspoon salt and 1/4 teaspoon pepper. Stir in bacon, remaining cheese and vegetable mixture into eggs. Pour egg mixture into pastry shell.
- Bake the quiche for about 1 1/2 hours, or until brown on top and the custard is just barely set in the center. I wiggle it in oven and there is a slight jiggle to the middle section; this will finish cooking upon cooling. Let cool slightly in the pan to be able to carve nicely. Run a small spatula between the pan and the baked crust to make sure it releases from pan before removing springform pan latch. Cut quiche into wedges and serve warm or at room temperature.
- Make Ahead The quiche can be cooled and refrigerated overnight. To serve, first cut quiche into serving size wedges, place pieces on a baking sheet and bake 350 oven about 12-15 minutes until warm.

- *Pastry Shell
- 1. In bowl of Standing Mixer or a Food Processor mix flour and salt. While machine running, add butter till mixed in. Add water, half at a time just until thoroughly incorporated. Flatten the pastry into an 8-inch disk, wrap in plastic and refrigerate until chilled, at least 1 hour or overnight.
- 2. Set a 9-inch springform pan on a baking pan with sides, lined with parchment paper or foil. Spray the inside of the pan with cooking spray.
- 3. On floured board, roll out pastry into a 16-inch round; transfer to the springform pan and press it firmly up to the top of pan, trimming as necessary. Refrigerate the pastry for 15 minutes to firm up.
- 4. Preheat the oven to 375°. Line the pastry shell plastic wrap or parchment paper; fill the shell with dried beans or rice. (I save a whole bag of this stuff and reuse it all the time) Bake the crust for about 40 minutes, or until lightly browned. Grab the plastic wrap or parchment paper and remove the beans. Bake crust for another 15 minutes until nicely browned. Cool Pastry shell. The pastry shell can be covered and held at room temperature overnight.

---

192.   Mini Tortillas

Serving: Makes 14 | Prep: | Cook: |Ready in:

Ingredients

- 1 tablespoon olive oil + extra for greasing
- 1 onion
- 100 grams artichoke hearts in oil
- 60 grams roasted red peppers in oil
- 7 pieces Serrano ham or prosciutto
- 6 eggs
- 100 milliliters cream
- 60 grams parmesan, grated
- salt and pepper

Direction

- Prep: 35min - Easy
- Preheat the oven to 160°C fan.
- Halve the onion and cut into thin slices. Heat the oil in a frying pan and fry the onion slices slowly for 10 minutes until soft. Set aside.
- Put the artichoke hearts and roasted red peppers onto a few pieces of kitchen towel to absorb the excess oil. Cut into bite sized pieces.
- Cut the ham or prosciutto slices into squares, to line the muffin holes.
- Grease the holes of a muffin tin with a bit of olive oil, line each hole with a slice of ham to cover the base and all sides. Distribute the onion, artichoke and red peppers between the 14 muffin holes.
- Beat together the eggs, cream and parmesan. Season with salt and pepper.
- Fill each muffin hole with the egg mixture and bake in the oven for 18 minutes.
- Leave the tortillas to cool in the muffin tin for 5 minutes, then take out with the help of a spoon and serve immediately or transfer onto a wire rack and leave to cool.
- TIP: You can play around with other flavor combinations. Try adding olives, sundried tomatoes and basil leaves instead of the artichokes and roasted pepper.

---

193.   Monte Cristo With Orange And Rosemary Maple Syrup

Serving: Makes 2 | Prep: | Cook: |Ready in:

Ingredients

- 1 1/2 tablespoons fresh squeezed orange juice
- 1/8 teaspoon orange zest
- 1/4 teaspoon fresh rosemary, very finely minced
- 1/2 cup pure maple syrup
- fresh ground black pepper
- 4   slices of brioche

- 6 thin slices of ham, turkey or both, cut to fit the bread
- 3/4 cup gruyere cheese, grated
- 2 egg yolks
- 3 tablespoons half and half
- 2 egg whites, whipped until stiff
- 1 cup panko bread crumbs
- 1 to 2 tablespoons unsalted butter

Direction

- In a small sauce pan combine the orange juice, zest, rosemary, maple syrup and pepper. Bring to a boil and remove from the heat.
- Make two ham and cheese sandwiches with the bread, cheese and ham.
- Combine the cream and the egg yolks in a flat container and whisk them together. Place the panko crumbs on a plate.
- Dip one side of each sandwich into the egg yolk mixture and let it soak up some of the liquid. Flip the sandwich to soak the other side.
- While it is soaking spread an even layer of the egg white across the top of the sandwiches and sprinkle with panko.
- Turn the sandwiches out onto the panko, panko side down. Coat the uncoated side of the sandwich with egg white and then flip it again.
- Place a nonstick skillet over medium heat and melt the butter in the pan. When it is bubbling add the sandwiches. Brown slowly so the interior gets warm and melty. Flip and brown the other side. Cut the sandwiches in half and plate them. Serve with hot syrup on the side.
- As you can see it would be easy to make these in larger quantities. Heat the oven to 250 and brown them a little faster, put them on a sheet tray and let the oven finish cooking them while you are onto making other sandwiches.

194. Moroccan Butternut Squash With Chicken, Chorizo, And Mussels

Serving: Serves 4 | Prep: | Cook: |Ready in:

Ingredients

- olive oil for pan
- 2 small chicken breasts
- 1/2 pound fresh chorizo, out of the sausage skin
- 18 black mussels, cleaned
- 2 cloves garlic, peeled and minced
- 1 large yellow onion, chopped
- 1 leek, chopped into rounds
- 1 inch fresh ginger, grated
- 2 teaspoons ground cumin
- 1/2 teaspoon ground coriander seed
- 1 teaspoon hot paprika
- kosher salt to taste
- fresh milled pepper to taste
- 2 fresh tomatoes, peeled
- 1 red bell pepper, cored and sliced into 1/2 inch strips
- 1/2 cup white wine
- 1 parsnip, peeled and chopped
- 1 turnip, peeled and sliced into chunks
- 1 carrot, peeled and chopped
- 1 large butternut squash, peeled, seeded and diced into inch or so size chunks
- 10 ounces chick peas, cooked
- 1 ounce dried cranberries
- 1 ounce sliced dried apricots
- 1 ounce yellow raisins
- 3 cups homemade chicken and mussel broth
- pinch of saffron
- serve with couscous, rice or other grain
- bunch of chopped cilantro and flat leaf parsley
- lemon wedges for garnish
- 1 tablespoon hot red pepper flakes
- 2-3 tablespoons olive oil
- 1/2 teaspoon ground coriander seed

Direction

- In a large Dutch oven brown the chicken with chorizo. Then remove the meat and set aside. When cool, cut up the chicken into small pieces. I keep the skin and bones.
- Saute the onion, garlic, leek in olive oil with spices. Add the red pepper and peeled tomatoes and stir over medium heat. Add the white wine and reduce. Next add the other vegetables and fruit; cook for a few minutes.
- Pour in the broth. Add the cut up chicken and cleaned mussels. Simmer over medium heat for 15 to 20 minutes. Take out a small amount of the broth and let the saffron infuse in it. Return to the pan and simmer gently until all the vegetables are tender, but not overcooked. Debone the chicken at this point, if you prefer.
- In a small pan heat the pepper flakes. Add the oil and stir in the coriander. Serve this in a small bowl on the side. When ready to plate the squash stew, serve over rice, couscous or other grains with chopped herbs and lemon wedges.

---

195. NOLA Muffaletta

Serving: Serves 4 to 6 | Prep: | Cook: | Ready in:

Ingredients

- For the olive salad
- 1 1/2 cups Kalamata olives, finely chopped
- 1 1/2 cups pimiento stuffed green olives, finely chopped
- 1 cup giardiniera, finely chopped
- 1 tablespoon brined capers, chopped
- 2 cloves finely minced garlic
- 1/4 teaspoon crushed red pepper flakes
- 1/4 teaspoon dried Italian seasoning
- 1/2 cup finely chopped red onion
- 1/2 cup chopped flat leaf parsley
- 1/2 cup extra virgin olive oil
- For the sandwich
- 1 loaf ciabatta bread (about 14 by 8 inches), sliced horizontally
- 1/2 to 3/4 pounds deli ham, sliced thin
- 1/2 to 3/4 pounds genoa salami, sliced thin
- 1/2 pound thinly sliced provolone cheese
- as much of the olive salad as you like
- extra virgin olive oil
- dried Italian seasoning

Direction

- For the olive salad
- Combine all ingredients and refrigerate for at least an hour in order for the flavors to blend.
- For the sandwich
- Brush the cut sides of the ciabatta loaf with the olive oil and sprinkle on some Italian seasoning.
- Layer the salami, ham, and cheese on the bottom side of the bread, finishing with a thick layering of the olive salad. (Or sprinkle the olive salad between each layer of meat and cheese -- no rules!)
- Place the top of the loaf on the sandwich, wrap tightly in plastic wrap, and place the loaf in the refrigerator with some weight on it for at least two hours. Slice and serve.

---

196. NW Applewood Smoked Pork & Sauce

Serving: Serves 20-30 | Prep: 1hours15mins | Cook: 0hours0mins | Ready in:

Ingredients

- NW Applewood Smoked and Braised Pulled Pork
- 8 pounds bone-in pork shoulder or butt
- 1 tablespoon kosher salt
- 2 teaspoons ground black pepper
- 2 teaspoons brown sugar
- 1 teaspoon smoked paprika
- 1 teaspoon crushed brown or yellow mustard seeds
- 1 teaspoon dried thyme
- 1 teaspoon dried and crumbled rosemary

- 1 teaspoon granulated garlic
- 2 large apples, cored and diced but not peeled
- 1 large sweet onion, sliced pole-to-pole
- 1/4 cup apple cider vinegar
- 1/4 cup Calvados or similar oak-aged apple brandy (or Bourbon if you can't find apple brandy)
- 10 lightly crushed juniper berries
- additional salt to taste
- Caramelized Apple and Onion Barbecue Sauce
- 2 medium apples, cored and finely chopped but not peeled
- 1/2 medium sweet onion
- 2 tablespoons butter
- 2 dashes ground white pepper
- 1 pinch baking soda
- 1/2 teaspoon smoked paprika
- 1 dash allspice powder
- 3 tablespoons brown sugar, divided
- 1/3 cup apple cider vinegar
- 1/2 cup smoked/pulled pork braising juices (from the accompanying recipe or substitute prepared stock with the addition of a little liquid smoke or more smoked paprika)
- 2 tablespoons molasses (or honey, maple syrup, etc.)
- 2 tablespoons ketchup (optional)
- salt to taste

Direction

- NW Apple wood Smoked and Braised Pulled Pork
- Set up smoker per manufacturer's directions. Include water in the liquid pan if it has one. Place a full charge of apple wood chips (pre-soaked in water) in the smoke box. Preheat to 225°F.
- Combine the measured salt, pepper, brown sugar, smoked paprika, mustard seeds, thyme, rosemary, and garlic in a small bowl and stir together to make a dry rub.
- Apply the dry rub (reserving 2tsp for later use) all over the pork and place it fat-side-up in a low-sided pan that will just fit it. I use disposable foil pans or a quarter sheet pan lined with parchment paper for this.
- Place the meat on a middle rack in the smoker and smoke at 225°F for about 4 hours, pausing to refill the water pan and recharge the smoke tray with fresh wood chips about three times (I do this on the hour). After 4 hours, the pork should have an internal temperature of 150°F, but it isn't necessary.
- Prepare a large (at least 7 quarts) enameled cast iron Dutch oven or a large crock pot for the braise: Place the sliced onion and apples in the bottom, sprinkle on the reserved 2tsp of dry rub and crushed juniper berries (use a mortar and pestle or the side of a chef's knife) and pour in the vinegar and Calvados. Place the pork on top of the bed of apples/onions and pour in any juices that collected in the pan while in the smoker.
- Cover with the lid and braise for at least 4 hours and up to 20 hours over low heat on the stovetop or high heat in a crock pot. Aim for a constant low boil. If you want to speed the cooking process for a shorter braise, cut the large chunk of meat into 4-8 smaller chunks in the pot.
- After about 4 hours, the meat should be tender enough to "pull" by simply stirring it with tongs. Remove the bone at this point. If it isn't soft enough yet to separate, give it more time and heat. If a lot of liquid has built up, crack the lid for the final hour of cooking and stir often to reduce and concentrate the juices. This is harder to accomplish in a crock pot because most products don't supply enough heat to keep a boil with the lid cracked. That's the main reason I prefer stovetop preparation. If you just can't get the juice reduced, pull some off with a ladle and keep it for another use such as a soup or the accompanying barbecue sauce.
- Adjust the salt, acid, and sweet seasoning as desired before serving. I often mix in half a cup of barbecue sauce to further moisten and flavor the meat.
- Caramelized Apple and Onion Barbecue Sauce

- Melt butter in a 1-2 quart saucepan over medium-high heat. Add onion, white pepper, a few pinches of salt, baking soda, and 1 tsp of the brown sugar. Stir and let it cook uncovered until the onions start to brown and stick to the pot a little (7-10 minutes).
- Have some water handy in a small cup. Pour in about 2 tsp of water, and deglaze the browned bits from the bottom of the pan using a flat-tipped wooden spoon. Let the onions cook and brown again undisturbed (but watch carefully--don't let them burn!) for about 5 minutes. Repeat the water deglazing. Again repeat the browning rest and deglazing a third time until a deep brown-colored paste is achieved. If you think it can get darker without burning, go for a fourth rest and deglaze.
- Now add half the apples with a little salt, stir, add a little water and quickly close the lid. This rapidly steams a portion of the apples and speeds up the breakdown process.
- After 5 minutes, remove the lid, add the remaining apples, cider vinegar, remaining brown sugar, smoked paprika, and allspice. Stir and continue to cook over medium-high heat while watching carefully to prevent burning.
- Once the apples are browned and starting to disintegrate (5-10 minutes later), add the pork braising juice or stock and cook for another 5-10 minutes. For a sweeter sauce, add molasses (my favorite), honey, maple syrup or any combination thereof. A tablespoon of ketchup or two is optional but really ties the flavors together well. Remove from heat and puree with an immersion blender then try a taste test. Adjust with salt, cider vinegar, or brown sugar as needed.

197.   Nearly Nikujaga Soup

Serving: Serves 2-4, depending on appetite | Prep: | Cook: | Ready in:

Ingredients

- For almost dashi:
- 3 ½ cups store bought or homemade chicken stock
- 4" x 4" piece dried kombu, wiped (but not washed) with a clean towel
- 1 1/2 inch piece fresh ginger (slightly thicker than your thumb), peeled, cut into six coins, lightly crushed with the back of a knife
- For potatoes and pork:
- 5 1/2 ounces piece of boneless pork belly
- 2 teaspoons canola oil
- 1 bunch green onions, white and light green parts only
- 2 large russet potatoes (11/2 - 1 3/4 lb)
- 2 1/2 cups mizuna, washed and thoroughly dried
- Shichimi Togarashi for serving
- For the braising liquid:
- 1/3 cup sake
- 2 tablespoons dark brown sugar
- 2 tablespoons reduced sodium, gluten free Tamari
- 1/4 cup water

Direction

- Start almost dashi: In a small saucepan, combine the chicken stock, Kombu and ginger coins. With cover slightly ajar, slowly heat the mixture over medium low heat.
- Prep potatoes and pork: Using a sharp knife, slice pork belly crosswise into ½" thick pieces. Lay each slice flat and cut in half. Place in a small bowl and set it next to your stovetop. Slice the green onions into thin rounds –you should have about 1/2 cup. Peel, quarter and cut potatoes into roughly 1" pieces –you should have about 4 cups. Chop mizuna (or other greens) into 1" lengths. Set vegetables in bowls near stove.
- Make braising liquid: In a glass one cup measure, combine sake, brown sugar and tamari. Stir to dissolve sugar. Set next to bowl of pork.

- Heat oil in a Dutch oven over medium heat, swirling pot to evenly coat. When oil is just shimmering, add pork and cook, allowing each side to brown for a minute or two before turning. Add green onion and potatoes, and continue to cook for about a minute, stirring gently to combine.
- Add the braising liquid, a few tablespoons at a time, to the pork and potato mixture. Stir after each addition and lower the heat if it starts to burn. Once you've added all the liquid, fill cup measure with ¼ cup of water and add that to the pot. Cover with lid and adjust heat as necessary to slowly simmer for 20 minutes.
- Remove Kombu from chicken stock and discard. Ladle enough stock into potato pot to just cover with liquid. Cover and continue cooking until potatoes are fully cooked and tender, about 15 minutes more. Ladle in remaining warm stock and stir in chopped mizuna. Allow soup to cook for a minute or two more to slightly wilt the greens. Serve immediately in soup bowls topped with a pinch of shichimi togarashi. Enjoy.

198. New Year's Day Ham And Beans

Serving: Serves 6 | Prep: | Cook: |Ready in:

Ingredients

- 1 pound Great Northern beans
- 1/2 onion, chopped, or more to taste
- 1 cup chopped celery leaves, and some of the inner ribs chopped if desired
- 1 ham bone with some ham still attached
- 2 pounds ham, cut in 1 inch chunks
- salt to taste

Direction

- Pick over beans and soak in water overnight.
- Drain and rinse beans.

- Put beans in large pot and cover with 6 cups of water.
- Add celery leaves, celery if desired, onion, ham and ham bone.
- Bring to a boil.
- Reduce heat to a simmer, and partially cover with lid.
- Simmer for 2 hours, until desired thickness (we like ours thick, but you could also make it soupier). Add salt at end depending on how salty your ham is.
- Serve with cornbread.

199. Okonomiyaki

Serving: Serves 4 | Prep: | Cook: |Ready in:

Ingredients

- Pancake
- 1 cup water
- 2 teaspoons dashi powder
- 1 cup all purpose flour
- 1 teaspoon sugar
- 1 teaspoon baking powder
- pinch salt
- 1/2 cup onion, thinly sliced
- 1 tablespoon canola oil
- 2 cups cole slaw mix
- 1 1/2 cups cooked chopped seafood, pork, or bacon, or a combination
- 3 large eggs
- 3 green onions, chopped
- Kewpie mayonnaise
- Katsuobushi (bonito flakes - optional)
- pickled ginger (optional)
- Okonomiyaki Sauce
- 3 tablespoons ketchup
- 3 tablespoons horseradish dijon mustard
- 3 Worcestershire sauce

Direction

- Bring the water to a simmer and add the dashi. Stir to dissolve and allow to cool to room temperature.
- In a large bowl, combine the flour, sugar, baking powder, and salt. Slowly add the cooled dashi to the flour mixture, stirring to make a batter. Cover and refrigerate batter for at least an hour and up to three hours.
- While the batter is resting, saute the sliced onion in a bit of canola oil with a pinch of salt until the onion has softened. Stir in shredded cabbage and stir fry for a few minutes until the cabbage gets limp. Remove from heat and set aside.
- After the batter has rested for an appropriate length of time, beat the three eggs and add them to the batter. Drain and discard any liquid that has accumulated from the cabbage and onion mixture; add vegetables to the batter along with any seafood or pork you wish to use. The batter will be very thick.
- Add a tablespoon of canola oil to an 8" nonstick frying pan and heat until it shimmers. Add okonomiyaki batter to a depth of about 3/4" inch. Cover pan and cook over medium-low heat, for about 5-7 minutes. Remove lid. Place a large plate over the pancake and flip out onto the plate. Cover the pancake with another plate and invert, so the pancake is uncooked-side down on the second plate. Carefully slide pancake into the pan. Cook the second side for another 10 minutes or so, turning heat down to medium-low.
- When the pancake is done, transfer to a serving plate. Drizzle with mayonnaise, sprinkle with bonito flakes and scallions, and serve pickled ginger on the side.
- Cut into wedges and serve with Okonomiyaki sauce.
- Okonomiyaki sauce: combine all ingredients in a bowl.

200.   Okonomiyaki (Savory Japanese Cabbage Pancake)

Serving: Makes 1 big pancake, large enough to split | Prep: | Cook: |Ready in:

Ingredients

- For pancake:
- 1/3 teaspoon dashi stock powder
- 2/3 cup water
- 1/2 cup all-purpose flour
- 1 egg
- 3 tablespoons tenkasu (tempura bits)
- 2 cups cabbage, chopped into thin strips
- 1/3 cup chopped green onions
- 3 to 4 strips bacon, chopped into 2 to 3 inch-long pieces
- For serving:
- Kewpie mayo (regular works fine too!)
- Okonomi sauce (or a homemade version: 3 tablespoons ketchup plus 1 tablespoon Worcestershire sauce plus 1 teaspoon soy sauce plus 1/2 teaspoon honey)
- Aonori (seaweed flakes)
- Sesame seeds

Direction

- In a large bowl, mix the dashi stock powder into the water until it dissolves. Whisk in the flour, egg, and tenkasu to make a batter.
- Add in the cabbage and most of the green onion (reserving a pinch). Fold into the batter until combined.
- Heat a large greased pan over medium-high. Dump the cabbage batter into the pan; using a small spatula, flatten batter top and edges into a round pancake about 1/2- to 3/4-inch thick. I've found that the less craggy the edges of the pancake, the easier it is to flip.
- Cover the top of the pancake with the bacon pieces in a single layer. Cook pancake this way for 3 to 4 minutes, then flip—using a big-old flat spatula—so the bacon-side is down. Cook until bacon has crisped, about 5 minutes, and

then flip again to cook for an additional 3 to 4 minutes, bacon side up.

- Slide pancake onto a large plate. If your mayonnaise and okonomi sauce aren't in squeeze bottles, scoop a spoonful of each into a bottom corner of separate plastic bags. Snip the corner with scissors to allow for precision-squirting. Zig-zag the okonomi sauce over the top in one direction, and the Kewpie (or regular) mayo in the other. Sprinkle remaining green onions, aonori, and sesame seeds over the sauces.

---

201.   Oriental Spaghetti

Serving: Makes about 30 2 inch meatballs | Prep: | Cook: | Ready in:

Ingredients

- 3 cups Thinly Shredded Cabbage (1/4 Head) or approx. a 12 oz package of coleslaw w/carrots
- Kosher Salt
- Freshly Ground White Pepper
- 1 Large Egg
- 1 1/2 pounds Ground Pork
- 3/4 cup Panko Crumbs
- 4 Scallions, minced
- 1 teaspoon Dried Ginger or 1 (1 inch) piece freshly grated.
- 3 tablespoons Low Sodium Soy Sauce
- 1 tablespoon Toasted Sesame Oil
- 2 teaspoons Cornstarch
- 2 tablespoons Water
- 4 teaspoons Chili Sauce
- 2 teaspoons Rice Wine Vinegar
- 1 tablespoon Sugar
- 3 tablespoons Toasted Sesame Seeds
- 1 packet (2 pouches) Stir Fry Noodles (KAME-Hokkien)
- 3 handfuls Cashews

Direction

- Preheat oven to 400° F. Line a baking sheet with parchment paper. Heat the sesame oil in a large nonstick pan. Add the cabbage and garlic. Season with Kosher salt and white pepper and ginger; cook until soft (~4 min). Set aside to cool. In a 2 cup measuring cup; mix together the soy sauce, sugar, chili sauce, rice vinegar, water and cornstarch. Put the pork into a mixing bowl. Add the scallions, garlic, egg, Panko crumbs, and cooled cabbage. Season with white pepper. Lightly roll mixture into 2 inch meatballs. Place onto baking sheet.
- Combine the sauce ingredients, set 1 cup aside for serving. Brush the meatballs with remaining sauce and sprinkle with sesame seeds. Bake until cooked through 20 to 25 minutes. Heat the stir fry noodles in 1 TBSP. Sesame oil with the cashews in a skillet with reserved sauce. Toss the meatballs and noodles with the sauce and serve.
- The meatballs freeze well.

---

202.   Our Favorite Chili

Serving: Serves 8 to 10 | Prep: | Cook: | Ready in:

Ingredients

- 2 tablespoons vegetable oil
- 1 1/2 cups chopped white or yellow onion
- 8 large garlic cloves, minced
- 1 pound ground beef chuck
- 1 pound bulk Italian sausage
- 1 pound ground veal
- 5 tablespoons chili powder
- 1 tablespoon ground cumin seed
- 1 teaspoon dried basil leaves
- 1/2 teaspoon dried oregano leaves
- 1/2 teaspoon dried thyme leaves
- 3/4 teaspoon kosher salt
- freshly ground black pepper
- 1 28-ounce can crushed tomatoes

- 1 3/4 cups low-sodium (or homemade) chicken stock
- 1 6-ounce can tomato paste
- 1 12-ounce bottle lager beer
- 1 16-ounce can kidney beans, drained
- 2 teaspoons finely minced canned chipotle chili
- 1 teaspoon adobo sauce, from the canned chipotle

Direction

- In a 7 to 8 quart, heavy Dutch oven or soup pot, heat the vegetable oil over medium-high heat. Add the chopped onion and garlic, with a large pinch of kosher salt, and sauté until softened. Add the ground meats and stir, breaking up the meat and cooking until the meat is no longer pink. (At this point, you can spoon out a little of the extra fat from the pot, if you like).
- Add the spices, stir to coat the meat, and cook an additional 2 minutes. Add the tomatoes, chicken stock, tomato paste, beer, and the 3/4 teaspoon salt. Simmer the mixture for about 1 1/4 hours, or until the consistency is to your liking. Add the drained beans, the minced chipotles and adobo sauce, and adjust the salt and pepper to taste.
- Cool and store in the refrigerator, or portion into freezer containers and freeze for future use. We like grated sharp shredded cheddar cheese, chopped red onions, and sour cream with our chili. It also makes great nachos, garnished with a little guacamole and cilantro. If you like a few more vegetables in your chili, feel free to add some chopped celery and bell pepper along with the onion and garlic. Adjust the spiciness with more or less chipotle chile.

203.   Oyster Stew With Chorizo And Spinach

Serving: Serves 3-4 | Prep: | Cook: |Ready in:

Ingredients

- 1 tablespoon olive oil
- 6 ounces chorizo sausage, cut in 1/4" slices
- 1 medium onion, chopped
- 1 1/2 cups whole milk
- 1 cup heavy cream
- 1 cup shucked oysters (about 12), liquor drained and reserved
- 3 cups spinach leaves, washed
- 1 teaspoon salt, or to taste
- 1 teaspoon freshly ground black pepper, or to taste

Direction

- Heat olive oil in a large sauce pan over medium heat. Add chorizo. Cook, stirring, until golden brown, 3-4 minutes. Transfer chorizo to a plate lined with a paper towel. Pour off all but 1 tablespoon fat from saucepan.
- Add onion to saucepan and sauté over medium heat until translucent, about 3 minutes.
- Add milk, cream and reserved oyster liquor to the onions. Bring to a boil and reduce heat to a simmer.
- Add spinach and cook briefly until wilted but still bright green.
- Add oysters and simmer until cooked through, about 2 minutes. Add salt and pepper to taste.
- Serve immediately in warm bowls.

204.   POLPETTINI: LITTLE MEATBALLS WITH MELTED FONTINA CENTERS

Serving: Serves 24 as an appetizer | Prep: | Cook: |Ready in:

Ingredients

- Meatballs
- 1 pound ground pork
- 1 pound ground veal
- 3 ounces prosciutto, minced
- 1 tablespoon diamond brand kosher salt
- 2 garlic cloves
- 1 teaspoon smoked paprika
- 1 teaspoon fennel seeds
- 1 tablespoon dried oregano
- 1 teaspoon dried thyme
- 1/2 yellow onion
- 1/4 cup parsley
- 1/2 cup Parmigiano-Reggiano, grated, plus more for garnish
- 1 1/2 cups Italian breadcrumbs
- 1 cup fresh ricotta
- 1/4 cup milk
- 2 eggs, mixed with a fork
- 4 ounces Fontina cheese, cut into 1/4-inch cubes
- Tomato, Garlic, Wine Braise
- 2 tablespoons olive oil
- 1 onion, chopped
- 1 carrot, minced
- 3/4 cup white wine
- 4 cups crushed tomatoes
- 1 cup chicken stock
- 1/2 cup basil, coarsley chopped plus more for garnish
- 2 tablespoons fresh oregano
- 2 teaspoons kosher salt
- 1 loaf crusty bread
- toothpicks

Direction

- Form Meatballs: In a large mixing bowl, combine pork, veal, prosciutto, salt, garlic, pepper flakes, fennel seeds, oregano and thyme. Add the onion, parsley and Parmigiano-Reggiano and mix by hand. Add the breadcrumbs, ricotta and milk. Mix by hand. Add the eggs and stir until just barely incorporated (don't overmix). Form the mixture into 1-inch balls. Poke a hole in the center of each ball and fit a piece of Fontina in the hole. Cover with meat and place on two

well-oiled sheet pans. Bake until browned, about 12 minutes. (Rotate pan halfway through).
- Prepare Tomato-Wine Braise: In a large saucepan, heat oil over medium heat. When the oil is hot, add the onion and carrot and cook until the carrot is softened and the onion is translucent, about 6 minutes. Add garlic, then deglaze with the white wine and cook for 1 minute to evaporate wine. Then add the crushed tomatoes, stock, basil, oregano and salt. Increase heat to high and simmer for 5 minutes.
- Finish Meatballs: Drain the fat off the meatballs. Transfer meatballs into a presentable ovenproof baking dish. Pour the braising liquid over them (it should barely cover the meatballs). Return to the oven and braise for 5-10 minutes until cooked through.
- Serve: Garnished with Parmigiano-Reggiano and basil. Put crusty bread around the edge of the serving dish to sop up all the liquid. Put out toothpicks for serving.

205.   PORK LOIN PASTIES WITH CARAMELIZED ONIONS, POTATOES AND ROASTED GARLIC

Serving: Serves 28 | Prep: | Cook: | Ready in:

Ingredients

- 10 pounds Pork loin roast, diced to ¼ inch
- 3 onion, halved and thinly sliced
- 1 bunch garlic cloves, roasted
- 10 Medium russet potatoes, peeled and cut in quarters
- 12 cups Flour
- 12 Sticks Butter
- 2 teaspoons Salt
- 4 cups ice water, plus more if needed
- 1 Onion (Chopped)
- 4 pieces Pork loin ribs

- 1 cup white wine, preferably pinot grigio or sauvignon blanc
- 2-3 teaspoons Ham rue, I use "better than bullion brand"
- 1 teaspoon Chicken rue, I use "better than bullion brand"
- 1/2 cup Flour
- Salt and pepper

Direction

- Early in morning, measure 6 cups flour in a bowl and cut up cold butter, salt and work together flour and butter until mealy. Add water slowly and just squeeze to bring together. Don't work dough or it will get too hard. Once it comes together, put into 4 small balls and put in fridge for at least 30 minutes. Repeat with other 6 cups flour.
- On stove top, heat medium sauté pan and add 2-3 T butter and melt. Add onion and cook down until caramelized.
- Heat oven to 350. In a sheet of foil, add a bunch of garlic cloves. Toss with olive oil, salt, and pepper and dot with a little butter. Roast until golden brown but shake foil packet 2-3 times while cooking.
- Cut up pork loin into small dice, ¼ inch. With a tabletop grinder or kitchen aide grinder attachment, grind potatoes. Put out 3 bowls and divide pork evenly. Add ⅓ potatoes without water and incorporate into meat. Season with salt and pepper. Fold in ⅓ onion and garlic. Repeat with other 2 bowls.
- Take 2 dough balls out and divide into 3 or 4 slices and start to roll out into individual rounds. Put a full scoop of meat plus a bit more. Brush with water. Top with butter and fold over. Trim extra dough and fold over and pinch together. Put on parchment lined baking sheet. Sheet should hold 5 pasties and each bowl should make about 9 pasties.
- Turn oven to 350 and brush top of pasties with milk. Cook for 45 min then switch for another 45 min.
- While making pasties, cook pork ribs with salt and pepper for 45 min to 1 hour.

- While pasties are cooking, put 1 stick of buttering Dutch oven over med heat.
- Add onion and sauté until translucent. Season with salt and pepper. Add drippings from ribs and ½ cup flour. Stir until rue. Add 1 cup wine and fill with water. Add ham rue to taste and a little chicken rue. Boil until thick and season as needed. Strain and return to pot.
- Serve pasties immediately with gravy and coleslaw.
- Can cut recipe down if wanting to make less but they freeze beautifully.
- If freezing, individually wrap each pasty in foil and place in a ziplock bag. Reheat at 300 degrees for 20-30 minutes or until heated through.

206.   Paleo Effect Asian Glazed Pork Sides, A Sweet & Crispy Appetizer

Serving: Serves 6-8 | Prep: | Cook: | Ready in:

Ingredients

- For the Pork Sides
- 2 pounds Pork Sides
- 2 tablespoons Organic Coconut Oil
- 1 teaspoon Sesame Oil
- 2 Green Onions
- to taste Coarse Sea Salt
- For the Sauce
- 1/4 cup Coconut Aminos
- 1/4 cup Paleo Sweet Chili Sauce
- 2 Bird's Eye Chili Peppers
- 1/4 teaspoon fresh Ginger
- 1 tablespoon Coconut Vinegar

Direction

- Slice the pork sides to ¼" thick strips.
- Combine the coconut oil and sesame oil in a saucepan and heat over medium-high (~6.5)

heat. While the oils are heating, lightly dust the pork sides with sea salt on both sides.

- Once the oil is very hot, so hot that it pops on its own, add the pork sides in a single layer. Cook on the first side until it is golden brown and crispy, then flip each pork side, place in a single layer, and cook until golden and crispy on the second side. This will take a little while, be patient…it's worth it.
- While the pork sides are frying, combine the coconut aminos, Paleo Sweet Chili Sauce, Bird's Eye chili peppers (1 if you like mildly spicy, 2 if you like spicy), ginger paste, and coconut vinegar in a food processor and blend until combined. Set aside for later.
- Once the pork has cooked, take it out of the grease and drain on a paper towel. Repeat this until all of the pork sides have been cooked to a crispy, golden brown on the outside, with a tender, chewy center. Once the pork is warm, but not molten, toss it in the sauce and serve with chopped green onions.

207.   Pan Roasted Brussel Sprouts With Bacon & Shallot

Serving: Serves 6 | Prep: | Cook: | Ready in:

Ingredients

- 2 pounds brussel sprouts, trimmed & halved
- 12 ounces smoked bacon, cut into thin strips
- 5 shallots, julienned
- 2 tablespoons dark brown sugar
- 1/4 cup cider vinegar
- kosher salt & pepper to taste
- 2 tablespoons canola oil

Direction

- Preheat oven to 400.
- In a very large skillet, preferably cast iron, cook bacon over med-low heat until crispy. Remove with slotted spoon and reserve.

- Add canola oil and sauté shallots until soft and beginning to caramelize. Remove with slotted spoon and reserve with bacon.
- Increase heat to med & add Brussels sprouts to skillet, having as many with the cut side down as possible. Allow to cook for 3 min, transfer to oven & roast for about 15 minutes, until tender.
- Remove Brussels sprouts from skillet. Add vinegar and sugar and cook until reduced by half and syrupy. Toss with Brussels sprouts, bacon, and shallots. Season to taste with salt & pepper, serve.

208.   Pan Seared Pork Chops With Mustard Cream Sauce

Serving: Serves 2 | Prep: 0hours20mins | Cook: 0hours10mins | Ready in:

Ingredients

- 2 Bone in, Frenched organic pork chops
- 1/2 cup Organic heavy cream
- 1 cup Homemade organic chicken stock
- 1+ tablespoons Organic stone-ground mustard
- 1/2 teaspoon Kosher salt
- 1/4 teaspoon Freshly ground black pepper
- 2 teaspoons Olive Oil

Direction

- Preheat oven to 375. Next, preheat a stainless steel skillet over medium-high heat, meanwhile rinse your chops with cold water and pat dry with clean paper towels. Once dry, season both sides liberally with kosher salt and freshly ground black pepper.
- Add 2 tsp. olive oil to your skillet. Once the oil shimmers, add your chops. Your pan should be VERY hot. Cook for 4 minutes and then turn over and cook for another 4 minutes. If the pork chop will not release from the skillet, it isn't ready to be turned. Sear it until it

144

releases willingly. Your chops should be well browned.

- Transfer chops to a an oven safe dish and cook in the oven until a thermometer inserted into the middle of the chop reads 155 degrees and juices run clear. Let the chops rest on a cutting board with a piece of foil tented over them.
- Meanwhile- deglaze the pan you seared the chops in with the chicken stock making sure to scrape up all those tasty bits at the bottom of the pan and lower heat to medium low. Let the stock reduce slightly.
- Add 1-2 TB. of mustard (depends on how mustard-y you want your sauce to taste) and whisk to incorporate the mustard into the stock. Add some salt and pepper to taste. Let the mixture reduce slightly.
- Add 1/2 cup of heavy cream and whisk to combine. Lower heat to lowest setting and cook until the sauce reduces and thickens slightly. Pour in any meat juices found in the baking dish, stir and adjust seasonings if needed. Plate your chops and spoon over your mustard cream pan sauce and enjoy!

---

209.   Panctta And Cider Vinegratte Green Beans With Pickled Onions

Serving: Serves 4 | Prep: | Cook: | Ready in:

Ingredients

- Green Beans
- 1 pound fresh green beans
- 4 ounces cubed pancetta
- 1/2 small onion
- 2 cloves of garlic chopped
- 8 shitake mushrooms
- 5 chanterelle mushrooms
- 3/4 cup fresh unfiltered apple cider
- 1/2 cup chicken stock (or water)
- 2 cider vinegar (or other white vinegar)
- 1 teaspoon chopped thyme
- 1 tablespoon flour
- 1 tablespoon butter
- salt and pepper
- Pickled onions (see recipe below, make ahead of time since they need to sit for at least two hours before serving).
- Quick pickled onions
- 2 small onions
- 1/2 cup red wine vinegar
- 2 tablespoons sugar
- 1/2 teaspoon mustard seeds
- 6 peppercorns
- 1 bay leaf
- 1 teaspoon Sumac (optional)
- 1 tablespoon salt
- 3/14 cup apple cider (or water, but then add another tablespoon of sugar)

Direction

- Green Beans
- In a pot bring water to a boil and add 2 teaspoons of salt. Trim the ends of the green beans and add to the water. Cook for about 7 minutes until soften but still bright green and still have some bite. Take out of the water and let cool in a bowl with ice water to stop the cooking.
- Put a tablespoon of oil in a pan and add the pancetta cubes. Sauté for 5 minutes to render some of the fat.
- Cut the mushrooms to lengthwise and chop the onion to small dice. Add to the pan with a bit of salt and sauté for 5 more minutes.
- Add the garlic, thyme and salt and pepper and sauté for 2 minutes.
- Add the butter and let it melt. Add the flour mix well and sauté for 2 minutes.
- Add the cider, chicken stock and the vinegar, mix well and let it thicken for few minutes. If it becomes too thick you can add more water or cider (but first taste to see it is not too sweet for your taste).
- Add the cooked green beans and mix well to cover with the sauce.
- For serving put some of the pickled onions without their liquids on top on each serving.

- This is great on top of grilled salmon, pork or chicken.
- Quick pickled onions
- Put all the ingredients except for the onion in a sauce pan and bring to a boil. Cook for few minutes on medium heat to reduce the liquids a bit.
- In the meantime cut the onions in half, peel them and then cut to thin half-moon slices.
- Remove the pan from the heat and add the onions. Let it rest for at least 2 hours.
- Remove from the liquids before serving.

210. Pappardelle With Prosciutto, Pine Nuts And Brown Butter

Serving: Serves 4 | Prep: 0hours15mins | Cook: 0hours15mins | Ready in:

Ingredients

- 3/4 pound Pappardelle pasta
- 1/2 cup Unsalted butter
- 2 teaspoons Fresh lemon juice
- 3 ounces Thinly sliced prosciutto, torn into small pieces
- 1/2 cup Finely chopped fresh parsley leaves
- 1/3 cup Pine nuts, lightly toasted
- Lemon wedges for garnish

Direction

- Cook the pappardelle pasta according to package directions in a pot of salted boiling water.
- While the pasta is cooking, in a skillet heat the butter over moderately high heat, swirling it, until it is golden brown. Remove the skillet from the heat and stir in the lemon juice, the prosciutto, the parsley and the pine nuts.
- In a serving bowl toss the drained pappardelle with the butter mixture. Salt and pepper to taste and serve with the lemon wedges.

211. Pappas Relenas (R.F.U.G.) Chubby Spud

Serving: Serves 8-10 | Prep: | Cook: | Ready in:

Ingredients

- potato prep
- 5 pounds potato; peeled
- 4 teaspoons blk.pepper
- 1 tablespoon salt
- .25 cups milk
- 4 cups breading
- 2 cups wash
- filling and breading
- 2.5 pounds chorizo; out of casing
- 1 bunch cilantro; chopped
- 1 shallot; diced
- 1 galic; diced
- 1 carrot; diced
- 1 celery; diced
- 1 cup don't forget the cheese
- 2 pints sour cream
- 1 packet onion soup mix
- 4 tablespoons ancho paste

Direction

- Boil potatoes 20 min. (till you can break), toss w/ seasoning and milk; I say toss, we're not making mashed. Cool to workable.
- Brown meat, add seasonings; sauté lightly set aside when cool mix in cheese.
- With measuring tablespoon as form, press out ten; taking two, indent using thumb (2 football halves) use 2tsp filling and form (football) (~)
- Breading: as breading goes: a wash and some crunch. Here we used egg and crushed matzo coconut/soy work well w/rice flour
- Refrigerate till firm or freeze fry @375 (5-7min) until golden
- Dipping sauce: combine cream, mix, and paste; fold well

212.   Paseo Style Cuban Pork Sandwich

Serving: Makes 2 | Prep: | Cook: | Ready in:

Ingredients

- 1/2 tablespoon butter
- 1 tablespoon EVOO
- 1 small-medium sweet onion- sliced in rings
- 1 tablespoon honey
- 1 large garlic clove- pressed
- 1/2 cup nonfat plain yogurt
- pinch of ground cumin
- 1 tablespoon fresh lemon juice
- 1.5 cups pulled pork (like Kayb's Caribbean Roast Pork)
- 4 thin slices of smoked deli ham
- 4 slices of Swiss cheese
- 1 French baguette- halved lengthwise and cut in 2 portions
- handful of cilantro
- salt and pepper

Direction

- For caramelized onions: in a skillet, heat EVOO and butter over medium heat. Add onions and slowly caramelize until golden. Take off of heat, and add in honey and a pinch of salt.
- For garlic-yogurt spread: whisk together pressed garlic, yogurt, lemon juice, cumin, and a pinch of salt.
- For sandwiches: On each baguette half, slather on garlic spread, and layer pork, ham, Swiss, onions, and cilantro. Top with other baguette half. Heat big skillet over medium. Place sandwiches in skillet, and press (I press w/a heavy cast iron skillet) for a few minutes on each side, until cheese is melt.
- Grab a bunch of napkins, a cold, minty mojito, and dig in!

213.   Pear And Prosciutto Pizza

Serving: Serves 2 | Prep: | Cook: | Ready in:

Ingredients

- 1 packet original Naan bread (2 per packet)
- 6 tablespoons olive oil
- 6 ounces fresh Mozzarella cheese, sliced
- 3 ounces prosciutto, torn into pieces
- 1 small pear, sliced
- 1-2 Roma tomatoes, sliced
- 1/4 cup shaved or sliced Parmesan cheese
- fresh basil leaves

Direction

- Preheat oven to 420 degrees Fahrenheit.
- Place Naan bread on an ungreased cookie sheet. Brush tops with olive oil. Top with mozzarella slices, about 3-4 per crust (it doesn't need to be completely covered with cheese). Add remaining ingredients ensuring not to overcrowd. You might have leftover ingredients but they make a great snack in between meals.
- Place in the oven and bake for 10 minutes or until the bread is browned on the edges and cheese has melted. Serve immediately. Enjoy!

214.   Pear, Pancetta, Parmesan, Pine Nut Tart

Serving: Serves 6 or 8, depending | Prep: | Cook: | Ready in:

Ingredients

- For the Crust
- 2 1/2 cups all-purpose flour
- 1/2 teaspoon salt
- 1/2 teaspoon Sugar
- 8 ounces Butter, 1" cubes

- 6 ounces Ice water
- For the Filling
- 3 Anjou pears, peeled whole, stems intact
- 1 Bottle Prosecco
- 4 ounces Pancetta, 1/4" cubes
- 1/4 cup Pine nuts, toasted
- 4 Large eggs, lightly whisked
- 2 ounces Parmesan, fine grate
- 4 ounces Whole milk (please!) ricotta
- 1/2 teaspoon white pepper

Direction

- Prepare crust. This recipe makes 2 crusts, so plan to freeze one for a time when you need to pull a rabbit out of a hat.
- Make ice water by filling a vessel halfway with ice, then fill with cold water. Swish around. Pour off 6 ounces of ice water. Hold the ice!
- Sift together flour, salt, and sugar into the bowl of a mixer fitted with the paddle. Distribute chunks of butter over. Mix on lowest speed only until butter is averages the size of hazelnuts (or garbanzo beans). Butter pieces will grow smaller as water is added and some greater friction results.
- With mixer running on lowest speed, add water in a steady stream, mixing only until no visible dry ingredients remain in bottom of bowl. Stop Mixer.
- Turn dough out onto a lightly floured surface. Gently round it up using the palms of your hands - they transfer much less heat than your fingers. Divide into equal halves. Again round up each half using your palms. Gently but quickly flatten, then round, then flatten. You are going for a disk whose edges are intact, and which is about 3/4" thick. Wrap each disk in plastic. If only using one, freeze the other. Refrigerate at least 30 minutes before rolling.
- While crust is refrigerating, prepare filling. Preheat oven to 375 degrees.
- Pour Prosecco into a stainless steel pot (wines are acidic and will react poorly with aluminum, producing an off taste and potentially gray color). Bring to a simmer. Holding pears by stems, gently immerse in Prosecco. Simmer for 15 minutes. Carefully remove pears from pot by grasping stems with tongs. Set in colander to drain and cool enough that you can easily handle them.
- While pears are poaching, cube pancetta. Spread out on baking sheet lined with parchment. Sprinkle over pine nuts. Bake together until pancetta is crisped and pine nuts are golden brown and fragrant. Remove from oven and cool baking sheet on a cooling rack.
- Remove crust dough from refrigerator. Unwrap and place on a floured surface. Dust the top of the dough with flour. Roll out dough to where it is 1" larger than tart pan. Use tart pan as template, and cut circle of dough with a knife. Roll circle of dough back onto rolling pin, then drape into tart pan. Quickly but gently press into bottom edge of removable bottom tart pan. Return to refrigerator while you finish the filling. Increase oven heat to 375 degrees.
- Whisk together eggs, Parmesan, and ricotta. Add white pepper and whisk to blend. Will the tart police burst through your door is you use black pepper? Well, try it and see!
- Halve pears and scrape out cores with a melon baller. Lay flat on a cutting board, and cut into 1/4" slices. Depending on how obsessive-compulsive you are, either arrange in perfectly matched slices in perfect concentric circles in tart pan, which you have removed from the refrigerator. Alternatively, scatter over surface of dough. Scatter cooled pine nuts and bacon over pears. Scrape those lovely drippings into the egg mixture and whisk. Set tart pan on a baking sheet.
- Pour the egg mixture over the top of pears, bacon, and pine nuts.
- Bake until puffed and lightly golden brown on top, about 30 minutes. Remove from oven and let sit for 5 minutes. Carefully lift removable bottom out of tart pan. Cut into 6 or 8 equal slices and serve immediately.
- Bon appétit!

215. Peas & Pancetta

Serving: Serves 4 | Prep: | Cook: | Ready in:

Ingredients

- 12 ounces fresh shelled sweet peas, rinsed
- 4 ounces pancetta, bacon or guanciale, cured pig's cheek (omit if vegetarian)
- 1 small onion, sliced
- 2-3 cherry tomatoes, halved
- small handfuls small parsley, chopped
- tiny bit of mint, chopped (optional)
- salt & pepper
- extra virgin olive oil

Direction

- Bring a medium pot up to boil. In the meantime, in a medium skillet on medium-low heat, slowly render down the pancetta for 4-5 minutes, trying not to brown it and not crispy. If it starts to brown remove the pan from the heat or lower the flame.
- Next add garlic & onion, sauté for 5-6 minutes. (Vegetarian Note: Just omit the pancetta & sauté the onions & garlic in olive oil.)When the onions & garlic are about 2 minutes from being ready, add the tomatoes.
- At the same time toss the peas in the water and blanch for 2-3 minutes. You want them approximately half-cooked. Strain the peas and throw them directly into the pan with the pancetta adding a spoonful of the pea-water. Allow to cook until peas are cooked but still have a bite.
- Taste and adjust the seasoning with salt & pepper. Just before you serve, toss in the herbs and drizzle with good extra virgin olive oil.

216. Penne With Asparagus, Proscuitto And Lemon

Serving: Serves 8 | Prep: | Cook: | Ready in:

Ingredients

- 1 pound penne rigate
- 3/4 cup pecorino romano cheese, freshly grated
- 3/4 cup fontina cheese, freshly grated
- 3 tablespoons ricotta cheese
- 1-1/2 cups heavy cream
- 1 cup rich chicken stock (2 cups good quality low-sodium stock, reduced by half)
- 1 bunch asparagus, washed, dried and root ends trimmed
- 3 tablespoons butter, melted
- 1 tablespoon grated lemon zest
- 1 tablespoon fresh tarragon, finely minced
- 5 ounces thinly sliced imported prosciutto, roughly chopped
- 1/2 teaspoon kosher salt and a few grinds of white pepper
- 1/3 cup seasoned breadcumbs

Direction

- Preheat oven to 500.
- Bring a large pot of salted water to boil for the pasta.
- For the breadcrumbs - in a sauté pan heat 2 tablespoons EVOO over medium heat and toast 1 cup of panko breadcrumbs, 1/4 teaspoon salt and 1/4 teaspoon pepper until golden brown. Spread on a plate to cool. (Keep the balance for 2 days in the fridge, or a long time in the freezer).
- In a large bowl, combine the cream, reduced stock, lemon zest, tarragon, cheeses, salt and pepper.
- Slice the asparagus on an extreme bias, about 1/8-1/4" thick and toss into a small bowl with the melted butter, mix to coat.
- Boil the pasta for 4 minutes, then drain and toss into the bowl with the cream and other ingredients, mix well.

- Pour the pasta into a large baking dish or roasting pan so that it fits comfortably in a thin layer no more than 1" deep. Sprinkle the sliced asparagus and chopped prosciutto on top and toss it into the oven for 10-12 minutes, until the sauce is bubbling, and the pasta is just starting to brown.
- Remove from the oven and serve, passing breadcrumbs to sprinkle on top if desired (highly recommended).

---

217.   Penne With Cauliflower And Pancetta

Serving: Serves 4 | Prep: | Cook: |Ready in:

Ingredients

- Bread Crumb Topping
- 1 cup panko bread crumbs
- 2 tablespoons butter
- 2 cloves garlic, minced
- Pasta and Sauce
- 1/4 cup EVOO (more or less)
- 2 cloves garlic diced
- 1/4 - 1/2 teaspoons red pepper flakes
- 2 anchovy filets crushed to a paste
- 2 tablespoons capers
- Juice from 1/2 small lemon
- 1/2 cup chopped flat leaf parsley
- 1/2 cup Freshly grated Romano Cheese
- 1/3-1/2 cups vegetable or chicken broth
- 3 ounces chopped pancetta
- 1/3 cup chopped walnuts
- 1 head of Cauliflower, broken into 1 1/2 inch pieces
- 2-3 tablespoons EVOO (for Cauliflower)
- Salt and Pepper to taste
- 8 ounces Penne pasta cooked, drained

Direction

- Bread Crumb Topping

- Brown the breadcrumbs in a frying pan on medium heat, stirring frequently until golden. Remove from pan, set aside. In the same pan, melt the butter, then add the garlic - cook for a few minutes medium low, until garlic is tender. Remove from heat, add the breadcrumbs and toss. Set aside.
- Pasta and Sauce
- Preheat oven to 450 degrees.
- Toss Cauliflower with 2-3 TBS of EVOO, place on baking sheet. Sprinkle with kosher salt and fresh ground pepper. Bake in a 450 degree oven for about 30 minutes, turning/stirring about every ten minutes or until brown. Set aside.
- Heat the EVOO for the sauce in a large pan - add the garlic and pancetta - cook over medium heat until the pancetta begins to brown.
- Add the red pepper, anchovies, capers. Continue cooking until pancetta is golden. Toss in the parsley, squeeze in the lemon juice, add the cauliflower and walnuts and combine all.
- Place pasta in a serving dish, and pour sauce over. Add about 1/3 cup broth, mixing until pasta is evenly coated. (It will "thin out" the pancetta/cauliflower mixture a bit and allow more even coating)
- Add Romano cheese, toss again.
- Garnish with a generous sprinkling of garlic breadcrumbs and serve immediately with extra Romano cheese for sprinkling.

---

218.   Pepper Peach Pork

Serving: Serves 8 or more | Prep: | Cook: |Ready in:

Ingredients

- 3 tablespoons kosher salt
- Freshly ground black pepper
- 1 tablespoon sugar
- 1 teaspoon ground cumin
- 1/2 teaspoon ground coriander

- 8 pounds Boston butt or pork shoulder roast
- 2 large sweet onions, peeled and thinly sliced
- 4 medium peaches, peeled, pitted, and chopped
- 1 tablespoon brown sugar
- 1/4 cup white miso
- 3 jalapeños, seeded and chopped fine
- 1/2 cup chopped cilantro stems (from the top, not the root end; you'll need the leaves, too)
- 6 cloves garlic, minced
- 4 tablespoons rice vinegar, divided
- 1/2 cup cilantro leaves, chopped
- 1 red onion, peeled and sliced

Direction

- Mix together salt, pepper, sugar, cumin, and coriander in a bowl; rub all over the Boston butt. Cover in plastic wrap and refrigerate overnight.
- In a large skillet, heat olive oil over medium-high heat. Sear pork for 3 minutes per side, until browned all over. Place in slow cooker.
- Reduce heat to medium-low. Add in onions and a little salt, and let cook until starting to brown, around 15 to 20 minutes. While onions are cooking, toss your peaches in a bowl with the brown sugar and let macerate.
- Add the peaches and sugar to the pan with the onions, raise heat to medium-high, and cook, stirring occasionally, about 5 minutes. Add in miso paste and stir until fully incorporated.
- Pour over the pork in slow cooker and turn it to coat. Add in jalapeños, cilantro, garlic, and 1 tablespoon rice vinegar. Cover and cook on low for 8 hours or until falling apart. Take off the heat and add in 1 tablespoon rice vinegar.
- Meanwhile, pickle your red onion slices by sprinkling with some salt and covering with remaining 2 tablespoons rice vinegar. When ready to serve the pork, sprinkle servings with some cilantro and slices of pickled onion.

---

219.   **Pig Pulled Over**

Serving: Serves 12~16 | Prep: | Cook: | Ready in:

Ingredients

- For the Pulled Pork
- 8 pounds organic pork shoulder
- 3 tablespoons kosher salt
- 2 cups your favourite barbeque sauce
- 2 cups mango juice
- For the Lime Slaw
- 125 milliliters white vinegar
- 125 milliliters raw sugar
- 1 lime zest and juice
- 2 pounds thinly shredded cabbage or coleslaw mix

Direction

- For the Pulled Pork
- To make the pulled pork, remove any string from the pork if it's in the form of a tied roast. Make a deep cut to butterfly the pork so it is about 3-4 inches thick throughout. Do not trim any of the fat.
- Rub the pork all over with salt and place, fat side facing up, in a roasting pan. Squeeze the barbeque sauce over the pork without smearing – you want the sauce to form a cap and sit on top of the meat. Fill the barbeque sauce bottle with the juice and shake it to dissolve the bit of sauce remaining. Pour the mixture around the pork.
- Seal the pan tightly with aluminum foil, overlapping a couple of sheets.
- Bake at 285 degrees F for 5-5 1/2 hours, until the fat is rendered and meat shreds effortlessly. Shred the pork with two forks while it's still hot in a separate large bowl and return it back to the pan of pork jus. Discard any visible lumps of fat.
- Bake at 300 degrees F, loosely covered for 1 1/2 – 2 hours, or until the sauce reduces into a thick glaze and the color intensifies.
- Serve on a demi-baguette, split horizontally, with the lime slaw.

- For the Lime Slaw
- To make the lime slaw, dissolve the sugar with the vinegar in a small sauce pan.
- While the vinegar syrup is still hot, pour it over the coleslaw blend and mix thoroughly with the remaining ingredients. Cover and chill at least overnight, though it will be best at least three days later.

---

220.   Pizza With Roasted Tomatoes, Oyster Mushrooms And Crispy Bacon

Serving: Serves 4 | Prep: | Cook: |Ready in:

Ingredients

- For the dough (recipe adapted from Jim Lahey's no-knead dough)
- 3 1/2 cups flour
- 2 teaspoons salt
- 1/4 teaspoon active dry yeast
- 2 teaspoons crushed rosemary
- 1 1/2 cups warm water
- For the toppings
- 1 cup ricotta
- 1/2 cup grated parmesean
- 2 medium sized tomatoes
- 8 cherry tomatoes
- 5 pieces thick-cut bacon
- 1 cup oyster mushrooms
- 1 tablespoon butter
- 1/4 cup scallions, chopped finely

Direction

- Whisk together the flour, yeast, salt and rosemary in a large bowl. While stirring, gradually incorporate the water until the dough is a round sticky mass. Transfer to clean bowl and cover with plastic wrap. Let the dough rise overnight until it's doubled in size and tiny bubbles have formed on the surface, at least 12 hours.

- On a floured work space, take the dough from the bowl and divide it in half. If you're only making one pizza, cover one of the halves in plastic wrap and store in the fridge for up to 3 days. Sprinkle flour over the remaining dough, cover with plastic wrap and let it sit for at least 1 hour. Set the oven to 475 degrees, generously sprinkle flour over the dough, and shape into a large disk, about 1/2 inch thick. Place it on a baking sheet while you prepare the rest of the ingredients.
- Cook the bacon in a skillet until it's almost crispy and transfer to a small dish to cool. Meanwhile, cook the oyster mushrooms in butter until they're golden brown in color.
- Combine the ricotta and parmesan in a small bowl, and then carefully spread over the dough with a rubber spatula. Thinly slice the tomatoes and arrange them on the dough. Chop the bacon into inch-long pieces and add them to the pizza, along with the oyster mushrooms. Finely chop the scallions and sprinkle evenly on top of the pizza.
- Bake for 10 minutes, or until the crust is golden and the toppings have crisped. Let cool, slice and serve.

---

221.   Pizza With White Wine Crust, Italian Sausage And Artichoke Hearts

Serving: Makes two 12-inch pizzas or one very large rectangle | Prep: | Cook: |Ready in:

Ingredients

- White Wine Dough
- 2 large onions, cut in half vertically, then thinly sliced (Also to become a pizza topping.)
- ¾ cup white wine, divided
- 2 teaspoons active dry yeast
- Pinch of sugar
- 2 tablespoons fruity olive oil
- 2 tablespoons honey

- 1/3 cup wheat germ
- 1 ½ teaspoon Kosher salt
- 3 cups all-purpose flour, plus up to another ½ cup for kneading
- ¼ teaspoon baking soda (to counteract acidity in the wine, which could affect the yeast)
- The Toppings -- and Instructions for Assembling and Baking
- 1 pound of sweet Italian sausages
- Olive oil for browning
- 2 large onions, sliced and cooked (the ones used to flavor the wine used in the dough)
- Two 4-inch branches of fresh rosemary
- 4 small or two large anchovy fillets
- 4 medium cloves of garlic, peeled and chopped finely
- 4 ounces of arugula, washed and spun or patted dry
- 1/4 cup flat leaf parsley, coarsely chopped
- One 12- ounce jar of marinated artichoke hearts, well drained (See note below.)
- Cheese (whatever you like, strictly optional, i.e., completely unnecessary)

Direction

- White Wine Dough
- Proof the yeast in 2 tablespoons of warm water with the pinch of sugar. Set aside.
- In a heavy skillet over medium heat, cook the onions in a few tablespoons of olive oil just until they begin to turn a light golden color. They shouldn't get too dark.
- Remove the onions – you will use them on the pizza -- and use 1/4 cup of the wine to deglaze the pan over medium heat, scraping up whatever bits you can. Bring to a boil, then turn off. Pour off, with all of the little bits, into a 2 cup liquid measuring cup and add the remaining ½ cup of wine, plus enough cold water to make 1 ¼ cup total.
- Put the wine and water mixture, the honey, olive oil, salt, wheat germ and one cup of flour in a large bowl. Stir it well to combine.
- Add the yeast and water mixture and beat well.

- Stir the baking soda into the remaining two cups of flour and add to the dough mixture. Stir, using the back of the spoon to press the flour into the dough to combine. When it becomes too difficult to stir, dump everything from the bowl onto your kneading surface and begin kneading to incorporate all of the flour from the bowl.
- Continue to knead for about ten or twelve minutes, until the dough is smooth and elastic. You may need to add up to another ¼ to ½ cup of flour, a bit at a time, while kneading. Don't add too much, or the dough will be flat and tough.
- Put the ball of dough into a well-oiled bowl, turn it over to coat, and let it rise for at least 2 ½ hours. Three is actually better, if you can manage it.
- (You can also make this dough in the morning and put it in the refrigerator all day, but if you do, please take it out at least an hour before you plan to roll it, and let it sit in a warm place. Also, coat it very well with oil and cover it tightly with plastic wrap while in the fridge.)
- After the dough has risen, punch it down and let it rest while you prepare the topping ingredients. I usually put it on a piece of parchment paper, and on cold days, put both in the microwave oven (but don't turn it on). If you have prepared your toppings in the interim, give the dough at least a fifteen minute rest before rolling it out.
- The Toppings -- and Instructions for Assembling and Baking
- Preheat the oven to 425 degrees Fahrenheit for a regular oven (or whatever adjusted temperature your convection oven manufacturer recommends). Put your pizza stones, if using, on the middle racks to preheat for at least twenty minutes after the oven is hot.
- In a tablespoon or two of olive oil, cook the sausages for about five minutes in a large skillet, turning frequently, until firm enough to slice.
- To the pan in which the sausages were cooked, add the (previously cooked) onion slices and

stir well, continuing to cook over medium heat.

- Remove the rosemary leaves from the branches and chop. Add to the onions in the pan. Toss to combine.
- Let the onions sit in the skillet, uncovered, while you slice the partially cooked sausages on the diagonal.
- Remove the onions from the skillet. Brown the sausage slices in the skillet over medium low heat at first. You should not need to add any more oil, but if you do, add some.
- When the sausage slices are nice and brown, remove and set aside.
- Turn the heat up to medium high, then put the arugula and chopped parsley in the hot pan and cover immediately. After 2 minutes (or when the arugula is wilted), remove it from the skillet using a slotted spoon, and put it into a bowl. Add the anchovy fillets and garlic and turn the heat on. Stir well until the anchovies appear to melt, taking care not to let the garlic burn. Turn the heat off and, using the back of a large spoon, press down on the arugula in the bowl to drain off as much liquid as possible into the skillet.
- Turn the heat back on and cook down the juices, taking care not to let the garlic burn. The anchovy should be disintegrating. Stir it well to mix with the garlic and pan juices. Return the arugula to the skillet and mix well with the anchovy and garlic.
- FOR EACH PIZZA: Roll out half the pizza dough into a 12-inch round, either on a peel or on a piece of parchment paper. (I usually just roll it right out on the parchment on which I let the dough rest. Then I just put the whole thing -- paper and all -- on the pizza stone when it's good and hot.)
- Put the arugula mixture on first, then the onions, then the sausage slices and artichoke hearts.
- (If using cheese, add it last.)
- Brush the outside edge of dough with olive oil. (The artichoke hearts I buy come in an herb-scented, lightly seasoned oil marinade that I use for this purpose.)

- Cook on the hot pizza stones for about 12 minutes. Check after 10, as they may be ready then. It could also take longer, up to 15 or even 18 minutes, depending on the efficiency and calibration of your oven.
- Enjoy!!
- N.B. If serving as an appetizer or at a casual gathering at room temperature, this is much, much better without any cheese. Or, you could grate some Parmigiano Reggiano and put it down first, as you would in a pissaladiere.

222. Polenta, Black Pudding And Red Onion Pomegranate Salad

Serving: Serves 6 | Prep: | Cook: | Ready in:

Ingredients

- Red onion and pomegranate salad
- 1 red onion, thinly sliced
- 1/2 teaspoon pink Himalayan salt
- 1/2 cup pomegranate seeds
- 1/3 cup cilantro
- freshly ground black pepper
- 1 tablespoon lime juice
- 1 tablespoon gape seed oil
- Polenta and black pudding
- 8 ounces (225 g) Yellow corn meal (instant)
- 1 pound black pudding sausage
- 1 (2 cups) red onion and pomegranate salad

Direction

- Red onion and pomegranate salad
- Slice onion and mix with salt, let sit for 20 minutes.
- Rinse the onion under cold water and squeeze out with hands (wear gloves)
- Clean pomegranate seeds.
- Wash and pick coriander leaves and coarsely chop them.

- In the mixing bowl put all ingredients and mix.
- Polenta and black pudding
- Polenta cooked (follow package instruction) before so it is firm and easy to slice or just bay polenta in the roll precooked, slice 1/2 inch thick.
- Make an onion-pomegranate salad.
- Slice polenta 3x3x1/2 inches and pan fry, keep worm.
- Peel and slice black pudding into 1/3 inch coins and pan fry 1 minute on each side.
- To assemble, put polenta on the plate 2-3 slice black pudding on it and salad on the top.

---

223.   Popovers With Bacon And Brussels Sprouts

Serving: Serves 4 | Prep: | Cook: | Ready in:

Ingredients

- Popovers
- 1 cup sifted flour
- 1 teaspoon salt
- 2 large eggs
- 1 cup whole milk
- Bacon and Brussel Sprout Filing
- 2 cups chopped brussel spouts
- 1 cup thick-cut bacon lardons
- 1 medium shallot, chopped
- Salt and pepper to taste

Direction

- Popovers
- Preheat oven to 450 degrees. Butter a muffin tin and put it in the oven to heat.
- Whisk flour and salt together. Beat the eggs in a separate medium bowl until they lighten a little, then whisk in half the milk.
- Gradually mix the flour in with a wooden spoon, then add the rest of the milk. Don't use a whisk; the batter may be a little lumpy. Pour the batter into the heated muffin tin; each cup should be about two-thirds full.
- Bake in the center of the oven for 15 minutes. Without opening the oven, lower the heat to 350 degrees and bake for another 20 minutes until the popovers are golden brown. Serve piping hot!
- Bacon and Brussels Sprout Filing
- Blanch the lardons for 1 minute in simmering water. Drain the bacon and reserve about 1/2 c. water.
- Heat a skillet on a medium flame and add the shallot. Sautee until it starts to turn translucent, then add the bacon. Fry the bacon until it just starts to brown on the edges.
- Add the sprouts and cook until they start to caramelize a little. Add the reserved blanching water and braise until the sprouts are tender. Season to taste and serve in the middle of steaming popovers. Add a fried egg if you feel like it...

---

224.   Pork & Mushroom Egg Rolls With Creamy Ginger Sauce

Serving: Serves 10 | Prep: | Cook: | Ready in:

Ingredients

- Mushroom Filling
- 1/2 pound ground pork
- 2 tablespoons 2 tsp olive oil
- 1/2 pound oyster mushrooms, chopped (~ 1/2-inch sized pieces)
- 1/2 pound shiitake mushrooms, stems discarded, caps sliced (~ 1/4 inch thick)
- 1/2 pound remini mushrooms, chopped (~ 1/2 inch sized pieces)
- 2 tablespoons cooking sherry
- 2 tablespoons soy sauce
- Salt and pepper
- 2 garlic cloves, sliced thin

- 1 plump lemongrass stalk, tender white inner bulb only, minced
- 1 red Thai chile, minced (** or 1/2 tsp dried chili flakes or cayenne pepper)
- 2 medium shallots, minced
- 1 tablespoon 1 1/2 tsp fresh ginger, minced
- 1/2 teaspoon finely grated lemon zest (** or 1 tsp lemon juice)
- 10 thin egg roll or spring roll wrappers
- 1 large egg, beaten
- Creamy Ginger Sauce
- 1/4 cup greek yogurt, plain
- 1/4 cup olive oil
- 1 tablespoon fresh tarragon, chopped (** or 1 Tbsp dried)
- 1 tablespoon fresh lime juice
- 1 tablespoon rice vinegar
- 10 Boston lettuce leaves, halved

Direction

- In a small skillet, brown the ground pork
- PREPARE THE MUSHROOM FILLING
- In a large skillet, heat 2 Tbsp olive oil. Add mushrooms, sherry, soy sauce, and season with salt & pepper.
- Cover, and cook over medium heat, stirring a few times, until the mushrooms have released their liquid and are tender (~ 8-10 minutes)
- Uncover, and cook 5 or 6 minutes longer, stirring occasionally, until they're browned
- In a small skillet, heat 2 tsp olive oil. Add garlic, lemongrass, chile, shallots and 1 Tbsp ginger. Cook over low heat, stirring occasionally, until the vegetables are golden brown, (~ 6-7) minutes.
- Add the lemon zest (or juice, if using), then stir the mixture into the mushrooms, along with the browned pork
- PREPARE THE CREAMY GINGER SAUCE
- In a blender, puree the Greek yogurt, olive oil, tarragon, lime juice, vinegar and the remaining 1 1/2 tsp ginger, until smooth. Season with salt and pepper.
- ASSEMBLE AND BAKE THE EGG ROLLS
- Preheat the oven to 400°F.

- Place an egg roll wrapper on your work surface with one corner pointing at you. Add 2-3 tablespoons of filling into a 2×4-inch rectangle just below the horizontal diagonal line that connects the right and left corners. Take the corner nearest you and fold it over the filling, rolling it away from you so that the filling is completely encased in wrapper. Fold the right and left corners in toward the center, keeping it snug, but not so tight that the wrapper breaks, and continue rolling until you have 2-inches of the last corner left
- Paint the edges of the last corner with a bit of egg, then quickly roll up the egg roll. (This will help hold it together). Lightly brush the top of the roll with beaten egg. Repeat with the remaining wrappers and filling
- Bake for 8-10 minutes, until they're beginning to brown, then flip them over and bake another 8-10 minutes.
- ** For added crispness, put the egg rolls under the broiler for 1-2 minutes, checking every 20-30 seconds)
- Cut the rolls in half on the diagonal, wrap them in lettuce leaves and serve with the ginger sauce.

225.   Pork Belly Pozole

Serving: Makes 8 to 10 servings | Prep: 0hours0mins | Cook: 0hours2mins | Ready in:

Ingredients

- 2-3 pounds pork belly or shoulder (fat trimmed and cut into 1 inch cubes)
- 1 pound tomatillos (husks removed and rinsed)
- 1 large onion (diced)
- 6 cloves garlic (minced)
- 2 30 oz cans hominy (drained and rinsed)
- 4 dried New Mexican Chilies (seeded and stems removed)
- 3 ears corn (kernals cut off)
- 1 small can died green chilies (hot)

- 3 cups low sodium chicken broth
- 1 tablespoon cumin + 1 tbsp
- 1 tablespoon coriander + 1 tbsp
- 1 tablespoon dried oregano + 1 tbsp
- 1 cup boiling water
- olive oil
- salt and pepper
- lime wedges (for serving)
- cilantro (for serving)

Direction

- Start by toasting your dried chilies in a sauté pan. Heat pan over high heat and toast each side of the chili until it bubbles and browns (it's okay if it burns a little bit!). Remove from heat and give a rough chop. Place in a bowl and cover with 1 cup boiling water. Cover bowl with a kitchen towel.
- While chilies are soaking, bring a salted pot of water to a boil and add tomatillos for 10 minutes. Drain and transfer to a food processor or blender.
- While tomatillos are boiling, sauté in olive oil, onion, garlic, 1/2 tbsp. each cumin, coriander and oregano, salt and pepper for 5 minutes in a large soup pot. Transfer to the blender. Add the chili peppers and their liquid to the blender as well, and pulse until smooth. Add salt and pepper to taste. (To clarify: tomatillos, onion/garlic mix, and New Mexico chilies go into blender to puree)
- In the big soup pot that you sautéed the onion in (trying not to use 1 million pots), heat the pan over medium high heat. Add the pork belly cubes, fat side down. Add remaining cumin, coriander and oregano to the pot with some salt and pepper. Sauté pork belly for 3 minutes on each side, until each is browned.
- Add the tomatillo/chile puree to the pork belly. Add chicken broth, green chilies, corn, hominy, and salt and pepper. Bring to a boil and then lower heat to a simmer. Let soup cook for 2 hours. Taste everyone once in a while and adjust seasoning.
- Serve the soup hot with lots of freshly squeezed lime juice and cilantro. We served it with warmed tortillas with melted cheese to dip into our soup! Enjoy!

---

226. Pork Brined In Rum And Cider With Apples

Serving: Serves 6 | Prep: 0hours0mins | Cook: 0hours0mins |Ready in:

Ingredients

- Brined Roast Pork
- 2 cups dark rum
- 2 cups apples cider
- 1/3 cup Kosher salt
- 15 juniper berries - crushed
- 15 peppercorns - crushed
- 3 garlic cloves - smashed
- 2 sprigs fresh rosemary
- 2 1/2 pounds boneless pork shoulder
- 2 tablespoons vegetable oil
- Sauteed Apples
- 2 tablespoons butter
- 1 large apple - peeled, cored, and cut into 1/2-inch wedges
- 3 tablespoons minced red onion
- 2 teaspoons finely minced fresh rosemary
- 1/2 cup dark rum
- 1/2 cup apple cider
- salt and pepper to taste

Direction

- Brined Roast Pork
- Combine all ingredients except pork and oil in a medium sauce pan. Place over medium-high heat, bring to a simmer, and cook until salt is dissolved. Cool to room temperature.
- Put the roast in a gallon zippered plastic bag, add brine, evacuate most of the air, and refrigerate for 18 - 24 hours — turning three or four times while brining to distribute the brine.
- Allow roast to warm on the counter for 2 to 3 hours before cooking.

- Heat oven to 250F. Rinse roast and pat dry with a lint-free kitchen towel. Discard brine.
- Heat oil in a heavy, oven-proof skillet over medium-high heat. Add roast and brown well on 3 sides — about 3 minutes per side. When you flip the fourth side down, place the skillet in the center of the oven. If the roast has a fatty side brown it first and end with it on top.
- For tender, medium-rare meat, cook roast to 145-150 degrees at its center according to an instant-read thermometer, 1 to 1 1/2 hours. Alternatively, for cooked through, succulent meat, cook to 165-170 degrees (we don't advise going for something in between). Remove from oven, place on a cutting board, and tent with foil.
- Sautéed Apples
- Heat a large skillet over medium heat. (Unfortunately the fond that accumulates in the bottom of the roasting skillet is too salty to use in a sauce, so use another large skillet.) Add butter and swirl to melt.
- Add apples and rosemary in a single layer and lightly browned - about 5 minutes. Flip and brown other side. Add minced onion and cook 1 minute longer.
- Add rum and reduce by half. Add cider and reduce by half. Taste and season with salt and pepper (light on the salt).

---

227.   Pork Chop Toastered

Serving: Serves 2 | Prep: | Cook: | Ready in:

Ingredients

- 4 pieces 1/2 inch thick pork chops
- 6 pieces peeled tomatoes
- 3 pieces red and green bell whole bell peppers
- 1/2 pound whole or sliced button or shiitake mushrooms
- 2 grams salt for boiling potatoes and chops
- 2 grams salt for rub
- 3 grams brown sugar

- 2 grams ground black pepper
- 3 grams garlic powder
- 2 grams nutmeg powder
- 1 gram coriander powder
- 2 grams dried thyme
- 30 milliliters EVOO (Extra Virgin Olive Oil)

Direction

- Line up chops in casserole then potatoes atop. Pour in enough tap water to cover top. Add in salt. Stir and dissolve then set to medium heat.
- Upon boiling, set timer to 10 minutes.
- When done scoop out potatoes and chops. Set aside.
- In a bowl, add salt, brown sugar, black pepper, garlic, nutmeg, coriander and thyme. Whisk to blend well. This is your meat rub.
- Lying unto toaster pan, brush EVOO unto both sides of chops. Scatter meat rub unto all sides and parts.
- Pre-heat oven toaster to 350deg.F (177deg.C). Slide in chops to topmost slot and heat for 20 minutes. Turn to other side and do the same. This is DONE. Set aside.
- In the same toaster pan with drippings, oil etc., line up mushroom, boiled potatoes, red & green bell peppers, onion, "labuyo", and "sili pansigang". Wedge unto toaster and in the same temp (350deg.F) cook for 15 minutes.
- Turn veggies and/or add little more EVOO if needed. DONE. Serve with pride your sumptuous and colorful creation.

---

228.   Pork Chops W/ Homemade Buttermilk Ranch

Serving: Serves 2 | Prep: | Cook: | Ready in:

Ingredients

- 4 tablespoons buttermilk
- 3 tablespoons mayo
- 2-3 tablespoons sour cream
- juice from 1 lemon

- 1 teaspoon white wine vinegar
- 1 anchovy filet, minced
- 2 tablespoons chives, chopped
- 1 tablespoon fresh dill, chopped
- salt and pepper to taste
- 2 bone-in pork chops
- 1-2 tablespoons olive oil

Direction

- In a small bowl, mix together the buttermilk, mayo, sour cream, lemon juice, and vinegar until smooth. Add in anchovy, chives, and dill. Season with salt and pepper to taste. Keep in fridge while preparing chops.
- Season both sides of chops with salt and pepper.
- Heat a large skillet under medium-high heat and add olive oil. Add pork chops and cook until nicely golden brown on both sides, about 4-5 minutes per side.
- Serve with ranch dressing and a side of mixed vegetables and/or rice.

229.   Pork Chops With Whiskey Onion Gravy

Serving: Serves 4 | Prep: | Cook: |Ready in:

Ingredients

- 4 pork chops
- 1 medium onion
- 1 tablespoon olive oil
- flour
- salt and pepper
- 1/2 cup whiskey
- 2 tablespoons flour
- 1 cup heavy cream

Direction

- Heat olive oil in a cast iron skillet over medium high heat. Add the onions and cook until they start to brown, about 10 minutes.

- While the onions are cooking, season your pork chops with salt and pepper and dredge in flour. Once the onions are brown add the pork chops to the pan and brown both sides, and mostly cooked. Once the chops have cooked most of the way, remove to a separate plate and start making the gravy.
- Lower the heat to medium low. With the onions still in the pan, de-glaze the pan with the whiskey and scrape the bottom with a wooden spoon or spatula to get all the yummy pieces that are stuck to the bottom up.
- Pour in the heavy cream and stir to combine. Add black pepper to taste, I like about 2 tsp of pepper in mine, then add in the 2 tbsp. of flour to make the roux. You can add more flour if you like thicker gravy. Lower heat to low and continue cooking for about 1 minute. Add the pork chops back in the pan, cover with a lid, and let simmer for about 10 minutes, to finish cooking.

230.   Pork Confit With Cider Veal Reduction

Serving: Serves 6 | Prep: | Cook: |Ready in:

Ingredients

- Pork Confit
- 5 pounds boneless Boston butt (pork shoulder), leave most of the fat on the meat
- Kosher salt
- 1 tablespoon fennel seeds
- 5 bay leaves
- 1 tablespoon juniper berries
- 1/2 tablespoon black pepper
- 6 cloves garlic, peeled
- Enough duck fat to cover meat (about 1 1/2 quarts)
- Cider Veal Reduction
- 2 tablespoons unsalted butter
- 1/2 cup shallots, peeled and chopped
- 6 cups cups cider

- 12 cups veal stock
- 10 fresh thyme sprigs
- A splash of apple vinegar
- Kosher salt

Direction

- Pork Confit
- Preheat the oven to 250? F. Warm the fat in a large deep pan by putting it in the oven while it preheats, or over low heat on the stove until it liquefies.
- Pull the pork out of the fridge and very liberally rub it with kosher salt. Pork likes salt, so do not be afraid of over salting. Let pork sit out and come to room temperature.
- Submerge the pork in the fat and add the fennel seeds, bay leaves, juniper berries, pepper, and garlic. It is very important that the pork is fully submerged throughout cooking. If you find you do not have enough, in a pinch, you can top it off with olive oil. Cook 4-5 hours, until extremely tender,
- The pork confit will be infinitely better if you let it sit in the fridge, cooled and covered in the fat for at least a week. However, overnight will suffice if you simply cannot wait!
- To serve the pork, heat the container to re-liquefy the fat, remove the pork and slice it into rectangle pieces, about 3"x1"x1". Taste a small piece to see if it needs more salt. Season according to your taste.
- In a stainless-steel sauté pan, heat a little of the duck fat, when it is hot add the pork pieces and sear on all sides until each surface has a golden brown crust.
- NOTE: The pork can be kept in the fridge, submerged in fat for up to 2 months. When you are finished with the fat, warm it and strain it, removing all of the garlic, spices and pork bits, store in your refrigerator and reuse for your next confit adventure!
- Cider Veal Reduction
- In a 4-quart pot briefly sauté the shallots. Add the cider and reduce by ¾. Add the veal stock and fresh thyme sprigs. Reduce over medium heat until the sauce coats the back of a spoon.

- Pour sauce through a fine strainer (straining out the shallots and thyme) into another pot. Taste your sauce. Adjust seasoning by adding apple vinegar and salt. Add butter to help round out the flavors. If your sauce does not reduce down to coat the back of the spoon, you can remove the thyme and whoosh it up in a blender with the shallots. This will give it a bit more body. Pass through a fine strainer.

---

231.   Pork Fillets W/Lentils & Charred Leeks

Serving: Serves 4 | Prep: | Cook: |Ready in:

Ingredients

- 4 medium-sized uncooked pork fillets (approx. 4oz. each)
- 1/2 teaspoon salt
- 1/4 teaspoon pepper
- 1/2 teaspoon paprika
- 2 sprigs fresh thyme
- 2 tablespoons olive oil
- 1 pound dried green lentils*
- 5 cups water
- 1 1/2 teaspoons salt
- 1/2 teaspoon pepper
- 1/2 teaspoon garlic powder
- 1/2 teaspoon liquid smoke
- 1/4 pound fresh, cleaned & dried leeks (may be sliced or chopped)*
- 2 tablespoons cooking oil
- 1 tablespoon butter
- 1 teaspoon minced garlic
- 1 pinch salt & pepper
- 2 tablespoons balsamic vinegar
- 4 tablespoons pepper jelly*
- 1 tablespoon fruit preserves (plum, apple or apricot)
- 3 tablespoons A-1 or other steak sauce
- 1/8 cup white wine
- 1 pinch salt

Direction

- Start w/ the lentils. Place the lentils in a large bowl or pot and run cold water over to clean and reduce some of the starch. You may have to change the water several times to rinse thoroughly. Check the lentils to make sure there are no small stones or other undesirable matter in them. Drain the water from the lentils. Put the lentils in a medium-sized pot and add all of the other ingredients (water and seasonings). Cook on medium-high heat for about 20 minutes--stirring occasionally--until the lentils are tender. Drain any excess water, cover with a top and set aside. *Lentils will triple in quantity once they are cooked. For this recipe you will only need two cups of cooked lentils. Store the remaining lentils in the fridge to use in other dishes (soups, cold salads, etc.).

- Clean the leeks. Trim the leek stalks by cutting the bottom close to the root and then cutting off the dark green tips. The white to very light green part of the leek is the best to cook with. You can use the dark green tips later for soup stock (be sure to wash them VERY well) or discard. Once the leeks are trimmed, peel back the layers and holding the stalk upside down, hold under cold, running water. Check between all the layers to make sure they are cleaned thoroughly. Drain the leeks in a strainer or on paper towels. Dry thoroughly-- blot dry with paper towels. Cut the leeks--slice into long strips as shown in the pic above or chop into 1/2 inch-thick rounds. *This step, cleaning the leeks, is the most time-consuming step in the recipe so to save time, you may want to prepare your leeks the day before or several days in advance.

- Cook the leeks and sauce. Heat the oil and butter in a large skillet under med-high heat. Add the minced garlic, leeks, salt and pepper. Cook the leeks without turning or stirring them for a minute or so on each side. You want them to char a little but watch them so they do not burn. When the leeks are tender and slightly charred, remove them from the pan--placing them on a small plate or paper towel. Leave the skillet on the heat and reduce flame slightly. Add the white wine and stir to deglaze the pan to get all the flavor bits off the bottom of the pan. Continue cooking the wine 2-3 minutes and then add the rest of the ingredients. Stir until all ingredients are thoroughly mixed in. *If you do not have the pepper jelly, you may substitute it with any flavor of jelly and add 1/2 teaspoon ground red pepper or red pepper flakes. Let the sauce simmer on a low-medium heat for 5-10 minutes.

- Cook the pork fillets. Note: For this recipe you can use a whole pork tenderloin and slice it into fillets, buy fillets at the butcher counter or bagged in convenient individually-wrapped portions. You may use plain or marinated fillets. The fillet is a very tender cut of meat but buying it in a marinade almost guarantees a more tender piece of meat. Beware, though, some marinades may contain a lot of salt/sodium so if you opt for the fillets in a marinade, you may want to reduce the salt in other areas of the recipe where you can. If using marinated fillets, you can omit the seasonings in this recipe. Otherwise, season both sides of the pork fillets with the salt, pepper and paprika. Heat the oil in a large skillet under high heat. Cut the sprigs of thyme in half and add two pieces to the skillet. Place a fillet on top of each sprig of thyme (cook two fillets at a time so the pan is not crowded). Sear the fillets on high heat-- approximately 2-3 minutes on each side. Remove from pan and set aside to rest. Repeat steps for the remaining two fillets. After the fillets have rested (about three minutes) slice them for plating.

- Plate the dish by putting 1/2 cup of the cooked lentils on the plate. Add the leeks and fillets and drizzle a little sauce over the pork. Garnish is optional but I used a teaspoon or so of chopped roasted red peppers just to give the plate a little color contrast. Enjoy!

232. Pork Loin With Cider Braised Leeks And Apples

Serving: Serves 4 | Prep: | Cook: | Ready in:

Ingredients

- 2 boneless pork loins
- Sea salt and freshly ground black pepper
- 1 tablespoon olive oil
- 1 tall glass hard, dry apple cider
- 1 1/2 tablespoons Cognac
- 1 tablespoon light brown sugar
- 1 white onion, diced
- 1 leek, quartered, sliced, and washed
- 1 green apple, cored, peeled, and diced
- 2 sprigs fresh thyme

Direction

- Take the pork out of the fridge 1 hour before cooking. Generously salt and pepper each side.
- Heat the olive oil in a Dutch oven until quite hot, over medium-high heat. Sear each loin for 2 to 3 minutes per side, until they are golden brown. Remove the pork to a plate.
- Deglaze the Dutch oven with the cider and the Cognac, making sure to scrape up all the brown bits. Add the brown sugar, and then let the cider reduce by half, about 10 minutes.
- Add the onion and then the leek, and let them simmer away for about 5 minutes. Add the apple to the pot, and incorporate. Add salt and pepper to taste.
- Toss in two sprigs of thyme, and then settle the pork loins on top of the onion, leek, and apple. Cover the Dutch oven with its lid completely, and cook for 20 minutes, or until the pork loin is just cooked through. Let the pork rest for 10 minutes before slicing it.

233. Pork Piccata

Serving: Serves 4 to 6 | Prep: 0hours5mins | Cook: 0hours10mins | Ready in:

Ingredients

- 1 package Smithfield Roasted Garlic and Herb Marinated Fresh Pork Loin Filet
- Salt, plus more to taste
- Freshly ground black pepper, plus more to taste
- 1/2 cup flour, plus more as needed
- 6 tablespoons butter, divided
- 6 tablespoons olive oil
- 4 tablespoons lemon juice
- 4 tablespoons chicken stock
- 4 tablespoons capers
- 3 tablespoons chopped parsley

Direction

- Slice pork loin into 1/4-inch slices and lightly pound out until thin. Season pork slices with salt and pepper on both sides, and then dredge slices in flour, shaking off the excess.
- Heat 4 tablespoons butter and the olive oil in large sauté pan over medium-high heat until hot. Sauté the pork slices for 3 minutes and flip, cooking the other side for 3 minutes, making sure that each side is nicely browned.
- Remove pork to a plate and deglaze the pan with lemon juice, chicken stock, and capers, using a wooden spoon to scrape the bottom of the pan. Cook until the liquid reduces by about 1/3.
- Season with salt and pepper, and stir in the remaining 2 tablespoons of butter to slightly thicken. Place pork on platter or plates and garnish with the lemon-caper sauce and parsley to serve.

234. Pork Tacos With Peach Salsa

Serving: Serves 2 | Prep: | Cook: |Ready in:

Ingredients

- For the pork:
- 2 pork loin steaks
- 1 teaspoon cinnamon
- 1 teaspoon cumin
- 1 teaspoon chilli powder
- 2 teaspoons smoked paprika
- 1/4 teaspoon kosher salt
- 1 tablespoon oil
- 2 tablespoons cider vinegar
- 1/4 red onion, minced
- cooking spray
- For the salsa and assembly:
- 1 small avocado, diced
- 1/4 red onion, finely minced
- 1 lime
- 1 ripe peach, chopped
- 1/4 teaspoon kosher salt

Direction

- For the pork:
- Combine everything except the pork in a medium bowl and mix until it is a smooth paste. Add the pork to the bowl and cover the steaks with the paste. Leave to marinate for 10 minutes.
- Heat a skillet over medium heat. Lightly spray each of the pork steaks and add to the pan rather than the pan to avoid smoking out your kitchen. Cook for 3-5 minutes per side, adding the onion and remaining marinade halfway through (i.e. when you flip them).
- Once cooked through, remove the pork steaks from the pan and chop into 1/4 inch cubes. Return the meat to the pan and stir until the onions are evenly dispersed.
- For the salsa and assembly:
- Place the avocado, peach, salt and onion in a small bowl, then juice the lime over the top. Stir gently to mix.

- Heat a large pan over medium heat. Lightly warm the tortillas by placing them in the pan for 15 seconds per side.
- To serve: spoon a little of the pork onto each tortilla, and top with peach salsa.

235. Pork Tenderloin With Raspberry And Lavender

Serving: Serves 2 | Prep: | Cook: |Ready in:

Ingredients

- 1 11 oz pork tenderloin
- ½ tsp pink peppercorns
- 1 dried bay leaf
- ½ tsp dried lavender flowers
- ½ tsp flaky sea salt
- 1 ½ tsp olive oil
- 4 heaping tablespoon fresh raspberries, crushed and strained, plus a few for garnish
- 1 ½ tsp honey
- 1 ½ tsp raspberry vinegar
- 2 tbs butter
- 1 tsp thyme (½ tsp if using dry)
- ½ tsp lavender flowers
- 1 ½ tablespoons crème fraîche
- 1 ½ tablespoon bacon fat

Direction

- With your meat at room temperature, make the rub. Crush peppercorns, bay leaf, ½ tsp lavender flowers, sea salt in a mortar till fine and powdery. Add olive oil. Rub all over the pork tenderloin, wrap it in plastic wrap and allow to rest for at least 1 hour at room temperature, but preferably several hours in the fridge.
- Crush and strain the berries in a sieve, basically to obtain a raspberry passata. Mix with raspberry vinegar, honey, thyme and lavender flowers. In a small saucepan, gently melt butter. Whisk in the crème fraîche. Add the raspberry passata, whisking slowly till all

the ingredients are combined and you smell the thyme and vinegar wafting, but never allow it to achieve a simmer. Turn off heat. If you want to garnish with raspberries, you can place them in the sauce now.

- Remove the meat from the fridge and allow to return to room temp. Unwrap and brown the meat on all sides in the bacon fat, till it appears to have a nice crust but remains raw inside. Remove from heat and cut into four even pieces. Set aside.
- You can do all of the above ahead of time, making this an excellent dish for a dinner party you actually want to participate in! When you are ready to eat, reheat the remaining bacon fat and start to cook the tenderloin chunks to the desired level of doneness using tongs to turn the chunky cubes around. You want them nice and brown on the outside, still tender and pink on the inside. Warm the coulis, and serve your meat in a pink puddle, garnishing with thyme, lavender and/or more raspberries.

236.   Pork So Dam Good You Won't Be Able To.....

Serving: Serves 6 | Prep: | Cook: | Ready in:

Ingredients

- 3 - 4 pounds Pork Shoulder
- 12 pieces flat bread.
- 1 bunch cilantro
- half pound bacon
- 3 cups greek yogurt
- 1 bunch cilantro
- 4 cloves of garlic
- 1 lemon

Direction

- If your shoulder has a fat cap remove it with a knife. Rub the meat all over with kosher or sea salt and black pepper. Fat cap side up lattice

the top and sides with bacon. With cooking string tie a few trusses around the meat to hold down the bacon. It will want to pull off as it renders.

- Set up a charcoal grill in the indirect method and place a disposable pie tin on the lower grate next to the coals. The shoulder will render quite a bit of fat. You may want to add some water to the tin to keep the grease from splattering. Place the shoulder on the grate away from the coals, add several lumps of apple wood to the fire and cover the grill with upper and lower vents open.
- Cook until the internal temperature reaches 180 degrees, approximately 1 ½ hours. Continue to cook the shoulder for 10 minutes after the meat reaches 180 degrees. Pork shoulder is heavily marbled. The high temperature and holding it at 180 degrees allows for most of the fat to render out of the meat and gives you a roast you can slice instead of pulling. A meat thermometer with a probe you can leave in while cooking is highly recommended.
- In a bowl combine yogurt, ½ cup minced cilantro, the juice of one lemon, and minced garlic. Season with salt, black pepper and additional lemon juice to taste.
- Remove the bacon and slice the shoulder against the grain. Crumble the bacon and offer it as a condiment with the yogurt sauce. Grill the flat bread on each side briefly. Let your guests each make their own sandwich.

237.   Pork With Peaches & Quinoa

Serving: Serves 2 | Prep: | Cook: | Ready in:

Ingredients

- 4 Organic Pork Chops
- 4 tablespoons Extra Virgin Olive Oil
- 1 Red Onion

- 2 Cloves of Garlic
- 1 pinch Salt
- 1 pinch Black Pepper
- 1 pinch Mixed Herbs
- 1 pinch Chilli Flakes
- 2 Fresh Peaches
- 1 handful Chives

Direction

- Grate the onion and garlic and add to the pork chops, along with the salt, pepper and mixed herbs.
- Heat a griddle pan and add the oil.
- Place the chops on the pan and fry on a high heat for several minutes, turning over, before lowering the heat to a medium heat.
- Continue frying the pork chops for approximately 10-15 minutes (or until cooked), turning over a couple more times and remove from the pan.
- Half the peaches, remove the stones and fry in the pan - on a high heat - for a few minutes.
- Serve with warm quinoa and vegetables and garnish with the peaches and chives.

238. Pork With Pear Sauce

Serving: Serves four | Prep: | Cook: | Ready in:

Ingredients

- 4 boneless pork chops 1/2" thick
- 2 tablespoons olive oil
- 1/2 cup flour seasoned with salt and pepper
- 1 tablespoon dried rubbed sage
- 2 pears, peeled, cored, thinly sliced
- 1/2 cup dry white wine, good quality
- 1 tablespoon sugar
- 2 tablespoons chrystallized ginger, minced
- salt and pepper to taste

Direction

- Heat olive oil in a large, heavy skillet over medium heat.
- Season pork chops by rubbing sage into the meat and then adding salt and pepper to taste. Dredge seasoned meat in the flour shaking off the excess.
- Once the oil is hot enough to shimmer in the skillet add the pork chops and brown on both sides. Remove the pork chops to a warm platter and tent with foil to keep warm.
- Pour off any excess oil, no more than 2 T. should remain. Add the sliced pears to the pan and sauté until starting to soften. About 3 min.
- Stir the wine, sugar and ginger into the skillet with the pears scraping up any browned bits from the pan. Simmer until a syrup like consistency is formed, about 3 min. Watch closely, do not boil dry.
- Add the reserved pork chops and any juices back into the pear sauce and cook for a minute or two until the pork is hot and cooked through.
- Place one chop on each of four plates and spoon pear sauce over the top.

239. Port Wine Glazed Ham

Serving: Serves 10 - 12 | Prep: | Cook: | Ready in:

Ingredients

- 1 8 -10 lb. ham, shank or butt. I prefer an uncooked ham, rather than a heat and serve ham.
- 11/2 cups Tawny Port Wine
- 1/3 cup honey
- 1/3 - 2/3 cups brown sugar (dark or light)

Direction

- Cut excess fat from ham and score, if you like.
- Marinate the ham in the Port Wine, refrigerated, for at least three hours or overnight.

- Bring ham to room temperature. Remove ham from marinade, reserve liquid, and pat ham dry. Brush honey on ham, and then pack all around with brown sugar. Place ham in roasting pan, and pour reserved liquid in bottom of pan.
- Bake, covered, at 375 for 1 hour. Remove cover, and continue to cook for about 1/2 hour, basting as necessary to develop a nice glaze. Allow to rest for 10 min before serving.

---

240.   Portuguese Cataplana

Serving: Serves 4 to 6, generously | Prep: 0hours0mins | Cook: 0hours0mins |Ready in:

Ingredients

- Shrimp Stock
- 3 pounds large, head-on shrimp
- 1 splash Olive oil
- 2 large onions, thinly sliced
- 3 garlic cloves, crushed
- 2 bay leaves
- 1 pinch saffron threads
- 1 tablespoon unsalted butter
- 1 tablespoon tomato paste
- 2 quarts water
- 5 sprigs parsley
- Cataplana
- 4 pounds littleneck clams
- 2 tablespoons olive oil
- 6 ounces linguica, chorizo, or other type of cured Spanish sausage, sliced into 1/4-inch coins
- 2 thin slices prosciutto, chopped
- 2 large onions, halved lengthwise and thinly sliced into half-moons
- 1 green bell pepper, thinly sliced
- 3 cloves garlic, minced
- 1 bay leaf
- 1 pinch saffron threads
- 1/4 teaspoon sweet paprika (omit if your sausage is seasoned with paprika)
- 14 1/2 ounces can (the small one) whole San Marzano tomatoes, drained and roughly chopped
- 1 splash dry white wine (vinho verde is perfect)
- 6 cups prepared shrimp stock, or high-quality store-bought shrimp or fish stock, (up to 8 cups)
- 2 pounds large shrimp (de-shelled, de-veined, and de-headed, from the shrimp used for the shrimp stock)
- 1/3 cup cream
- 1 pinch Fresh parsley to garnish

Direction

- Shrimp Stock
- Clean your shrimp under cold running water. Remove the head with a sharp knife, then de-shell the bodies. You'll be using the heads and shells as the flavor base of the stock. (Reserve the bodies for the cataplana!)
- Heat a large, deep saucepan or Dutch oven on the stove over medium-high heat. Coat the bottom of the pan with a thin layer of oil, then add the shrimp heads and shells and cook until browned. Add the onions, garlic, bay leaves, and saffron, sweating until the onions are soft but not browned. Add the butter and tomato paste, cooking for a minute or so, then cover with 2 quarts water. Heat to a simmer, and let bubble away (at a moderate, not aggressive) simmer, for about 30 to 45 minutes.
- Remove from the heat, add the parsley sprigs, and let stand for 15 minutes.
- Strain through a fine-mesh strainer, pressing on the solids to release all of their flavor. Discard the solids. You can use the stock immediately, refrigerate for up to 2 days, or freeze for up to 2 months.
- Cataplana
- Soak your clams in a large bowl filled with ice and water for at least 15 minutes — this will help them release some of the sand in the shells. Then scrub and rinse under cold water.

- Heat olive oil in a cataplana pot (or a Dutch oven or other large pot with a tight-fitting lid) until shimmering, then add sausage and prosciutto. Brown, stirring occasionally, until the sausage gets a little color and the prosciutto starts to look like it's crisping, about 5 to 7 minutes. Add the onions and pepper and continue to cook, stirring now and then, until the onions are soft but not brown, about 4 minutes. Add the garlic, and cook one minute more. Add the bay, pinch of saffron, paprika, tomatoes, and splash of white wine, stirring to deglaze the pan. Slowly add the shrimp stock, then cook at a low simmer for about 20 minutes, until the tomatoes lose their tinniness and all the flavors have sufficiently co-mingled.
- Increase the heat to bring to a boil, add in the shrimp and clams, lock the cataplana, and cook about 5 to 10 minutes, shaking occasionally. If using a Dutch oven, cook, covered, stirring occasionally until the clams pop open, 5 to 10 minutes. Once the clams have opened, slowly stream in the cream and stir, then shower with fresh parsley.
- Serve the cataplana right at the table, with bread, little fried potatoes, or white rice.

---

241. Potato Pastry Stuffed With Kale, Pork & Feta

Serving: Serves 4 | Prep: | Cook: | Ready in:

Ingredients

- Potato Pastry
- 1 cup cooked, mashed potatoes (you can use leftovers!)
- 1/2 cup unsalted butter
- 1 1/2 cups all purpose flour*
- 3/4 teaspoon salt
- The Stuffing
- 1 bunch kale, washed, trimmed & shredded (large bunch)
- 1/4 cup onion, finely diced
- 2 tablespoons shallots
- 1 teaspoon garlic, minced
- 1/2 pound ground pork
- 3 cups cremini mushrooms, chopped
- 1/2 cup celery, finely diced
- 1/2 cup carrots, shredded
- 1/4 cup red pepper, finely diced
- 2 teaspoons fresh sage, finely chopped
- 2 teaspoons fresh rosemary, finely chopped
- 2 teaspoons fresh thyme, finely chopped
- 3/4 cup crumbled goat feta
- 1/4 cup grated parmesan cheese
- salt & pepper to taste
- 1 tablespoon olive oil
- 2 tablespoons butter
- 1 egg, beaten

Direction

- Potato Pastry
- Heat potatoes and butter in a saucepan, stirring constantly until butter is melted.
- Slowly add the flour, mixing to make a smooth, stiff dough.
- *The amount of flour depends on a couple of things, like how much moisture is in your potatoes. Adding it slowly allows you to adjust the quantity as you get the dough to a stretchy consistency.
- Let dough rest 30 minutes.
- The Stuffing
- Steam shredded kale to tender, about 10 min. set aside.
- Sauté ground pork with a little olive oil, until cooked through, about 15-20 min. Set aside.
- Sauté mushrooms in 1 tbsp. butter until cooked and golden brown and the liquid has evaporated, about 10-15 min.
- Sauté onion, shallots, garlic, celery, carrots, red pepper in 1 tbsp. butter until tender, about 7-10 min.
- Remove from heat and mix in cooked pork, mushrooms and fresh herbs. Once well blended add kale, feta and parmesan, salt and pepper.

- On a lightly floured surface, roll dough to ½ inch thickness (about 9x12 rectangle shape), adding flour if needed to keep the dough smooth (not sticky)
- Transfer to a piece of parchment cut for a 12x18 inch cookie sheet.
- Continue rolling to ¼ inch thickness, about 12x18.
- Leaving a 4 inch strip down the middle, slice 12-14 1 inch strips down each side of the dough for braiding. (Careful to not cut the parchment paper)
- Carefully transfer dough, with parchment paper, to 12x18 inch cookie sheet.
- Spread stuffing evenly down the middle of the dough in a mound.
- Starting at one end, take strips and crisscross/braid down and over the stuffing. Gently tug each strip to stretch it as you overlap.
- When you get to the end if you have a bit of extra dough you can trim it off.
- Brush with beaten egg and sprinkle with kosher salt.
- Bake in a 375°F preheated oven for 30-40 min or until golden brown

---

242. Pressed Muffuletta Sandwich

Serving: Serves 8-10 | Prep: | Cook: | Ready in:

Ingredients

- 6 cloves garlic, chopped
- 4 tablespoons olive oil
- 2 cups green olives, pitted and chopped
- 1 cup black olives, pitted and chopped
- 4 ribs celery with leaves, chopped
- 2 tablespoons capers
- 1 sprig lovage, chopped
- 2 sprigs basil, chopped
- 3/4 cup olive oil
- 2 tablespoons sherry vinegar
- salt and pepper
- 1/2 teaspoon red pepper flakes
- 1 cup red Peppadew peppers
- 1 cup artichoke hearts in oil, thinly sliced and well drained
- 1/2 pound prosciutto, sliced
- 1/4 pound mortadella
- 1/4 pound roasted parma cotto
- 1/4 pound sweet sopressata
- 1 pound fresh mozzarella
- 3 loaves of strong, crusty bread

Direction

- Warm the garlic in the olive oil. It should not color at all, in fact it should not sizzle. This takes the acrid edge off it. Let it cool while you prepare the rest of the salad.
- Mix all ingredients down to Peppadew pepper together. Add the garlic. Taste for seasoning and adjust as desired. This is your olive salad.
- Cut each loaf of bread in half horizontally. Some recipes will tell you to pull out the crumb, but this is heinous. Spoon olive salad onto the bottom half of the bread. You just want a thinnish layer, one olive shard deep.
- Slice the Peppadew peppers and artichoke hearts and lay over the olive salad.
- Thinly slice the mozzarella and place over the peppers and artichoke hearts.
- Layer on three slices of cold cuts. I think it's best to use either prosciutto or the cotto but not both together.
- Cover the cold cuts with another layer of olive salad and top with the top half of the bread.
- Repeat with the other loaves of bread.
- This step requires a leap of faith. Wrap the loaves in foil or cut them into sections that will fit in a Ziploc bag. Then sit on them until they are nicely squished, about 15 minutes. Some people will apply heat to the sandwiches instead, but again, this is heinous.
- Enjoy these with a seltzer. Afterwards, be sure you either brush your teeth or chew some sugarless gum if you will be interacting with the public.

243. Prosciutto And Fontina Panini With Arugula Pesto

Serving: Serves 4 sandwiches | Prep: | Cook: |Ready in:

Ingredients

- For the Sandwich
- ¼ cup cider vinegar
- 2 tablespoons sugar
- 1/2 teaspoon salt
- 1 large shallot, thinly sliced
- 1 loaf ciabatta, sliced lengthwise
- 1/3 pound prosciutto (about 10 slices)
- 1/3 pound fontina, thinly sliced
- For the pesto
- ¼ cup toasted pine nuts
- 2 garlic cloves
- 2 cups baby arugula
- ½ lemon, juiced
- 1/2 teaspoon salt
- ¼ cup olive oil

Direction

- Make the pickled shallots: bring the cider, sugar, and salt to a boil in a small saucepan over a medium flame. Simmer for a minute, until the sugar has dissolved, then pour the hot liquid over the shallots in a small bowl or jar so they are fully submerged. Allow to sit for 20 minutes, then place in an airtight container until ready for use. This can be done up to a week before.
- Make the pesto: in a small food processor, pulse the pine nuts and garlic until coarsely chopped. Add the arugula, lemon juice, and salt and pulse to combine. Stream in olive oil and continue to blend until all the ingredients are finely chopped and the pesto is smooth and creamy. Taste for seasoning and add more salt if necessary.
- Preheat the broiler. Place the two slices of bread crust side down on a baking sheet and toast in the oven for 3-5 minutes, until beginning to crisp but not totally browned. Slather the bottom half of bread evenly with pesto and arrange the cheese slices in a single layer. Return just this slice of bread to the oven and continue to toast until the cheese has melted, about 3-5 minutes.
- Slather the other slice of bread with the remaining pesto and arrange the pickled shallots on top, followed by the prosciutto. Sandwich the halves together.
- Heat a large skillet over medium-high heat. Depending on the size of your pan and the size of the ciabatta, you may have to cut the sandwich in half. Set the sandwich top side down in the pan and weight it with a smaller skillet and/or a heavy bowl so the bread is crushed and flattened as it toasts. When the bread has browned, repeat on the other side. When finished, the panini should be browned, crisped, and flattened, and should have cheese oozing from it. Toast the remaining half (if necessary), and then cut it again to create four sandwiches.

244. Puff Pastry Pizza

Serving: Serves 2-4 | Prep: | Cook: |Ready in:

Ingredients

- 1 sheet of thawed puff pastry, rolled out to 3-4mm thick
- fig jam/preserves
- pesto of choice. I used leftover Springtime Pesto
- 2 medium balls of fresh mozzarella or 1 large ball
- parmigiano reggiano, grated
- 10-12 very thin slices of prosciutto

Direction

- Heat oven to 425 degrees F.
- Roll thawed puff pastry on a floured surface until it is a rectangle roughly 3-4mm thick.

Place on top of parchment paper, silpat or foil and place on cookie sheet.

- Put a thin layer of fig jam on one half and a thin layer of pesto on the other half. The key is a thin layer. The jam is very sweet and the pesto has a lot of olive oil.
- Slice the mozzarella thinly and scatter over entire sheet. Sprinkle a thin layer of parmesan over the top. Lastly, add the prosciutto in heaps on top of everything.
- Bake for 12-15 minutes or when the edges of the pastry turn golden brown.

---

245.   Pulled Pork

Serving: Makes a mess of pulled pork, enough for 10-12 | Prep: | Cook: |Ready in:

Ingredients

- Garlic Brined Pork Shoulder
- 4 quarts boiling water
- 8 ounces sea salt
- 9.6 ounces sugar
- 20 cloves of lightly crushed garlic
- 2 tablespoons black peppercorns
- 2 tablespoons yellow mustard seed
- 2 teaspoons chile flakes
- 2 teaspoons allspice berries
- 8 whole cloves
- 4 bay leaves
- 1 skinless, boneless pork picnic shoulder, butterflied
- Black Coffee and Bourbon Barbecue Sauce
- 1 1/2 cups red wine vinegar
- 1 1/2 cups ketchup
- 1 cup pork broth
- 1/2 cup brown sugar
- 1/2 cup strong black coffee
- 1/4 cup bourbon
- smoky meat drippings if available

Direction

- Bring a little more than 4 quarts (3.8 liters) of water to a boil over high heat. Place the salt and sugar into a large non-reactive container. Make a sachet with the garlic, spices and bay and tie securely with string. Pour 4 measured quarts (3.8 liters) of boiling water into the container with the salt and sugar. Stir to dissolve. Add the sachet to the brine. Cover the container loosely and let sit for at least four hours, or overnight.
- The following day, lightly rinse and pat dry the pork in preparation for brining. Submerge the pork in the brine. Weight with a plate and refrigerate for three days.
- Remove the picnic from the brine, place on a towel-lined tray and refrigerate uncovered overnight to dry. Discard the brine.
- Make the sauce. In a saucepan over medium heat simmer the red wine vinegar until it has reduced in volume by about half. Add to the pot the ketchup, pork broth, brown sugar, coffee and bourbon along with any smoky meat drippings, if available. Simmer the ingredients together for roughly thirty minutes, stirring frequently, until the flavors blend harmoniously. Taste for seasoning.
- Heat your smoker to 180°F (82°C). Place the picnic in the smoker on a rack. Open it up fully so as to expose a maximum of surface area. Put a pan underneath it to catch any juices that drip out as it cooks. Tend to the fire and maintain a consistent temperature as needed.
- Slowly smoke the picnic for about four hours, far beyond well done or until a meat thermometer inserted into the thickest part of the meat registers 175°F (79°C). The connective tissue should be nearly collapsed and the meat tender and obscenely flavorful.
- Remove the picnic from the smoker and set it on a tray to rest. When it is cool enough to handle, break it apart into chunks about the size of your thumb. Place the shredded meat into a pot and stir in enough of the barbecue sauce and drippings to coat the meat well. Place over a very low flame and barely simmer it for 30 minutes to allow the sauce to absorb.

Taste for seasoning and add more sauce as desired.

---

246.   Pulled Pork Baps With Apple Slaw And Tangy BBQ Sauce

Serving: Serves 6-8 | Prep: | Cook: | Ready in:

Ingredients

- For the Pork and Slaw
- 3kg Pork Shoulder Joint, bone in
- 2 tablespoons Olive Oil
- 1/2 tablespoon Smoked Paprika
- 1 Dried Ancho Chile
- 2 Cloves of Garlic
- 1 tablespoon Dark Brown Sugar
- 1/2 Red Cabbage, Shredded
- 2 Carrots, peeled and grated
- 2 Sticks of Celery, finely sliced
- 1/2 Red Onion, finely sliced
- 1 Apple, such as Braeburn/ Granny Smith, peeled and grated
- 2 tablespoons Mayonnaise
- 4 tablespoons Buttermilk
- 2-3 tablespoons Cider Vinegar
- Salt & Pepper, to taste
- Bread Baps, to serve
- For the BBQ Sauce
- 1 White Onion, diced
- 4 Cloves of Garlic, finely grated
- 1 tablespoon Olive Oil
- 1 tablespoon Mustard Seeds, ground to powder
- 500 milliliters Tomato Ketchup, I used Heinz
- 150 milliliters Cider Vinegar
- 8 tablespoons Dark Brown Sugar
- 3 tablespoons Honey
- 1 tablespoon Smoked Paprika
- 1 Dried Chipotle Chilli
- 2 tablespoons Dark Soy Sauce
- 2 tablespoons Worcestershire Sauce
- 1 tablespoon Cayenne Pepper

Direction

- Preheat your oven to 220 degrees Celsius. Line a roasting tin with tin foil and place the roasting joint in it. If your butcher has not already scored the crackling skin, do so with a sharp knife, with lines 1cm apart. Drizzle the olive oil over the meat, sprinkling the paprika with some salt and pepper over. Rub the mixture into the meat, coating all over and into the crevices. Cut the garlic cloves in half and rub over the meat, before pushing the pieces into gaps in the meat and underneath during cooking. After soaking the dried ancho chile in hot water until soft, rub it over the meat, massaging the flavours in. Pop it into the oven for half an hour at the high heat for the crackling to crisp. Remove from the heat and turn the oven down to 170 degrees Celsius. Take what cooking juices have come from the meat and place in a saucepan with the sugar. Stir on a high heat until the sugar has melted and pour over the meat. Cover the joint with tin foil and return to the oven. Continue to cook for 5 hours, occasionally basting the meat, making sure to always cover with tin foil before returning to the oven.
- While the meat is cooking, make the barbecue sauce. Heat the olive oil in a large saucepan, tossing in the onions and garlic with some salt, before reducing to a low heat. Cook until the onions become translucent. Add the ground mustard seeds and cook for one minute to gain fragrance. Next, add three tablespoons on the sugar, allow to caramelize for a moment, before adding the ketchup and vinegar. The sharp aroma of the vinegar will hit the back of the nose with a punch, so stand back.
- Bring the heat down to let the mixture simmer, and stir in the paprika, cayenne pepper, two tablespoons of the honey and the chipotle chili. Allow the mixture to simmer for a further ten minutes to cook off some of the vinegar. Add another three tablespoons of sugar, all of the soy sauce and Worcestershire sauce. Keep on a low heat for another twenty minutes, by which time the sauce should have

thickened and darkened, the vinegar now a pleasant undertone when tasted. The rest of the honey and sugar should be added to taste, as the taste of the sauce depends on the quality of ketchup and vinegar used. Set aside and allow to cool before pouring into jars. It will keep in the fridge for up to a month.

- Next, prepare the coleslaw. Put the cabbage, onion, celery, apple and carrot into a large bowl. In a separate bowl, combine the mayonnaise, buttermilk and two tablespoons of the vinegar. Season to taste with salt and pepper, before adding to the vegetable mixture. Stir to combine, and taste. Depending on the sweetness of your apple, you may add the extra tablespoon of cider vinegar. Chill in the fridge until serving.
- After five hours of cooking and basting, take the pork from the oven. Remove the foil from the meat and return to the oven for 20 minutes at 200 degrees Celsius to crisp the crackling. Remove from the oven and allow to rest, tin foil replaced, for 15 minutes. This will moisten the meat, making it easier to pull apart. Remove the crackling and serve separately. Pull the meat apart, shredding with two forks, putting pieces of fat to the side.
- Slice the bread baps in half and toast under the grill. Pile the meat in a large serving dish and serve on the table, letting your group serve themselves and pile those baps high!

---

247. Pulled Pork Cuban Sandwich

Serving: Makes 2 sandwiches | Prep: | Cook: | Ready in:

Ingredients

- 1 ½ cup pulled pork - I like this "Cuban Adobo" style pulled pork: https://food52.com/recipes...
- 4 slices Black Forest ham (or Canadian bacon, or even regular bacon, if you like)

- 1 cup grated cheese, or more to taste – we use a sharp cheddar, but you can use whatever you like. Feel free to slice it instead.
- 2 Cuban rolls; I highly recommend this: https://food52.com/recipes...
- Mayo, to taste
- Mustard, whatever kind you prefer, to taste
- 6-8 sweet pickles, or 4 kosher dills, or ¼ cup sweet and sour red onion jam, or any other fruit chutney

Direction

- Slice the rolls lengthwise. Slather mayo and mustard on to taste.
- Very important: Warm up the pulled pork. We do this in a microwave for about 2 minutes on 70% power. You need the pulled pork to be good and hot before you put it on the sandwich, and then, don't waste any time cooking the sandwich itself.
- While the pork is heating, put two slices of ham on one side of the Cuban roll.
- Divide the pork between the rolls. Immediately put the grated cheese on the warm pulled pork. Put the pickles on. Bring the two sides of the sandwich together.
- We use our Panini press for these. If you don't have one, cook the sandwiches in a dry skillet, that you've gotten nice and hot, pressing down on the sandwiches using a second heavy skillet, putting a piece of plain (not waxed) parchment between the sandwich and the top skillet; turn the sandwich over after the bottom has toasted up nicely and replace the skillet.
- Enjoy! ;o)

---

248. Quiche In Winter White And Blue

Serving: Makes one 10 inch quiche | Prep: | Cook: | Ready in:

Ingredients

- for the tart crust
- 1 1/4 cups all purpose flour
- 1/2 teaspoon salt
- 1   stick unsalted butter
- 2 tablespoons ice cold water
- for the filling
- 3   slices thick, applewood smoked, uncured bacon
- 1 1/2 cups cauliflower, cut into individual florets (halving large ones)
- 2 teaspoons minced garlic
- 1 tablespoon apple cider vinegar
- 1 tablespoon water, plus more if necessary
- 1/3 cup Fuji apple, peeled, cut into ¼ inch dice (can substitute another late season variety) drizzled with juice from 1 lemon wedge to prevent oxidation
- 1/3 cup finely grated Emmentaler (grate right before adding to quiche)
- 1/4 cup finely grated Buttermilk Blue Cheese (grate right before adding to quiche)
- 1 cup half-and-half
- 3 large eggs
- Freshly ground black pepper

Direction

- For the tart crust
- Combine flour and salt in a mound on a cool, clean surface. Place stick of butter on top of mound. Slice butter into ¼-inch thick pieces. Dip each slice of butter in flour, coating top and bottom.
- Using your thumbs and index fingers, flatten each slice, gently squeezing. As you do this, sections of each slice will fall on to the flour mound. Repeat until you have flattened every slice.
- You should now have a pile of thin, flour coated butter flakes on top of your flour. Slide both hands, palms facing up, under the edges of the flour mound and bring your hands together, raking floury butter flakes and gently combining pieces by pressing your thumbs down against your other fingers. Repeat until you have mostly saw dusty clumps with a few larger flakes.
- Sprinkle 1 T of ice-cold water over pile. Gently work mixture together with your hands to combine dough. If dough gets sticky, dip fingers in flour. Add remaining tablespoon of ice cold water and gather, eventually rolling dough into a smooth ball (be careful not to overwork, or dough will be tough). Wrap ball in a large piece of plastic wrap and flatten into disc (about 1 inch thick and 4 inches across). Fold plastic wrap around edges of disc to seal and refrigerate for at least 30 minutes and up to 1 day.
- When ready to use, remove from refrigerator and allow disc to sit at room temperature for about ten minutes before rolling out. Roll out dough (slightly larger than tart pan) and carefully wind around pin while sliding ceramic tart pan under. Unwind dough from pin into tart pan, carefully pressing into the bottom and up the sides. Trim excess with kitchen shears. Place in the freezer for 10 minutes.
- Preheat oven to 350 degrees F. Line dough with parchment, fill with at least 1 cup of rice or dried beans and bake for 15 minutes. Remove pan from oven, remove parchment and weights, and poke surface of dough all over with a fork. Return to oven for 12 more minutes. Remove and set aside to cool before filling and baking. Do not turn off oven.
- For the filling
- Place bacon slices in a cold pan that is large enough to fit all three slices in a single layer and turn heat to low. Slowly cook bacon, turning up heat if necessary. You want to cook the bacon to the point that the fat just begins to render, without burning. Remove bacon slices to a paper towel lined plate. Do not turn off burner.
- Pour off all but 1 T of drippings and briefly rest pan on a cool burner. Add cauliflower pieces and return pan to hot burner. Cook cauliflower, constantly turning to prevent burning, about a minute. Add apple cider vinegar and cook for a few seconds, add 1 T of water and continue cooking, stirring. Mix in garlic and cook until cauliflower is tender and

golden, about 3 minutes more, adding another tablespoon of water if necessary to prevent burning. Remove pan from heat.

- Cut each bacon slice in half lengthwise and then chop crosswise.
- Assemble tart by sprinkling half of the Emmentaler onto the bottom of the crust. Layer in the bacon, then the cauliflower, and then the diced apple. In a large Pyrex measure, combine the half-and-half with the eggs and the blue cheese. Add fresh ground pepper. Pour egg-cheese mixture over cauliflower filling and top with remaining Emmentaler.
- Transfer to oven and bake for 25-30 minutes, until golden and slightly puffed. Allow quiche to cool for at least 10 minutes before serving. Enjoy!

249.   Quickie Chili

Serving: Serves 4 hungry folks | Prep: | Cook: | Ready in:

Ingredients

- 1 1/2 pounds ground beef or round
- 1/2 pound ground pork, mild (or hotter to your liking)
- 2 16 oz bush's chili beans, mild
- 2 14 oz del monte zesty chili style diced tomatoes
- 1 tablespoon creamy peanut butter

Direction

- Brown beef and pork, Drain.
- Add rest of ingredients. Slow cook until ready to eat.
- Serve with your favorite toppings. EX: Diced onions, cheese, croutons, etc.

250.   Rad Raddish BLT

Serving: Makes 1 sanwich | Prep: | Cook: | Ready in:

Ingredients

- 2 tablespoons Guacamole
- 2 pieces Bread, toasted
- 4 pieces Bacon, cooked
- 1-2 Radishes, sliced
- 1 bunch Watercress, rinsed

Direction

- Toast your two slices of bread to a desired done-ness. While that's going on you can assemble the other ingredients. In a microwave safe dish, put a paper towel down on the plate and lay the bacon slices side by side, cover with a paper towel and cook for 5 minutes. (Or cook it how you usually do)
- Wash and slice the radish into thin rounds. Rinse and trim the leaves off of the bunch of water cress.
- To assemble your sandwich, spread the guacamole on one side of the bread and lay the bacon on top. On the other piece of bread lay out 7-8 leaves of watercress (or just a bunch) and layer the sliced radishes on top. Fold together, cut in half and enjoy!

251.   Raise The Red Lantern (Red Braised Pork, Slow Cooker Style)

Serving: Serves 2-4 | Prep: | Cook: | Ready in:

Ingredients

- 1 1 1/2 pound pork shoulder
- 1/2 cup sliced okra
- 3-4 large leaves of collard green, washed and stemmed
- 26 ounces pork or beef stock
- 1 leek

- 5 garlic cloves, peeled and smashed
- 8-10 szechuan pepper corns
- 1 tablespoon gochujang (Korean hot pepper/soy bean paste)*
- 1 tablespoon gochugaru (Korean hot pepper powder)*
- peanut oil
- chili sesame oil
- salt

Direction

- Mise en place. In small dishes portion out the pepper powder and pepper paste. Crush the garlic but leave the cloves intact.
- Wash the collard leaves and roll into "cigars", then slice into chiffonade ribbons.
- Slice the leeks into coin shapes (white and pale green parts only) reserving the tough green parts for another day, such as making stock.
- Using paper towels, wipe down the pork shoulder completely so that it's kind of dry. Rub all over with the hot pepper powder.
- In a Dutch oven or some other high capacity killing machine---I'm talkin' to you Kim Jong Un---heat the peanut and sesame oil to the point where they begin to shimmer. Browning is a necessary step. So do that on all sides of the shoulder. Season with salt as you go.
- Meanwhile spread the sliced leeks on the bottom of your crock. When the shoulder is browned and very aromatic transfer to the crock. Surround it with the collards and sliced okra. Add the stock and if necessary, depending on the volume of your slow cooker, add water just so that the liquid comes half way up the side of the shoulder. It shouldn't be submerged. Throw in the Szechuan pepper corns while you're at it.
- Set the cooker to low and the dial to 6 hours. Go to work or to the local karaoke bar. When you get home steam up some rice for about 20 minutes. Cut up the shoulder and plate with sauce spooned over. Turn off the slow cooker. Its work is done.
- *The Korean ingredients will be the most difficult components to find. Here are some imperfect substitute suggestions; for the hot pepper powder try a Spanish pimenton de la vera (maybe a smoked style, i.e. ahumado) and for the pepper paste try sriracha aka "rooster sauce".

252.   Really Good Pizza

Serving: Serves 14" pizza | Prep: | Cook: |Ready in:

Ingredients

- 1 cup warm water
- 2 teaspoons yeast
- 2 1/2 cups flour
- 1 teaspoon sugar
- 1 teaspoon salt
- 2 teaspoons oil
- 1 handful cornmeal
- 2 tablespoons olive oil
- 12 ounces tomato sauce
- 1 packet pepperoni slices
- 8 ounces fresh mozzarella cheese

Direction

- Mix yeast and water.
- Let sit for 5 minutes.
- Mix dry ingredients (except cornmeal) in medium bowl.
- Add water/yeast mixture and stir.
- Knead dough for 1 minute.
- Let rise in warm place for 20 minutes.
- Sprinkle cornmeal on pizza pan. Press into pizza pan and roll out to edges.
- Brush lightly with olive oil.
- Spread tomato sauce (spaghetti sauce works great).
- Add pepperoni and whatever else you may like...
- Top with thinly sliced mozzarella cheese.
- Bake at 400 degrees for 26 minutes or until crust is golden brown.

- Remove from oven, allow to cool slightly and enjoy!

253.   Red Beet Char Siu Pork

Serving: Serves 4 (or 2 for dinner with leftovers) | Prep: 24hours0mins | Cook: 0hours20mins | Ready in:

Ingredients

- 3 roasted red beets
- 1 tablespoon soy sauce
- 1 tablespoon ketchup
- 1 tablespoon rice wine vinegar
- 1 tablespoon dark brown sugar, packed
- 2 tablespoons fresh ginger, grated on a microplane
- 1 clove of garlic
- 1/2 teaspoon toasted sesame oil
- 1/2 teaspoon ground fennel (I actually buy seeds and grind them fresh with a mortar and pestle)
- 1/4 teaspoon white pepper
- 1/8 teaspoon ground clove
- 1/8 teaspoon cinnamon
- squirts of Sriracha, to your taste
- 4 tablespoons vegetable oil or other neutral oil, divided
- 1 pork tenderloin, silver skin removed, about 1 lb
- 2 scallions, thinly sliced for garnish (optional)

Direction

- To roast the beets, remove the stems and greens (if present), peel with a vegetable peeler and cut into a 1/2 inch dice. Place on a foil-lined baking sheet, drizzle with olive oil, a touch of salt and pepper, and roast in a 400F degree oven for 45 minutes.
- Puree the roasted beets in a blender or food processor. Add the soy sauce through Sriracha and 2 tablespoons of neutral oil and blend until smooth (this will not be liquid, more like a bright fuchsia paste.)

- Empty the paste into a large zip top bag. Pat the pork tenderloin dry, lightly coat with salt and pepper, and add to the bag, massaging the paste into the meat. Seal and refrigerate to marinate overnight (or at least 4 hours - and up to 24, the longer the better in my book.) Bring to room temperature before cooking.
- Preheat the oven to 400F and prepare a foil-lined baking sheet. Heat a large cast iron or other heavy bottomed sauté pan with the remaining 2 tablespoons of neutral oil over medium-high heat. Add the pork to the pan to brown, 2 minutes per side (8 minutes total). Remove the pork, place on the sheet tray and cook in the oven about 20 minutes, or until the internal temperature reads 140F. Once out of the oven, let the meat rest for 10 minutes loosely tented with foil; the internal temperature should read 150F after the rest. Slice into rounds and enjoy!

254.   Red Beans And Rice

Serving: Serves 12 or so | Prep: | Cook: | Ready in:

Ingredients

- 1 pound small red beans, dried
- 1 medium onion, diced
- 2-4 cloves garlic, minced
- 3 15-oz cans petite diced tomatos
- 1 can diced tomatos and green chiles
- 1 pound andouille sausage, sliced 1/4 inch thick
- 1 cup diced or shredded cooked chicken or turkey
- 1 cup diced or shredded smoked ham (or 2 hamhocks)
- 1 tablespoon smoked paprika
- 1 teaspoon seasoned salt
- 1/2 teaspoon Aleppo pepper or cayenne
- 2-3 dashes hot pepper sauce (preferably Pick-a-Peppa)
- 4 cups cooked white rice, for serving

- 1 tablespoon olive oil

Direction

- Soak beans overnight in water; drain and rinse.
- Put beans in stock pot with enough water to barely reach the top of beans. Add tomatoes, tomatoes and chiles, paprika, pepper, seasoned salt and cooked chicken. Bring to a boil over medium high heat, and lower heat to medium low.
- Saute onion in olive oil over medium heat until soft. Add sliced andouille and saute over medium high heat until beginning to brown. Add ham and saute until meats are browned. Add to stockpot.
- Simmer over medium low heat until beans are completely done, about two hours. Can hold over low heat for hours longer. Serve in large soup bowls over a mound of white rice, with a good crusty bread or old-fashioned cornbread on the side.

255. Rich N' Cheesy Smoked Sausage Cheese Dip

Serving: Serves 28 | Prep: | Cook: |Ready in:

Ingredients

- 16 ounces skinless smoked sausage, cut into small 1/4 inch triangle pieces
- 2 pounds processed cheese, cubed
- 10 ounces diced tomatoes with green chili peppers, drained
- 2 teaspoons ground cumin
- 1 cup sour cream
- 1/2 cup chopped cilantro
- tortilla, pita or bagel chips

Direction

- Combine smoked sausage, processed cheese, tomatoes and cumin in a large saucepan; mix well.
- Heat mixture over low heat until melted and hot, stirring occasionally.
- Add sour cream and cilantro; stir well.
- Heat through and transfer to a medium-sized slow cooker on low heat.
- Serve with tortilla, pita or bagel chips. Dip may be served in a large bowl at room temperature for up to two hours.

256. Roasted Breakfast Tart

Serving: Serves 6-8 | Prep: | Cook: |Ready in:

Ingredients

- Garnish (Candied Bacon and Fried Sage)
- 7 slices of Bacon
- 1/4 cup Sugar
- 1/4 cup Cinnamon
- 1 bunch fresh Sage
- 3 tablespoons Olive oil
- Crust and Filling
- Crust
- 3 cups Spelt flour
- 1 teaspoon Salt
- 2 tablespoons Pure cane organic raw sugar
- 1 cup Olive Oil
- 6 tablespoons Organic Fat Free Milk
- Filling
- 9 Organic Egg whites
- 1/2 cup Organic Fat Free Milk
- 2-3 Cloves of roasted garlic(Press)
- 2-3 Oven roasted Organic Tomatoes
- 1/4 teaspoon Salt
- 1/4 teaspoon Pepper
- 1 teaspoon Olive oil
- 1/2 cup Fresh Mozzarella
- 1/2 cup grated Parmigiano Reggiano

Direction

- Garnish (Candied Bacon and Fried Sage)

- Combine sugar and cinnamon in bowl, set aside. From filling recipe below please roast head garlic and 3 sliced tomatoes and seasoned with olive oil, salt and pepper at 375 on a parchment lined baking pan. Rotate until garlic is golden brown and tomatoes are roasted until desired look.
- In medium frying pan add olive oil on high heat quickly fry clean and dry sage. Only takes 15-20 sec. will be dark green. Set aside.
- In the same frying pan drain extra oil and add bacon. Start frying on med-high heat. Lightly brush sugar and cinnamon and flip bacon. Turn heat to med-low and finish cooking bacon brushing each side. Remove and drain on paper towel. Set aside
- Crust and Filling
- This is your Pie Crust: in a large bowl sift flour, salt and sugar. Add Olive Oil and slowly add Milk (you might not need it all).Mix until it combines together, then kneed. Work in 1 cup of chopped fried sage (leave some sage for garnish). Press into a greased baking pan. (9 inch. round spring pan) Blind Bake @ 350 for 8-10 min. Remove and cool.
- This is your Filling (while your crust cools):In a large bowl add egg whites, milk, press 2-3 cloves of garlic, olive oil, salt and pepper. Whisk this mixture pour into baked pie shell and layer oven-dried tomatoes, fresh Mozzarella and Parmigiano Reggiano. Adding toppings should be done to your desire. Bake in 350 degree oven for 12-15 minutes. Start on the top rack for the first 6 min. Lower to bottom rack and finish until egg sets. Remove and cool for 5 min. cut into pie slices and garnish with fried sage and candied bacon.

257. Roasted Pork Belly

Serving: Serves 6-8 | Prep: 0hours45mins | Cook: 2hours30mins | Ready in:

Ingredients

- Roasted Pork Belly
- 2 1/2 lb pork belly (choose a meaty piece)
- 1 Tbsp kosher salt
- 2 tsp thyme
- 1 tsp sage
- olive oil
- small wire rack
- large roasting rack or cookie sheet
- heavy duty foil
- Hoisin Mushroom Sauce
- 1 onion, chopped
- 8 ounces fresh shiitake mushrooms, sliced
- 2 Tbsp Hoisin Sauce
- 2 Tbsp rice wine (or sherry)
- 1 cup chicken stock
- 1/2 tsp salt
- 1 tsp cornstarch
- olive oil

Direction

- Roasted Pork Belly
- Preheat oven to 450 degrees.
- Rinse pork belly then dry thoroughly with paper towels. Place on a cutting board. Using a skewer, poke the skin all over as much as possible. If the bamboo skewer stops piercing the skin it has probably become blunt at the end so discard it and use another. Repeat until you've used 5-6 skewers Do this for at least 5 minutes to really get lots of holes deep into the skin. I don't think you can pierce the skin too much!
- Mix together salt and herbs. Flip pork belly over so skin side is down and rub half of the salt mixture into the meat. Drizzle with olive oil
- Roll pork belly into a cylinder so that the skin is on the outside and the meat is all tucked inside. Tie the cylinder with the kitchen string in 3 places along the length of the cylinder.
- Rub outside of skin with some olive oil, then rub the rest of the salt and herb mixture into the skin.
- The next set of steps is to help with the spattering that will occur when you cook the pork belly. First, take very generous piece of

foil out that is at least a half a size too large for your large roasting try or cookie sheet. Place that foil on the rack and tent the edges of the foil upwards. This will create some walls that help catch some splatters. With a smaller piece of foil, make a little 'tray' that is large enough for your rack. Place on the cookie sheet, then place the wire rack down into it and the pork belly on top of that.

- Roast at 450 degrees for 1 1/2 to 2 hours. The skin will become bubbled and crispy and a lot of fat will render into the pie/cake pan beneath.
- Let pork rest for 10 minutes before cutting twine and slicing.
- Hoisin Mushroom Sauce
- Sauté onions in olive oil until translucent and soft. Add mushrooms and continue to cook. They will absorb the oil and then shrink down. Let them brown a little.
- Mix together hoisin, rice wine, salt, and the chicken stock. Add to the mushrooms once they have browned. Let the mixture come to a boil and reduce by quarter.
- Mix cornstarch with 1 Tbsp. of water or broth. Add to hoisin/stock mixture and stir vigorously. Cook until the sauce has thickened and no cloudiness remains. Add more broth or water if necessary to thin to desired consistency.

---

258.   Roasted Red Pimento Peppers With Hazlenuts, Prosciutto And Campo D Montal

Serving: Serves 4 | Prep: | Cook: | Ready in:

Ingredients

- 8 small pimento peppers or 2 red bell peppers
- 2 red onions, peeled, root end in tact and cut into 6 pieces each from root to stem, this is so

they will stay together when cooked, you should have 12 wedges
- 3 thin slices of prosciutto, torn into strips
- 1/3 cup hazlenuts
- 1 tablespoon roasted pumkin seed oil
- 1 tablespoon grape seed oil
- 2 1/2 teaspoons good balsamic vinegar
- thin slices of Campo D Montal cheese
- salt and fresh ground pepper

Direction

- When you have time roast the peppers over direct flame and char them. Place them in a container with a lid and let them rest for 20 minutes. Once they have cooled peel them and then put a slit in one side and reach in with a finger and remove the seeds. If you are using red bell peppers cut them into wedges leaving the seeds behind. (If you don't have gas burners use your broiler with the top rack put as close to the burner as you can get it.)
- Preheat the oven to 400 degrees. Place the hazelnuts onto a sheet tray and roast them for 12 minutes. Remove them from the oven and dump them into a clean dish towel and fold the corners of the towel to the center. Using the palm of your hand roll the nuts around with enough pressure to remove the skins.
- In a sauté pan add enough canola oil to coat the pan. Place the pan over medium heat and then place the onion wedges flat side down into the oil. Once they start to simmer cook them until they are good and caramelized and then turn them to the other flat side and brown it. When they are done remove them from the heat to cool.
- In a small bowl whisk together the oils and balsamic vinegar. Season it with salt and pepper.
- To plate: Place the peppers and onions on the plate. Drizzle each with some dressing. Crush some of the hazelnuts and sprinkle them around and then a couple of whole nuts. Twist and drape the prosciutto around the peppers and onions and then shave big thin hunks of

cheese onto the salad. Season with salt and pepper and serve.

---

259. Rosemary Roasted Pork Tenderloin

Serving: Serves 2-3 | Prep: | Cook: |Ready in:

Ingredients

- 1 pound pork tenderloin
- 2 tablespoons extra virgin olive oil
- 1 tablespoon fresh rosemary, chopped
- 1/2 teaspoon sea salt
- 1/2 teaspoon ground black pepper
- 1 head of garlic, minced
- 2 tablespoons butter

Direction

- The day before: In a bowl, mix together olive oil, rosemary, sea salt, and black pepper. Spread mixture all over the pork and let marinade in refrigerator overnight.
- Before baking, let pork sit in room temperature (about 30 minutes).
- Preheat oven for 400°F. Pan sear all sides of the pork until browned. Put pork in oven to roast for 25 minutes or until internal temperature reaches 150°F-160°F.
- Let pork rest at least 10 minutes before carving.
- Make sauce: On medium-low heat, melt butter and add garlic. Cook until garlic is fragrant (not burnt). Drizzle over pork tenderloin and serve.

---

260. Rotini With Andouille, Pine Nuts, Raisins And Spinach

Serving: Serves 4 | Prep: | Cook: |Ready in:

Ingredients

- 1/4 cup Italian pine nuts
- kosher salt
- 3/4 pound rotini
- 2 tablespoons olive oil
- 1 rope (13 1/2 ounces) Andouille sausage, cut into 1/2-inch slices
- 10 ounces baby spinach
- 1/3 cup raisins (golden and/or regular), soaked in warm water for 10 minutes, then drained
- 1/4 cup grated Pecorino cheese, plus more for serving

Direction

- Toast the pine nuts in a 12-inch skillet over medium, stirring frequently to make sure they don't burn, about 3 minutes. Remove and set aside.
- Bring a large pot of water to a boil. Add 2 tablespoons of salt and bring back to a boil. Add pasta and cook until al dente according to package directions.
- While the pasta cooks, prepare your sauce. Wipe the skillet clean. Heat 2 tablespoons of olive oil over medium. Add the sausage and cook until it begins to brown, about 7 minutes.
- Add the spinach to the skillet and toss together with the sausage until it begins to wilt, adding in small amount of pasta water to help it along if needed.
- Add the pasta directly to the skillet along with the raisins and pine nuts, tossing to coat, adding in adding in ¼ cup of pasta water or more (up to 1 cup) as needed to loosen up the sauce. Add in the Pecorino cheese and toss again. Season with salt and pepper.
- Plate in bowls. Pass Pecorino at the table, if desired.

---

261. Roulade Of Pork Loin

Serving: Serves 6 | Prep: | Cook: |Ready in:

Ingredients

- 2 pounds Pork Loin Roast, boneless
- 1 1/2 cups Apple cider (non alcoholic)
- 1/2 cup Tart green apple, peeled and chopped
- 2/3 cup Bread crumbs finely processed
- 1/4 cup Calvados or apple brandy
- 3 Garlic cloves, minced
- 2 Medium Shallots, finely chopped
- 1/4 cup Finely chopped parsley
- 1 teaspoon Salt
- 1/2 teaspoon Black pepper
- 1/4 cup Olive oil + 3 tablespoons
- Cotton cooking twine
- 1 tablespoon Butter

Direction

- Start by preparing your filling. Chop all your ingredients as suggested. In a frying pan, heat the oil over medium high heat.
- Sauté the shallots and garlic for a couple of minutes, stirring so as not to burn. Add the apples and continue to sauté for another 2 minutes reducing heat to medium.
- Stir in the bread crumbs so all ingredients are well mixed. Add 1 cup of the cider and mix well. Add the pepper and 1/2 of the salt, mix well.
- Transfer mixture to a mixing bowl, add the parsley and a couple tablespoons of the remaining cider. Mix well and allow to cool. Preheat oven to 400.
- Next, we will get our roast ready. With the fat side down, begin to slice down the center of the roast lengthwise. Slice down until about 1/2 inch from the bottom. Do not slice all the way through! Now spread the roast open and on each half, make two slits evenly apart, slicing down to within 1/2 inch of the bottom. Do this for the left and right sides. You should now be able to flatten your roast open.
- Take your ball of filling and slice into 5 equal parts. Proceed to fill each cavity of the roast, careful to not fill completely to the edge, that way, when you close it up, it won't squeeze out of each end.

- Once you have filled the cavities, gently put your roast back together again. Realize that since you've added "stuffing", the roast will be fatter around. Take kitchen twine (cotton) and cut 5 or 6 even length pieces long enough to go around the roast. At this point, there is a professional way of twining a roast with one single string; however, I always have problems with that, so I find it easier to just cut separate pieces. Begin by tying the ends about an inch in from each end. Be careful to not tie it too tight around so as not to squeeze the filling out. But be sure it will securely keep the roast closed up. Now that you've done each end, tie the remaining strings around the roast, evenly apart, like the illustration. Once your roast is all tied up, cut any excess string and turn your roast over, cut side down.
- In a frying pan, heat the remaining olive oil over medium high heat. Sear your roast, turning 1/4 turn every 2 minutes or until roast is nice and golden brown. Transfer roast to a baking dish.
- Add the butter to the frying pan, reducing heat to medium. Once butter is melted, carefully add the apple brandy or Calvados and deglaze your pan. Add the remaining cider, and reduce heat to low.
- Once the liquid has reduced by half, pour it over the roast and sprinkle remainder of salt over the top. Transfer to middle rack of oven, reduce heat to 350 and bake uncovered for 1 hour (for a 2 lb. roast).
- Once finished baking, remove and set aside for 10 minutes to allow juices to set into the meat. Serve, making 1 inch thick slices. Pour any pan juices over the meat for added flavor. Enjoy.

262.	**Rustic Ricotta And Peach Tart**

Serving: Serves 8 | Prep: | Cook: | Ready in:

Ingredients

- 1 pie crust (I like the Pillsbury's unroll and fill crust)
- 3 peaches sliced
- 1/2 cup ricotta cheese
- 3 tablespoons honey
- 4 ounces prosciutto
- 1 pinch kosher salt
- 1 tablespoon olive oil
- 1 tablespoon milk

Direction

- Preheat the oven to 425 degrees (F)
- Roll out the pie dough onto a greased cookie sheet or a floured pizza stone.
- Add a thin layer of prosciutto on top of the crust, leaving a 1-2 inch ring of dough exposed.
- Spread the ricotta cheese on top of the prosciutto. Drizzle with honey.
- Toss the peaches in the olive oil and salt. Lay the peaches on top of the cheese.
- Fold the exposed crust over the layered peaches and cheese. Brush the crust with milk. Bake in the oven for about 20 minutes.
- When the crust starts to brown, remove the tart from the oven and sprinkle sliced prosciutto on top of the peaches, tucking pieces into the peaches and the crust. Return to the oven for 5 minutes.
- Cook the tart for 5 more minutes then remove and allow to come to room temperature. Slice and serve!

263. Rustic Penne With A Wine Mystery Solved

Serving: Serves 4 | Prep: | Cook: |Ready in:

Ingredients

- 1 red onion
- 2 tablespoons olive oil
- 1 pound plum tomatoes, more if you like

- 1/2 pound sausage. Any kind will do but as noted above I like to use D'Artagnan's non-pork sausage, like boar.
- 1/2 cup white wine
- 2/3ds packets penne
- 1 yellow pepper
- 1 pinch hot pepper
- pamesan cheese

Direction

- Chop onion and pepper into medium dice, roughly chop tomatoes.
- Squeeze out sausage meat from casings into bite sized chunks
- Heat two tablespoons of oil in sauce pan. Add onions and sauté till translucent, 7 minutes or so.
- Boil water for pasta and cook while the sauce is cooking. I like to do it about a minute under what's recommended on the box but it is very much to personal taste.
- When onions are tender, add sausage and red pepper. Brown for a few minutes. Then add wine, reducing by half or so over high heat. Add tomatoes and peppers. Salt to taste. Cook until it has an almost creamy consistency, 15 or 20 minutes.
- Dump sauce over the pasta and stir for a minute or two in a pot. Check for salt. Serve with cheese.

264. Sage + Prosciutto Tartines

Serving: Makes about 2 cups | Prep: | Cook: |Ready in:

Ingredients

- 1 cup packed sage leaves
- 3/4 cup toasted walnuts
- 3-4 ounces prosciutto (I used sliced)
- 1 cup grated parmesan
- 5 cloves of garlic, roughly chopped
- 3/4 cup olive oil

- Juice from half a lemon
- 1 pinch crushed red pepper flakes
- Kosher or sea salt, to taste
- Freshly ground black pepper, to taste
- Baguette or sourdough boule, to serve

Direction

- Add the garlic to a food processor or blender and pulse until it's nicely minced, about 20 seconds.
- Roughly chop the sage, walnuts, and prosciutto. Add them to the food processor with the red pepper flakes and blend until the mixture is coarsely and evenly chopped.
- Add the lemon juice and start the food processor. Add the olive oil in a slow, steady stream.
- Once all of the olive oil is in, add the parmesan and blend until just incorporated.
- To serve, toast or grill sliced of your bread. (If using a pan, brush both sides of the bread with a little oil.) Once they come off the grill or pan, rub the top side with a garlic clove cut in half. Sprinkle with salt and pepper. Spread each slice with pesto and garnish with a light dusting of lemon zest and parmesan. Now tuck in and enjoy.

265. Salami, Pepperoncini, And Chevre Sandwich

Serving: Serves 2 foot-long sandwiches | Prep: | Cook: | Ready in:

Ingredients

- 1 24-inch baguette
- 2-3 ounces chevre
- 3 ounces salami
- 3 ounces provolone
- 1 roasted red pepper, sliced
- 3-4 artichoke hearts, quartered
- 2-3 sun-dried tomatoes, julienned
- 2-3 tablespoons black or green olive tapenade

- 2-3 pepperoncini, sliced
- 2 cups arugula

Direction

- Slice the baguette horizontally and pull out some of the bread from inside each half and discard (or save for breadcrumbs!). Spread chevre on the bottom half of bread. Arrange meats and cheeses on top of that.
- Top with red peppers, artichoke hearts, sun-dried tomatoes, and pepperoncini. Top with arugula, piled up to keep it in place. Smear top half of bread with tapenade and place on top of arugula, catching any stuff that fell out and stuffing it back in. Slice the whole thing in half with a serrated knife. Wrap tightly with plastic wrap and again with foil, then refrigerate until needed, preferably 24-36 hours to allow flavors to meld.

266. Salsiccie Con Uova

Serving: Serves 4-6 | Prep: | Cook: | Ready in:

Ingredients

- 1 pound pasta, cooked
- 4 medium links of sweet Italian sausage (about 3/4 pound)
- 1 1/2 cups seedless red or black grapes
- 2 tablespoons balsamic vinegar
- salt and pepper to taste (may not be needed)

Direction

- 1. Prick sausages all over with a fork. Cook sausages in two tablespoons of oil and a couple of ounces of water in skillet, turning frequently. As the water evaporates, sausages will begin to brown, and a nice fond will form on the bottom of the pan. Deglaze with more water, scraping up the browned fond, and continue cooking until sausages are nicely colored and firm.

- 2. Remove sausages to cutting board. Slice the sausages at an angle, about a quarter-inch thick. Return the slices to pan. If the pan seems dry, add remaining olive oil. Brown the cut sides of the sausage, then add grapes. Cook, stirring, until a few of the grapes begin to burst, giving up a bit of their juice.
- 3. Deglaze with balsamic vinegar.
- 4. Toss with hot drained pasta, adjust seasoning if necessary, and serve.

---

267. Sam Sifton's Momofuku Bo Ssäm

Serving: Serves 6 to 10 | Prep: 6hours5mins | Cook: 6hours20mins |Ready in:

Ingredients

- For the pork
- 1 whole bone-in, skin-on pork butt or picnic ham, 8 to 10 pounds
- 1 cup granulated sugar
- 1 cup plus 1 tablespoon kosher salt
- 7 tablespoons brown sugar
- For the ginger-scallion sauce
- 2 1/2 cups thinly sliced scallions, both green and white parts
- 1/2 cup minced fresh ginger
- 1/4 cup neutral oil, such as canola or grapeseed
- 1 1/2 teaspoons light soy sauce
- 1 scant teaspoon sherry vinegar
- 1/2 teaspoon kosher salt, or to taste
- For the ssäm sauce
- 2 tablespoons ssamjang fermented bean-and-chile paste (available in many Asian markets and online)
- 1 tablespoon gochujang chile paste (available in many Asian markets and online)
- 1/2 cup sherry vinegar
- 1/2 cup neutral oil, such as canola or grapeseed
- Accompaniments

- 2 cups plain white rice, cooked
- 3 heads Bibb lettuce, leaves separated, washed and dried
- Kimchi, if you can find it at the market

Direction

- Prepare the pork. Place the pork in a large, shallow bowl. Mix the granulated sugar and 1 cup of the salt together in another bowl, then rub the mixture all over the meat. Cover the meat with plastic wrap and place in the refrigerator for at least 6 hours or overnight.
- When you're ready to cook, heat the oven to 300°F. Remove the pork from the refrigerator and discard any juices. Brush off the meat to remove the bulk of the remaining sugar and salt. Place the pork in a roasting pan and cook in the oven for about 6 hours, basting hourly with the pan juices, until it collapses and yields easily to the tines of a fork. Remove the meat from the oven and allow to rest for up to an hour.
- Meanwhile, make the ginger-scallion sauce. In a large bowl, combine the scallions with the ginger, oil, soy sauce, vinegar, and salt. Mix well and taste, adding more salt if needed.
- Make the ssam sauce. In a medium bowl, combine the chili pastes with the vinegar and oil, and mix well.
- Prepare rice and wash lettuce. Put kimchi and sauces into serving bowls.
- When your accompaniments are prepared and you are ready to serve the food, turn oven to 500°F. In a small bowl, stir together the remaining tablespoon of salt with the brown sugar. Rub this mixture all over the cooked pork. Place in oven for approximately 10 to 15 minutes, or until a dark caramel crust has developed on the meat. Serve hot, with the accompaniments.

268. Sandwich W/ Ham, Proscuitto, Crispy Gruyere & Lemon Aioli

Serving: Serves 1 | Prep: | Cook: | Ready in:

Ingredients

- 1 egg yolk
- 1/2 cup olive oil
- 1/4 cup olive oil, extra virgin
- 1 garlic clove, minced
- 1/2 - 1 lemon, fresh sqeezed juice
- 1/4 teaspoon kosher salt
- 2 pieces brioche, sliced for sandwich (approx. 1/2")
- 3 pieces ham, thinly sliced (deli or black forest)
- 3 pieces proscuitto, thinly sliced (Parma, San Daniele, or Spanish variety Jambon Serrano)
- 10 pieces gruyere cheese, sliced thin with vegetable peeler or cheese slicer
- red onion, thinly sliced

Direction

- Gruyere crisps: Heat oven to 350 degrees. Place sliced cheese on baking sheet lined with parchment paper. Bake for 12-15 minutes, until lightly brown. Remove from oven and let cool.
- Aioli: I use a cuisinart food processer to make the aioli, but you could also whisk this by hand in a medium size bowl. Separate the egg yolk, discard egg white. Place the egg yolk in the cuisinart with a splash of water. Pulse until smooth.
- With the cuisinart on, slowly stream / drizzle olive oils into the egg yolk. Adding the oil too fast will not allow the mixture to emulsify / thicken properly. Once the olive oils have been incorporated it should resemble a thick mayonnaise.
- Pulse in the salt and garlic. Pulse lemon juice a little at a time. Vary the amount of lemon juice to get the correct consistency. Add enough lemon juice to thin the aioli to be spreadable, but not a soupy liquid.
- Sandwich: Toast brioche to lightly browned. Remove gruyere crisps by lifting up the parchment and pushing upwards. They will likely break into pieces which is fine (feel free to snack on a some too as you will have extra!). Spread a generous amount of aioli on both pieces of brioche. On one brioche side, add sliced ham, prosciutto, and gruyere crisps, alternating each component. Top with red onions and second brioche side. Serve sandwich halved.

269. Santa Margherita's Pork With Tart Balsamic Cherries

Serving: Serves 2 | Prep: 0hours30mins | Cook: 1hours0mins | Ready in:

Ingredients

- 2 Bone-in porkchops
- 1/3 cup Balsamic Vinegar
- 4 tablespoons Balsamic Vinegar, kept aside
- 2 teaspoons Butter
- 2 Shallots, thinly sliced
- 1/3 cup Low-salt chicken broth
- 1 cup Fresh tart cherries, pitted

Direction

- Coat pork in vinaigrette and allow to rest. Minimum 10 minutes up to 1 hour.
- In a pan melt 1 tbsp. of butter over medium high heat.
- Sauté pork until brown, about 3 minutes per side. Set pork aside, covered.
- Add remaining butter to pan and melt. Add sliced shallots and sauté until lightly golden.
- Add stock, pitted cherries and the remaining marinade to the onions. Deglaze pan and bring contents to a boil. Reduce heat to a simmer.

- Add pork to the pan and simmer until cooked through - about 2 minutes per side. Check temp for doneness. Plate the pork chops and spoon sauce over to serve. Note: If using sweet cherries - Taste test the sauce prior to adding pork and add extra balsamic vinegar to taste.

---

270. Sausage Acorn Squash Egg Bake

Serving: Serves 4 | Prep: | Cook: | Ready in:

Ingredients

- 1 acorn squash
- olive oil, salt and pepper (for roasting squash)
- 2 garlic asiago pork sausages (you can choose any sausage of your liking)
- 2 heads of broccoli - steamed
- 12 eggs
- 1/4 cup half and half
- 1/4 teaspoon red chili flakes
- 1/4 teaspoon white pepper
- 1/2 teaspoon dried cilantro
- 1/2 cup pepper jack cheese

Direction

- Preheat the oven to 375
- Cut your acorn squash in half & scoop out seeds (an ice cream scooper works really well). Slice the squash into 1/2 inch thick half-moons. Toss in olive oil, salt and pepper. Arrange them on a lined baking sheet & roast for about 30 minutes. Remove from oven once you can easily stick a fork through them.
- Heat a pan with a small amount of olive oil over medium heat. Cook the sausages for about 10 minutes (flipping them halfway through). They should be just starting to get crispy. Cut the sausages into 1/2 inch rounds and set aside.
- In a large bowl crack all of the eggs and add the half and half, red chili, white pepper and cilantro. Whisk until everything is combined.

- In a baking dish (I used a 9x13 oval dish), grease the bottom and sides with olive oil. Arrange half of mix-ins on the bottom of the sheet (squash, sausage and broccoli), then pour the entire egg mixture over. Sprinkle all of the cheese evenly. Add the remaining mix-ins to the top (makes sure they're at least a little submerged in the eggs). Transfer to the oven and bake for 45-50 minutes (or until the center is no longer runny)

---

271. Sausage And Pepper Crescent Pockets

Serving: Serves 2 people | Prep: 15hours0mins | Cook: 15hours0mins | Ready in:

Ingredients

- 1 Roll of Jumbo Sized Crescent Dough
- 3 Tuscan Kale Sausages
- 1 Red Pepper
- 0.5 Banana Peppers
- 1 Large Spanish Onion
- 4 tablespoons Extra Virgin Olive Oil
- 1 tablespoon Parmigiano Reggiano Cheese
- 3 Slices of Fresh Mozzarella Cheese
- 1 tablespoon Salt and Black Pepper
- 0.5 teaspoons Dried Basil
- 0.5 teaspoons Garlic Powder
- 3 tablespoons Pinot Grigio

Direction

- Step One: Lay two large Crescent Rolls out on a baking sheet which has been lightly greased with Extra Virgin Olive Oil. Brush the Crescent Rolls with Olive Oil and temporarily place to the side.
- Step Two: Take three room temperature sausages and remove them from their casings. Disregard the casing and place the Sausage meat into a medium-hot frying pan with Two Tablespoons of Olive Oil. Season the meat and

sauté it down until brown. When finished — place to the side in a medium sized bowl.

- Step Three: In the same pan, add another two Tablespoons of Olive Oil. Chop your Peppers and Onions — adding them into the frying pan over a Medium Heat. Once they begin to brown, add a few tablespoons of Pinot Grigio to help the vegetables cook down and develop a luscious texture and flavor. Once finished, add your sautéed vegetables to the bowl of cooked Sausage.
- Step Four: Once the cooked Sausage, Peppers and Onions are combined in a bowl — add in a Tablespoon and a Half of grated Parmigano Reggiano cheese — and toss all ingredients together until they form a cohesive mixture. Place Two Tablespoons of your Mixture directly on top of your Crescent Dough. Be sure to evenly distribute just enough filling on top the dough, without overfilling it. Next, gently tear up your slices of fresh Mozzarella — and add approx. three to four dollops of Cheese to each crescent roll. The Mozzarella should be sitting comfortably on top of the Sausage and Pepper mixture. Once enough filling and Mozzarella has been added to the dough — pinch each end of the Crescent Dough closed — until a sandwich pocket is formed.
- Step Five: Brush each Sandwich Pocket with a little more Olive Oil. Place into a 375 Degree Oven for 15–18 Minutes or until Golden Brown. Serve with a Garnish of Chopped Basil or Fresh Parsley.

272.   Sauteed Brussel Sprouts With Shallots And Proscuitto

Serving: Serves 4 | Prep: | Cook: | Ready in:

Ingredients

- 1 pound brussel sprouts - if they're the little ones (about the size of a nickel), leave them

whole. If they're slightly larger cut them in half.
- 2 large shallots, chopped
- 8 pieces proscuitto, cut into 1 1/2 inch pieces - or more if you love proscuitto!

Direction

- Cut the stems off the Brussels sprouts and cut them in half if they are on the larger side.
- Put the chopped shallots in a deep pan with olive oil and cook on medium until softened.
- Add the Brussels sprouts to the pan and brown them slightly, then turn the stove down to low, cover the pan and let them soften a bit. You may need to add a little more olive oil so they don't dry out.
- Add the prosciutto and let it crisp up around the Brussels sprouts. Cook for a few minutes on low so that all the flavors meld together. Throw some salt and pepper on them to finish. Serve and Enjoy!

273.   Savory Ham And Swiss Cornbread Bake

Serving: Serves 6 | Prep: | Cook: | Ready in:

Ingredients

- Crust:
- Filling:
- 2 tablespoons butter
- 2 tablespoons all-purpose flour
- 1 cup milk
- 8 ounces swiss cheese, shredded or cubed
- 1 tablespoon dijon mustard
- 1 pinch salt
- 1 pinch white pepper
- 1 1/2 cups diced ham
- 2 hard boiled eggs, sliced
- 8 asparagus spears, grilled or sautéed with olive oil and salt, and cut into bite sized pieces
- 1/2 cup crushed swiss cheese flavored crackers

Direction

- Preheat oven to 375 degrees F.
- Prepare the crust: In a medium bowl, mix together melted butter, cornbread mix, water, egg and sour cream. Set aside.
- Prepare the filling: In a medium saucepan, melt butter over low heat. Add flour and stir to combine. Cook, stirring constantly, for 3 minutes. Increase the heat to medium and whisk in the milk, a little at a time. Cook until thickened, about 4-5 minutes, stirring frequently. Reduce heat to low; add cheese, mustard, salt and pepper. Stir until cheese is mostly melted (I like to leave some chunks of unmelted cheese).
- Spread cornbread mixture into greased 10-inch cast iron skillet. Place ham, eggs and asparagus over cornbread. Pour cheese sauce over the asparagus. Top with crushed crackers. Bake at 375 degrees for 35-40 minutes, or until crust is golden brown and middle is set. Remove from oven and cool 5 to 10 minutes. Cut into wedges.

---

274.   Savory Sausage And Potato Pie

Serving: Serves 6-8 | Prep: | Cook: | Ready in:

Ingredients

- Your favorite double pie crust large enough to accommodate a 9-inch, deep dish pie
- Oil
- 2 large red onions, skinned and julienned
- 2 teaspoons sugar
- 2 Tablespoons Worcestershire sauce
- 2 teaspoons Colman's mustard powder
- Recommended amount of good quality vegetable stock powder (I like Seitenbacher Vegetable Broth and Seasoning) and water to make 20 ounces of broth
- Bacon fat

- 8 local country pork sausages (I like to use a mixture of basic country and pork and apple)
- 1 pound of fingerling potatoes, sliced in half, lengthwise
- 2 cups button mushrooms, sliced thinly
- 1, 12-ounce bottle of nut brown ale (I like Smuttynose's Old Brown Dog Ale.)
- Salt and black pepper
- 1 egg

Direction

- Set your oven at 375 degrees.
- Toss the julienned onions with 2-3 teaspoons of olive oil. Spread them on a baking sheet and sprinkle with sugar. Roast the onions until soft and somewhat caramelized, about 20 minutes or so. You do have to stir them about once or twice during the cooking process. When they've colored nicely, set them aside to cool.
- Heat 20 ounces of water in a kettle and add the broth crystals and set liquid aside.
- Mix mustard powder and Worcestershire sauce together to make a sort of slurry.
- Put about two tablespoons of bacon fat (you can substitute olive oil if you need to) in a large sauté pan. First brown your sausages whole until they've got some nice color on the outside. They don't need to be cooked through. Remove from pan and set aside to cool. When they are cooled, cut them on the diagonal, in two-inch pieces.
- In the same pan in which you cooked the sausages, place the potatoes cut side down and cook them until almost fork-tender and golden brown. Remove them from pan, sprinkle with salt and pepper and set aside to cool.
- In the same pan, sauté the mushrooms until they are caramelized on one side, adding more fat if necessary. When caramelized, remove from pan and set aside to cool.
- Make certain there are about two tablespoons of fat in the hot pan and add two tablespoons of flour to make a roux. Cook the roux until it's fragrant – about 2-3 minutes. And then whisk in the broth. Add the

mustard/Worcester sauce slurry. When the gravy is thick, slowly pour in the beer, taking care that it does not foam out of the pan. When the beer is settled and incorporated, add the roasted onions. Taste for seasoning at this point.

- Roll out the bottom crust and place it in a 9-inch deep, glass pie plate. Layer the sausage pieces, potatoes and mushrooms into the pie plate. Pour the gravy over them. Cover with a top crust. Brush with a salted egg wash.
- Place the pie on a low rack in the oven. Lower the temperature from 375 to 350 degrees, immediately upon closing the door. Cook the pie for 45 minutes. Then move the pie to a top rack and cook for another 10 minutes or a bit longer until the crust is golden.
- Cool the pie slightly 10 to 15 minutes before serving.

---

275.   Savory Waffles With Goat Cheese And Lardons

Serving: Makes 10 waffles | Prep: | Cook: | Ready in:

Ingredients

- 2.5 tablespoons butter
- 170 milliliters Milk
- 1 cup flour
- 2 teaspoons baking powder
- 2 eggs
- lardon/baking strip
- 1/3 goat cheese log, cut into dices
- 1 handful chives, finely chopped

Direction

- Fry the bacon strips in a pan and strain on paper towel.
- Melt the butter and heat the milk in a saucepan, do not boil.
- In a bowl, combine flour and baking power. Add the egg yolks and stir. Add the

butter/milk mixture a little bit at a time, stirring constantly.
- Beat the egg whites until stiff and careful fold into the waffle dough.
- Add the bacon strips, crumbled coat cheese and chives. Do not mix too much. Make the waffles in your waffle maker, you should have about 10.

---

276.   Scallion And Coconut Rice With Pork

Serving: Serves 4 | Prep: 0hours20mins | Cook: 0hours45mins | Ready in:

Ingredients

- 4 large scallions, thoroughly washed, trimmed just above root
- 3 tablespoons canola oil, divided
- 3/4 pound ground pork
- 1 tablespoon good quality fish sauce (like Red Boat or Three Crabs)
- 1 tablespoon plus 1 teaspoon minced ginger
- 1 tablespoon plus 1 teaspoon minced garlic
- 1 1/4 cups medium grain Calrose rice
- 1 1/4 cups chicken stock
- 3/4 cup coconut milk (shake can before opening)
- 1 head of baby bok choy (optional), end trimmed, leaves separated, washed, and sliced crosswise
- 1 wedge of lime, for finishing

Direction

- Prep scallions by slicing 1/3 cup of white and light green parts. Thinly slice dark green part of scallions for 3/4 cup, divided into 1/2 cup and 1/4 cup. Set aside.
- Heat 1/2 tablespoon of canola oil over medium heat in a Dutch oven or similar pot. Add ground pork, 1 tablespoon of minced garlic and 1 tablespoon of minced ginger and cook, breaking up meat with a wooden spoon.

When meat is no longer pink, add fish sauce and cook for another minute or two, stirring. Transfer meat to a bowl and cover with foil.

- Add 1/2 tablespoon canola oil to pot, followed by remaining 1 teaspoon of garlic, 1 teaspoon of ginger and 1/3 cup of sliced white and light green scallions. Cook, combining with wooden spoon, until fragrant, about a minute. Add rice and stir to coat, until rice is shiny. Add stock and coconut milk, stir to combine and cover. When rice begins to bubble, turn heat down to simmer. Set your timer for 20 minutes.

- While rice is cooking, heat remaining 2 tablespoons oil in a small skillet over medium heat. When oil shimmers, add 1/2 cup of sliced dark green scallions. Crisp up scallions by stirring frequently, remembering that they will go from crisp to burned in a second. Since they are dark, you won't have as obvious a visual clue as with onions or shallots; I usually rely on smell. Once they start to smell dark and smoky I start to look for golden brown charred edges and begin to remove onions by the forkful to a paper towel lined plate until they are all done. It's not the most delicate maneuver but they are delicious and worth it.

- If you are using the baby bok choy, add it to the still hot skillet once you've removed the crispy scallions. Cook in scallion oil until leaves are wilted and stem begins to soften, about 2 minutes. Remove from heat.

- When timer goes off, remove lid from rice pot and give mixture a stir. Rice should be perfectly cooked, plump, and almost risotto like, though without the extra liquid. Stir in reserved pork, crisped scallions, remaining 1/4 cup sliced dark green scallions, and bok choy if using. Finish with a squeeze from a lime wedge. Serve immediately and enjoy.

277. Schnitzel Of Pork

Serving: Serves 4 | Prep: | Cook: |Ready in:

Ingredients

- 3 cups (385 g) all-purpose flour
- Salt and pepper
- 4 eggs
- 1 cup (250 ml) sour cream
- 1/4 teaspoon freshly grated nutmeg
- 4 cups (170 g) panko (Japanese bread crumbs), pulsed until the texture of regular bread crumbs
- 1 cup (115 g) grated sbinz or grana padano cheese
- 4 large pork schnitzels (loin cutlets), pounded by the butcher to 1/4 inch (6mm) thickk
- 1/4 cup (60 m) canola oil or more if needed

Direction

- Prepare 3 flat containers, each big enough to contain 1 schnitzel at a time. Put the flour and a good pinch each of salt and pepper in the first container. In the second container, whisk together the eggs, sour cream, nutmeg, and another good pinch each of salt and pepper. In the third container, mix together the processed panko and the cheese.

- Dip a schnitzel in the flour and shake off the excess; drop it in the egg mixture and drain off the excess; and lay it in the third container with the panko mixture and coat it well. Shake off the excess crumbs and put it on a platter. Repeat with the remaining schnitzels, then put the platter, uncovered, in the fridge, and leave it to dry a little.

- Heat the oil in a big frying pan over medium-high heat. Do not wait until the oil smokes, but it should be hot enough so that a pinch of crumbs sizzles on contact. Place 1 schnitzel in the pan. Remember to lay it down away from you, so you don't splash yourself. Cook, turning once, for 3 minutes on each side, or until golden brown. You want to maintain a steady sizzle the whole time the schnitzel cooks, but you don't want it to over color. Transfer to paper towels to absorb the excess oil, and season with salt and pepper. Repeat with the remaining schnitzels, adding more oil to the pan if needed.

- Serve the schnitzels one at a time as they are ready, or leave them on the paper towels and place in a low oven until serving.

278.   Scrumptious Stuffing/anytime Of Year

Serving: Serves 6-8 | Prep: | Cook: |Ready in:

Ingredients

- 1 pound Best Italian Sweet Sausage, casings removed
- 2 tablespoons Olive oil
- 1 Large Onion, chopped
- 2 Large celery stalks, chopped
- 2 Apples, peeled and chopped
- 1 cup Chopped walnuts
- 1 bunch Parsley
- 5 Sage Leaves, finely chopped
- 1 packet Stuffing Mix or 8 cups of cubed old bread
- 1 Egg, lightly beaten
- 1 1/2 cups Chicken broth
- 1 teaspoon Poultry Seasoning
- Pinch Thyme or Herbs de Provence or both (optional)
- Salt & Pepper
- Raisins

Direction

- Sauté sausage in olive oil until cooked through. Remove from pan into a large bowl. In the same pan add butter, onion and celery and salt and pepper. Cook till onion is translucent. Allow to cool slightly.
- Mix all remaining ingredients with the sausage and add the cooled onions last. Mix well, adjust seasoning and either stuff your bird or cook on the side.

279.   Shredded Pork And Chinese Celery Lo Mein

Serving: Serves 4 to 6 | Prep: | Cook: |Ready in:

Ingredients

- 2 tablespoons canola oil
- 1 1/2 cups yellow onion, julienned
- 3 tablespoons fresh garlic, minced
- 1 cup green onion, sliced thinly
- 3 cups Chinese celery, stem and leaves, finely chopped
- 2 cups cooked shredded fatty pork
- 2 tablespoons Chinese rice wine or sherry
- 1/3 cup soy sauce, less salt variety
- 2/3 cup chicken or pork stock
- 16 ounces Fresh Hong Kong Style thin egg noodles
- 1/2 teaspoon sesame oil

Direction

- Have all the ingredients chopped and ready on a tray next to the stove.
- Bring a large pot of water to a boil.
- Heat a 14 inch wok or sauté pan over high heat. Add the oil and then the onions. Cook until they start to caramelize. Add the garlic and stir.
- Add the Chinese celery, pork and half the green onions. Stir to combine and continue to sauté and stir until the celery becomes tender, 3 to 5 minutes.
- Add the rice wine and let the alcohol burn off. Then add the soy and stock. Bring to a boil and then reduce the heat.
- Add the noodles to the boiling water and cook according to the package instructions. When they have finished cooking remove a half cup of the cooking liquid and then drain the noodles. Add the noodles to the pork and celery. Add the sesame oil and toss to combine and if needed add a little noodle cooking liquid to thicken the sauce or add volume if it has reduced too much. Serve in a bowl or

bowls and garnish with the remainder of the green onions.

280. Shredded Pork With Bell Peppers

Serving: Serves 2 as a main dish, or 4 as a side dish | Prep: | Cook: | Ready in:

Ingredients

- Marination
- 2 pork chops, sliced thinly, and stack the thin layers together, slicing it thinly again until shredded
- 2 teaspoons dark brown sugar
- 2 teaspoons regular soy sauce
- 2 cloves of garlic, minced finely
- 1 tsp of chinese cooking wine
- Stir-Fry
- 1 large bell pepper, or 2 medium
- 1 green onion, sliced thinly
- 1 tablespoon oyster sauce
- 1 teaspoon dark soy sauce
- 1 teaspoon chinese dark vinegar
- 1 tablespoon vegetable oil
- Dash ground white pepper
- 1/4 cup of water, simmering
- big wooden chopsticks

Direction

- Marinate the shredded pork for about 1 hour, up to 24 hours in the fridge.
- To prepare: with wooden chopsticks, swirl and mix in the shredded pork in boiling water until cooked half way, about 2 min; set aside (reserve the juice of the water-stock, and add in to the stir-frying if you find the dish too dry- I didn't have to).
- Heat wok with oil and stir-fry green onion until fragrant; mix in the bell peppers and stir-fry about 30 seconds, put in the rest of the ingredients and finish up with a generous dash of white ground pepper.

- Serve with rice.

281. Shrimp And Pork Dumplings

Serving: Makes approximately 50 dumplings | Prep: | Cook: | Ready in:

Ingredients

- 1 pound large shrimp. Cleaned, shelled, deveined and chopped
- 1 pound ground pork
- 1/4 cup fresh cilantro (if there are roots, even better)
- 1/8 cup shallot
- 1/8 cup ginger
- 4 garlic cloves
- 1/8 cup sesame oil
- 1/4 cup Tamari or Soy Sauce
- 1 tablespoon black pepper
- 2 egg whites, whipped
- 1/8 cup tapioca flour
- 1 lemon (juice)
- 50 round shu mai wrappers

Direction

- In a blender, mix together cilantro, shallots, ginger, garlic, sesame oil, soy and black pepper until an even and smooth consistency.
- In a large mixing bowl whip 2 egg whites, add tapioca flour and lemon. (I use my stand mixer)
- Add blended spices, pork and chopped shrimp and mix together.
- To wrap the dumplings, place about 2 teaspoons of filling in the middle of a wrapper. Set the dumpling bottom on a flat surface and pinch the sides together until it is standing.
- Fill the bottom pot portion of a steamer with water. Use parchment paper to line the steamer tray (and poke holes in the paper). Place the dumplings in the steamer tray.

- Bring the water to a boil and cover the steamer with the dumplings and steam for 45 minutes.
- Enjoy with soy sauce, hoi sin, and/or sambal oelek chili.

282. Simple Paleo Scotch Eggs

Serving: Serves 4 | Prep: | Cook: |Ready in:

Ingredients

- 6 whole pork sausages, 100% organic butchers meat
- 1 teaspoon paprika
- 1 teaspoon salt
- 1 pinch pepper
- 2 tablespoons ground almonds
- 100 grams mixed seeds
- 6 large eggs

Direction

- Turn oven on to 180°c
- Place 4 large eggs in to boiling water for 6 minutes (medium eggs: 5 minutes, small eggs: 4 minutes). Take off heat and place in to ice-cold water whilst you carry on with the rest of the preparations
- In to a blender place the almond meal, pinch of salt and mixed seeds, blitz until coarse and crumbly, place aside
- In to the blender place all sausage meat (make sure to de-skin beforehand), spices, salt and pepper, blend until fully combined and sticky
- Peel the cold eggs, gently (as they will still be soft-boiled)
- Now break sausage mixture in to 6 balls. Using the palm of your hand create a "cup", flat patty shape. Place one egg into the middle and work the sausage mixture around it making sure to fully seal all the sides
- Now dip the ball in to the egg mix (1 whisked egg) and fully cover smoothing all the sides (this is how your meat and egg will stay bound)

- Roll the ball straight in to the mixed seeds / almond mixture
- In to a shallow frying pan over high heat up about 1/2 cup olive oil and place scotch egg in to the oil. Brown each side for around 1-2 minutes until golden brown, then place on to a baking sheet and bake for 5 – 6 minutes
- Serve straight away with homemade chutney, rocket and avocado

283. Simple Roast Pork And Vegetables

Serving: Serves 6 | Prep: 0hours50mins | Cook: 2hours30mins |Ready in:

Ingredients

- 3-4 pounds pork shoulder roast with bone
- 2 cloves garlic, smashed and minced
- 1 tablespoon fresh thyme, minced
- coarse sea salt
- coarsely ground black pepper
- 4-5 carrots, peeled and chopped into 1-2 inch chunks
- 2 celery ribs, chopped in 1-2 inch chunks
- 1.5 pounds small potatoes (I used Baby Dutch yellow potatoes)
- 1 bag frozen pearl onions (or you can blanch and peel fresh ones if you prefer)

Direction

- Slather the pork roast with garlic, thyme, salt and pepper. Let it sit for about 30 minutes to get to room temperature.
- Preheat the oven to 325° F. Place the pork roast on a roasting rack, fat side up.
- Roast the pork for 35 minutes per pound or in this case about 2 1/2 hours.
- About 45 minutes before the end of the roasting time, place the chopped vegetables on the roasting pan and roast them until tender, stirring at least once during that time.

- Once the vegetables and roast are tender, remove them to a serving platter and let it rest for 5 to 10 minutes.
- Pour the pan juices over the roast and serve with some good crusty bread.

284.   Simple Sausage Pasta

Serving: Serves 4-6 | Prep: | Cook: | Ready in:

Ingredients

- Simple sausage pasta
- 1 lb of Italian sweet sausage (squeezed out from casing)
- 1lb of fresh papadelle or tagliatelle
- Olive oil 1/8 of a cup
- 3 cloves fresh and pounded garlic
- 1 tsp chilli flakes
- 1 tsp of fennel seeds (optional)
- ½ cup of white wine
- ¼ cup of starched water from the pasta
- Glazing the tomatoes
- 4 vine ripened tomatoes (sliced in to 4 pieces length)
- 1 tbsp butter

Direction

- Simple sausage pasta
- 1) Heat the oil and add the garlic. Sauté on low heat for a few minutes and until the garlic softens. Add the crushed chili and fennel seeds to toast them and extract the full flavor
- 2) Coarsely crumble and add the sausage to the garlic oil adding the wine after 3 minutes and cook until golden brown (usually 7 minutes)
- 3) Boil the pasta as per directions and add ¼ cup of the pasta water to the sausage
- 4) Toss the pasta with the sausage
- Glazing the tomatoes
- 5) In a separate pan, glaze the tomatoes by heating the pan and melting butter. Add the tomatoes and cook for 3 minutes on low heat.

- 6) When serving, garnish with a couple of pieces of tomato and sprinkle with the parsley.

285.   Slab Muffuletta

Serving: Serves a crowd | Prep: | Cook: | Ready in:

Ingredients

- 1 sheet pan focaccia (see note)
- 6 tablespoons finely chopped castelvetrano olives (or other green olives)
- 6 tablespoons finely chopped oil-cured black olives (or other black olives)
- 6 tablespoons finely chopped roasted bell peppers
- 3 stalks celery, roughly chopped, plus any leaves that might be attached
- 3 tablespoons drained capers
- 3/4 cup flat-leaf parsley, roughly chopped
- 5 tablespoons extra-virgin olive oil
- 3 tablespoons red wine vinegar
- 1 1/2 teaspoons dried oregano
- Kosher salt, to taste
- 1 pound sliced capicola
- 1 pound sliced soppressata
- 1 pound sliced mortadella
- 1 pound sliced provolone

Direction

- Make the olive spread. Combine the olives, roasted peppers, celery, capers, parsley, olive oil, vinegar, and oregano in a bowl. Season with salt to taste.
- Build the muffaletta. Cut the focaccia in half (so you have two 9 x 13 pieces). Now halve each piece horizontally—a big serrated knife and a slow, sawing motion works best here. Flip the 4 pieces over, so the fluffy interior is facing up. Spread the olive mixture evenly over each. On 1 bottom piece, layer half the meat and cheese in this order: capicola, soppressata, mortadella, provolone. Repeat

with the other bottom piece. Cap both with the remaining 2 pieces.

- Wrap each sandwich tightly in plastic or foil. Place onto a sheet pan and top with another sheet pan. Load up the top sheet pan with some cans or jars. Weigh down for at least 1 hour (at room temperature) or up to 12 hours (in the fridge).
- When ready to serve, cut each half into 8 to 16 pieces (so, 16 to 32 total) and arrange together to reflect the original, slab focaccia shape.

---

286. Slow Cooked Pork Carnita Tacos With Corn And Avocado Salsa

Serving: Serves 8-10 people | Prep: | Cook: | Ready in:

Ingredients

- Slow Cooked Carnitas
- 4 pounds pork butt
- 1 can evaporated milk
- 1 can cola soda
- 2 cinnamon sticks
- 1 orange (rind and juice)
- 2 bay leaves
- 4 crushed garlic cloves
- 2 tablespoons chicken base
- 1 teaspoon nutmeg
- 1 teaspoon cumin
- 1 teaspoon dried oregano
- 1 teaspoon red pepper flakes
- salt and pepper to taste
- Corn and Avocado Salsa
- 1 packet frozen corn or 4 ears of fresh corn off the cob
- 1 jalapeño small dice with seeds and membrane discarded
- 1/2 red onion small dice
- 8 radishes cut in half and then sliced in half moons
- handful of chopped cilantro
- juice of two fresh limes

- 3 tablespoons white vinegar
- 1/2 teaspoon cumin
- 1/2 teaspoon dried oregano
- 1 teaspoon granulated garlic
- salt and pepper to taste
- 1-2 avocado, chopped

Direction

- Slow Cooked Carnitas
- In a separate bowl mix evaporated milk, cola, nutmeg, cumin, oregano, chili flakes, chicken base, orange zest and juice from 1 orange, crushed garlic, salt and pepper.
- In a large saute pan pour about 1 tbsp. of neutral oil and sear the salt and peppered Pork Butt for 8-10 minutes (or until all sides are nicely browned. Put Pork Butt in the Slow Cooker. Add cinnamon sticks and bay leaves. Pour marinade over the pork butt and put lid on slow cooker. Put slow cooker onto the lowest setting and let it cook for 8-10 hours.
- When cooking is done, take out of slow cooker and shred with a fork and put a little bit of the cooking liquid on the shredded pork to stay moist. Serve immediately as a taco or burrito with either corn or flour tortillas. Top with salsa and queso fresca
- To serve, warm up either corn or flour tortillas. Put a couple of spoonfuls of pulled pork in the tortilla and top with the Corn and Avocado Salsa and some Queso Fresco (or any cheese of your choosing).
- Corn and Avocado Salsa
- In a small bowl mix the juice of two limes, vinegar, oregano, cumin, garlic powder, salt and pepper. Set aside.
- Put your diced jalapeño and red onion in a medium bowl. Add the sliced radishes and corn. Sprinkle in the chopped cilantro and lightly toss. Add the vinegar, lime, spice mixture to the medium bowl and mix. Take a small taste and readjust seasoning. Right before serving, stir in chopped avocado.

287. Slow Cooker Barbecue Pulled Pork With Mango Salsa

Serving: Serves 6-8 | Prep: | Cook: | Ready in:

Ingredients

- BBQ Pulled Pork
- 2.5-3 pounds pork butt (shoulder)
- 1 1/2 teaspoons Smoked Paprika (1tsp goes into spice rub, 1/2 goes into cooking liquid)
- 1 1/2 teaspoons ground cumin (1tsp goes into spice rub, 1/2 goes into cooking liquid)
- 1 teaspoon salt
- 1/2 teaspoon ground black pepper
- 1 bottle of beer (I used Newcastle Brown Ale)
- 4 garlic cloves (smashed)
- 2 bay leaves
- 1/2 cup BBQ sauce (I used Annie's Sweet and Spicy)
- salt to taste
- soft corn tortillas, soft regular or slider rolls
- Mango Salsa
- 2-3 just ripe mangos
- 1/2 jalapeno pepper
- 1/4 red onion
- 1 lime
- 1 handful of fresh cilantro

Direction

- Mix together the 1 tsp smoked paprika, 1 tsp ground cumin, 1 tsp salt and 1/2 tsp pepper and rub on the pork butt. Brown the pork in a skillet over medium high heat, then transfer the meat into a slow cooker.
- Pour the beer over the pork, add the four garlic cloves, two bay leaves, 1/2 tsp smoked paprika and 1/2 tsp of cumin. Turn the slow cooker on low and cook for at least 9 hours.
- About an hour before the pork is done, dice the mango, onion, and jalapeno, roughly chop the cilantro, mince the garlic and mix all of these together in a medium-sized bowl. Squeeze the lime over the salsa and mix in.
- Remove pork from the slow cooker and pull apart using two forks. Also discard any large pieces of fat. Add back enough of the cooking juices to make the meat nice and moist. I also mush up the garlic cloves and mix with the pork.
- Add about 1/2 cup of barbecue sauce to the meat and mix until all of the meat is coated, and add a little salt if necessary. You can add more barbecue sauce if you'd like, but I usually mix in a little bit and keep the bottle handy for people who want to add more.
- Serve the pork onto the warmed up rolls (softer and slightly sweet rolls work really well e.g. challah/brioche), slider buns, or corn tortillas and top with the salsa. If making tacos, I usually brush the tortillas with a sparse amount of oil and heat in a skillet until slightly browned.

288. Slow Cooker Italian Pork Stew

Serving: Serves 9 | Prep: | Cook: | Ready in:

Ingredients

- 1 Butternut Squash (small)
- 2 cups Chopped fresh kale
- 1 Onion (large) chopped
- 1 Garlic and herb sirloin
- 1 cup Dried lentils
- 1/2 teaspoon Each of salt and pepper
- 32 ounces Chicken Both

Direction

- Place the butternut squash, kale, onion and garlic in a 5-qt. slow cooker. Place roast on vegetables. Add the lentils and seasonings. Pour broth over top. (You can add additional water a ½ cup at a time if it looks necessary. You can do this later after it's absorbed some of the chicken broth as well.)
- Cover and cook on low for 8-10 hours or until meat is tender.
- Remove meat; cool slightly.

- Shred pork with two forks and return to slow cooker to heat through.

| 289. | **Slow Cooked Pork Tacos** |

Serving: Serves 4 to 6, depending on hunger level | Prep: | Cook: | Ready in:

Ingredients

- Pork Tacos
- 2 teaspoons cumin seeds
- 1 teaspoon coriander seeds
- 2 teaspoons ancho chili powder
- 1 teaspoon chipotle chili powder
- 1/2 teaspoon dried oregano
- 2 pounds boneless pork shoulder (not too lean), cut into 3/4-inch chunks
- Kosher salt
- Vegetable oil
- 1 medium yellow onion, finely chopped
- 1 poblano pepper, finely chopped
- 1 serrano chili, seeded and finely chopped
- 2 garlic cloves, minced
- 1 cup canned diced tomatoes, with their juices
- 1 1/2 cups chicken stock (homemade or low sodium)
- 2 large limes
- Corn tortillas
- 2 avocados
- Pickled onions (recipe below)
- Cilantro, washed and dried
- Sour cream (optional)
- Pickled Onions, à la aargersi
- 1 medium red onion
- 1 tablespoon kosher salt
- 2 tablespoons sugar
- 1/4 medium beet, peeled
- Handful cilantro
- Cider vinegar

Direction

- Pork Tacos

- Put the cumin and coriander in a small pan and set over medium heat. Toast the spices for a minute or two, shaking the pan occasionally, until they're fragrant. (Be careful not to scorch them.) Grind the spices finally using a spice grinder or a mortar and pestle. Transfer to a small bowl, stir in both chile powders and the oregano and set aside.
- Heat a tablespoon of oil in a large, heavy pot or Dutch oven over medium-high heat. Season the pork well with salt and add about half of the meat to the pot. Brown it well on all sides, about 4 minutes total, and transfer it to a bowl using a slotted spoon. Add more oil and brown the second batch of meat, adding it to the bowl once it's done.
- Lower the heat to medium and add another tablespoon of oil to the pot. Add the onion, poblano, serrano and a generous pinch of salt. Cook, stirring frequently, until softened, about 5 minutes. Add the garlic and cook for a minute or so, until fragrant. Stir in the spice mixture and cook for another minute.
- Return the meat to the pot, with any juices that have accumulated, and add the tomatoes and chicken stock. (The meat should be covered in liquid – if it's not, add a little water.) Squeeze in the juice of half a lime and add 2 teaspoons of salt. Turn the heat up to high and bring the liquid to a boil. Turn down the heat, cover the pot and simmer gently for an hour. Uncover the pot and continue to simmer until the pork is very tender and the sauce is reduced and thick, 30 to 60 minutes longer. Taste for seasoning, adding salt if needed, and squeeze in the juice of another half a lime.
- To serve, heat the tortillas in the oven or in a dry pan. Peel and roughly chop the avocados and cut the remaining lime into thin wedges. Fill each taco with some of the pork, pickled onions, avocado, cilantro and sour cream if you like. Serve with lime wedges for squeezing.
- Pickled Onions, à la aargersi
- Slice the onion thinly and put it in a microwaveable container. Add the salt, sugar, beet and cilantro. Cover everything with 1 part

water to 2 parts vinegar. Microwave for 1 minute, stir, and microwave for another minute. Cool, then cover and refrigerate overnight.

290. Slow Cooker Citrus Pulled Pork Tacos

Serving: Serves 6 | Prep: 0hours20mins | Cook: 6hours15mins | Ready in:

Ingredients

- Citrus Rubbed Pulled Pork
- 2 pounds boneless pork roast
- 3 tablespoons kosher salt
- 1 tablespoon ground black pepper
- 1 tablespoon granulated garlic
- 1 tablespoon onion powder
- 2 limes, zested
- 2 tablespoons oil
- Citrus Slaw
- 3 tablespoons fresh lime juice
- 2 tablespoons olive oil
- 1 1/2 tablespoons sugar
- 1 tablespoon fresh grated ginger
- 3/4 teaspoon kosher salt
- 1/2 teaspoon fresh ground black pepper
- 8 ounces raw cole slaw mix (or make your own)
- 12 pieces corn tortillas

Direction

- Citrus Rubbed Pulled Pork
- Combine all dry ingredients and the lime zest.
- Rub on the pork roast to coat evenly, you may not use all of the mixture.
- Heat a nonstick crock pot insert or a sauté pan with the oil.
- Once the oil is hot, sear all sides of the pork roast.
- Once the meat is seared, cover entirely with water (if using a sauté pan, transfer to crock pot first). Place in insert in crock pot and cover.
- Cook on high heat for 6 hours in the crock pot.
- Once the meat is done, transfer to a 9" x 13" pan and shred with a pair of tongs.
- Spoon some liquid from the crock pot over the shredded meat to keep juicy. Cover until use.
- Citrus Slaw
- In a medium bowl, mix everything together but the cabbage and the corn tortillas.
- Add the cabbage and coat well.
- Warm the corn tortillas and fill with pulled pork and slaw. Garnish with a lime spritz, jalapenos, or green onions.

291. Slow Cooker Peruvian American Pork Adobo

Serving: Serves 6 to 8 | Prep: 8hours0mins | Cook: 8hours0mins | Ready in:

Ingredients

- Marinade
- 1 large red onion, quartered
- 4 large cloves garlic
- 6 allspice berries
- 1 teaspoon salt
- 1/2 teaspoon black pepper
- 1/2 teaspoon dried oregano
- 2 tablespoons ají panca paste, or to taste (see Note below for substitution)
- 1 (12-ounce) bottle hard cider
- Adobo
- 3 pounds pork shoulder, trimmed and cut into 2 to 3–inch chunks
- 3 large red onions, sliced into 1/2-inch half moons
- 3 cups pork or beef stock
- Salt, to taste

Direction

- For the marinade, place all of the ingredients in a blender and blend until smooth.

- Place the pork into a large container. Pour the marinade onto the pork and coat all the pieces well. Cover the container and place in the refrigerator overnight or up to 24 hours. (This can also be done in a resealable plastic bag.)
- Place the pork into a slow cooker along with all of the marinade. Add the stock and sliced onions and stir to combine. Cook on high for 6-8 hours, or until fork tender.
- Serve in bowls with crusty bread.
- Note: Ají panca is a dried chile that imparts a deep, mildly spicy flavor to many Peruvian dishes. It's typically soaked and ground into a paste. You can find jars of ají panca paste at many Latin American groceries or online, and it's worth getting if you want to make many other Peruvian dishes. If you cannot find ají panca paste, use 1 tablespoon sweet paprika and one teaspoon cayenne pepper.

---

292.   Slow Cooked Carnitas Chili Verde

Serving: Serves 8-10 | Prep: | Cook: |Ready in:

Ingredients

- for the sauce
- 2.5 pounds tomatillos
- 8   cloves garlic, unpeeled
- 3-4   jalapeno peppers, seeded and chopped
- 1   can Hatch green chilies
- 1 bunch cilantro, roughly chopped
- for the chili
- 1   5-6 lb. pork shoulder/pork butt
- 3-4 tablespoons oil
- 2   large onions, chopped
- 4   cloves garlic, peeled and minced
- 1   beer (I used a Negro Modelo, but anything will do!)
- 1 teaspoon ground cumin
- 1/2 teaspoon cayenne pepper
- 1/2 teaspoon ground cloves
- 3 tablespoons fresh oregano, finely chopped
- 3 cups chicken stock

Direction

- For the Verde Sauce: Preheat the broiler. Husk and rinse the tomatillos, then slice in half and place, cut-side down, on a lined baking sheet along with the unpeeled garlic cloves. Put the lot in the oven under the broiler until lightly blackened (about 7 minutes in my oven, but keep an eye on them!). When everything's cooled a bit, peel the roasted garlic cloves and add them, the tomatillo halves, the chopped jalapenos, the can of chilies (with sauce!), and the chopped cilantro to the bowl of a food processor. Pulse several times until everything's chopped up and mixed well. (Wasn't that easy?)
- For the Chili: Trim the pork shoulder of excess fat (meaning that very thick band on the outside) and cut the meat into ~1" cubes. This is the trickiest part if you're using a bone-in shoulder, but don't worry about it if some of the pieces are different sizes! Pork shoulder is very forgiving.
- Salt and pepper the cubed pork. Heat a few tablespoons of oil on medium-high in the bottom of a Dutch oven or other heavy-bottomed pot (a large one - everything's going in eventually!). Brown the pork cubes in batches (but don't worry about cooking them through! This is just for flavor). When the pork is all browned and removed, turn the heat to medium and add the chopped onion and garlic to the pot, sauteing until softened.
- When the onion is nicely softened, "deglaze" the pan with a can of beer (this step is optional, but it's a nice way to add all the browned pork bits back to the sauce and my excuse for drinking while cooking). Add the browned pork to the onion mixture, then dump in the tomatillo sauce and stir to coat everything. Add the fresh oregano and spices (as well as salt and pepper to taste). Add chicken stock until pork is covered. Bring everything to a boil over medium heat, and

then reduce to a simmer. Simmer for several hours until the pork is meltingly tender.

- To serve: Serve in bowls over rice, with chili-style toppings: sour cream, grated cheese, chopped jalapenos, and fresh cilantro. As with all chilis, the flavors are even better the next day! (And the next, and the next...if it lasts that long)

293. Smoked Pork Rillettes

Serving: Makes about 1 1/2 cups | Prep: | Cook: | Ready in:

Ingredients

- To make the cold smoker and smoke the pork:
- unlined "tin" can
- Brand new soldering iron - make sure it's not been used for soldering!!
- wood chips (smallish ones) or wood pellets - I used applewood chips
- 2 boneless country-style pork ribs (fatty ones are better) - about 1.25 lbs
- To make the rillettes
- The pork you just smoked
- 1 cup rendered pork fat or lard – not the kind that comes in a box and doesn't need refrigeration, please!
- 1 tablespoon minced garlic
- 2 teaspoons Diamond kosher salt, divided
- ¾ to 1 teaspoon freshly grated nutmeg, divided
- ½ to ¾ teaspoon freshly ground black pepper
- 1 bay leaf
- 2 tablespoons whiskey, divided
- ¼ cup minced shallot
- water

Direction

- To make the cold smoker and smoke the pork:
- Preferably using a safe edge can opener, cut the lid most of the way off the can. Think of the can lid as a clock face; you want to open

from about 7 o'clock to about 5 o'clock cutting in a clockwise direction. Use a pliers to bend the lid open. Empty and rinse the can. Use a keyhole opener to open a hole in the lid at the 6 o'clock position.

- Fill the can about a quarter to a third full with your wood chips/pellets. Wiggle the tip of the soldering iron through the keyhole, as far in as you can get it. Put the can on the grate of your grill on its side with the keyhole toward the bottom; again like the 6 o'clock position of an ordinary wall clock. Make sure the tip of the soldering iron is well-covered by the chips. You are now ready for cold smoking!!
- Cut each of the ribs in half lengthwise. This exposes more of the meat and fat to the smoke to help develop a well-balanced smoky flavor. Rest the pork on a grate in your grill, making sure it doesn't touch the smoker apparatus. I use the warming rack provided inside my grill, but you can use whatever will work for your particular grill.
- Plug the soldering iron in. It will take a bit to warm up, but you should start to see smoke in 5 to 10 minutes. If not, wiggle the soldering iron around a bit; it may not be in good contact with the chips.
- Once you start to see smoke, put the lid down on your grill and set your timer for 30 minutes. Try not to open the lid during this time – you should see and smell smoke coming from the grill. After 30 minutes your meat should have developed a good amount of smoke aroma. Remove the meat from the grill. Unplug your soldering iron, but wait until the chips burn out and the can cools down before handling it.
- To make the rillettes
- Cut the pork into ¾- to 1-inch cubes. Massage the garlic, 1 teaspoon kosher salt, ½ teaspoon nutmeg, and ¼ teaspoon black pepper into the meat. Allow the meat to rest at room temperature for 45 to 60 minutes or refrigerate overnight.
- Combine the lard and 1 cup of water in a 2 to 3 quart saucepan. Melt the lard over medium-low heat. Once it has mostly melted add the

pork, bay leaf, and 1 tablespoon whiskey. If needed add more water so pork is just covered. Bring to a simmer over medium heat, then reduce heat to maintain a gentle simmer.

- Continue to simmer, skimming off foam and stirring occasionally, for 2 hours adding more water if needed. The water should not boil off before the meat is tender and the fat has rendered. After 2 hours check to see how tender the pork is. If it is easily shredded add the shallots, if not check again in 15 minutes.
- The rillettes are done when the pork is easily shredded and the fat has become "clear and beautiful." This will take about 2 ½ to 3 hours. Once the water has cooked off, continue to cook the meat in the fat for 5 to 10 minutes, stirring frequently. The meat should not become crispy.
- Strain the meat in a fine mesh strainer, collecting the fat in a bowl or large glass measure. Allow the meat to rest in the strainer for 5 to 10 minutes, then transfer to a medium sized bowl. Use 2 forks to shred the pork.
- Add the remaining whiskey, kosher salt, ¼ teaspoon nutmeg, and ¼ teaspoon black pepper. Add ¼ cup of the reserved fat back into the meat. Mix vigorously to thoroughly combine and further break down the meat.
- Stir in additional fat 1 tablespoon at a time until your mixture is like stiff cookie dough in texture. Taste and add more nutmeg or black pepper if desired. In my experience the rillettes will taste saltier now than they will taste after a night in the fridge.
- Pack the rillettes into jars or ramekins. Seal the top with ¼-inch layer of the reserved fat – this will help to preserve the rillettes, so they will keep for several weeks in the refrigerator. Refrigerate the rillettes overnight or longer. Allow to come to room temperature before serving. Enjoy!
- Now, go smoke some cheese!!
- 5-spice variation: Add several broken up star anise pods to the chips when smoking. Eliminate the bay leaf. Use Chinese 5-spice in place of the nutmeg and black pepper. Use kirsch or brandy in place of the whiskey.

294. Smokey Tea Pork With Sweet Potatoes And Shiitake Mayo

Serving: Serves 6-8 | Prep: | Cook: | Ready in:

Ingredients

- 3.5 pounds boneless pork shoulder
- 1 medium onion, chopped
- 4 garlic cloves, chopped
- 3 tablespoons fermented black beans, rinsed, chopped
- 3 tablespoons ginger, grated or finely chopped
- 2 cups boiling water
- 2 lapsang souchong teabags (or 2 T loose tea)
- 2 tablespoons soy
- 2 tablespoons maple syrup
- 2 tablespoons dry sherry
- 2 sweet potatoes, cut into fries
- 2 tablespoons shiitake powder (from dried shiitakes ground in spice grinder)
- 1/2 cup mayo
- 1/2 teaspoon sriracha
- 1/2 teaspoon soy
- 2 teaspoons lemon juice
- oil for frying
- cilantro, chopped for garnish
- green onions, thinly sliced for garnish

Direction

- Cut pork into large chunks and brown in batches in the pot of a pressure cooker (or large pot). Remove to a bowl and add onions, garlic, ginger and black beans to fat. Stir for a few minutes.
- Steep tea in boiling water about 5 minutes. Remove tea bags and add soy, maple syrup and sherry. Add to onion mixture, scraping up any brown bits on bottom. Return pork. If using pressure cooker, cook on high for about

201

20 minutes, then place in sink under cold water to release pressure. Otherwise, cover and simmer over low for about an hour and a half or until pork is very tender. Remove lid, crank up heat and reduce sauce to a glaze. When cool enough to handle, break/shred pork into smaller pieces.

- If frying sweet potatoes: heat 2" of oil in a heavy bottomed pot to 375. Add a small batch of fries and cook until the edges start to crisp. Remove to newspaper or paper towels. Make sure heat is around 375 and add fries again until browned. It happens fast so pay attention. Drain on paper towels, then toss in bowl with salt, and a bit of cilantro and green onion. Finish cooking remaining sweet potatoes. If baking: heat oven to 425. Toss sweet potatoes in a couple tablespoons olive oil, season with s&p and bake about 20 minutes, flipping halfway through.
- Mix mayo, mushroom powder, sriracha, soy and lemon, adding just enough water to make it drizzle-able.
- Place a mound of fries on a plate, top with pork, a drizzle of mayo and an extra sprinkle of cilantro and green onion. Eat with a fork, right away.
- If you don't have a group partaking in this dish, there will be leftovers. As mentioned, the pork is great over rice with something simple and green like broccoli or kale. I usually freeze a packet or two for later. You can also use ribs: baby back, spare, boneless country...the possibilities are endless!

295. Southern Greens Crostini With Crumbled Bacon And Remoulade Aioli

Serving: Serves 4-6 | Prep: | Cook: |Ready in:

Ingredients

- For the Greens and Bacon
- 3 slices good bacon
- 1/2 pound collard greens, washed, stems removed, leaves cut into ribbons
- 1/2 pound Swiss chard, washed, stems removed, leaves cut into ribbons
- 2-3 large garlic cloves, peeled, put through a press
- salt
- 1 pinch red pepper flakes
- For the Remoulade Aioli and Crostini
- 1 large egg yolk
- 1 tablespoon fresh lemon juice
- salt
- 1 clove garlic, peeled, put through a press
- 3/4 cup canola oil
- scant 1/4 cup(s) extra-virgin olive oil
- 3/4 teaspoon mustard seeds, toasted, coarsely ground
- 2-3 teaspoons Dijon mustard
- sprinkly cayenne pepper
- 1 baguette, sliced on the diagonal into 1/2" ovals

Direction

- In a skillet, cook the bacon until crispy done. Remove from skillet and drain on paper towels. Let cool and then crumble. Reserve 1 T drippings in skillet; discard the rest.
- In the same skillet with the 1 T bacon drippings and over medium-high heat, add the garlic, red pepper flakes and a generous dash of salt. Stir and before anything can burn, add the greens and stir well to combine. Cover, reduce heat to medium and cook 4-5 minutes. Then remove from heat, but keep covered until you are ready to use them.
- Make your remoulade aioli: in a medium bowl, whisk together the egg yolk, lemon juice, garlic and salt. Add the canola oil, a few drops at a time, whisking vigorously. The aioli will soon thicken, and at that point, slowly pour in the rest of the canola oil, whisking mightily all the time. Once all the canola oil is incorporated, slowly whisk in the olive oil. Once the olive oil is in, whisk in the ground mustard seed and Dijon. Whisk to incorporate

and sprinkle lightly but firmly with cayenne. Stir. Taste and season with more salt, lemon or mustard if you'd like. You want this to have a flavor burst from the mustard and lemon and a back-end kick from the cayenne. Whisk to make sure it's smooth and everything is incorporated. Your arm will be tired.

- Get your greens and put them in a bowl. Toss with a healthy-sized spoonful of the remoulade aioli.
- Toast or grill the baguette slices. Cover the surface of each toasted piece with a light gloss of aioli. Spoon a nice amount of greens on top and sprinkle with crumbled bacon. Voila!

296. Southwest Smoked Pork Loin

Serving: Serves 8 | Prep: | Cook: | Ready in:

Ingredients

- 3 cups hickory wood chunks
- 1 (2 1/2 lb) boneless pork top loin, trimmed
- 2 teaspoons minced garlic
- 1 teaspoon chili powder
- 1 teaspoon cumin
- 1/2 teaspoon freshly cracked black pepper

Direction

- Soak wood in water at least 1 hour.
- Stir together garlic and next 4 ingredients. Rub evenly over pork.
- Prepare charcoal grill for medium-low indirect-heat. Sprinkle half the drained wood over the coals. Place pork on rack not over direct heat. Cover, with grill lid, and smoke for 90 minutes or until a temperature inserted into thickest portion registers 155 degree F. Add more coals and remaining wood chips as needed.
- Remove roast from grill, cover with foil and let stand at least 30 minutes.

297. Southwestern Pork Chile

Serving: Serves 6 | Prep: | Cook: | Ready in:

Ingredients

- 3 tablespoons canola oil, divided
- 2 onions, chopped
- 4 large garlic cloves, minced
- 3 tablespoons flour
- 1 teaspoon Kosher salt
- 2 teaspoons ground cumin
- 1 teaspoon freshly ground black pepper
- 3 pounds boneless pork butt, trimmed and meat cut into cubes
- 8 large dried red New Mexico chiles, seeded ground in spice grinder
- 4 cups reduced sodium chicken broth
- 1 bay leaf

Direction

- Preheat oven to 350 degrees F. Heat 2 tbsp. oil in a large, heavy-bottomed, ovenproof pot over medium-high heat. Add onions and cook, stirring, until onions are golden, about 6 minutes. Add garlic and cook for an additional minute or two. Transfer onions and garlic to a bowl with a slotted spoon.
- In a large bowl, stir together flour, salt, cumin, and pepper. Add pork and toss to coat. Return pot to medium-high heat, add remaining 1 tbsp. oil, and working in batches, lightly brown meat on all sides. Transfer meat to a separate bowl as you go.
- Return onions and garlic to pot. Sprinkle onion mixture with ground chiles and cook, stirring for about 2 minutes. Add broth, stirring to loosen browned bits from bottom of pot. Whirl sauce in a blender until smooth. Return sauce to pot and add bay leaf and reserved pork.
- Cover pot. Place in preheated oven and cook for 1 hour. Set lid slightly ajar and cook until pork is fork=tender, about 1 more hour. Remove bay leaf before serving.

- Serve over rice or in flour tortillas with sour cream.

298. Souvlaki Meat On A Stick

Serving: Makes four sticks | Prep: | Cook: | Ready in:

Ingredients

- 1 1/2 pounds pork tenderloin cut in cubes about 1 to 1 1/2 inches
- 3 lemons (the third reserved for squeezing on the meat at serving time)
- 1/2 cup olive oil
- 2 cloves minced garlic
- 1 teaspoon salt
- 1 teaspoon black pepper
- 2 teaspoons dried oregano
- 1 teaspoon dried basil
- 1 teaspoon Hungarian paprika
- Green bell pepper and white onion slices (optional)

Direction

- Marinate the meat in the olive oil, garlic, salt, pepper, oregano, basil, paprika and the juice of 2 of the lemons for 4 to 6 hours.
- Soak 4 wooden 12 inch skewers in water for 1/2 hour or more before grilling.
- Skewer 1/4 of the meat on each skewer, adding the slices of onion and pepper here and there if desired.
- Grill on a medium heat to your desired degree of doneness (about 15 minutes).
- Squeeze the juice from the third lemon over all four skewers before serving. OPA!!

299. Spaghetti Carbonara

Serving: Serves 4-6 | Prep: 0hours5mins | Cook: 0hours30mins | Ready in:

Ingredients

- 1/4 pound guanciale or pancetta, cut into 1/3-inch cubes
- 7 large egg yolks
- 1 large egg
- 1 pound spaghetti
- Kosher salt
- Freshly ground black pepper
- 1/2 cup freshly-grated Pecorino, plus more for garnish

Direction

- Put guanciale in a large skillet and place over medium-low heat. Cook, stirring frequently, until fat renders but guanciale is not browned, about 5 minutes. Transfer the guanciale to your serving bowl; reserve the drippings.
- Add egg yolks and egg to your serving bowl; whisk to blend.
- Meanwhile, cook pasta in a large pot of boiling salted water, stirring occasionally, until al dente. Drain, reserving around a 1/2 cup pasta cooking liquid.
- To egg mixture, immediately add spaghetti, 2 tablespoons pasta cooking liquid, and 1 teaspoon guanciale drippings; toss to coat. Working in 3 batches, gradually add Pecorino, stirring and tossing to melt between batches. Add lots of black pepper (around 2 teaspoons). Toss until the sauce thickens, adding more pasta water by tablespoonful if needed. Season to taste with salt and black pepper.
- Divide among bowls (or don't). Garnish with Pecorino.

300. Spaghetti Carbonara With Peas

Serving: Serves 2 | Prep: | Cook: | Ready in:

Ingredients

- 1 tablespoon olive oil

- 1 tablespoon bacon fat
- 3 ounces prosciutto (or pancetta or bacon) cut in 1" strips
- 8 ounces spaghetti (or any thin pasta i.e. linguini, etc.)
- 3 large garlic cloves
- 1 egg (we prefer pasture raised eggs)
- 1/2 cup Parmesan cheese
- 1 pinch red pepper flakes
- 1/2 teaspoon fresh ground black pepper
- 6 ounces baby peas (we use the organic frozen)
- Garnish with Italian parsley

Direction

- Mix the egg and ½ cup of the Parmesan cheese thoroughly. Reserve at room temperature until needed.
- Boil the spaghetti in oiled and salted water until cooked al dente; about 8 to 10 minutes. While this is cooking, start the sauce. When the spaghetti is cooked, drain, dry and set aside at room temperature until needed. Reserve some pasta water in case it is needed to thin the sauce.
- Put the bacon fat and olive oil in a 10 inch sauté pan and heat to medium. Put in the sliced prosciutto and red pepper flakes and sauté until prosciutto just starts to brown, about 2 to 3 minutes. When the prosciutto has cooked about 2 minutes, add the garlic slices and cook for 1 minute more.
- Turn the heat to low, add the peas and cooked and dried spaghetti and mix into the oil and prosciutto until the spaghetti is warmed thoroughly, about 2 minutes more. Keep stirring so nothing burns or overcooks.
- Move the pan from the hot burner to a cool burner and stir in the egg and Parmesan mixture and combine thoroughly. Keep stirring so that the egg doesn't fry. If this mixture is too dry add a little reserved pasta water until the sauce is the consistency that you like.
- Place the spaghetti carbonara on warmed plates. Garnish with a few kalamata olives and/or some Italian parsley either chopped or in sprigs. Serve with fresh grated Parmesan, salt and fresh ground black pepper.

301.   Spanish Carbonara

Serving: Serves 2 | Prep: | Cook: | Ready in:

Ingredients

- 2 handfuls dried spaghetti
- 1/4 pound cured Spanish chorizo, roughly chopped
- 3 egg yolks
- 25 +/- grams butter
- 1 pinch Thyme, dried or fresh
- 1/4 cup grated parmesan cheese
- cracked black peper

Direction

- In a sauce-pan, bring water to a boil and cook spaghetti to taste.
- While spaghetti is cooking, mix in a bowl the butter, egg yolks, parmesan cheese, and thyme together. It should be the consistency of a thick cake batter. If not, add a bit more butter.
- Drain the pasta and set aside. Add the chorizo to the sauce pan over a medium heat, no need for oil. Once the chorizo is lightly brown, turn the heat to low.
- Add the pasta and butter egg mixture to the pan quickly. Toss until coated then remove from heat.
- Serve with fresh cracked black pepper.

302.   Spanish Lentil Soup With Sausages And Apples

Serving: Serves 8 | Prep: | Cook: | Ready in:

Ingredients

- 2 cups brown or green lentils that hold their shape (I used lentils de puy)
- 5 cups water
- 2 tablespoons Spanish extra virgin olive oil, but not a super pricey one
- 1 pound sweet Spanish style chorizo, casing removed and sliced into half moons
- 1 pound Morcilla (Spanish style blood sausage), casing removed and either sliced or slightly crumbled
- 2 medium onions, chopped
- 4-6 cloves garlic, minced
- 2 medium tomatoes, peeled and chopped
- 1 teaspoon sweet smoked Spanish paprika
- 2-3 crisp, sweet apples, such as Fuji, peeled and sliced
- salt and pepper to taste
- 4 cups chicken stock, plus more as needed
- 1 tablespoon good quality chicken stock base (such as Minor's low sodium)
- 1/2 cup Amontillado Sherry
- 3 Bay leaves
- 2 tablespoons apple cider vinegar, plus more to taste

Direction

- Place the lentils in a medium-large saucepan with 5 cups of water. Bring to a boil, skim any foam, and then reduce heat to simmer for 15 minutes.
- In the meantime, heat a large Dutch oven over medium-high heat. Add the oil, heat through, and then add the sausages. Cook to release the fat from the sausages, about 7 minutes, stirring. Using a slotted spoon, remove the sausages and set aside.
- Add the onions with a pinch of salt to the sausage-flavored oil. Reduce the heat to medium and cook, stirring, until the onion is golden, about 7 minutes.
- Add the garlic and cook, stirring, for 1 minute.
- Then add the tomatoes and smoked paprika. Simmer briskly for 5 minutes.
- Then add the apple slices and mix in for 1 minute.

- Add the sherry and then dump the lentils with their cooking liquid into the pot. Add salt and pepper to taste, along with the chicken stock.
- Add the bay leaves and bring to a boil. Cover the Dutch oven and reduce the heat to simmer. Check occasionally to make sure there is enough liquid in the pan, and cook for 20-30 minutes, until the lentil are completely tender (they should not fall apart).
- Add the sausages back into the pot and stir through. Taste for salt and pepper. This soup was good the first day, but it was fantastic the second day.

303.   Special Cheesy Pasta

Serving: Serves 4 | Prep: | Cook: | Ready in:

Ingredients

- 3 cups pasta
- 8 tablespoons butter
- 1 onion, sliced thin
- 4 pieces bacon
- 1 tablespoon bacon grease
- 1/4 cup all purpose flour
- 2 cups milk
- 1/2 cup cream
- 2 egg yolks
- 1/2 cup gruyere cheese
- 1/2 cup cheddar
- 1/2 cup parmesan cheese

Direction

- Pre-heat oven to 350. Make the white sauce using half of the butter
- Beat the egg yolks in a small bowl and stir in 1/4 cup of the sauce whisking all of the time. Add back into the white sauce.
- Add the cheeses to the sauce and cook until melted.
- Fry the bacon and then remove to a plate and chop.

- Add the remaining butter to the frying pan along with the tablespoon of grease from the fried bacon. Fry the onions in this until soft.
- Add fried onions and bacon to the sauce and season to taste.
- Cook the pasta for half the amount of time it says on the packet then add to the sauce.
- Put in an oven dish and bake for 15-20 mins.

304. Speck + Arugula Pizza

Serving: Serves 4 | Prep: | Cook: | Ready in:

Ingredients

- Cornmeal, for dusting
- 1 pound pizza dough
- 2 medium tomatoes, cored and crushed
- 6 ounces fresh mozzarella cheese, pulled apart
- Just before serving, scatter with 2 cups baby arugula and 3 ounces thinly sliced speck
- Olive oil, for serving
- Sea salt, for serving

Direction

- Preheat the oven to 475°F with a rack in the bottom position. Place a large rimmed baking sheet upside down on the rack to preheat, 8 minutes.
- On a piece of parchment paper dusted with cornmeal, using a lightly floured rolling pin, roll pizza dough into a large circle, about 1?4 inch thick. Scatter it with toppings. Carefully remove the hot baking sheet from the oven and slide the parchment with the dough onto it. Bake until the dough is golden and crisp, 8 to 10 minutes. Before serving, add the remaining fresh ingredients, a drizzle of olive oil, and a sprinkle of sea salt.

305. Speck And Provolone Wrap With Fig, Grape And Pear Relish

Serving: Makes 2 wraps (one for who you're making the lunch for, and one for yourself!) | Prep: | Cook: | Ready in:

Ingredients

- Fig, Grape and Pear Relish
- 3 firm fresh figs, finely chopped
- 10 green grapes, halved or quartered
- 1/4 pear, peeled and seeded, and finely chopped
- 1 tablespoon pear chutney (you can use pear jelly, apple jelly or apple chutney with equal success)
- squeeze of lemon juice
- pinch of salt
- Speck and Provolone Wrap
- 2 flour tortillas
- 2 tablespoons herbed chevre, divided
- 1 package of speck ham (8-10 slices)
- several slices provolone cheese
- arugula or baby greens
- Fig, grape and pear relish

Direction

- Fig, Grape and Pear Relish
- Combine all ingredients in a small bowl. Let sit for 30 minutes to mingle flavors.
- Speck and Provolone Wrap
- Spread the chevre on each tortilla. Layer on the speck and provolone. Shmear on the relish and finish with arugula or baby greens.
- Wrap it up and wrap in foil.
- Pack the wrap for a loved one. Keep one for yourself.

306. Spiced Pan Roasted Pork Chops With Sumac Vegetables

Serving: Serves 4 | Prep: | Cook: |Ready in:

Ingredients

- Spice Mix
- 2 tablespoons Sweet paprika
- 1 teaspoon Garlic powder
- 1 teaspoon Cinnamon
- 2 teaspoons Ground coriander
- 2 teaspoons Ground turmeric
- 1 tablespoon Ginger powder
- 2 teaspoons Ground cardamom
- 1 teaspoon Ground allspice
- 1/4 teaspoon Ground cloves
- Pork Chops and Vegetables
- 3 tablespoons Olive oil
- 2 Large sweet potatoes, peeled and cut into 1 1/2-inch pieces
- 1 Medium red bell pepper, seeded and chopped into large pieces
- 2 Fennel bulbs, fronds removed and sliced
- 1 Small red onion, peeled and sliced
- 2 teaspoons Sumac
- 4 Bone-in pork chops
- Fine kosher salt, to taste
- Freshly ground pepper, to taste
- 2 tablespoons Finely chopped cilantro leaves
- Lemon wedges to garnish

Direction

- Preheat oven to 400 degrees.
- Line a large, rimmed sheet pan with parchment paper.
- In a small skillet, combine all of the spice mix ingredients and place over medium heat. Toast, stirring constantly, for about 2 minutes or until the spices become very fragrant. Remove from the heat and set aside.
- Toss the sweet potatoes, red bell peppers, fennel, onion, and sumac with 2 tablespoons of the olive oil and a pinch of salt. Spread in a single layer onto the prepared sheet pan. Make a well amongst the vegetables for the pork

chops and place them amongst vegetables. Sprinkle with another pinch or two of salt, then sprinkle generously with the spice mix. Drizzle the chops with remaining olive oil.

- Cover the pan loosely with foil and place in the oven. Roast for 20 minutes until the potatoes are slightly tender (but not mushy) and the pork chops are shiny. Remove the foil, lightly toss the vegetables, and return to the oven. Roast uncovered for another 10 minutes. Remove from the oven.
- Sprinkle everything on the pan with chopped cilantro leaves to taste and serve with lemon wedges.

307. Spiced Pork Belly With Apple Cider Glaze

Serving: Serves 4 | Prep: | Cook: |Ready in:

Ingredients

- Spiced Pork Belly
- 4 whole cinnamon sticks
- 1 whole star anise
- 1 tablespoon sichuan peppercorns
- 1/2 teaspoon cumin seeds
- 2 black cardamom pods
- 3 tablespoons kosher salt
- 2 pounds pork belly
- 1 bunch fennel fronds removed from bulb
- 1 red onions, halved
- 1 garlic bulb, broken into cloves
- Apple Cider Glaze
- 1 cup chicken stock
- 1 1/2 cups apple cider
- 1/3 cup vermouth

Direction

- Spiced Pork Belly
- The day before: toast spices (only 1 of the cinnamon sticks) together in cast iron pan just until they start smoking.

- Grind all spices in spice grinder (or in a coffee grinder; clean afterward by grinding 1/4 cup rice).
- Combine spices with 1 tablespoon of the salt and then rub over all sides of pork. Cover and refrigerate for at least 24 hours.
- The next day: preheat oven to 450 degrees. Rinse spices from pork.
- Pierce fat all over (avoid piercing the flesh below) and rub salt into incisions. Turn over and season with salt and pepper.
- Roast fat-side down in a large pan for about 30 minutes, until much of the fat has melted and skin on top is crackling. Then turn down oven to 350 degrees and roast for another hour.
- Remove from oven and move pork to a plate. Stir vegetables in melted pork fat, add remaining three cinnamon sticks, and place pork on top of vegetables. Baste with fat and roast another hour.
- Apple Cider Glaze
- Remove pan from oven and gently move pork to a plate. Cover with foil and set aside.
- Drain fat from pan and place over stove burner. Discard just the fennel fronds and the cinnamon sticks.
- Put roasting pan with remaining vegetables on the burner. Pour liquids and simmer, scraping the bottom to pick up the bits. Stir constantly as sauce thickens for about 45 minutes.
- Strain the sauce. Smoosh as much of the juices out of the vegetables as you can by pressing them against a mesh strainer. Taste before salting.
- Shred and serve with mashed root vegetables or brown rice. You can also use some of the melted pork fat to cook some greens as a side.

---

308.   Spicy Apple Chorizo Hash

Serving: Serves 4 | Prep: | Cook: | Ready in:

Ingredients

- 1 (about 1/2 pound) large tart, crisp apple
- 1 (about 1/2 pound) large red potato
- 3 tablespoons tablespoon olive oil (divided, plus more as needed)
- Salt and pepper, to taste
- 9 ounces raw Mexican pork chorizo
- 1 red bell pepper (halved, seeds and ribs removed, and cut into 1/2-inch dice)
- 1 onion (peeled and cut into 1/2-inch dice)
- 1 medium jalapeño (halved, seeds and ribs removed, and cut into tiny dice, optional)
- 1 clove garlic (peeled and minced)
- 4 to 8 soft-poached eggs (optional)
- Halved radishes (optional)

Direction

- Preheat the oven to 425° F.
- Cut the apple and potato into 1/2-inch dice. Place them into a medium bowl and drizzle with 2 tablespoons of the olive oil, season with salt and pepper, toss to combine. Spread apples and potatoes onto a parchment-lined, rimmed baking sheet, keeping them in as close to a single layer as possible. Roast in the heated oven 30 to 40 minutes until tender and beginning to brown on the edges. Toss them once or twice during roasting to ensure even cooking.
- Meanwhile, put a large, heavy bottom cast iron or non-stick skillet over medium heat. Heat the remaining 1 tablespoon olive oil and add chorizo to the skillet, breaking it up with a wooden spoon. Cook, stirring and breaking up chorizo, until lightly browned and beginning to look dry and crumbly, about 10 minutes. Use a slotted spoon to transfer chorizo to a paper towel-lined plate to drain. Leave the fat in the skillet, adding extra olive oil to bring the volume of fat to about 2 tablespoons if necessary.
- Add the diced bell pepper, diced onion, and diced jalapeño (if using) to the skillet in which the chorizo was cooked. Cook over medium heat, stirring often, about 5 minutes. Stir in minced garlic and cook 1 minute more. Turn off the heat. Gently fold in roasted apples,

potatoes, and cooked chorizo. Turn the heat to low and cook, folding gently, until the flavors come together, about 2 minutes.

- Serve warm with poached eggs on top (if using) and halved radishes on the side (if using).

with candied cherry halves. This dish does not require basting as the juices and sauce, combined with the pineapple, will keep it moist. The juices from the cooked ham go well with mashed potatoes or rice and can also be used for a ham and potato layered casserole the next day.

309. Spicy Mustard Pineapple Baked Ham

Serving: Serves 8 | Prep: | Cook: | Ready in:

Ingredients

- 12-16 pounds Spiral-sliced ham
- 1 can Dole crushed pineapple
- 3/4 cup yellow mustard
- 1/2 cup honey
- 3 tablespoons ground horseradish
- 1 tablespoon Tony Tchatcher's New Orleans seasoning
- 1 tablespoon hot curry powder
- 1 teaspoon white pepper
- candied cherry halves to garnish

Direction

- Preheat oven to 350 degrees. Mix together the mustard, honey, horseradish curry powder, Thatcher, pepper and juice from the pineapple-- stir until well-blended.
- Place the ham in a foil-lined pan at least 4 inches on the sides. Pour about a cup of hot water in the pan, then pour the sauce slowly over the top and make sure all of it gets covered, saving back about 1/4 cup.
- Pat the pineapple all over the top and front of the ham, then pour on the 1/4 cup of sauce. Carefully cover the entire ham with foil, making sure it does not touch the top or front (don't want it to stick during baking--you want a good, tight seal on the foil so tuck it over the edges and end of the pan.
- Place the ham on the center of the rack, and bake for at least 4 hours. Remove and garnish

310. Spicy Pork Ramen Noodles

Serving: Serves 4 | Prep: 0hours25mins | Cook: 0hours15mins | Ready in:

Ingredients

- 10 ounces fresh ramen noodles
- 1 tablespoon vegetable oil
- 8 ounces ground pork
- 1/4 cup low-sodium chicken broth
- 3 tablespoons chili garlic sauce, such as Huy Fong
- 2 tablespoons low-sodium soy sauce
- 1 tablespoon honey
- 1 teaspoon minced fresh ginger
- Blanched bok choy, chopped roasted peanuts, sliced scallions, and toasted sesame seeds, for serving

Direction

- Bring a large pot of water to a boil; add noodles and cook until tender, about 2 minutes. Drain and rinse under cold water.
- Meanwhile, heat oil in a medium skillet over medium-high. Add pork and cook, breaking up meat with the back of a spoon, until cooked through, about 6 minutes. In a small bowl, whisk together stock, chili sauce, soy sauce, honey, and ginger; add to pan; simmer until thickened slightly, about 1 minute. Add noodles and toss to combine. Serve with blanched bok choy and sprinkle with peanuts, scallions, and sesame seeds.

311. Spinach & Zucchini Pizza

Serving: Serves 3-4 | Prep: | Cook: | Ready in:

Ingredients

- 250 grams spelt flour
- 200 milliliters luke-warm water
- 5 grams dry yeast
- pinch of salt
- 2 tablespoons olive oil
- 1 cup tomato sauce
- 100 grams ham
- 1 medium-size zucchini
- 1 cup raw spinach
- 1 cup grated cheese
- 1 cup grated mozzarella

Direction

- Prepare the dough: add luke-warm water to dry yeast and add a teaspoon of flour. Mix well, cover with a cloth and let rise for about 10 minutes. In a separate bowl, place flour and a pinch of salt. When the yeast rises, add it to the flour. Add olive oil and combine well with a fork, then proceed to kneading the dough by hand for about 10 minutes, until the dough is smooth and flexible. Cover with a cloth and let rise for an hour.
- After an hour, knead out the dough and divide into 2 pieces. Roll each dough piece out into a pizza shape (round, rectangle or free-style).
- Cover baking tray with baking paper to prevent sticking. Preheat oven to 220°C / 428°F. Place pizza dough on baking tray. Spread tomato sauce onto the dough, then top the pizza with ham, sliced zucchini, spinach leaves, grated cheese, and mozzarella.
- Place pizza in preheated oven and bake for about 12-16 minutes, or until the pizza dough is golden brown. Remove from oven and serve hot.

312. Spinach Basil Salad With Applewood Smoked Bacon And Honey

Serving: Serves 4 | Prep: | Cook: | Ready in:

Ingredients

- 4 large cage-free eggs
- 2 thick slices applewood smoked, nitrate-free bacon
- 1 medium sweet onion, sliced
- 2 garlic cloves, crushed with side of knife
- 2 tablespoons honey
- 1 tablespoon apple cider vinegar
- 1 bag (1 pound) pre-washed baby spinach
- 1 cup basil leaves
- sea salt and crushed red pepper flakes

Direction

- Bring water in a saucepan to a boil. Remove the pan from the burner. Gently lower the eggs into the water and return the pan to the hot burner. Lower the heat and simmer for 5 minutes. Drain the water and cool the eggs in cool water. Peel the eggs. Eggs may also be poached or sauteed as desired.
- Meanwhile, cook bacon for 4 minutes over medium heat. Remove bacon from pan to a plate leaving the rendered oil in the pan.
- Add the onion and garlic and cook for 5 to 6 minutes, until softened. Add honey and apple cider vinegar and sauté until the onion has caramelized, about 5 more minutes.
- Place the spinach and basil into the pan. Season with sea salt and red pepper flakes. Toss with tongs until the leaves are just wilted, about 30 seconds. Pour the mixture into a bowl and crumble bacon into chunks over the salad. Halve the soft-cooked eggs and arrange on top of the salad.

313. Spinach Or Ham Quiche

Serving: Serves 6 | Prep: | Cook: |Ready in:

Ingredients

- 1 frozen pie crust
- 1/2 pound boiled ham, cut into small pieces
- 1 package frozen spinach, defrosted and drained of liquid
- 1/4 pound Swiss cheese, grated
- 4 eggs
- 1 tablespoon flour
- 1 cup milk
- 1/2 cup heavy cream
- 1/4 salt
- freshly ground black pepper
- 3 tablespoons unsalted butter, melted

Direction

- Preheat oven to 400F.
- Add ham OR spinach and grated cheese to uncooked crust.
- Combine eggs, flour, milk, cream, salt and pepper.
- Pour mixture over the ham OR spinach and cheese.
- Drizzle melted butter over the egg mixture.
- Bake in a 400F oven for 30+ minutes.

314. Spiralized Potato Carbonara

Serving: Serves 4 | Prep: | Cook: |Ready in:

Ingredients

- 2 Lbs. Yukon Gold Potatoes, cut in half and spiralized using the spaghetti blade
- 2 Large Eggs- room temp
- 2 Egg Yolks
- 1/3 cup Shredded pecorino Romano, plus additional for serving
- 1/3 cup Grated Parmesan

- Coarsely Ground Pepper
- 3 1/2 ounces Pancetta or bacon small diced

Direction

- In a mixing bowl, whisk together the whole eggs, egg yolks and pecorino and Parmesan. Season with a pinch of salt and black pepper.
- Place a large non-stick skillet over medium-high heat. Add the pancetta or bacon and sauté until the fat just renders. Remove from skillet and set aside.
- Leaving the rendered fat in the pan, return the same skillet back to medium heat and add in the potato noodles. Let cook, covered, for 7-10 minutes or until cooked through.
- Remove potato noodles to a large bowl and vigorously toss with the egg and cheese mixture, until noodles are well coated and a creamy sauce is formed. Add the cooked pancetta and top with more cheese to taste. Serve immediately.

315. Steamed Mussels With Spicy Portuguese Sausage

Serving: Serves 4 | Prep: | Cook: |Ready in:

Ingredients

- 3 pounds fresh mussels, live
- 1/3 cup flour
- 1 pound chourico, casings removed and sliced (other semi-hard cooked sausage will work too)
- 4 tablespoons unsalted butter
- 4 garlic cloves, minced
- 1 small yellow onion, chopped (about 1/2 cup)
- 1 teaspoon fennel seeds, crushed
- 1/3 cup bourbon
- 1/2 cup cream
- 1 tablespoon tarragon, chopped

Direction

- Whisk the flour in 6 cups of cold water. Place the mussels in there for about an hour. I've found that not only will the mussels spit out any grit, they'll plump up because the mussels will get nourishment from the flour. This is not a necessary step if you just need to dive into those mollusks, but it does make a noticeable difference in how ample the mussels will be.
- Sauté the slices of chourico in butter on medium heat until fragrant and hot (about 4-5 minutes). Add the garlic, onion, and fennel. Stir for about 5 minutes, until the onion is soft. Be careful not to burn the bottom. Turn the burner on low. Add the bourbon.
- Drain the mussels and add them to the pot and cover. Stir occasionally to make sure the bottom isn't burning until the mussels open.
- Divide the mussels and sausage into bowls. Add the cream to the pot and stir. Ladle the sauce over the mussels and sausage.

316. Stir Fried Rice Noodles With Minced Pork And Black Bean

Serving: Serves 3 to 4 | Prep: 0hours15mins | Cook: 0hours20mins |Ready in:

Ingredients

- 200 grams rice noodles
- 300 grams minced pork
- 1/2 cup chopped baby corn
- 1 head of broccoli, chopped into florets
- 1-inch pieces of ginger, finely sliced
- 5 cloves of garlic, finely chopped
- 1 small onion, chopped
- 3 stalks of spring onions, chopped (set the tops aside to use as garnish)
- 3 teaspoons black bean paste
- 1 1/2 teaspoons soya sauce
- 1 teaspoon rice vinegar
- 1/2 teaspoon chile flakes

- 2 tablespoons olive oil (plus extra for the eggs)
- 3 eggs, lightly beaten
- 2 dried red chiles, halved and de-seeded
- 1 teaspoon sesame oil
- 2 teaspoons sesame seeds, lightly toasted
- 2 tablespoons peanuts, coarsely chopped
- Freshly ground black pepper
- Salt

Direction

- Cook the rice noodles in a pot of boiling water. Immerse the baby corn into the same pot as the noodles 3 minutes before the noodles are done. Blanch the broccoli a minute before both are done, and drain out all together. You want the noodles and vegetables to be al dente and still have a bite to it.
- Pour the olive oil into a wok/pot over medium heat and toss in the dried red chiles, onions, spring onions (the bottom part), ginger, and garlic. Sauté for a few minutes until translucent and lightly browned.
- Add the pork into the wok and, using a spatula, break up any clumps that are stuck together. Brown the meat thoroughly for a few minutes. Add in the black bean paste, soya sauce, rice vinegar, pepper, and chile flakes. (Note: Start by using 2 teaspoons each of soya sauce and rice vinegar, and taste before adding more). Cook for a few minutes until the rawness of the sauces are cooked off. Taste and adjust seasoning; set aside.
- In a skillet, lightly toast the sesame seeds and peanuts; set aside to sprinkle on top later. In the same skillet, add a few teaspoons of olive oil and lightly scramble the eggs, keeping it just a teeny bit runny.
- Toss in the noodles and vegetables into the minced pork mixture; add the scrambled eggs and mix through to combine evenly. Add a little water if necessary to loosen the consistency.
- Tip into your serving dish and garnish with the spring onion tops, peanuts, sesame oil, and seeds.

317. Stuffed Acorn Squash

Serving: Serves 4 | Prep: | Cook: |Ready in:

Ingredients

- 2 medium acorn squash
- 3 tablespoons olive oil, divided
- 1 cup chopped white onion
- 1 clove garlic, chopped
- 1 pound loose spicy Italian sausage
- 1 bunch Swiss chard
- 1 cup canned chopped tomatoes, drained
- 2 teaspoons chopped fresh thyme leaves
- 1 teaspoon chopped fresh oregano
- 1 cup shredded Pecorino-Romano cheese
- salt & pepper to taste

Direction

- Heat oven to 375 degrees. Cut squashes in half lengthwise, and scoop out the seeds (save for roasting!). Slice a small piece off the bottom of each squash half so that it is stable. Brush inside of each squash with olive oil and season with salt and pepper. Place squash, cut side down, on a roasting pan or rimmed baking sheet. Bake for 25 to 30 minutes, or until squash is tender but not mushy. You should be able to easily pierce it with a sharp knife.
- While the squash is in the oven, prepare the stuffing. Remove stems and thick ribs from chard leaves. Chop chard stems/ribs into ¼ inch pieces. Set aside. Roughly chop chard leaves.
- Heat remaining olive oil in a large skillet over medium heat. Add onions and chopped chard stems. Cook until onions are translucent and chard stems are soft, about 5 minutes. Add garlic and cook until fragrant, about 30 seconds.
- Add sausage, breaking apart with a spatula as it cooks, if necessary. Once sausage is just cooked through, add tomatoes, chard and herbs. If there seems to be too much liquid from the tomatoes, allow it to cook off for a minute or two. Otherwise, remove skillet from heat and add salt and pepper to taste.
- Spoon sausage mixture into each squash half and sprinkle with a quarter cup of cheese.
- Return to squashes to oven, and turn heat up to 450 degrees. Bake until cheese is melted, about 5 to 7 minutes.

318. Stuffed Italian Zucchini Boats

Serving: Serves 4 | Prep: | Cook: |Ready in:

Ingredients

- 4 smallish zucchini - about 4"-5" long
- 2 cloves garlic
- 1 cup roughly chopped onions
- 1/2 cup finely minced canadian bacon or ham
- 1/2 teaspoon fennel seed
- pinch of red pepper flakes
- 1/4 teaspoon black pepper
- 1/4 teaspoon salt
- 4 tablespoons olive oil, divided
- 1/2 cup finely chopped tomato
- slice bread (I used a dense piece of whole wheat)
- 2 tablespoons chopped parsley
- 2 tablespoons basil chiffonade + extra for serving
- 1/4 cup shredded part-skim mozzarella + extra for sprinkling
- sprinkle of parmesan cheese (optional)

Direction

- Preheat the oven to 375°. Spray a baking sheet with cooking spray and set aside.
- Slice the zucchini lengthwise down the middle. Use a melon-baller to carefully scoop the flesh out of the zucchini and transfer to a mini prep food chopper. Pulse several times until the zucchini flesh is finely chopped. Transfer to a bowl.

- Add the onions to the food processor and pulse until they are about the size consistency of the zucchini. Transfer to the same bowl as zucchini and add the minced Canadian bacon.
- Crush the fennel seed either by using a mortar and pestle, a spice grinder, or place a piece of plastic wrap on a cutting board, add the fennel to the center and fold the plastic wrap over it. Use a rolling pin or mallet to crush the fennel seed. Add crushed fennel to the zucchini mixture, along with red pepper flakes, black pepper and salt.
- Heat a medium skillet over medium high heat, add the olive oil. When the oil is hot, stir in the zucchini mixture and cook down until it's given up most of its liquid, about 5-6 minutes. Add the chopped tomato and cook a few minutes more. Remove from heat and set aside.
- Tear the bread into small chunks and add them to the food processor along with the parsley. Pulse 3-5 times until coarsely chopped and transfer to the zucchini mixture. Add the mozzarella and basil, stir to combine.
- Lightly coat the interior of each zucchini half with a little olive oil. Spoon filling liberally into each zucchini and arrange on a baking sheet. Take a look at the tray and if you see a zucchini leaning in a particular direction -- instead of sitting straight up, prop the zucchini against one of the sides of the sheet pan to hold it erect and prevent it from spilling over in the oven. If most of your zucchini are persnickety - find a shallow casserole dish that will fit them snugly against one another and prevent them from toppling. Drizzle with remaining olive oil and sprinkle with a little mozzarella and parmesan. Bake for 20-25 minutes or until golden. Sprinkle with fresh basil and serve.

319. Stuffed Peppers With Sausage

Serving: Serves 4 | Prep: | Cook: | Ready in:

Ingredients

- 4 large green bell peppers
- Salt to taste
- 1 3/4 cups chicken stock
- 1 teaspoon garlic powder
- 1 teaspoon onion powder
- 1 bay leaf
- 1 scant cups long-grain white or brown rice
- 1 tablespoon olive oil
- 1 pound raw Italian sausage (sweet or hot)
- 1 small red onion, diced
- 2 large carrots, finely diced
- 3 medium zucchini, diced
- 1 cup (8 oz) can tomato sauce
- Salt and freshly ground black pepper to taste
- Finely grated Parmesan for topping

Direction

- Cut off the tops of the bell peppers, remove the stems, and set the tops aside. Remove the seeds and ribs from each bell pepper, then sprinkle the cavity with salt and place upside-down on paper towels. Leave to drain while you assemble the stuffing. Finely dice the reserved bell pepper tops, and set aside.
- In a saucepan, combine chicken stock, garlic powder, onion powder, and bay leaf. Bring to a boil over medium-high heat, then add rice and a large pinch of salt. Reduce heat to low, cover, and simmer until the rice is cooked--20-25 minutes for white rice, 30-40 minutes for brown rice. Remove from the heat and set aside.
- Preheat the oven to 400° F, and place a rack in the middle position. Line a baking sheet with aluminum foil. Heat oil in a large skillet over medium heat. Cut or squeeze the sausage out of its casing and add to the pan. Cook, breaking up the meat with your spoon or spatula, until the last traces of pink disappear.

Add reserved bell pepper tops, onion, carrots, and zucchini, and cook for 5-7 minutes, or until the vegetables are soft. Add cooked rice, tomato sauce, and salt and pepper to taste.

- Arrange peppers, cut side up, on the baking sheet, and distribute the stuffing mixture evenly among them. Sprinkle the top of each pepper generously with cheese. Bake for 15-20 minutes, or until the peppers are just tender and the cheese is golden. Remove from the oven and let sit for 10 minutes before serving.

320. Stuffed Deboned Chicken Roll

Serving: Serves 6 | Prep: | Cook: |Ready in:

Ingredients

- 1 3-4 pound chicken, deboned
- 1 pound ground pork
- 1/2 cup panko bread crumbs
- 1 teaspoon baking powder
- 1 egg
- 2 cloves of garlic, minced
- 1/2 cup parsley, chopped
- 1 teaspoon salt
- 1/2 teaspoon black pepper
- 1/2 teaspoon chili flakes
- 4-5 fresh thyme sprigs
- 2 tablespoons sunflower oil
- salt and black peper for chicken

Direction

- Mix ground pork, panko, baking powder, egg, garlic, parsley, 1 tsp salt, ½ tsp black pepper and chili flakes, cover and place in the fridge.
- Debone chicken the best way you know
- To the point before staffing, I did butterfly legs and breast to extend roll.
- To make rolling easier, place chicken on the baking sheet covered with saran wrap or parchment paper and put in the freezer for an hour or so but not longer than two (depend on

your freezer) for the chicken to dray and firm up. It will be much easier to handle.

- Take out and staff chicken with pork mixture that you shaped into one tick sausage, place crossway, roll, tide and season with ½ tsp salt, ½ tsp black pepper, 2 tbsp. oil, 4-5 sprigs fresh thyme
- Roast at 400 F for 70-80 minutes, every 15 to 20 minutes baste chicken with oil.
- Take out, cover with aluminum foil and let rest for 10-15 minutes.
- Discard the string and slice.

321. Sugar Bush Maple Coffee And Cocoa Rubbed Pork Tenderloin

Serving: Serves 6-8 | Prep: | Cook: |Ready in:

Ingredients

- Sugar Bush Maple Coffee Rub
- 3 tablespoons Sugar Bush Maple coffee
- 2 tablespoons Sweet paprika
- 1 teaspoon Smoked paprika
- 1/2 teaspoon Chipotle chile powder
- 1/2 tablespoon Kosher salt
- 1/2 teaspoon Freshly ground black and white pepper
- 2 tablespoons Unsweetened cocoa
- 1 tablespoon McCormick onion powder, California Style
- 1/4 teaspoon garlic powder or granulated garlic
- Mustard marinated pork tenderloins
- 2 Whole pork tenderloins, thin end tucked under and tied
- 2 tablespoons Dijon mustard
- 4 tablespoons Yellow mustard
- 1 tablespoon EVOO
- 1 medium shallot, minced
- 2 garlic cloves pressed through garlic press
- 2 + tablespoons Asian sweet chili sauce, according to your taste

- 1 teaspoon Soy sauce
- 1 tablespoon Worcestershire sauce

Direction

- Sugar Bush Maple Coffee Rub
- Thoroughly blend the dry rub ingredients and spread on a sheet pan.
- Mustard marinated pork tenderloins
- Remove fat and silver skin from tenderloins and dry with paper towels. Completely blend the next 8 ingredients and slather both tenderloins with the marinade.
- Roll the mustard marinated tenderloins in the coffee/cocoa rub, covering completely and wrap tightly in plastic wrap, set in a baking dish large enough to hold both, refrigerate overnight. When cooking time rolls around, the tenderloins can be pan seared and finished in a 350°oven, but my favorite method is on the grill rotisserie, takes about 40 minutes on MOM or you can slow roast on LOL for a longer period of time, checking the meat with an instant read thermometer to a temperature of 140-150°, my preference. A ten minute rest under heavy duty foil tent, slice and serve. You can serve with a sauce of your choice; I made a reduced apple cider sauce that was just perfect with the rotisserie tenderloins. I tried the recipe with a BBQ type sauce and felt that it was too tart for my taste.

322.　　　Sunday Pork Ragu

Serving: Serves at least 4 with lots of leftover sauce | Prep: | Cook: | Ready in:

Ingredients

- 3/4 pound pork bones (see head note), cut into approximately 2-inch pieces
- 1-2 tablespoons salt (or more to taste), divided
- 5 links sweet Italian sausage
- 3 links, spicy Italian sausage
- 1 medium yellow onion
- 6 small garlic cloves (about 3/4 ounce)
- 2 tablespoons Extra Virgin olive oil
- 1 small can (5.5 oz) tomato paste
- 2 large (28 ounces each) cans good-quality tomatoes (see head note)
- 1 bay leaf
- 1/2 cup fresh parsley, chopped
- Freshly ground pepper to taste
- 1 pound dried pasta (a shape such as rigatoni or penne is best -- see head note)
- 1/2 cup fresh basil, julienned
- 1/2 cup Pecorino Romano cheese (or more to taste)

Direction

- Preheat oven to 400 degrees. Line a baking sheet with sides with aluminum foil. Place a baking rack over the foil and place the ribs on the rack. There should be a little space between each rib. Sprinkle with 1/2 teaspoon salt. Place baking pan in oven and roast for 30-40 minutes (the bigger pieces you may have to turn halfway through) until nicely browned and caramelized. Remove pan from oven and with tongs take each rib off the rack. Place on a paper-towel lined plate to further drain.
- On cutting board, carefully remove casings from sausage. Slice each link into four pieces, or simply pinch off balls of sausage about 1 to 1 1/2 inches in diameter. Set each piece of sausage on wire rack (no need to wash the rack beforehand). Place baking pan in oven and roast for about 30 minutes, or until sausage is browned and caramelized. It usually is not necessary to turn the sausage, but you can if you wish. Remove pan from oven and turn off oven.
- On cutting board, cut onion into medium-small dice. Thinly slice garlic cloves, then roughly chop. (You don't want the garlic pieces too small or they will burn.) Heat a large, heavy saucepan or Dutch oven over medium-low heat. Add olive oil. When oil has warmed, add onion and sauté until just beginning to turn golden brown (about 10 minutes), stirring occasionally with a wooden

spoon. Add garlic to pan and stir frequently. When the garlic aroma becomes heady and fragrant (watch carefully to make sure garlic is not browning too quickly), clear a hot spot in the pan with your wooden spoon. Add tomato paste and sauté until the tomatoes begins to release their fragrance. Mix tomato paste with onion and garlic mixture and add 5.5 ounces of water to pan. (Easiest way to do this is to simply fill tomato paste can with water.) Drain juice from canned tomatoes and reserve about a cup of it. Add bay leaf and tomatoes to pan. You can add tomatoes whole -- they will cook down. Or simply cut each tomato into about four pieces with kitchen shears before adding them to the pot.

- Bring tomato-onion-garlic mixture to a simmer and add pork bones and sausages, nestling them carefully into the sauce. You want enough meat to flavor the sauce, but not so much that it overwhelms the tomato sauce. Lower heat and cook tomato sauce at a low simmer for about two hours, stirring occasionally. During the first hour of cooking, if level of sauce in the pan begins to evaporate, add reserved tomato liquid, as needed. After the first hour of cooking, add water to the sauce instead if sauce is looking too thick. The sauce will smell wonderful as it cooks, infusing your home with pork and tomato aromas. Inhale and savor, and pour yourself a glass of your favorite red wine.

- After about two hours of cooking, begin to add salt, about 1 teaspoon at a time. Let sauce cook for about 15 minutes, so that the salt's flavor can be absorbed before adding more. Add a few grinds of fresh black pepper and the parsley. Taste and adjust the seasonings until the flavors are to your liking. Continue to cook for another half hour or so. (Total cooking time should be at least 2 1/2 to 3 hours, but honestly you cannot cook this sauce too much. The longer it simmers, the better it will taste.)

- About half an hour before you are ready to eat, fill a large stockpot with water. Bring to a boil and add a tablespoon or two of salt. Taste

it and see if you can taste the salt. If you can't taste the salt, then add a little more. When water is rapidly boiling, add dried pasta. Give a good stir with a slotted spoon and bring back to a boil. Cook for about eight minutes, then begin tasting the pasta. When it is al dente (just slightly chewy, but not hard) drain pasta, but reserve a cup or two of the cooking water.

- If the sauce looks too thick, add a ladle or two of pasta water. Warm a big spaghetti serving bowl with some of the pasta water. Add a ladleful of sauce to the bottom of the bowl. Top with a tablespoon or two of cheese. Add a few large spoonfuls of pasta. Top with sauce, more cheese and a sprinkling of basil. Add another layer of pasta, sauce, cheese and basil. Keep layering the ingredients until the bowl is full. Add bones and sausage around the edges of the bowl. Top with a handful of basil and more cheese.

- Serve pasta in bowls with additional grated cheese and basil. Pour some more red wine, and serve with warm bread. Enjoy!

323. Suppli Sotto Cieli Di Roma

Serving: Serves 4-6 | Prep: | Cook: | Ready in:

Ingredients

- 1 cup Arborio (or other short grain) rice
- 1 tablespoon butter
- 1/4 cup chopped red onion
- 2 cups chicken stock
- 1 pinch saffron threads
- 3 eggs (2 for the rice plus 1 for your frying station)
- 1/3 cup grated pecorino cheese
- 1/4 pound prosciutto or speck or spicy capacola (have it sliced thick), cut into ¼ inch dice
- 5 ounces low moisture mozzarella

- 1/2 cup bread crumbs (panko)
- 1/2 cup all purpose flour
- 3 cups frying oil (olive oil would be Roman, but you can use canola or peanut oil as well)
- Salt and ground pepper

Direction

- Prepare the rice. Bring your chicken stock to a boil, add the saffron threads and lower heat to a simmer. Meanwhile melt the butter in your rice pan and add the onion. Allow the onion to color
- Stir the rice into the butter with a wooden spoon. Continue to stir until the rice is translucent.
- Over medium heat add stock to rice and onion a ladleful at a time. Allow 25 minutes for rice to become al dente and remove from heat.
- Turn your rice out into a large bowl and allow to cool. Beat two eggs and add them to the rice with several spoons of pecorino, plus salt and pepper. Using your clean hands squish everything together into a lumpen proletariat like mass.
- In a large pot, preferably cast iron, enameled or not, heat frying oil to 370 degrees.
- Again using your clean hands, shape the rice into egg shaped balls and insert a piece of mozzarella and a chunk of your preferred hammage. Close the ball tightly.
- Your frying station consists of a plate of flour, the remaining egg (also beaten) in a bowl, and a final plate of bread crumbs mixed with more pecorino.
- One by one, roll the suppli into flour first, dip into egg and finally roll in bread crumbs.
- Carefully lower your suppli into your hot cooking oil. If you displace too much oil you won't be yelling "Eureka" like Archimedes. You'll be dialing 911. Allow your suppli to get nice and golden brown. Serve hot but with care.
- Note to cook: There are many variations for suppli and they remain open to argument. Welcome to Rome. Among my favorites

would be a ragu of regaglie (chicken giblets), which you could substitute for ham.

---

324. Suzanne Goin's Grilled Pork Burgers

Serving: Makes 6 burgers | Prep: | Cook: | Ready in:

Ingredients

- For the burger:
- 1 1/2 teaspoons cumin seeds
- 3 tablespoons extra-virgin olive oil, plus more for grilling
- 1/2 cup diced shallots
- 1 tablespoon minced garlic
- 1 tablespoon thyme leaves
- 2 chiles de arbol, thinly sliced on the bias
- 2 pounds ground pork
- 1/4 pound fresh Mexican chorizo, casing removed
- 3 ounces applewood-smoked bacon, finely diced
- 2 tablespoons chopped flat-leaf parsley
- 6 slices Manchego cheese
- 6 brioche buns or other good burger buns
- Aioli (recipe follows)
- Romesco (recipe follows)
- 2 ounces arugula
- Kosher salt and freshly ground black pepper
- For the aioli and the romesco:
- 1 extra-large egg yolk
- 1/2 cup grapeseed oil
- 1/2 cup extra-virgin olive oil
- 1 small clove garlic
- 1/4 lemon, for juicing
- Pinch cayenne pepper
- Kosher salt
- 5 ancho chiles
- 2 tablespoons raw almonds
- 2 tablespoons blanched hazelnuts
- 1 1/4 cups extra-virgin olive oil
- 1 slice country bread, about 1-inch thick
- 1/3 cup San Marzano canned tomatoes

- 1 clove garlic, chopped
- 1 tablespoon chopped flat-leaf parsley
- 1/2 lemon, for juicing
- Kosher salt

Direction

- For the burger:
- In a medium sauté pan, toast the cumin seeds over medium heat a few minutes until the seeds release their aroma and darken slightly. Pound the seeds in a mortar or spice grinder until coarsely ground.
- Return the pan to the stove over high heat for 1 minutes. Add the olive oil and shallots. Turn the heat down to medium-low, and cook for a few minutes, stirring, once or twice, until the shallots start to soften. Add the garlic, thyme, cumin and sliced chile. Season with 1/4 teaspoon salt and a few grindings of black peppery, and cook 3 to 4 minutes, until the shallots become translucent. Set aside to cool.
- In a large bowl, use your hands to combine the ground pork, chorizo, bacon, shallot mixture, and parsley, being careful not to overmix the meat. Season with 1 1/4 teaspoons salt and lots of freshly ground black pepper. Shape the meat into six 6-ounce patties. Chill in the refrigerator if not using right away.
- Light the grill 30 to 40 minutes before cooking and remove pork burgers from the refrigerator to come to room temperature (if you made them in advance).
- When the coals are broken down, red, and glowing, brush the pork burgers with olive oil and grill them 3 to 4 minutes on the first side, until they're nicely browned. Turn the burgers over, and place a piece of cheese on each one. Cook another 3 minutes or so, until the pork is cooked through. (It should still be slightly pink in the center.)
- Slice the buns in half, brush them with olive oil, and toast them on the grill, cut side down, for a minute or so, until they're lightly browned.
- Spread both sides of the buns and the aioli. Place a burger on the bottom half of each bun, and dollop with a generous amount of romesco. Place some arugula leaves on top, and finish with the top half of the bun.
- For the aioli and the romesco:
- For the aioli: Place the yolk in a stainless steel bowl. Begin whisking in the grapeseed oil drop by drop. Once the mixture has thickened and emulsified, you can whisk in the remaining grapeseed and olive oils in a slow steady stream. If the mixture gets too thick, add a drop or two of water.
- Pound the garlic with 1/4 teaspoon salt with a mortar and pestle. Whisk the garlic paste into the aioli. Season with 1/4 teaspoon salt, a squeeze of lemon juice, and the cayenne. Taste for balance and seasoning. If the aioli seems thick and gloppy, thin it with a little water. In addition to thinning the aioli, this will also make it creamier.
- For romesco: Preheat the oven to 375° F. Remove and discard the stems and seeds from the chiles, and then soak them in warm water for 15 minutes to soften. Strain the chiles, and pat dry with paper towels.
- Meanwhile, spread the nuts on a baking sheet and toast for 8 to 10 minutes, until they smell nutty and are golden brown.
- Heat a large sauté pan over high heat for 2 minutes. Add 2 tablespoons olive oil and wait a minute. Fry the slice of bread on both sides until golden brown. Remove the bread from the pan and cool. Cut it into 1-inch cubes and set aside.
- Return the pan to the stove over high heat. Add 2 tablespoons olive oil and the chiles and sauté for a minute or two. Add the tomatoes. Season with 1/2 teaspoon salt and cook 2 to 3 minutes, stirring often, until the tomato juices have evaporated and the tomato starts to color slightly. Turn off the heat, and leave the mixture in the pan.
- In a food processor, pulse together the toasted nuts, garlic, and fried bread until the bread and nuts are coarsely ground. Add the chile-tomato mixture and process for a minute more.

- With the machine running, slowly pour in the remaining 1 cup olive oil and process until you have a smooth purée. Don't worry, the romesco will "break" or separate into solids and oil; this is normal. Add the parsley, and season to taste with lemon juice and more salt if you like.

325. Suzhou Style Mooncakes

Serving: Makes 12 | Prep: | Cook: | Ready in:

Ingredients

- For the water and lard doughs:
- For the water dough
- 1 1/2 cups all-purpose flour
- 2 tablespoons sugar
- 1/3 to 1/2 cups cold water
- 1 egg, beaten
- 20 grams lard
- For the lard dough
- 1 cup plus 2 tablespoons all-purpose flour
- 100 grams lard
- For the pork filling:
- 250 grams lean ground pork
- 2 tablespoons finely chopped scallions
- 1/2 teaspoon salt
- 1/2 teaspoon minced fresh ginger
- 1/4 teaspoon dashi powder (optional)
- 1.5 teaspoons cornstarch
- 1 tablespoon light soy sauce
- 1/2 tablespoon sugar
- 1 dash white pepper
- 1 tablespoon sesame oil
- 1 teaspoon Shaoxing wine

Direction

- Combine meat ingredients and shape into 12 balls. Cover lightly with cling wrap and place in the fridge to firm up.
- For the water dough, mix all of the ingredients together and knead until very smooth. Add water or flour as needed. The dough should be soft with no lumps. Divide into 12 balls. Set on table, cover with cling wrap, and let rest for 30 minutes.
- For the lard dough, mix all of the ingredients together until they form a dough. Divide into 12 balls. Cover in cling wrap and set aside. The lard dough will be much drier, yet still oily. It'll almost flake apart but it should hold together.
- Roll the hybrid ball of dough into a long, thin oval. Then roll it into a log, widthwise.
- Repeat with the remaining 11 balls of dough, making sure to keep the finished logs under cling wrap to prevent drying out. Let the logs rest for 20 minutes.
- Take one log and press your finger down the middle so that the two edges bends upward. Now flatten this semicircle with your palm so that you see two spirals—the two flattened ends of the dough logs—along the surface. Use a rolling pin to roll the dough into a thin circle.
- Place one of the firm balls of meat inside the circle and bring the sides of dough up.
- Pleat and scrunch the edges of the dough together, making sure to press tightly to seal. Use scissors to cut off any excess dough. Flip the ball over and set it aside, covering it loosely with cling wrap to prevent drying out. Repeat with all of the logs of the dough and balls of meat.
- Heat a dry pan over low heat. Place the moon cake, their smooth sides up, in the pan. Once the bottoms are nicely browned, flip and continue to fry. The outer layer will start to split. Once both sides are golden brown, remove the moon cakes from the pan and serve hot.
- You can also bake the moon cakes: Preheat oven to 375° F, brush the moon cakes with an egg wash made from 1 egg beaten with a splash of water, and bake for 25 to 30 minutes, until golden brown.

326. Sweet & Savory "Vesper" Bread

Serving: Serves 1 | Prep: | Cook: | Ready in:

Ingredients

- 1 slice of your favorite bread
- unsalted, high butterfat butter
- your favorite honey
- Brie or Camembert, white rind removed
- 2 slices ham

Direction

- Warm, but do not toast your slice of bread.
- Slather it with a little butter, and then top with a little honey.
- Smear the brie cheese on top and cover with some sliced ham.
- Enjoy the melting of flavors in your mouth. (You can slice it in half and fold it over like a sandwich if it's easier to eat than open-faced)

327. Sweet & Sour Pineapple Spareribs

Serving: Serves 4 | Prep: | Cook: | Ready in:

Ingredients

- 2 pounds spareribs, "chinese" cut
- 4 cloves garlic
- 1/3 cup soy sauce
- 6 tablespoons sugar
- 1/4 cup rice vinegar
- 1/2 teaspoon salt
- 1 tablespoon vegetable or peanut oil
- 1 tablespoon cornstarch
- 1 can pineapple chunks, drained

Direction

- Combine soy sauce, sugar, vinegar and salt. Set aside.

- In a medium saucepan, heat spareribs and 1 c water. Boil then simmer for 20 minutes (longer if chunks are large). Drain spareribs.
- In a clean pan, heat oil. Add garlic and spareribs. Fry for a few minutes. Add soy sauce mixture. Cook on low heat for 25 minutes.
- Combine cornstarch and a little water. Add to spareribs and stir until sauce thickens. Garnish with pineapple chunks.

328. Sweet Potato, Pork, And Black Bean Stew With Prunes

Serving: Serves 6-8 | Prep: | Cook: | Ready in:

Ingredients

- 1 pound boneless pork loin or boneless chops
- 1 large sweet potato
- 1/4 cup packed chopped prunes
- 1 can black beans
- 2 slices bacon
- 1/2 medium onion
- ground black pepper

Direction

- In a large stock pot, fry the bacon until crisp (metal tongs help). Remove bacon, pour off all but 2 tablespoons of bacon fat (save that! It's liquid gold! Pour it into a ceramic or glass custard cup with a lid and stick it in the fridge).
- Cut the pork loin into cubes. Brown in the bacon fat. Remove pork loin from pot.
- Dice onion, and add to the pot with remaining bacon fat.
- Peel and cut sweet potato into bite-sized cubes.
- Chop cooked bacon and add with sweet potatoes, pork loin, prunes, and undrained beans to the stock pot.
- Add water to cover. Then add black pepper (at least a 1/8 teaspoon).

- Bring to a boil, then reduce heat and simmer until sweet potatoes are tender and flavors have combined.
- Serve hot with whatever starchy accompaniment you'd like.

329. Swiss Chard Quiche With Lardon And Lancashire

Serving: Serves 1 quiche | Prep: | Cook: | Ready in:

Ingredients

- 1 pie crust
- 1 tablespoon canola oil
- 1 tablespoon butter
- 1/2 onion, sliced
- 4 branches of swiss chards
- 2 cloves of garlic, thinly sliced
- 2 tablespoons white wine
- 1 cup lardon (thick bacon bits)
- 2 eggs
- 1/2 cup milk (low-fat is fine)
- 1/2 cup 15% cream
- salt and pepper
- 3/4 Lancashire or Monterrey Jack cheese

Direction

- Cut the Swiss chard: separate the leaves and the stems. Heat the canola oil and butter in a large skillet. Add the onion and the stems. Cook on medium heat until Swiss chard is tender.
- Add the garlic, the leaves, and the white wine. Cook for 5 minutes until liquid has evaporated. Drain the mixture if needed.
- Press the dough into a pie dish (9 po).Spread the Swiss chard and onions on the dough and toss lardon on top.
- In a bowl, whisk together cream, milk, eggs and season with salt and pepper. Pour the mixture over the Swiss chard and bacon.
- Sprinkle the grated cheese on top and bake on 350F for 30-35 minutes or until mixture is firm

and cheese is golden. Serve warm or cold with a salad.

330. Taiwanese Braised Minced Turkey/Pork Over Rice (滷肉飯 Lu Rou Fan)

Serving: Serves 4 | Prep: | Cook: | Ready in:

Ingredients

- 1 pound ground turkey or pork
- 1/2 cup fried shallots
- 4 cloves garlic, minced
- 1 teaspoon five-spice powder
- 1 teaspoon brown sugar
- 1/2 cup soy sauce
- 1 cup rice or shaoxing wine
- water
- 1 package pickled sour mustard, diced

Direction

- In a pan, heat oil to medium-high heat. Add pork and cook, stirring occasionally, until meat browns.
- Add garlic and fried shallots to the pan and cook until fragrant. Add the five-spice powder, sugar, soy sauces, rice wine, and just enough water to cover the meat. Then, bring to a boil. Reduce heat to a gentle simmer and cover partially. Cook until meat is completely tender and sauce has thickened, 3 to 4 hours. Add pickled sour mustard.
- Serve with steamed rice.

331. Tandoori Chicken Sausage

Serving: Makes 5 lbs of sausage | Prep: | Cook: | Ready in:

Ingredients

- 3.5 pounds chicken thigh meat, diced
- 1.5 pounds pork back fat, diced
- 2 onions, grated
- 2 tomatoes, grated
- 4 bay leaves
- 1 cinnamon stick
- 2 cardamon pods
- 5 cloves
- 1/2 tablespoon turmeric
- 2 tablespoons yogurt
- 1/2 tablespoon cayenne pepper
- 7 garlic cloves, minced
- 2 tablespoons grated ginger
- 2 serrano chiles
- 1 tablespoon garam masala
- 1 lime, juiced
- 40 grams of kosher salt
- 1/4 cup freshly chopped cilantro
- 3 tablespoons paprika
- 1 cup ice cold water
- 10 feet of hog casings

Direction

- First, you have to cook the masala. Heat some canola oil in a pot over medium heat and add the bay leaves, cinnamon stick, cardamom pods, and cloves. Allow the aromas to fill your kitchen and for the spices to toast a little. Add the grated onion and tomatoes. Season with salt and cook until nicely brown and caramelized, about 10 to 15 minutes. Add the turmeric and cayenne pepper and cook for another minute. Add the yogurt, garlic, ginger, serrano chiles, lime juice and garam masala. Cook the masala until it is completely dry and there is no visible moisture. This is key to ensuring your sausage becomes the correct texture. The finished masala should look like a seasoning paste.
- Take the masala off the heat and let cool to room temperature. If you add hot masala to the chicken, the chicken will cook, so make sure the masala is extremely cold before adding it to the diced chicken and pork fat.

Add cilantro and the salt to the chicken masala and let sit in the fridge overnight so everything gets really, really cold.
- Put the chicken mixture through the small die on a meat grinder. Once all is ground, put the mixture in the bowl of your kitchen aid and start the mixture with the paddle attachment. Slowly add in the water until the mixture becomes very sticky, about 1 minute.
- Put the hog casings on the tube of your sausage stuffer and stuff into one huge link. Then, twist the casing to create 6 inch links.
- Cook the sausages to 160 degrees either by grilling or roasting.
- I served mine with some yogurt, green chutney (cilantro, mint, jalapenos, lime juice, cumin, and water blended together), some sliced red onions, and lemons.

---

332.   Tantanmen

Serving: Serves 4 - 5 | Prep: | Cook: | Ready in:

Ingredients

- Sichuan Chili Oil
- 1 cup canola, grapeseed, or some other neutral flavored oil
- 4 large cloves garlic, peeled and lightly crushed
- 3 half inch thick slices fresh ginger
- 2 star anise
- 3 black cardamom pods
- 2 tsp fennel seeds
- 2 tbsp Sichuan peppercorns
- 1/4 cup coarse Korean pepper flakes
- Ramen Broth
- 3 quarts chicken stock (low sodium canned or boxed is fine)
- 2 lbs chicken wings or chicken thighs
- 1 3 inch long piece kombu (optional but recommended)
- Sesame Tare

- 1/4 cup roasted sesame paste (though tahini works too)
- 1/4 cup miso - white or yellow is milder, red more assertive and salty
- 2 tsp roasted sesame oil
- 1 tbsp Sichuan chili oil
- 2 tsp sugar
- 1 tbsp soy sauce
- 1 tsp fresh ginger, grated on a microplane
- Pork Topping
- 1 tbsp neutral oil
- 1 clove garlic peeled and minced
- 2 scallions, finely chopped
- 1 tsp fresh ginger, grated on a microplane
- 1 lb ground pork
- 2 tsp soy sauce
- 2 tbsp chicken stock (you can use a bit of the ramen stock)
- 1 tbsp chili broad bean paste (doubanjiang)
- Garnishes
- 3 scallions, finely chopped
- 4 baby bok choi, steamed until just cooked (4-5 minutes), then shocked in ice water
- Sichuan chili oil

Direction

- Chili oil instructions: Place the oil and all of the ingredients except for the chili flakes into a medium sized saucepan. Heat over medium low heat until the garlic is soft and beginning to turn golden and the end of a clean, dry bamboo chopstick placed in the oil creates tiny bubbles. While waiting for the oil to heat, put the chili flakes in a large, clean, dry heatproof jar. A Mason jar works well. Carefully strain the hot oil into the jar with the chili flakes. The oil will bubble up as it hits the chili (hence the large jar) and the chili will smell toasty. Set the oil aside to cool.
- Broth instructions: Put the stock, chicken, and kombu in a large pot over medium heat. Bring to a simmer, then turn down the heat to keep it there. Simmer for 2 - 3 hours, until the stock is reduced by 1/4. Strain the broth and discard the kombu and chicken parts. If you're using

chicken thighs, you can take the meat from the bones, cool it, and save it for another use.
- Tare instructions: Combine the tare ingredients and stir until combined into a thick paste.
- Pork topping instructions: Heat a skillet with the oil over medium high heat until the oil is nearly smoking. Add the garlic, ginger, and scallion and cook, stirring, until fragrant, about 20 seconds. Add the ground pork and cook until no pink remains, stirring and breaking the meat up into tiny pieces. Stir in the soy, stock, and chili bean paste, coating the meat completely.
- Assembly: Cook the ramen noodles according to package directions. Put 2 tbsp. of the tare in the bottom of 4 large bowls. Add a ladleful of hot broth and stir until smooth. Add more broth until the bowl is 1/3 to 1/2 full (depending on the amount of noodles you're using).Put the ramen in the bowls with the broth. Top with ground pork, scallions, and baby bok choy, and drizzle each bowl with a few teaspoons of the chili oil. Serve immediately.

---

333.   Tasty Tonjiru For 20 Under $10 Japanese Pork Hot Pot

Serving: Serves 20 | Prep: | Cook: | Ready in:

Ingredients

- Traditional Tonjiru
- 1.5 pound pork, (700 g) thinly sliced, see Note 1
- 12 cups water or vegetable soup stock
- 3 large carrots, scrubbed or peeled, sliced
- 2 gobo roots (burdock)
- 2 large onions, or leeks, peeled, thickly sliced
- 1 package konyaku or shirataki, see Note 2
- 1 pound satoh imo or russet potato or sweet potato, see Note 3

- ½ cup miso, blend (beige) or koji miso preferred. If using white miso, add salt to taste.
- Tasty Tonjiru Feast Version
- 3 cups daikon radish (about 9" long) bottom part, peeled
- 1 can bamboo, drained, sliced
- 2 aburage, (fried tofu)
- 1 package tofu, (try to find Morinaga brand) silk or not
- 1 bunch nira, Japanese chives, or spring onions, cut 1-inch pieces
- If budget permits, shiitake mushrooms, caps & stems chopped

Direction

- Thinly slice pork. Stack about 5 pieces at a time, and slice into pinkie-sized matchsticks. (Every bite of soup should have some pork in it.)
- In your largest soup pot bring half the water to a boil. Add pork, mixing so that the pieces don't stick together. Bring to a boil, and skim any scum off the top. When soup is clear, lower heat to low.
- Carrots can be cut thick julienned or in moon shapes. Scrub gobo burdock roots well (or peel). Have a large bowl of tap water ready. Slice burdock 1/4 inch on a diagonal or thick julienne. After every 5 or 6 slices, soak in the water. When all the burdock has been cut, drain, and replace water in bowl for soaking another 10 minutes. Slice onions. Drain burdock, add all veggies to soup.
- Cut shirataki into 2-inch strands. (Cut konyaku into matchsticks.) Pour a little boiling water over, then add to the soup pot.
- Add potatoes. Add the rest of the water. Bring to a boil, then simmer until potatoes are slightly falling apart.
- If using sato imo, the Traditional Tonjiru ends here, so go to Step12. If using other potatoes, might as well add other ingredients for the Feast Version.
- Slice daikon into 1 1/2 inch circles. Lay each circle flat, then cut in 6 slices. Stack half on

sides and cut to julienne. OR cut circles thinner, stack and cut like a pie. Add to the soup.
- Add bamboo. (If using, add shiitake mushrooms)
- Rinse aburage with boiling water (easy in microwave), drain, slice into half lengthwise, then slice into pinkie sizes. Add to soup.
- Smash tofu with a whisk or fork. Add to pot. Everything should be cooked at this point.
- Right before serving add nira or spring onions.
- Add miso to a big ladle. Smash miso with whisk, adding a little soup in top of the ladle. Pour off and keep adding soup water until miso has been totally mixed. Turn off heat.
- Note 1: Traditionally, a fatty cut of pork, like pork belly, is used but any cheap cut is fine. No time to cut, then ground pork works fine.
- Note 2: Shirataki or Konyaku are available in Asian markets, might be frozen.
- Note 3: Eliminate potatoes for low-glycemic/ low carb version. Sato imo is traditionally used but they cause an itchy reaction to my hands. Sweet potato is delicious but don't use more than 2 large ones.
- Note 4: If you can find a fresher version of cooked bamboo frozen, or in the vegetable section, it is worth it.

---

334. Tex Mex Braised Pork Stew

Serving: Serves 6 | Prep: | Cook: | Ready in:

Ingredients

- 3 pounds boneless pork shoulder (Boston Butt), cubed into bite size pieces
- 1 tablespoon olive oil
- 1 red onion, halved and sliced
- 2 large cloves garlic, minced
- 2 tablespoons cumin
- 2 teaspoons oregano
- 1 1/2 teaspoons chili powder

- 1/2 teaspoon salt
- 1/4 teaspoon black pepper
- 2 cups chicken broth
- 1 15-ounce can black beans, rinsed and drained
- 1 cup roasted, peeled and seeded hatch chilies, diced or one cup of canned mild-medium green chilies
- 1 cup corn off the cob, or frozen corn
- diced tomatoes
- diced avocado
- fresh cilantro leaves

Direction

- Preheat the oven to 325°.
- In a large Dutch oven, heat the olive oil over medium high heat. Add the pork and cook until browned. Add the garlic and onions, stir into the pork, cover and simmer for 3-4 minutes until tender. Add the cumin, oregano, chili powder, salt, pepper, chicken broth, black beans and chilies. Stir to combine, cover tightly with lid and place in the oven.
- Cook for 2 1/2-3 hours until pork is tender. Stir in the corn and serve in bowls with tomatoes, avocado and cilantro to garnish.

335.   The BLT Benedict

Serving: Serves 2 to 4 depending on appetites | Prep: | Cook: | Ready in:

Ingredients

- The BLT Benedict
- 4 slices thick-cut bacon
- 4 eggs
- 2 English muffins, split
- 4 thick slices fresh tomato about the same size in diameter as the English muffins (editor's note: if not in season, you can leave them off!)
- Approximately two cups of a Spring lettuce mix
- The hollandaise (recipe follows)

- Eric Ripert's Blender Hollandaise
- 2 1/2 sticks butter
- 2 egg yolks
- 2 tablespoons fresh lemon juice
- 1/4 teaspoon salt and black pepper (more, to taste)
- 1/8 teaspoon cayenne pepper
- 1/2 teaspoon dry ground mustard
- A pinch of white pepper

Direction

- The BLT Benedict
- Preheat your oven to 400°F. Line a rimmed baking sheet with foil and lay the strips of bacon on it. Bake the bacon for 10 to 15 minutes until crispy. Remove the strips to paper toweling to drain.
- Start toasting your English muffin halves in the toaster. Poach your eggs in your favorite way. I have an egg poacher insert that sits atop a 10 inch sauté pan filled with water. I lightly spray the cups with oil and slip the eggs in and then cover with a lid. Bring the water in the sauté pan up to a boil and cook until the egg whites are set and the yolks are still runny.
- Set the toasted English muffin half on a plate and place a tomato slice and 1/4 of the lettuce mix over. Cut each bacon strip in half and lay two halves over the lettuce. Top with a poached egg and drizzle with the hollandaise.
- Eric Ripert's Blender Hollandaise
- Melt the butter on the stove or in the microwave until piping hot.
- Warm the blender bowl by filling with hot water and then emptying and drying the bowl.
- Add the egg yolks, lemon juice, cayenne, salt, white pepper and mustard and blend at medium speed. Slowly drizzle in the hot melted butter with the machine still running until emulsified.

336. The Crispiest Cutlets

Serving: Serves 4 | Prep: | Cook: |Ready in:

Ingredients

- 1 pound turkey, pork, or chicken cutlets, pounded to about 1/4 inch thick
- Kosher salt
- Freshly ground black pepper
- 2 cups flour
- 1-2 eggs, beaten
- 2 cups Panko breadcrumbs
- 1 cup canola or vegetable oil

Direction

- Lay meat out on a cutting board and sprinkle generously with salt and pepper on both sides.
- Dip cutlet in flour and shake off excess. Next, dip in egg mixture and let excess drip off. Lastly dip into breadcrumbs and make sure it's completely covered. Transfer back to cutting board. Repeat with remaining cutlets.
- In a large frying pan, heat oil over medium-high heat until dropping a little bit of water causes it to sizzle. Add cutlets, working in batches if needed, and fry until crispy and brown (about 3-4 minutes). Flip and repeat on other side. Add more oil if needed before next batch.
- Transfer cooked cutlets to plate with paper towel to drain out some oil. Serve immediately.

337. The Legendary Ma Po Tofu

Serving: Serves 8 | Prep: | Cook: |Ready in:

Ingredients

- 1 pound ground pork
- 1 tablespoon wine (for marinating meat)
- 3 tablespoons soy sauce (for marinating meat)
- 1/2 teaspoon sugar (for marinating meat)
- 1/4 teaspoon black pepper (for marinating meat)
- 1 teaspoon sesame oil (for marinating meat)
- 1 1/2 tablespoons cornstarch (for marinating meat)
- 3 tablespoons vegetable oil
- 2 boxes of tofu (regular or silken)
- 3 garlic cloves
- 4 green onions (chopped – separate white and green parts)
- 6 tablespoons soy sauce (for sauce)
- 1 tablespoon cornstarch (for sauce)
- 1 tablespoon hot sauce (for sauce - Chinese black bean chili sauce in a jar is preferred, regular chili sauce is okay. This can be omitted or can be increased)
- 1/2 teaspoon sesame oil
- 1/2 teaspoon black pepper

Direction

- Marinate pork with wine, soy sauce, sugar, pepper, sesame oil, and cornstarch.
- Heat oil in large frying pan. Sauté garlic and white part of green onion in oil for less than 1 minute.
- Stir fry the marinated ground pork for 5-6 minutes. You may cover 1-2 times to steam the pork. Do not add any water. Open the cover to stir-fry the pork continuously until done.
- Add diced tofu, stir gently, and cover for 3 minutes with medium temperature to simply "warm up" the tofu. Open the cover, mix and stir gently, tofu will be little mashed, which is okay.
- Mix soy sauce, cornstarch, hot sauce and pour over the tofu/meat in the pot. Stir gently and quickly with high heat until the sauce is thickened. Taste and adjust seasoning – add more soy, salt, pepper, or hot sauce as needed.
- Remove to a large bowl. Sprinkle with ½ ts sesame oil, ½ tsp black pepper and the green part of the chopped onion.
- Serve hot with white rice. Enjoy!

338. The Recipe Critic's Creamy Garlic Pork Marsala

Serving: Serves 4 to 6 | Prep: 0hours10mins | Cook: 0hours20mins | Ready in:

Ingredients

- 1 package Smithfield Roasted Garlic and Herb Marinated Fresh Pork Loin
- 1 tablespoon olive oil
- 8 ounces sliced mushrooms
- 3 garlic cloves, minced
- 3/4 cup Marsala wine
- 1 cup chicken broth
- 1 1/4 cups heavy cream
- 1 teaspoon ground mustard
- 1 teaspoon garlic powder
- 1 teaspoon cornstarch
- 1 handful fresh parsley, chopped

Direction

- Start by cutting your pork loin filet into about 1-inch cubes. In a medium-size skillet over medium-high heat, add the olive oil and pork cubes. Cook 3 to 4 minutes on each side, until pork is brown and cooked throughout. Remove and set aside on a plate.
- Add the minced garlic and mushrooms to the skillet and cook for 2 to 3 minutes or until tender. Set aside on the plate with the pork.
- Add the chicken broth and Marsala wine, bring to a boil, and allow it to deglaze for about 1 to 2 minutes. Add in the heavy cream, ground mustard, and garlic powder. Add in a cornstarch slurry (mix the cornstarch with 2 tablespoons water in a small bowl) by pouring into the sauce. Let simmer until thick for about 5 to 7 minutes.
- Put the pork and mushrooms back into the sauce and heat through. Serve over rice, noodles, or mashed potatoes.

339. Three Cheese Monte Cristos

Serving: Serves 4 | Prep: | Cook: | Ready in:

Ingredients

- 1 cup flour
- 1 tablespoon sugar
- 1/2 teaspoon salt
- 2 teaspoons baking powder
- 2 tablespoons melted butter
- 1 egg
- 1 cup milk
- 8 slices Gouda cheese
- 8 slices gruyere cheese
- 1/2 cup parmesan cheese
- 8 slices thin deli turkey
- 8 slices thin deli ham
- 8 slices thick white (French toast) bread
- Dijon mustard
- butter for griddle

Direction

- Mix together the first 4 ingredients. In a separate bowl, whisk together butter, egg, and milk. Add dry ingredients to wet, and stir until flour is dampened. Set aside.
- For each sandwich, spread one slice bread with mustard, and layer with (in following order) 2 slices gruyere, 2 slices ham, sprinkle parmesan, 2 slices turkey, ground pepper, 2 slices gouda, other piece of bread. Repeat for all 4 sandwiches.
- Heat butter in skillet or griddle to medium heat.
- Pour half of batter in shallow dish, and for each sandwich, dip in batter in shallow dish, and pour batter over top to coat. Grill each sandwich- about 2-3 minutes on each side until batter is golden brown and cheese is melted.
- Serve dusted with powdered sugar.

340. Three Meat Tomato Sauce

Serving: Makes 1 big pot | Prep: | Cook: | Ready in:

Ingredients

- for the meatballs
- 1/2 pound ground beef (85/15)
- 1/2 pound ground pork
- 2 large eggs
- 3/4 cup bread crumbs
- 1/2 cup Parmesan (grated)
- 1 tablespoon Dijon mustard
- 1 tablespoon Worcestershire sauce
- 3 cloves garlic (minced)
- 2 tablespoons dried shallots or 1 tsp onion powder
- a few pinches crushed red pepper flakes
- salt and pepper
- for the rest of the sauce
- 3/4 pound hot Italian sausage (removed from casing)
- 1 pound boneless, skinless chicken breast (cubed)
- 1 yellow onion (diced)
- 6 cloves garlic (minced)
- 2 tablespoons tomato paste
- 3/4 cup dry red wine
- 1 28 ounces can crushed tomatoes
- 1 28 ounces can whole peeled tomatoes
- 1 14.5 ounces can fire roasted tomatoes
- 2 tablespoons dried oregano
- 3 bay leaves
- 1 teaspoon crushed red pepper flakes
- salt and pepper

Direction

- Start by making the meatballs. Add all meatball ingredients in a mixing bowl and mix with hands until all ingredients are combined. Don't over mix, it will make the meatballs dense. Heat a Dutch oven or soup pot over medium-high heat with olive oil. Form meatballs and drop into the pot. Turn meatballs to cook on all sides, about 2 minutes per side. Remove from heat to a plate and set aside. Pro Tip: To make the meatballs extra delicious -- sauté the onions and garlic in olive oil before putting them in the meatballs.
- Add the chicken breast cubes and add salt and pepper. Let brown on all sides for about 8 minutes total. Remove from heat to a plate and set aside.
- Add Italian sausage and let cook only for about 4 minutes, breaking it up with a wooden spoon into small pieces. Lower heat to medium and add onions, garlic, salt, pepper, oregano and crushed red pepper flakes. Let cook for about 5 minutes, until onions are translucent.
- Add tomato paste and red wine. Bring to a simmer and let cook for about 5 minutes. Add all tomatoes, oregano, bay leaves, and a good amount of salt and pepper. Add chicken and meatballs back to the pot. Bring to a simmer. Lower heat and cover. Let simmer for 1 and a half hours.
- Serve with crusty bread or over pasta.

341. Tiny Meatballs

Serving: Serves 15 | Prep: 0hours30mins | Cook: 3hours0mins | Ready in:

Ingredients

- Tiny Meatballs
- 1/2 cup parsley, finely chopped
- 1/2 cup basil, finely chopped
- 1/2 head of garlic, finely chopped
- 1/2 cup breadcrumbs
- 1/2 cup ricotta
- 1/2 teaspoon nutmeg
- 4 egg yolks
- 1 teaspoon salt
- 1 teaspoon pepper
- 1/2 teaspoon cayenne
- 2 pounds italian sausage, uncased.
- Kat's Marinara

- 2 28 oz can's whole peeled tomatoes
- 1 vidalia onion, cut in 8ths
- 1 stick of salted butter
- 1/2 teaspoon salt
- 2 bay leaves
- 1/2 head of garlic, peeled
- 1 cup broth (I like the bone broth)
- 2 dried chile's
- 1 teaspoon peppercorns
- 4 sprigs parsley and basil
- 1/4 cup chopped parsley and basil
- 1/2 bottle of red wine (chianti, montepulciano, something lighter)

Direction

- So I threw my whole peppercorns, dried chile and herbs into my blender to combine them which to be honest didn't work, don't do that. Next time I will put the peppercorns and the chile in the spice grinder and finely dice the herbs and combine in a bowl with the breadcrumbs, salt, and nutmeg. "If you don't have a spice grinder, regular ground pepper and some cayenne or chile flakes are fine" in my best Ina Garten voice.
- In a much larger bowl, mixing with your hands, combine the uncased sausage with the egg yolks and the ricotta. Then add your herbs, spices, and breadcrumbs. Do a test cook on a dime sized piece of sausage mixture, to test your seasoning and adjust where you wish. On a large sheet tray shape your meatballs, I did mine in maybe the size of a quarter in diameter.
- I also coated my meatballs in cornstarch and fried them (3-5 minutes in a half inch of oil and then rolled them over for another 3 to 5 minutes) and then kept them overnight to use in my sauce the next day. This made about 110 meatballs, you totally could halve this recipe, this many meatballs was 12-14 servings.
- In a big (preferably cast iron) pot heat two tablespoons of olive oil and toss in the onion followed by the garlic cloves to release their aromatics, put everything else in the pot, bring it to a boil, reduce to a simmer, cook for two

hours stirring occasionally. You will probably need to add more salt.
- If you want a heartier chunkier sauce you can really just use a wooden spoon to break up the tomatoes and the garlic, if you choose this method I would use cracked pepper instead of whole peppercorns, for a smooth sauce throw the whole cooked down mixture in the blender, make sure you dig out the bay leaves. I added the chopped herbs after pureeing to give my sauce some more color. If you're serving this with your meatballs add them in to heat the meatballs up again, serve with fettuccini or a big rigatoni and parmesan.

---

342. Tostadas De Jamón Ibérico

Serving: Serves 2-3 | Prep: | Cook: | Ready in:

Ingredients

- 1 large sliced tomato
- 6 crusty slices of bread
- 3 tablespoons exra virgin olive oil
- 4.25 ounces jamón ibérico
- 2 cloves raw garlic
- 1 pinch coarse salt

Direction

- Toast the pieces of bread and vigorously rub raw garlic on the slices while they are still hot.
- Drizzle extra virgin olive oil over each toasted bread.
- Top each toast with freshly sliced tomato.
- Sprinkle the tomatoes with coarse salt.
- To finish them, cover the tomatoes with the jamón.

343. Tourtiere For A Cold Winter's Day

Serving: Serves 8 | Prep: | Cook: |Ready in:

Ingredients

- The Crust
- 250 grams all-purpose flour
- 225 grams (2 sticks) salted butter
- 1/4 cup cold water
- 1 egg, beaten
- The FIlling
- 2 tablespoons vegetable oil
- 1 medium onion
- 1 large apple
- 1 pound ground pork
- 2 tablespoons fresh sage
- 1/2 teaspoon freshly grated nutmeg
- 1 1/2 teaspoons salt
- 1/2 teaspoon freshly ground black pepper
- 1/2 cup breadcrumbs
- 1 cup water

Direction

- Start your pastry. Cut the butter into the flour (I like to use my trusty pastry blender, but I imagine the food processor would work just fine, too). Once the mixture is crumbly, rub the butter in with your hands a bit, just to make sure it's really smeared into the flour. This will help it get super flaky later on.
- Once the mixture is like wet sand, add the 1/4 cup cold water and stir everything together with a fork until it forms a ball of dough. A lot of pastry recipes warn against overmixing the dough, but I haven't had any problems with this one. There's such a high butter-to-flour ratio that you'll be fine. Put the dough in the fridge for 20-30 minutes.
- In the meantime, gather the ingredients for your filling. Chop up the apple and onion pretty small so they'll blend into the pork later on. Chop the sage as small as possible so it gets distributed throughout the filling.
- Start sautéing the onions and apples in a little bit of vegetable oil, then get going on the next step of the pastry.
- Pull the dough out of the fridge and roll it out into a long, thin rectangle (just a few rolls of the pin should do). Then, fold the dough in on itself in thirds, like you would fold a letter to fit in an envelope. Turn the new rectangle 90 degrees and repeat the process a few times, rolling into a rectangle, folding, and turning. This is what gives you millions of little tiny layers later on. I think I did it 3 or 4 times. It only takes a few minutes. Once you're done, divide the dough into two even rounds and put back in the fridge.
- Once the onions and apples have softened, pull them out and set aside in a bowl. Add a little more oil and brown the pork. Add the sage, nutmeg, salt, and pepper and mix thoroughly. Add the onions and apples back to the pan, along with the breadcrumbs and water, and simmer the whole mixture for 20 minutes or so.
- Preheat your oven to 400 degrees once the pork is simmering.
- When the pork is almost done, pull out your dough one last time. Roll out one round to a couple inches wider than your pie pan and drape it in, leaving some pastry hanging over the edges. Add the filling, then top with the remaining round of dough, rolled out to the same size. Crimp the edges and cut some slits in the top to let out steam. Brush the egg wash on the top of the pie.
- Bake for 30-40 minutes, until golden brown on top. Let cool for 20-30 minutes before slicing.

344. Tuscan Turkey Roulade

Serving: Serves 4-5 | Prep: | Cook: |Ready in:

Ingredients

- 1 Boneless turkey breast, skin removed
- 4 cups sliced onions

- 2 tablespoons fresh rosemary leaves
- 1 tablespoon fennel seeds
- 1/2 cup dry white wine, more as needed
- 1/2 pound pork sausage (for example, sweet Italian)
- salt and black pepper

Direction

- Butterfly and flatten turkey breast with a meat mallet. You want it flat enough to roll.
- Spread sausage over the flattened turkey. Sprinkle rosemary leaves over the sausage. Tightly roll up the turkey and tie securely with kitchen/butcher's twine. Lightly sprinkle the roulade with salt and pepper. Set aside.
- Place sliced onions in a baking pan. Sprinkle with fennel seeds and 1 teaspoon of salt. Put turkey roulade on top of the onion bed. Add white wine to the pan.
- Bake in a 375°F oven until the internal temperature reaches about 160°F. This usually takes about an hour or so. Add more wine if the onions start to dry out and burn.
- Let the roulade rest for at least 10 minutes before slicing. Don't forget to remove the string. Serve with braised onions, spooned over the slices.
- Variation: this can be made with chicken breasts. Note: if you don't have fennel seeds, you can use fresh sliced fennel bulb. Please do not use dried rosemary. Omit if you don't have fresh rosemary.

---

345. Vietnamese Egg Rolls (Cha Gio)

Serving: Serves 2 | Prep: 0hours30mins | Cook: 0hours10mins | Ready in:

Ingredients

- 2 eggs
- 1/2 cup wood ear mushroom
- 1 cup ground pork
- 1/2 taro
- 1 tablespoon pepper
- 1 teaspoon salt
- rice papers

Direction

- Step 1: Make the filling 1. Finely shred wood ear mushroom, carrot and taro. 2. Beat the egg and separate the yolk from the white. Save both for later. 3. Mix together ground pork, taro, egg yolk and carrot in a bowl. Add peppers and salt and marinate them in 10 minutes by hands until perfectly mingled.
- Step 2: Wrap the rolls 1. Place a rice paper on a dry, flat surface. Rotate it a bit so you look at it in a diamond shape. 2. Use a pastry brush or simply your fingers to brush egg whites all over the wrapper. This helps soften its texture for easier rolling. 3. Scoop a tablespoon of filling near the bottom of the nearest corner to you. Lift the bottom up and start rolling until it covers up all the filling. 4. Fold over the left side and the right side one after another, towards the center. Remember to pull both sides tightly, but not too tight, because the paper could be torn into small holes (which will make it messy once you bring your rolls to fry). 5. Keep folding it up to the other corner, and carefully tuck the wrapper as you're rolling to keep it tight enough. 6. Once finished, lay it side down and let chill. The seam will seal itself as the egg white wash begins to dry.
- Step 3: Fry 1. Fill the frying pan with an inch of high-heat cooking oil. Heat the oil to 350°F (175°C). 2. Gently slide the raw egg rolls in, seam-side down. Fry each side for 2 minutes and keep turning occasionally until they're golden brown and crispy. 3. Put them out on wire rack or paper towels to drain oil.
- Step 4: Serve. Serve the rolls onto plate immediately when they're still hot. Occasionally, put on some slices of cucumber and tomato for an appealing display.

346. Vietnamese Meatball Sandwiches

Serving: Serves 6 | Prep: | Cook: | Ready in:

Ingredients

- Meatballs
- Ground Pork
- Panko Bread Crumbs
- Shallots
- Scallions
- Salt
- Black Pepper
- Fish Sauce
- Lime Juice
- Sugar
- Quick Pickles
- Cucumbers
- Radishes
- Salt
- Rice Wine Vinegar
- Thai Chili
- Sugar

Direction

- Meatballs
- Mince scallions and shallots.
- Combine all ingredients thoroughly
- Quick Pickles
- Thinly slice vegetables
- Salt and drain vegetables for at least 30 minutes.
- Rinse and purge vegetables and combine with other ingredients. Let stand for 20 minutes.

347. Waiting For Bonaparte Muffaletta (The Remix Edition)

Serving: Serves an army | Prep: | Cook: | Ready in:

Ingredients

- For the olive salad:
- 1/2 cup Spanish pimento olives
- 1/2 cup pitted black olives (Kalamatas work fine)
- 4 to 6 cornichons
- 2 cloves garlic (see note below)
- 2 teaspoons dried Italian oregano
- 1/2 cup extra-virgin olive oil
- 2 tablespoons red wine vinegar
- 1/4 teaspoon ground black pepper
- For the sandwich components:
- one 6-ounce crusty Italian roll
- A little creole mustard
- 1/4 pound thinly sliced premium cooked or cured ham (even prosciutto or jamon Serrano)
- 1/4 pound thinly sliced capicola (as the name suggests, this is most often made from pig neck)
- 1/4 pound sliced provolone cheese

Direction

- It's easy to make the olive salad in the bowl of a food processor using the olives, cornichons, garlic, oregano, olive oil, vinegar, and black pepper. Give everything a few quick pulses. It should remain a bit chunky -- somewhat coarser than a tapenade.
- Spoon the olive salad into a non-reactive bowl and cover it with cling wrap. It should then go into the refrigerator to rest for at least 5 to 8 hours, and it will keep overnight.
- To assemble, use a sharp bread knife to divide the loaf into two halves horizontally like a giant hamburger bun. Smear some mustard on the bottom half and top with ham, capicola, provolone, and a generous amount of olive salad. Cover with the top portion of the roll and divide into halves or quarters. Bring napkins.
- Notes to the cook: For the garlic, I use a "garlic confit". What that consists of is about 40 peeled cloves of garlic covered in canola oil and poached for about forty minutes -- a flame tamer is advised. Store the garlic and oil in a

sealed container in the refrigerator. After a few days the oil will be highly perfumed. I think the little Corsican would like that touch. It's handy to have on hand and you can add a little of the oil to the salad. Otherwise, use fresh garlic cloves.

- The cornichon included in the olive salad is untraditional but one of my New Orleans friends really liked it, so I think it really works. Don't be stingy with the olive salad.

348. Warm Lentil Salad With Sausage And Potatoes Salade De Lentilles À La Lyonnaise

Serving: Serves 4 | Prep: | Cook: |Ready in:

Ingredients

- 9 ounces Green lentils, preferably "Lentils du Puy"
- 1 onion studded with a clove and 3 black peppercorns
- 1 bouquet garni (3 sprigs of thyme, 3 sprigs of parsley and 1 bay leaf)
- 18 ounces pork Lyon Sausage or dry sausage
- 2 medium potatoes
- Parsley leaves for decoration
- Fleur de Sel for finishing touch
- 6 tablespoons Extra Virgin Olive Oil
- 2 tablespoons Cider vinegar
- salt
- pepper

Direction

- Make the bouquet garni by making a bundle with 3 sprigs of thyme, 3 sprigs of parsley and 1 bay leaf tied with kitchen string.
- Pick through and wash the green lentils and cook in a large pot with 8 cups of water. Bring to a boil and cook for 5 minutes.
- Drain. Put back in the pot with the onion with the clove and the bouquet garni. Cover with boiling water, bring to a boil, cover with lid,

allow to simmer for 15 minutes (for cooking time please check the instructions in your package). Season with salt and cook 3 minutes more covered with lid.

- Wash the potatoes thoroughly leaving them whole with skin on.
- Prick the sausage piercing the skin.
- Bring a pot with water to a boil and add the potatoes with the skin and the pork sausage and allow to cook at medium low heat until potatoes are cooked through.
- Make a vinaigrette sauce by whisking together the olive oil, the vinegar, salt and pepper.
- Peel the potatoes and cut in slices or in cubes (this depends how rustic or modern you want to serve the dish). While still hot, drizzle with some vinaigrette.
- Peel the sausage and cut in slices or in cubes.
- Drain the lentils and season with some vinaigrette. Check seasoning and keep warm.
- Serve still warm.
- For a rustic presentation put the lentils in a serving dish with potato slices and sausage slices and sprinkle with some parsley.
- For a modern presentation, put on the center of the plate some lentils, potatoes and sausage pieces, drizzle a little olive oil, sprinkle some Fleur de Sel and garnish with a parsley leaf.

349. Warming Red Pozole

Serving: Serves 10 to 12 | Prep: | Cook: |Ready in:

Ingredients

- 4 dried New Mexico chiles, stems and seeds removed
- 1 tablespoon olive oil
- 1 large onion, coarsely chopped
- 6 cloves of garlic, peeled
- 3 pounds pork shoulder or country style ribs, cut into 3/4-inch cubes
- 2 teaspoons cumin
- Salt and pepper

- 2 cups chicken stock
- 1 teaspoon dried oregano
- 2 cans hominy, drained and rinsed
- Water
- Cabbage, shredded finely
- Radishes, sliced thinly
- Limes, quartered for squeezing
- Avocado, cut into small chunks
- Tortilla chips or corn tortillas
- Cilantro, coarsely chopped
- Crumbled queso fresco or your cheese of choice

Direction

- Toast chiles in a dry pan over high heat for a few minutes until slightly browned. As you heat them, they should puff up, soften, and become fragrant. Remove from pan, let cool, and cut or tear roughly. Pour 1 cup boiling water over them to soften them for 15 minutes.
- Add oil to a large, heavy pot and turn the flame to medium high. Add onions and garlic and sauté until onions have soften and colored. Remove from heat.
- Add onions and garlic to a blender with the chiles and their liquid. Purée until smooth.
- Put pot back on high heat and brown the pork in two batches. Add 1 teaspoon cumin, salt, and pepper to each batch as the pieces brown. Add all pork back to pot along with chile liquid, chicken stock, oregano, and hominy. The liquid should completely cover the pork. Add water or more stock if necessary. Bring to boil then lower to simmer. Taste for seasoning and add more salt, pepper, or cumin to suit your taste. Cover the pot and cook the stew over low heat for 2 hours.
- While the pozole cooks, get toppings ready.
- To serve: Ladle pozole into bowl. Top with cabbage, radishes, and any other toppings. Squeeze a healthy dose of lime juice into your bowl and dig in!

350. White Bean And Cabbage Soup

Serving: Makes 3 to 4 quarts | Prep: | Cook: | Ready in:

Ingredients

- 1 meaty ham bone (or ham shank)
- 1/2 pound dried Great Northern beans
- 3 tablespoons olive oil
- 1 cup diced onion
- 3 cloves minced garlic
- 2 large carrots sliced into thin rounds
- 1/4 to 1/2 teaspoons crushed red pepper flakes
- 1 bay leaf
- 4 cups chicken broth (and up to 2 cups more)
- 1/2 head small cabbage, chopped
- Salt and pepper to taste

Direction

- Soak the beans overnight in water and then the next day, change the water and bring them up to a boil in a medium sauce pan and then simmer for about 45 minutes until tender. Save about 2 cups of the bean broth.
- Place the ham bone or shank in a large soup pot and cover with about 4 quarts of water. Bring to a boil and then simmer for 45 minutes to an hour. Remove the bone, cool a bit and then pick off the meat and reserve. Save the ham broth.
- Sauté the onion, carrot and garlic in the olive oil until softened in a large soup pot.
- Add the bay leaf and crushed red pepper and give everything a good stir.
- Add the bean, ham and chicken broths to the pot, bring up to the boil and then simmer for about 20 minutes.
- Add the cooked beans and reserved ham bits and bring back up to the boil. Add the chopped cabbage and simmer another 15 to 20 minutes. If you'd like your soup "soupier" add the extra 2 cups of chicken broth at this time. Season to taste with salt and pepper.

351. Wholesome Pea & Ham Soup

Serving: Serves 8 | Prep: | Cook: | Ready in:

Ingredients

- 1 smoked ham hock, skin removed
- 1 leek
- 8 peppercorns
- 3 bay leaves
- 1 zucchini
- a splashes olive oil
- 2 carrots, diced
- 1 1/2 cups pumpkin, diced
- 2 cloves garlic, sliced
- 2 1/2 cups dried green split peas
- a handfuls parsley, chopped
- Sea salt & freshly cracked pepper

Direction

- To prep your leek, cut the green part off and wash well, reserve the white part.
- In a large pot add ham hock, green part of leak, peppercorns, bay leaves, zucchini and fill the pot with cold water until three quarters full. Bring to the boil then simmer for almost 2 hours.
- Take it off the heat and let it cool. Once cooled put it in the fridge overnight.
- The following day, remove the soup from the fridge, remove all of the solidified fat off the top of stock using a spoon. Discard fat. Put on a high heat to melt the jellied stock.
- Meanwhile dice the white part of the leek.
- Take ham hock out of the stock, let it cool, then pull apart and chop the meat. Set aside.
- Strain stock through a fine sieve into another large pot, this will ensure no grit is in the stock from the green park of the leek.
- Bring sieved stock to the boil then add leek, carrots, celery, pumpkin, garlic, split peas, parsley and season. Reduce to a simmer stirring occasionally so the peas don't stick to

bottom. Return the pork. Add boiled water if it gets too thick. Simmer until dried peas are soft.

352. Yum Dogs

Serving: Makes 6 dogs | Prep: | Cook: | Ready in:

Ingredients

- Bean Sprout Slaw
- 1 pound (approximatey 4 big handfuls) bean sprouts
- 2 teaspoons kosher salt
- 1 large carrot, grated on the large holes of a box grater
- 1 small red onion, very thinly sliced
- 1 jalapeño pepper, seeds and ribs removed, very thinly sliced (keep some of the ribs and seeds if you'd like your slaw a little spicier)
- 1/2 cup roughly chopped cilantro
- 1/3 cup rice wine vinegar
- 1 tablespoon sugar
- 1/2 teaspoon freshly ground black pepper
- Yum Dogs
- 1/2 cup mayonnaise or aioli
- 2 tablespoons Sriracha
- 6 good quality hot dogs of choice (I use a very juicy organic chicken dog)
- 6 slices good quality bacon of choice (I have found maple bacon particularly luscious)
- 6 hot dog buns or rolls, preferably ones that are large and sturdy
- 4 scallions, thinly sliced
- 1/2 cup roasted, salted peanuts, roughly chopped

Direction

- Bean Sprout Slaw
- In a large colander, thoroughly wash the bean sprouts, then shake off the excess water. Set the colander over a bowl or in the sink. Toss the salt with the bean sprouts to distribute evenly, then let the liquid drain from the

sprouts, turning them periodically. Let the sprouts drain for at least 30 minutes. Their volume should decrease significantly.

- In a large bowl, combine the sprouts and the rest of the ingredients. Adjust seasoning as necessary. Keep refrigerated until ready to use.
- Yum Dogs
- Combine the mayonnaise and Sriracha and keep covered in the refrigerator until ready for use.
- Heat a cast iron skillet over medium heat. Score each hot dog a few times. Wrap each hot dog in a slice of bacon, starting at one end and corkscrewing it around to the other. If you find the bacon isn't adhering, you can use a wooden toothpick to pin it to the ends of hot dog.
- Cook the dogs, rotating to cook the bacon thoroughly on all sides. Depending on the thickness of your meats, this will probably take 2-4 minutes on each side. Transfer the hot dogs to a newspaper- or paper towel-lined platter. If you used toothpicks, remove them.
- Depending on the size or density of your buns (tee hee hee), you might need to hollow them out a little or not. Spread each bun generously with the Sriracha mayonnaise, then fill them with the Bean Sprout Slaw (I use tongs to gently squeeze out excess liquid).
- Place the dogs on the slaw and top with scallions and peanuts. Then open wide! It's a mouthful!

---

353.   Zucchini Farci With Nepalese Minced Pork Curry

Serving: Serves 4 | Prep: | Cook: |Ready in:

Ingredients

- 4 pieces round or normal medium sized zucchinis
- 400 grams minced pork
- 1 cup pine nuts
- 1 tablespoon olive oil
- 2 tablespoons yellow mustard seeds
- 1 teaspoon cumin seeds
- 1 teaspoon coriander seeds
- 1/2 teaspoon coriander powder
- 1 teaspoon ground cumin
- 1/2 teaspoon ground turmeric
- 3 pieces garlic clove (crushed)
- 2 tablespoons fresh grated ginger
- 1 cup finely chopped onion
- 1/4 cup water
- 1 cup fresh coriander, coarsely chopped
- 1/4 cup mint leaves, coarsely chopped
- 4 pieces lime wedges
- Cooking oil e.g. olive oil or grapeseed oil

Direction

- Wash the zucchinis and trim of the ends. Cut the zucchinis tops and keep them for use as a cover, scoop out the seeds with a spoon. Rub the inside and outside of the zucchinis with olive oil. Set aside.
- Toast the pine nuts by tossing them in a small pan at medium high heat until they turn golden brown. Transfer the nuts to a small bowl and set aside.
- Heat a little oil in a pan, add in the mustard seeds, cumin seeds and coriander seeds, stir fry for about 2 mins., when the seeds start popping, add in the cumin, turmeric, and garam masala and stir fry for another 2 mins until you smell the fragrance from the spices.
- Add the garlic, ginger and onion to the curry mix, sauté until the onion becomes translucent.
- Add in the minced pork and continue to stir fry. Pour in the water, bring to boil and turn to medium heat and simmer for about 15 mins, until the water is evaporated. In the meantime, preheat the oven at 350F.
- Season the minced pork with a little salt and stir in the pine nuts, coriander and mint. Turn off the heat.

- Spoon the pork curry into the zucchinis, place them in a baking tray and bake in the middle rack for about 15 mins.
- Serve with steamed plain rice and lime wedges. Alternatively, you can mix in camargue (red rice)

354. Chickpea Sauce And Sauage With Pasta

Serving: Serves 6 | Prep: | Cook: |Ready in:

Ingredients

- 2 chickpea cans (about a pound each, drained of water)
- 6 sweet onions - roughly chopped
- 1 pound italian sausage loose - not in casing
- 3 tablespoons olive oil
- spicy italian seasoning to taste
- salt and pepper
- 1 pound pasta such as ziti
- grated pecorino cheese

Direction

- Brown sausage in pan until most of pink is gone. Remove and set aside
- Add oil to same pan if there is not enough fat left from sausage and cook onions until very soft and just beginning to caramelize.
- Blend onions and one can of chickpeas in blender or food processor until smooth and return to pan. Add sausage and additional can of chickpeas and warm together for about ten minutes on medium to medium low heat add seasonings to taste
- Meanwhile pasta water should be boiling - add pasta and cook as directed. Save a cup of the pasta water. Add pasta to chickpeas /sausage mixture add reserved pasta water if appears dry add cheese and serve

355. Greens With Dates, Nuts & Harissa

Serving: Serves 2 | Prep: | Cook: |Ready in:

Ingredients

- for the salad:
- 2 cups kale, tough stems removed
- 2 cups romaine lettuce, roughly chopped
- 1 carrot
- 1/4 english cucumber
- 1 eggs, lightly beaten
- 3 dried dates
- 3 slices proscuitto
- 1/4 cup salted cashews
- for the harissa vinaigrette:
- 1 lemon, zested and juiced
- 4 tablespoons olive oil
- 1 tablespoon honey
- 1/2 teaspoon harissa
- 1/2 teaspoon kosher salt
- grind or two of black pepper

Direction

- In a small saucepan, cover an egg with cool water. Bring to a boil over high heat and cook for one minute. Remove the pan from heat and let the egg steep in the water for 10 minutes.
- Meanwhile, place kale on a cutting board and massage it for about 10-15 seconds until it softens and becomes fragrant. Roughly chop the kale and transfer it to a salad bowl. Add the romaine lettuce.
- Peel the carrot and use either a julienne scraper or a box grater to julienne/grate the carrot. Add to the lettuce.
- Slice dates in half lengthwise. Remove the pit, then dice the dates into small pieces and add to the salad.
- Either slice or tear the prosciutto into pieces and sprinkle over the salad. (Prosciutto tends to stick to itself, so it's better to separate the pieces in the salad to avoid getting one big ball of it on your plate.)

- Cut the English cucumber in half, lengthwise and then cut into 1/4" half-moon slices and transfer to the salad bowl.
- Drain the water from the pan, run the egg under cool water. Gently crack the shell and peel the shell from the egg. Slice the egg in half and set aside.
- Roughly chop cashews and sprinkle over the salad.
- In a small bowl combine the lemon zest and juice, olive oil, honey, harissa, salt and pepper. Whisk until well combined. Taste for seasonings -- if you like it sweeter, add honey. If you want more spice add harissa etc.
- Pour the dressing over the salad and toss. Place boiled egg on the salad to serve.

356.   Indiana's Treasure Tart

Serving: Serves 10-14 | Prep: | Cook: | Ready in:

Ingredients

- 10-12   phyllo dough sheets 14x18 inch
- 1/3 cup   olive oil
- 1/4 cup   plain bread crumbs
- 4 tablespoons   pesto,homemade or commercial
- 4 slices   bacon,chopped
- 1   onion,diced
- 2 tablespoons   garlic,diced
- 1/2-3/4 cups   crumbled gorgonzola
- 2-3   tomatoes,any kind,large
- to taste   salt,kosher if available
- to taste   ground black pepper
- 10 med   basil leaves juilianned

Direction

- Pre-heat oven 400 F
- Line large cookie baking sheet with parchment paper
- Chop bacon and fry till starting to crisp, about 5 min @med-hi setting. Add onion and sauté until just tender, about 5 minutes, add garlic for last minute of sauté. Remove and drain

well on paper toweling. When drained add 1/4 cup gorgonzola to bacon/onion/garlic in a bowl.
- Wash and THINLY slice tomatoes about 1/8 inch thick. Drain in colander so excess juices drain away.
- Wash and dry basil leaves on paper towel
- Lay sheet of phyllo on prepared pan, brush with olive oil, and sprinkle with 1/4 tsp bread crumbs. Repeat with all but last sheets of phyllo (10 for less thick crust).on final top sheet first brush with oil then roll 3/4 inch of each side of stacked sheets toward center to create a rim.
- Brush pesto, using same brush, over inside of tart. Sprinkle bacon/onion/garlic/gorgonzola mix over tart. Lay tomato slices overlapping slightly, use all. Season with salt and pepper. Sprinkle remaining gorgonzola over tart, don't ignore the outer edges.
- Bake 30-35 min, till crust golden brown and crispy flaky. Cool on wire rack 5 min. Lift by parchment paper to cutting board or other flat serving piece. juilianne basil leaves over entire tart. Served warm is best, room temp is ok. Cut in 2x3 inch rectangles, this is really rich & a little goes a long way
- Thaw frozen phyllo in frig at least 8 hrs. before using. Keep phyllo sheets covered as you use them so they don't dry out.

357.   Miso Ramen With Char Siu Pork And Soft Boiled Egg

Serving: Serves 4 | Prep: | Cook: | Ready in:

Ingredients

- char siu
- 1   pork tenderloin
- 1/4 cup   soy sauce
- 1/4 cup   rice vinegar
- 1 tablespoon   chinese five spice
- 1/4 cup   brown sugar

- Dash sriracha
- ramen
- 1/2 pound ramen noodles
- 1 ounce canola oil
- 2 quarts seafood stock / dashi stock
- 2 tablespoons bonito flakes
- 1 tablespoon red miso
- 1/4 cup thinly sliced scallions
- 1/4 cup enoki mushrooms, trimmed, a few reserved
- 1 small bunch baby bok choy, trimmed and sliced into 1/2 inch strips
- 1 large egg
- 1 pinch togarashi
- 1 pinch furikake

Direction

- Char siu
- Combine all ingredients in a bowl save pork and whisk thoroughly to incorporate. Add pork and marinate overnight. (Can be marinated as little as an hour or two if you're in a time crunch)
- Preheat oven to 450 and place pork on a foil-lined half-sheet/sheet pan. Roast until meat registers approximately 140-145 in the thickest part. Remove, rest, and slice into 1/4 inch pieces.
- Ramen
- Heat a small sauté pan over high heat. Add oil and heat. Reduce to medium. Add bok choy and sauté until just wilted. Remove from heat. Set aside.
- Bring a pot of salted water to boil. Add 1 tsp baking soda. Once at a gentle boil, add egg and cook for six minutes. Remove with a slotted spoon or spider strainer and cool in ice bath. Peel. Slice in half.
- In a large pot, combine stock with miso and bonito, bring to a gentle boil. Add noodles and cook until just tender. Remove from heat.
- In individual bowls, place the bok choy and sautéed enoki in the bottoms. Add noodles, then ladle broth to just about the tops of the noodle pile. Garnish with pork, remaining enoki, soft-boiled egg, togarashi, and furikake.

358.   Pasta Al Coccio

Serving: Serves 4 | Prep: | Cook: | Ready in:

Ingredients

- 350 grams short pasta
- 1 clove of garlic, finely chopped
- 1 onion, finely chopped
- 1 cup fresh peas (if you use frozen ones blanched for 5 min
- 3 fresh mushrooms porcini or 1 packet dried mushrooms
- 3 tablespoons cream
- 100 grams thick cut bacon, diced
- 1 cup white wine
- salt and pepper to taste
- 3 tablespoons of Extra-Virgin olive oil
- 2 tablespoons truffle olive oil, to taste
- 1 cup grated Parmigiano cheese

Direction

- Start by cleaning the porcini mushrooms if they are fresh, by eliminating the soil-covered end of the stalk. Separate the stalks from the caps and eliminate any bruised parts. Then delicately pass a brush over all the parts needing to be cleaned. Finally, gently wipe the entire mushroom with a cloth or with the absorbent kitchen paper. Then chop the mushrooms.
- If you are using dried porcini mushrooms put them in a bowl with warm water and allow them to plump up for about 20-30 minutes. Drain the mushrooms and chopped them. In the coccio pot (earthenware pot) heat the extra virgin olive oil over medium heat, add the garlic and onion. When they begin to brown, add the bacon and mushrooms. Add white wine and let it cook for at least 5 minutes, until the mushrooms release their water. Then add the peas and cook under low heat, stirring occasionally. While the mushroom sauce is

setting, boil a pot of water and add pasta. Cook the pasta for half the cooking time on the package. Drain the pasta reserving the water (you will use it to finish cooking the pasta).Toss the pasta in the pot with mushrooms sauce. Mix the cream into the sauce and keep on cooking until pasta is al dente, adding little by little the pasta-water. Before serving, season with truffle olive oil and grated parmigiano cheese. Tips: if you don't have an earthenware pot, you can use a stainless – steel or cast iron sauté pan.

359.   Pork With Port And Star Anise Cherry Sauce

Serving: Serves 6 | Prep: | Cook: |Ready in:

Ingredients

- 3 pounds pork tenderloin
- 2 pieces star anise pods
- 2 cups tawny port
- 1/2 pound pitted cherries
- 2 tablespoons olive oil
- salt and pepper
- 3 tablespoons heavy cream

Direction

- 1. Heat the olive oil in a large sauté pan on medium high heat until hot. Blot tenderloin with paper towel to remove surface moisture. Rub salt and pepper onto tenderloin.
- 2. Sear the pork tenderloin on all sides. Remove tenderloin to a plate.
- 3. Put port, star anise, and cherries into sauté pan and bring to a simmer, scraping up any brown bits in sauté pan left from searing pork.
- 4. Nestle tenderloin in sauce, add juices on plate to sauce, and simmer until sauce is reduced by half and pork is cooked through, turning pork occasionally and basting with sauce.

- Remove sauté pan from heat. Remove pork. Remove star anise pods. Stir in heavy cream.
- Slice pork and arrange on platter. Spoon sauce over top. Serve warm.

360.   Roasted Italian Sausage, Veg And Pasta

Serving: Serves 6 | Prep: | Cook: |Ready in:

Ingredients

- 3 cups grape tomatoes (I used red and yellow)
- 1   red bell pepper
- 1   yellow bell pepper, cut to 1/2" dice
- 1   orange bell pepper
- 1   medium zucchini, sliced vertically, then crosswise into 1/2" pieces
- 1   medium yellow squash, sliced vertically, then crosswise into 1/2" pieces
- 1   small red onion, cut into 1" chunks
- 3   cloves garlic, minced
- 1 teaspoon dried basil
- 1 teaspoon fennel seed
- 1 teaspoon dried oregano
- 1/4 teaspoon red pepper flakes
- 3 tablespoons olive oil
- 3/4 teaspoon kosher salt
- 1/2 teaspoon black pepper
- 1 pound italian sausages, casings removed and cut into 1" chunks
- 1 pound corkscrew pasta, cooked to al dente
- 1/2 cup kalamata olives, seeded and halved or quartered
- 2 tablespoons capers, rinsed and drained
- 1 tablespoon red wine vinegar
- 2 tablespoons freshly chopped parsley
- 2 tablespoons freshly chopped basil

Direction

- Preheat oven to 425 degrees.
- Place bell peppers into oven and cook until skin is papery and blackened, about 35-45

minutes. Remove and transfer peppers to a bowl. Cover with plastic wrap and let the peppers steam in the bowl.

- On a large baking sheet combine the zucchini, squash, onion, garlic, basil, fennel, oregano, red pepper flakes, olive oil, kosher salt and black pepper. Toss the vegetables until well coated with the oil, herbs and spices. Add the sausage and spread everything into an even layer on the baking sheet. Roast for 35-40 minutes. (Note the vegetable/sausage mixture can roast in the oven at the same time the peppers are cooking)
- While vegetables are roasting, prepare the pasta and cook until al dente. Rinse with cool water to stop the cooking process and drain. Set aside.
- When the peppers are cool enough to handle, remove the skins, stems and seeds and cut the peppers into thin strips. Transfer peppers to a large bowl. Add the roasted vegetables and sausage to the peppers. Scrape the pan to get all of the juicy goodness into the bowl. Add the olives, capers and red wine vinegar. Toss to combine.
- Transfer the pasta to a large serving bowl. Top with the vegetables and all the juices. Sprinkle with fresh basil and parsley. Serve.

| 361. | Spaghetti And Meatball Soup (with Roasted Canned Tomatoes) |

Serving: Serves 10 | Prep: | Cook: | Ready in:

Ingredients

- FOR THE SOUP
- 2 28 ounce cans whole tomatoes (san marzano preferred)
- 2 teaspoons olive oil
- 1/2 large red onion
- 4 garlic cloves, minced or grated

- 1 tablespoon dried oregano (or 1/2 tablespoon fresh, minced)
- 1/2 tablespoon red chili flakes (or less, if you can't stand the heat)
- 1/2 tablespoon fennel seeds
- 1 teaspoon pepper
- 1 28 ounce can crushed tomatoes
- 7 cups chicken brother (or other broth, or water - in a pinch)
- 2 large sprigs fresh basil, leaves removed & finel slices
- salt, to taste
- FOR THE MEATBALLS (and to complete the soup)
- 2 pounds lean ground pork (or beef, chicken, etc - but i find the pork most moist)
- 2 large eggs
- 1 teaspoon salt
- 1 tablespoon fresh thyme, finely minced
- 1 teaspoon pepper
- 4 garlic cloves, finely minced or grated
- 1/4 large red onion, finely minced or grated
- 1 teaspoon red chilli flakes
- 2 tablespoons olive oil (to be used in pan)
- Cooked Spaghetti (For Serving)
- Grated Good Parmesan

Direction

- FOR THE SOUP
- Preheat oven to 375 degrees F.
- Drain whole tomatoes, reserving the liquid. Remove whole tomatoes from can, scraping seeds from each and squishing them so they can spread open and lay flat(ish) and place onto roasting pan. Roast, turning a few times to allow the brown bits to be scraped from the pan, watching carefully that they don't burn. This process can take 30 minutes to an hour, depending on the amount of liquid in your tomatoes. The end result should have no liquid left in the pan, and the tomatoes should be shriveled up, with browned parts throughout.
- Place olive oil, roasted whole tomatoes, sliced garlic, oregano, fennel seeds, chili flakes, and diced onions into large Dutch oven or stock

pot and sauté over medium heat, stirring frequently, until onions are transparent.

- Use immersion blender to blend soup to incorporate onions and garlic (Note: This step is optional, if you don't have access to immersion blender. You can either blend in a standard blender, or mush mixture with a spoon to get the tomatoes as broken down as possible. This will just result in a chunkier soup overall - no biggie!)
- Add crushed tomatoes, reserved whole tomatoes juice (strained of seeds if you prefer), fresh basil and stock and allow to simmer for 15 minutes or so, stirring frequently.
- Season with salt and allow to simmer while you make the meatballs.
- FOR THE MEATBALLS (and to complete the soup)
- In a large bowl, place all ingredients except olive oil, and mix with your hands until well incorporated.
- Pinch off about 1 teaspoon of pork mixture and roll into meatballs + set aside. You want these to be pretty tiny, as they need to fit onto a soup spoon for easy eating. Continue until you use up all of the pork mixture.
- Heat olive oil in large cast iron or frying pan over medium-high heat. Test oil with one of your meatballs to ensure it is heated enough that the meatball sizzles when it hits the oil.
- Leaving about 1/2 inch space between each, place as many meatballs as you can into pan. Allow each meatball to brown on one side, then flip over to at least one other side so it keeps its shape well. Once meatballs are seared, drop into the soup to finish cooking. Continue until all meatballs are done.
- Allow soup to simmer over medium heat for 15-20 minutes.
- Test one of the meatballs by removing it from the soup and cutting it in half to ensure it is cooked through.
- To serve, ladle soup (don't forget to make sure there's a good portion of meatballs!) over bowls prepared with a serving of pre-cooked spaghetti noodles + a sprinkle of good parmesan cheese. Buon appetito!

---

362.   Springtime Tarte

Serving: Serves 6 to 8 people | Prep: | Cook: | Ready in:

Ingredients

- 1   refrigerated pie crust
- 6   slices fully cooked bacon, chopped
- 1 packet (8 oz.) shredded sharp cheddar cheese
- 2 tablespoons of fresh chopped chives
- 8   fresh asparagus sprears
- 4   large eggs
- 1 1//2 cups half and half
- 1/4 teaspoon salt
- 1/4 teaspoon black pepper

Direction

- Preheat oven to 350' F. Unroll dough onto work surface. With rolling pin, for a 9 1/2 inch tart pan, roll dough into 12 inch round. Transfer dough to an ungreased tart pan, gently pressing dough into bottom and up side of pan. Run rolling pin over top of pan to trim excess dough. Sprinkle bacon, cheese and chives over bottom of crust. Cut tough ends from asparagus, trimming to fit into tart pan. Place asparagus spears in spoke pattern over cheese, with asparagus alternately tip to stem. In medium bowl, with whisk, lightly beat eggs. Add half and half, salt and pepper and whisk until well blended. Pour egg mixture over asparagus. Bake 40 to 45 minutes or until golden and set in center. Cool tart in pan on wire rack 10 minutes to serve warm.

---

363.   Sweet Potato And Bacon Hash

Serving: Serves 2 | Prep: | Cook: | Ready in:

Ingredients

- 2 sweet potatoes, peeled and cut into 1/2" cubes
- 1/2 green pepper, seeded and chopped
- 1/2 yellow onion, peeled and chopped
- 1 clove garlic, minced
- 3 slices bacon, chopped
- 2 tablespoons butter, divided
- 1 teaspoon kosher salt, divided
- 1/2 teaspoon black pepper
- 1 teaspoon smoked paprika
- 4 4 eggs
- 2-3 green onions, thinly sliced on a diagonal, for garnish
- fresh chopped parsley for garnish
- hot sauce to taste

Direction

- Preheat oven to 400 degrees.
- Fill a medium saucepan halfway with water, cover with a lid and bring to a boil. Salt the water with 1/2 teaspoon kosher salt and add the diced potatoes. Reduce heat to a simmer and cook potatoes about 10-12 minutes until just tender. Drain the potatoes completely and allow any moisture to evaporate - you don't want the potatoes to be wet, because they will become mushy. Heat an oven safe nonstick or cast iron skillet over medium heat. Add the bacon and cook until brown and crisped. Use a slotted spoon to transfer the bacon to a paper towel lined dish. Set aside.
- Add 2 teaspoons of the butter to the pan with reserved bacon fat and heat over medium heat. Add the diced peppers and onions and sauté until vegetables are softened, about 3-4 minutes. Transfer the vegetables to a small bowl and set aside.
- Add remaining butter to the pan and heat until the butter is melted and foamy. Add the sweet potatoes in a single layer. Sprinkle the potatoes with smoked paprika, salt and pepper and cook for 3-4 minutes. Do not stir, just let them get a nice crust before disturbing them. Use a thin, flexible spatula to turn the

potatoes over in the pan to crust the other sides, cooking for 2-3 more minutes per turn (about 12 minutes total).
- Add the raw, chopped garlic, peppers and onions to the potatoes and carefully fold them in, so that you don't break up the potatoes. Cook for 3-4 minutes. Crack the eggs on top of the hash - spaced a few inches apart. Lightly salt and pepper the eggs and cook on the stovetop for 1-2 minutes. Transfer the pan to the oven and cook for 2 minutes. Turn on the broiler and heat the eggs for 1-2 minutes until whites are cooked through, but yolks are still jiggly. (YUM!)
- Sprinkle with reserved bacon, green onions and parsley. Serve with hot sauce, I recommend Crystal brand - it has a nice vinegary taste that cuts through the fat in this dish.

---

364. Tomato Bacon And Onion Quiche

Serving: Serves 10 | Prep: | Cook: |Ready in:

Ingredients

- 2 refrigerated pie crusts
- 1 cup caramelized onions (recipe on site)
- 1 1/2 teaspoons kosher salt
- 2 large ripe tomatoes, seeded and sliced into 1/4" thick rounds
- 8 eggs, whisked
- 2 cups half and half
- 1 tablespoon fresh thyme, chopped
- 1/2 pound cooked bacon, diced or crumbled
- 2 cups shredded gruyere cheese

Direction

- Preheat oven to 450 degrees. Roll out the pie crusts and fit them into two pie plates, pressing the bottom and sides to the plates. Crimp the edges with your fingers, or use the tines of a fork to create a nice border on the crust. Bake the pie crusts for 8-9 minutes until lightly browned. Remove from oven and set aside to cool.

- Turn oven down to 350 degrees.
- Lay the tomatoes on a sheet pan lined with paper towels. Sprinkle with 1/2 teaspoon kosher salt and let tomatoes sit for 20 minutes until the liquid has been released. Blot the tomatoes dry with fresh paper towels.
- In a medium bowl combine the eggs, half and half, thyme, remaining teaspoon of kosher salt and pepper. Whisk to combine thoroughly.
- Stir in the bacon, onions and cheese. Divide the mixture between the two pie crusts. Arrange the tomato slices on top of the quiche mixture, overlapping if necessary.
- Bake the quiches for 45-50 minutes. Remove from oven and let cool 10-15 minutes before serving.
- Can be made a day ahead. Cool to room temperature, cover and refrigerate. Reheat in a 300 degree oven for 20 minutes before serving.

- 2 cups fresh or frozen peas

Direction

- Position rack in the middle of the oven and preheat to 350°F.
- Add onions, celery, peppers, garlic, thyme and oil in a deep baking dish, mix and cook in the oven for 20 minutes.
- In meantime cut and season the chicken with salt, black pepper and chili flakes, cut sausage and add to the vegetables with chicken, mix and bake for another 20 minutes.
- Take out of the oven and add crushed tomato and rice, mix and add 3 cups of water, 1 tsp salt and cook for additional 30-35 minutes.
- Check for seasoning, add peas and parsley, mix and cover for 10-15 minutes, you don't have to cook peas.

365.	Đuveč

Serving: Serves 8-10 | Prep: | Cook: | Ready in:

Ingredients

- 8 chicken thighs, cut into large pieces
- 4 smoked sausages, sliced
- 1 pound onion, diced
- 1 pound mix peppers, diced
- 4 ounces celery, diced
- 10 cloves of garlic, sliced
- 1/2 cup sunflower oil
- 2 teaspoons sea salt
- 1 cup parsley, chopped
- 2-3 sprigs thyme
- 1 1/2 cups arborio rice
- 3 cups crushed tomato
- 3 cups water
- 1/2 teaspoon black pepper
- 1 teaspoon chili flakes

Index

Conclusion

Thank you again for downloading this book!

I hope you enjoyed reading about my book!

If you enjoyed this book, please take the time to share your thoughts and post a review on Amazon. It'd be greatly appreciated!

Write me an honest review about the book – I truly value your opinion and thoughts and I will incorporate them into my next book, which is already underway.

Thank you!

If you have any questions, **feel free to contact at:** *author@shellfishrecipes.com*

Carla Moore

shellfishrecipes.com

Made in United States
Orlando, FL
09 March 2023

30870709R00139